THE GIGANTIC READER

Overstuffed with Irresistible Information

WEST
SIDE
PUBLISHING

Contributing Writers: Michael Allen, Jeff Bahr, Robert Bullington, Ryan L. Cole, Katherine Don, Mary Fons-Misetic, Anne Holub, Erika Cornstuble Koff, Shanon Lyon, Susan McGowan, Art Montague, JR Raphael, Russell Roberts, Lawrence Robinson, Allen Smith, Pamela D. Toler, Ken White, Jennifer Plattner Wilkinson, Kelly Wingard

Cover Illustrator: Adrian Chesterman

Additional Interior Illustrators: Hye Lim An; Erin Burke; Erin Burke/ National Baseball Hall of Fame Library, Cooperstown, NY; Nicole Lee; Robert Schoolcraft; Shavan Spears

Fact Verification by: Darcy Chadwick and Kathryn Holcomb

Contents

❖ ❖ ❖ ❖

A Noble Pursuit Made Fun

Welcome fellow fact seekers to *The Gigantic Reader,* the second book in our annual Armchair Reader™ series. We've worked long and hard to ensure that this edition (which, if we may toot our own horn, will doubtlessly become your favorite Reader) is totally huge, immense, and ginormous in every way.

As with the first volume, *The Colossal Reader,* this compendium runneth over with fascinating articles and lists. Inside, you'll find small, neatly wrapped nuggets of information on a whole mess of topics, covering science, celebrities, art, sports, history, food, animals, and plenty of just plain weird stuff. We have it all, from Polish mummies to the history of long-gone candy bars.

This is tantalizing trivia for our troubled times, an eclectic collection that will leave you satisfied, but still hungry for more. And *The Gigantic Reader* has something for just about everyone, whether you're male or female, young or old, an Elvis or Beatles fan...well, you get the picture.

You see, unlike many of the books in the Armchair Reader™ series, the focus of this book is, well, *unfocused*—basically, it's about anything and everything. Working together as a team, the editor and writers came up with story topics that set their brains on fire, and they thought it only polite to share with the readers. Seriously, we get into everything: Some of the most dangerous jobs, the world's biggest living thing (which just may be under your feet as you read this), and unusual facts about opossums (which are seriously weird).

We've constructed the book so that you can open *The Gigantic Reader* to a random page and find something interesting. We want this book to spark your interest in a new subject and perhaps lead you on your own exploration. You can decide to take the next step and become the expert. Or not. It's all there for your pleasure and it was our pleasure to create it for you.

Not intriguing enough for you? Check out these topics:

- Civil War veteran William Minor contributed thousands of definitions to the *Oxford English Dictionary*—from his cell in an insane asylum.

- Being attacked by a bear? Here's how to escape.
- What happens when surrealism meets slapstick? Find out about the completely wackadoo friendship between Salvador Dalí and Harpo Marx.
- Learn what it takes to be on a crime scene decontamination crew.
- Did you know Alfred Hitchcock, the master of suspense, has a fear of eggs? Take a look at some other surprising celebrity phobias.
- Meet a professional Abe Lincoln impersonator.

See what we mean? *The Gigantic Reader* is jam-packed with interesting information—stuff that will make you the envy or bane of all your quiz-loving friends. Soon enough, you'll find yourself itching for more. But don't worry; we're already working on the next annual Armchair Reader™! So for now, just prop up your feet, settle back, and dig into *The Gigantic Reader*.

Until the next Reader,

Allen Orso

Allen Orso

P.S. Please let us know what you think of the Armchair Reader™ series—both good and bad. You can contact me personally at **www.armchairreader.com.**

"If we value the pursuit of knowledge, we must be free to follow wherever that search may lead us. The free mind is not a barking dog, to be tethered on a ten-foot chain."

—*Adlai E. Stevenson Jr.*

"It is no good to try to stop knowledge from going forward. Ignorance is never better than knowledge."

—*Enrico Fermi*

What's In a Name?

❖ ❖ ❖ ❖

A rose by any other name may smell as sweet, but a book with a bad title could end up on the sale table instead of the bestseller list. After all, Tolstoy's War and Peace *has a far more dignified ring to it than his first choice,* All's Well That Ends Well. *Luckily, these original titles didn't make it to the bookstore shelves.*

- Long after the publication of *The Great Gatsby,* F. Scott Fitzgerald regretted not going with his preferred title, *Trimalchio in West Egg.*

- William Faulkner proposed *Dark House* as the title for both *Absalom, Absalom!* and *Light in August.*

- Peter Benchley and his editor discarded more than 100 titles for Benchley's first novel, including *Great White, The Shark, Leviathan Rising, The Jaws of Death,* and *A Silence in the Water.* Pressured to make a decision because the book was ready to go to press, they agreed that the only word they liked in any of the proposed titles was *Jaws.*

- Charles Dickens's classic *Tom-All-Alone's Factory that Got Into Chancery and Never Got Out* was published as the more succinctly titled *Bleak House.*

- Stephen Crane's great Civil War novel, *The Red Badge of Courage,* was originally titled *Private Fleming, His Various Battles.*

- Jane Austen thought about the implications of *First Impressions* and renamed her novel *Pride and Prejudice.*

- *Main Street,* Sinclair Lewis's classic exposé of small town hypocrisy was originally called *The Village Virus.*

- Margaret Mitchell's *Gone with the Wind* was almost published as *Pansy,* the inappropriate (yet original) name of the main character, now known as Scarlett O'Hara.

Frankenstein's Flattop

❖ ❖ ❖ ❖

Pity poor Frankenstein's monster. Cursed with a head as flat as a tabletop, unable to find a hat or glasses that fit, he must wonder what happened. After all, the monster described in Mary Shelley's novel looked relatively normal (except for that whole reanimated-corpse thing). So why does the movie version have the flat head?

Lugosi's Lament

It was late spring of 1931 in Hollywood, and actor Bela Lugosi and Universal Studios had struck box office gold with *Dracula*. The film company, sensing a potential bonanza in horror films, immediately cast their new star in the upcoming *Frankenstein*—but, to Lugosi's dismay, he was to play the role of the monster rather than Dr. Frankenstein. Angrily, he wondered why a star of his caliber should play a grunting creature that "any half-wit extra could play."

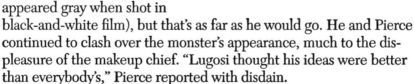

More problems awaited Lugosi in the form of Universal's chief makeup artist Jack P. Pierce. Pierce and Lugosi had previously clashed on the set of *Dracula*, when the star refused to alter his appearance with pointed teeth and a beard (as author Bram Stoker had described the character).

For *Frankenstein,* Lugosi reluctantly agreed to apply blue-green greasepaint to his face (an effect that appeared gray when shot in black-and-white film), but that's as far as he would go. He and Pierce continued to clash over the monster's appearance, much to the displeasure of the makeup chief. "Lugosi thought his ideas were better than everybody's," Pierce reported with disdain.

When the film's director, Robert Florey, finally shot 20 minutes of *Frankenstein* test footage in June, costar Edward Van Sloan described Lugosi's appearance as "something out of *Babes in Toyland*"; commenting that the broad wig made the star's head look four times its normal size, and that his skin was "polished and clay-like."

Lugosi—who, during the shooting, had threatened to get a doctor's excuse so he wouldn't have to play the part—was through. "Enough is enough," said the Hungarian actor. "I was a star in my country and will not be a scarecrow over here!"

A Monster Makeover

After Universal executives screened the test footage, they banished both Lugosi and Florey to a lesser project and appointed Englishman James Whale the new *Frankenstein* director. On Whale's recommendation, they selected an actor Whale had spotted in the Universal commissary—a fellow named Boris Karloff—to play the monster.

Over the next three weeks, Karloff and Pierce worked for three hours every night to develop the monster's signature appearance. The result, including the now-trademark flat head, was one of the most famous makeup jobs in Hollywood history. The unique noggin was no whim: Pierce had spent months researching surgery, anatomy, and other related fields. As he told *The New York Times,* "My anatomical studies taught me that there are six ways a surgeon can cut the skull in order to take out or put in a brain. I figured Frankenstein, who was a scientist but no practicing surgeon, would take the simplest surgical way. He would cut the top of the skull off straight across like a pot lid, hinge it, pop the brain in and then clamp it on tight. That is the reason I decided to make the Monster's head square and flat."

When released in December 1931, *Frankenstein* became an instant smash, and Karloff's rising star quickly eclipsed that of Lugosi. Throughout Karloff's career, he always knew who (or what) to thank for his golden opportunity: the infamous monster, flat head and all.

The Times They Are A-Changin'

1903

- On January 1, the Commercial Pacific Cable Company opens the first direct telegraph connection from San Francisco to Honolulu using undersea cables.

- The first teddy bear is introduced by Morris and Rose Mitchum.

- On November 3, Panama declares its independence from Columbia.

- Pierre and Marie Curie win the Nobel Prize in physics for their studies of radiation.

- Henry Ford incorporates the Ford Motor Company, with 12 shareholders and capital totaling $28,000. Ford is just one of 88 auto manufacturers founded that year.

- On December 17, brothers Orville and Wilbur Wright make the first manned flight in an engine-powered airplane at Kitty Hawk, North Carolina. They fly 852 feet in 59 seconds, reaching an altitude of 15 feet.

- Henri Desgranges, editor of the French sports journal L'Auto, organizes the first Tour de France as a publicity stunt to win readers from its popular rival, Le Velo. Sixty cyclists ride 2,500 kilometers in 19 days.

- "Sweet Adeline" is sung for the first time on December 27. Barbershop quartets are never the same.

- Dr. Horatio Nelson Jackson makes the first transcontinental crossing of the United States by car, accompanied by his dog and a mechanic. The trip takes 65 days; all three wear goggles while traveling.

- An epidemic of typhoid fever in New York City is traced to Irish immigrant and cook Mary Mallon. Nicknamed "Typhoid Mary," Mallon continues to take jobs that involve handling food, often using false names. She is placed in quarantine in 1915 as a public health measure.

- Publisher Joseph Pulitzer founds the Pulitzer Prize as a condition of endowing the new School of Journalism at Columbia University.

A New Leash on Life: Surprising Service Animals

Move over, Lassie. Step aside, Rin Tin Tin.
Service animals are real-life heroes.

A Friend in Need

A service animal is generally defined as any animal that is trained to aid a disabled handler, specifically in regards to their disability. While the general populace is accustomed to seeing a well-trained, behaved dog fulfill this function, the definition of the typical animal trained for service work is far broader than just dogs being used as seeing-eye, hearing-ear, seizure-alert, or wheelchair assistance animals.

High-Ho ... *Cuddles?*

Since 1999, miniature horses have been formally trained as service animals for persons who have visual impairment. Cuddles, the first guide horse, went into service two years later. Guide horses are an excellent alternative for people who are allergic to or fearful of dogs, or are simply horse enthusiasts. Guide horses, which are comparable in size to a medium to large dog, are intelligent, docile, have excellent memories, provide stable physical support to individuals with balance problems, can be house-trained, and on average have a lifespan three to four times that of a service dog. Some drawbacks to the miniature horse include their limited dexterity in comparison to a typical service dog and their more limited portability.

The Monkey Business

Since the introduction of the first service monkey in 1979, the use of Capuchin monkeys as service animals has increased with the development of a more codified training system. Their longevity, portability, intelligence, and extraordinary dexterity make them superior choices for people whose disability requires assistance with a wide variety of daily activities. More than just handy for turning on and off lights or picking up dropped items, monkeys can be trained to retrieve meals from the refrigerator, dishes from the cupboard, load CDs, or press the start button on a computer or microwave. As long as they're on a harness or leash and they're well behaved, service monkeys can even have their own seat on an airplane.

While cats are generally not recognized as service animals, some cats do serve as emotional support animals. Emotional support animals assist people with severe emotional or mental disabilities, often by simply providing company.

When Pigs Fly

Pigs are occasionally used as emotional support and therapy animals as well. They're extremely intelligent, albeit limited in what practical services they can perform—unless of course, their handler is a devotee of truffle hunting.

One service pig, technically a "therapeutic companion pet," caused an uproar in 2000 when US Airways transported it from Philadelphia to Seattle. As service animals, they don't need to be certified, nor is it permissible to ask what function the animal fulfills. Thus, the airline had to take on good faith that the pig wasn't just a pet. The woman who owned the pig did make prearrangements and presented a doctor's note, which was never publicly released, that allegedly indicated that the pig had a calming effect on the woman, who had a heart condition. Whether or not the pig had been specifically trained to calm the woman is debatable. Furthermore, the service swine's owner misrepresented its size to a significant enough degree that the pig protruded into the aisle, and she had no means of restraining or controlling the animal.

Although the flight was uneventful, during deplaning the pig panicked, not only causing distress to the 200 other passengers with its squealing and erratic behavior, but also leaving behind an unpleasant mess for the flight crew to deal with before the next flight. US Airways has since revised their policy concerning service pigs. People, leave your pigs at home.

Fast Facts

- A typical American dog owner spends more than $14,000 on his or her pet by the end of its life.

- In 1869, visionary inventor Thomas Edison patented the first electronic vote recorder. The recorder registered voters' choices as they were made and provided total vote counts, as well as a paper trail. His invention was such a radical departure from voting tradition that it was a commercial failure.

- Ten percent of Dalmatians are considered deaf.

- Flies taste with their feet.

- The idea of a "tip" for a waiter or waitress comes from 17th-century boxes in restaurants labeled "To Insure Promptness." Diners would put some cash in the box before eating to get better service.

- Lyndon B. Johnson was the first U.S. commander-in-chief to wear contact lenses.

- That early morning jolt of caffeine can be costly in Moscow. The price of an average cup of coffee is $10.19 US, the highest in the world.

- Barbed wire played a large part in the formation of the American West. In 1873, an Illinois farmer named Joseph Glidden was credited with designing the most popular barbed wire, winning out in court battles and in the marketplace, beating over 570 other patented designs.

- The human body contains approximately four ounces of salt.

- Louisa May Alcott, author of the best-selling classics Little Men and Little Women, actually disliked children. What's more, Alcott was a schoolteacher.

How to Kill the Undead

It's getting so you can barely drive to a remote wooded location or let a teeny-weeny little mutant virus loose without attracting the undead. Zombies and vampires are seemingly everywhere, from big cities to rural hamlets, and from the frozen tundra to the blazing desert.

A person needs to be prepared—knowing how to kill the undead can prevent them from ruining your day.

I Have Met the Enemy, and It Is Grandma

In order to kill the undead, it's first important to know which type of creature you're facing. For example, there are numerous types of zombies. Imagine how you'd feel if you thought you were facing the slow, shambling zombies from *Shaun of the Dead* or a George A. Romero flick and figured you could easily outmaneuver them, and instead they turned out to be the fast-paced zombies of *28 Days Later.* Wouldn't your face be red! (Granted, as they ate your brain.) Vampires are similar: Some vampires turn into crispy critters in the sunlight. However, Dracula himself walked around London in the daytime. A vampire's aversion to sunlight is strictly a 20th-century invention.

By the same token, you should realize that any former affiliations you may have had with the undead have no meaning anymore. If you see grandma lurching toward the house or floating outside your window—and she's been dead since last May—it's likely she's not back to offer you a plate of fresh-baked chocolate chip cookies. Common sense is key.

Killing Them Softly... Sort Of

Weapons for killing the undead abound. For zombies, the best weapon is a shotgun or any other type of firearm that can dispatch the creature with a headshot from a distance. (As Romero put it: Kill the brain, kill the ghoul.) Of course, loading up with fresh ammunition is annoying, which is why a machete is a popular choice. A chainsaw also works well, but with the price of gasoline nowadays, you may not want to waste it on zombies. A baseball bat, crowbar, or other bludgeoning implement also gets the job done.

Setting a zombie on fire may look pretty, but until the flames melt the brain, all you've really done is create an animated torch. The same for explosives—since a zombie's dead already, it will simply shrug off the loss of a limb or the inconvenience of shrapnel wounds.

When battling zombies, always wear tight-fitting clothing. Zombies are like babies; they'll grab whatever they can and stick it in their mouths. Your clothes should be heavy, like leather, to provide bite protection. Taunting is also encouraged. Phrases like "Oh, you want some of this?" and "Hey, dead thing! Let's go!" can bolster your confidence.

Vampires: Old-School Slaughtering

Killing a vampire is more old-school, organic work. To kill a vampire, a stake made of aspen, ash, hawthorn, or maple through the heart usually does the trick. Decapitation also works; sometimes the head is placed under the arm or between the legs to make it harder to rejoin the body. Some Slavic traditions specify that only a sexton's or gravedigger's shovel can be used for this purpose, so plan accordingly. Burning a vampire can be effective, but again it may take awhile.

Unlike zombies, vampires can be deterred. A simple smearing of garlic often does the trick. According to legend, a vampire is compulsively neat, so throwing a handful of seeds, salt or sand into its path will force it to pick up every grain before resuming its pursuit. Another legend says that a vampire will stop and read every word of a torn-up newspaper thrown in its way.

However, there is no word as to how well this works with an illiterate vampire.

HOW IT ALL BEGAN

The Meter Men
We can blame Carl Magee of Oklahoma City for one of the great curses of urban living. No, he didn't cause the first toxic smog, nor did he engineer the first axle-snapping pothole. Worse, in 1932 he invented the coin-operated parking meter.

As if that wasn't enough, in 1953, a Colorado violinist named Frank Marugg invented the Denver Boot, a device that immobilizes vehicles until the associated parking tickets are paid. Thanks a lot, fellas.

Tea Time
Tea and politics have never mixed well. Ever since the infamous Boston Tea Party, many Americans have been slow to hop on the tea bandwagon. Yet it was an American, Thomas Sullivan, who came up with the first tea bag in 1908, which was, one could say, a revolution in its own right. On the other hand, perhaps because it was an American invention, the British didn't accept it for many years.

Sullivan's original tea bags were decidedly upscale, featuring hand-sewn silk. In other words, the bag was more costly than the tea leaves it contained. Hemp bags were tried, but they were discontinued in favor of the tasteless paper bags used today.

Breathing Easy
Being tongue-tied can be plenty embarrassing for a person but for race-horses it can be an advantage. Tying the tongues of racehorses has been a common practice for many years. The tie prevents the horse's tongue from flipping over the bit and impeding its breathing during races.

Sweets for a Sweetie
Sugar was once marketed in large, rock-hard chunks, which was inconvenient and messy. It certainly didn't suit Juliana Rad, a housewife in Dačice, Czechoslovakia. Somewhat accident prone, Juliana cut herself one day while trying to whittle off enough sugar for her cup of tea. Mercifully, her husband Jakub took charge. Alas, he wasn't any great shakes at either first aid or patience, so, in 1843, he created the sugar cube.

Broadway's Biggest Losers

❖ ❖ ❖ ❖

Broadway is known for producing some of the world's largest shows ever seen on stage. Still, they can't all be Cats. Here are some of the biggest tankers in Broadway history.

Probably the worst play on Broadway, the stinker that all subsequent bombs have been compared to, was Arthur Bicknell's **The Moose Murders.** The script included one character who tried to have sex with his mother; meanwhile another character, dressed in a moose costume, was kicked in the groin by a quadriplegic. *New York Times* theater critic Frank Rich called it "the worst play I've ever seen on a Broadway stage." It had one performance at the Eugene O'Neill Theatre on February 22, 1983, before it was closed down.

Another early closer was the 1966 stage version of the movie classic **Breakfast at Tiffany's.** Although it had big-name star Mary Tyler Moore playing Holly Golightly, the musical still stood at nearly four hours long and was constantly being revised. *Breakfast* had its first preview on December 12, but producer David Merrick shut it down only four nights later, saying the show's closing was preferable "rather than subject the drama critics and the public to an excruciatingly boring evening."

Another movie adaptation to bomb big on Broadway was a 1988 musical version of Stephen King's horror novel, **Carrie,** which closed after a measly five performances. Actress Barbara Cook was actually nearly decapitated by a set prop, and lead actress Linzi Hateley's body microphone stopped working after the show's climactic blood-soaked scene. The $7 million show was the most expensive quick-to-close flop in Broadway history.

An older stinker on Broadway was **Portofino,** a confusing musical that combined an auto-racing storyline with witches, priests, and the devil. Opening on February 21, 1958, it seemed destined to bomb. It closed after only three shows. Famed theater critic Walter Kerr wrote, "I will not say that *Portofino* was the worst musical ever produced, because I've only been seeing musicals since 1919."

Beefed Up

❖ ❖ ❖ ❖

You're probably familiar with the terms "juiced," "roid-raged," "hyped," and "pumped"—all used to describe the effects of anabolic steroids. For better or for worse, steroids have invaded the worlds of professional and amateur sports, and even show business.

Better Living Through Chemistry

Anabolic steroids (also called anabolic-androgenic steroids or AAS) are a specific class of hormones that are related to the male hormone testosterone. Steroids have been used for thousands of years in traditional medicine to promote healing in diseases such as cancer and AIDS. French neurologist Charles-Édouard Brown-Séquard was one of the first physicians to report its healing properties after injecting himself with an extract of guinea pig testicles in 1889. In 1935, two German scientists applied for the first steroid-use patent and were offered the 1939 Nobel Prize for Chemistry, but they were forced to decline the honor by the Nazi government.

Interest in steroids continued during World War II. Third Reich scientists experimented on concentration camp inmates to treat symptoms of chronic wasting as well as to test its effects on heightened aggression in German soldiers. Even Adolf Hitler was injected with steroids to treat his endless list of maladies.

Giving Athletes a Helping Hand

The first reference to steroid use for performance enhancement in sports dates back to a 1938 *Strength and Health* magazine letter to the editor, inquiring how steroids could improve performance in weightlifting and bodybuilding. During the 1940s, the Soviet Union and a number of Eastern Bloc countries built aggressive steroid programs designed to improve the performance of Olympic and amateur weight lifters. The program was so successful that U.S. Olympic team physicians worked with American chemists to design Dianabol, which they administered to U.S. athletes.

Since their early development, steroids have gradually crept into the world of professional and amateur sports. The use of steroids have become commonplace in baseball, football, cycling, track—even golf and cricket. In the 2006 Monitor the Future survey, steroid use was measured in eighth-, tenth-, and twelfth-grade students; a little more than 2 percent of male high school seniors admitted to using steroids during the past year, largely because of their steroid-using role models in professional sports.

Bigger, Faster, Stronger—Kinda

Steroids have a number of performance enhancement perks for athletes such as promoting cell growth, protein synthesis from amino acids, increasing appetite, bone strengthening, and the stimulation of bone marrow and production of red blood cells. Of course, there are a few "minor" side effects to contend with as well: shrinking testicles, reduced sperm count, infertility, acne, high blood pressure, blood clotting, liver damage, headaches, aching joints, nausea, vomiting, diarrhea, loss of sleep, severe mood swings, paranoia, panic attacks, depression, male pattern baldness, the cessation of menstruation in women, and an increased risk of prostrate cancer—small compromises in the name of athletic achievement, right?

While many countries have banned the sale of anabolic steroids for non-medical applications, they are still legal in Mexico and Thailand. In the United States, steroids are classified as a Schedule III controlled substance, which makes their possession a federal crime, punishable by prison time. But that hasn't deterred athletes from looking for that extra edge. And there are thousands  of black-market vendors willing to sell more than 50 different varieties of steroids. Largely produced in countries where they are legal, steroids are smuggled across international borders. Their existence has spawned a new industry for creating counterfeit drugs that are often diluted, cut with fillers, or made from vegetable oil or toxic substances. They are sold through the mail, the Internet, in gyms, and at competitions. Many of these drugs are sub-medical or veterinary grade steroids.

Impact on Sports and Entertainment

Since invading the world of amateur and professional sports, steroid use has become a point of contention, gathering supporters both for and against their use. Arnold Schwarzenegger, the famous body-builder, actor, and politician, freely admits to using anabolic steroids while they were still legal. "Steroids were helpful to me in maintaining muscle size while on a strict diet in preparation for a contest," says Schwarzenegger, who held the Mr. Olympia bodybuilding title for seven years. "I did not use them for muscle growth, but rather for muscle maintenance when cutting up."

Lyle Alzado, the colorful, record-setting defensive tackle for the Los Angeles Raiders, Cleveland Browns, and Denver Broncos admitted to taking steroids to stay competitive but acknowledged their risks. "Ninety percent of the athletes I know are on the stuff. We're not born to be 300 lbs. or jump 30 ft. But all the time I was taking steroids, I knew they were making me play better," he said. "I became very violent on the field and off it. I did things only crazy people do. Now look at me. My hair's gone, I wobble when I walk and have to hold on to someone for support and I have trouble remembering things. My last wish? That no one else ever dies this way."

Recently, a few show business celebrities have come under scrutiny for their involvement with steroids and other banned substances. In 2008, 61-year-old *Rambo* star Sylvester Stallone paid $10,600 to settle a criminal drug possession charge for smuggling 48 vials of Human Growth Hormone (HGH) into the country. HGH is popularly used for its anti-aging benefits. "Everyone over 40 years old would be wise to investigate it (HGH and testosterone use) because it increases the quality of your life," says Stallone.

"If you're an actor in Hollywood and you're over 40, you are doing HGH. Period," said one Hollywood cosmetic surgeon. "Why wouldn't you? It makes your skin look better, your hair, your fingernails. Everything."

FROM THE VAULTS OF HISTORY

Toilet Truths

If there was ever a contest for a person whose career was defined by their name, then Thomas Crapper would win hands down. Crapper was a 19th-century plumber who, despite the urban legend, did not invent the flush toilet. And, although his name has often been associated to the first references of "crap" and "crapper," both terms date back before career. What Crapper *did* do was promote and increase the popularity of the flush toilet (a fairly new invention until they were installed at the Great Exhibition in 1851), promoted sanitary plumbing, and was the first to come up with the idea of a bathroom fittings showroom. Crapper's most affluent client was Prince Edward, and he installed all of the plumbing, cedarwood toilet seats, and enclosures (including 30 lavatories) in the prince's country estate.

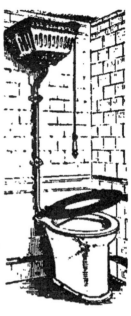

After his death in 1910, Thomas Crapper & Co. was sold and reacquired a number of times until it was purchased by Simon Kirby, a collector of antique bathroom fixtures. Kirby has since opened a company that sells authentic reproductions of Thomas Crapper's Victorian bathroom fixtures.

Star Search

"I know what you're thinking—'Did he fire six shots or only five?'...you've got to ask yourself one question: 'Do I feel lucky?' Well, do ya, punk?" Those infamous words from the 1971 hit film *Dirty Harry* were responsible for skyrocketing Clint Eastwood to stardom. But, according to the original plan, those words should have been uttered by someone else. The role of Dirty Harry was first offered to Frank Sinatra. After he refused, the role was offered to John Wayne and then Paul Newman. It wasn't until the studio exhausted their search that Clint Eastwood finally accepted the part of the rogue San Francisco detective.

Tasty (but Troublesome) Foods

Some of the most common foods are the worst when it comes to digestion. Learning what the body can and can't handle may help you avoid those dreaded post-meal pains.

Sure, to some people the foods below might seem like a list of all-time favorites. But some of those classic American dishes are actually causing your body to protest. Start listening to it now and save yourself some misery two hours after dinner.

Chocolate
Unfortunately, this sweet treat tops the list of digestive downers. Chemicals in chocolate cause some of the digestive muscles to relax, allowing burning acid to creep back up out of the stomach. It's not all negative, though: A small amount of chocolate shouldn't do much damage. Eating too much of it, nutritionists say, is when people start to see problems.

Beans
It's no surprise that the so-called "magical fruit" doesn't sit well in the stomach. The reason? Beans require a specific enzyme in order to break down, and most people don't have enough of it to properly digest them.

Broccoli
The fiber in this frequent salad addition can leave the tummy feeling funny long after the meal's finished. It's the sulfur in broccoli that causes all the discomfort. The solution is simple, though: Cooking the broccoli can break up the sulfur and keep your stomach from doing turns.

Chicken Nuggets
Doctors say the fried chicken nugget is just plain bad for your insides. The grease and high fat make it a chore for your system to digest, especially if you are already prone to stomach problems. Bake 'em instead, and your belly will thank you.

Gum

Dieticians and dentists are at war on this one. Sugar-free gum, it turns out, is not problem-free for your digestive system. Sorbitol, the sugar substitute used in many brands, can really get things rumbling above your belt. Gums that have ten grams or more of Sorbitol are the most troublesome.

Ice Cream

If you aren't careful, frozen goodies can lead to terrible bellyaches. The fat found in ice cream takes too long for the stomach to process, which can leave you feeling full and bloated. Plus, many people have problems digesting dairy—another red flag in the frozen food aisle.

Mashed Potatoes

Dairy is also the downside to this familiar food. The milk and cream mixed into most mashed creations can cause all sorts of gastrointestinal upsets. When eating at a restaurant, you may just be out of luck. At home, though, you can switch to lactose-free milk to make it easier on your digestive system.

Onions

Eating these tear-inducing vegetables raw isn't just bad for your breath—the nutrients in the fragrant fixings can send your stomach into overdrive. Like broccoli, however, cooking the onions first can cut back their kick. Your significant other will also be appreciative.

Orange Juice

Mr. Simpson isn't the only OJ associated with danger. The beloved morning beverage can coat your esophagus with acid, causing irritation. Avoiding citrus juice on an empty stomach can help dilute its effects, so grab a bagel before you gulp that glass.

Peppers

Sure, spice can be nice, but you may pay the price. The burning thirst that jalapeños and other peppers bring isn't just a feeling—it's a sign from your body. The spice can do some serious damage on its way down, and once that process starts, there's not much you can do to stop it.

Fast Facts

- *Think you can go a long time without eating? Adult crocodiles can go an entire year without a bite.*

- *The word "nerd" comes from Dr. Seuss, who first used the term in his 1950 book* If I Ran the Zoo.

- *A racehorse from the early 1900s named Lolly Pop provided the inspiration for the lollipop candy name.*

- *The average dog runs about 19 miles per hour.*

- *Prior to becoming a dictator, Fidel Castro spent some time in the ballpark: He played baseball for the University of Havana during the 1940s.*

- *On the first slot machines, the symbols on each reel were suits from playing cards. After slots were banned in 1902, the machines were changed to offer gum, candy, and drinks—and the card suits were covered over with images of gum and fruit. The cherries are still used, but the sticks of gum turned into the black bars seen on many slot machines today.*

- *Safe driving is a major concern for legislators: New York State has made it illegal for blind people to drive. Meanwhile, Tennessee took matters a country mile further when legislators prohibited driving while asleep.*

- *The McDonald brothers—founders of the billions-sold fast food chain—sold their business to Ray Kroc for $2.7 million in 1961.*

- *Wine bottles are tinted to keep the liquid from being exposed to light. Even small amounts of exposure can cause the stuff to spoil.*

The Talk of the Tracks: Hobo Slang

Has someone ever said to you: "I'm one John Hollow Legs. I don't even have an ace spot to my name, which is why I need to find a doughnut philosopher and beg him for a dukie."

No? Then you've never conversed with a hobo.

Hobo, a word used to describe a wandering homeless person, became particularly iconic during the Great Depression. Hoboes had a language all their own. The sentence at the top, for example, translates to: "I'm a hungry stiff. I don't even have one dollar to my name. I need to find a hobo who is satisfied with his coffee and food so I can beg him for something to eat."

First heard in the American Pacific Northwest in the late 1800s, the term differentiates migrants who are willing to work from "bums" or "tramps," who will not. The term **hobo** itself is possibly slang for "Ho boy," "Hello Brother," or even "hoe-boy" (an itinerant farm worker). By the 1890s, hobo was an accepted term, a fraternity growing in tandem with the miles of railroad tracks springing up across the United States.

Some hobo terms are still common enough. A **cathouse** is still a brothel, while a **coffin nail** still describes a cigarette. A burial site for the destitute is called a **potter's field**, and **glad rags** means nice clothing. Other hobo jargon, however, is a bit more incomprehensible. For instance, **axle grease** means butter, and a **dog robber** is not someone who steals a pooch but rather a term for a boarding house keeper. **Flintstone kids** describes the latest generation of hoboes instead of the cartoon characters Pebbles and Bam-Bam, and a **town clown** means a policeman rather than a municipal jester.

Hoboes have by and large faded from the American scene. However, that doesn't mean their lingo has, too. Who knows, maybe someday you'll get a request to hand out some **toadskins**. If you know that means paper money rather than the actual hide of a toad, you'll be much better off.

Word Histories

President: Originally the title of the leader of the United States was supposed to be "His Highness the President of the United States of America and Protector of the Rights of the Same." George Washington, however, disliked the use of "His Highness" and settled upon simply "Mr. President" as an appropriate title for the leader of the new democracy. The word itself is derived from the Latin *praesidere* meaning "to govern."

Acid Test: Now more commonly associated with 1960s LSD culture, the phrase originally referred to the use of nitric acid by frontier prospectors and traders to determine whether an object or rock contained gold. Similar substances such as copper or iron will corrode upon contact, but gold is not affected.

Acrobat: Acrobat is derived from the Greek words for "aloft" plus "climbing or walking"; the best Greek acrobats were called *neurobats* and used a length of catgut that was comparable to modern fishing line in thinness, so that they appeared to be walking through the air.

Xmas: Those who believe that this word is a cheap and potentially blasphemous abbreviation for "Christmas" forget that since at least A.D. 1100 the symbol X, derived from the Greek word for Messiah, has been used in reference to Jesus Christ. In fact, the word "Xmas" has been around since at least the mid-1500s.

Love Apple: One of the first terms used to refer to tomatoes, which until the 19th century were believed by most Europeans to be poisonous.

Aftermath: This derives from the 15th century term *after mowth,* which referred to the second harvest of hay cut every summer.

Ahoy: First recorded in Tobias Smollett's *The Adventures of Peregrine Pickle* (1751), the word was by then a common greeting among sailors though it originated with hog farmers who used it to call to their animals. Alexander Graham Bell wanted the term to be the standard greeting for telephone calls.

Managerial Musical Chairs

For Chicago Cubs fans in the early 1960s, the question
wasn't "Who's on First?," but rather, "Who's in the dugout?"
If ever there was an idea that deserved a failing grade,
it would be Philip K. Wrigley's College of Coaches.

Hibernation

The Chicago Cubs were once one of
baseball's elite teams. But that was
many years ago; by 1961, the team
hadn't had a winning record for over a
decade. This was despite the presence
of some good ballplayers on the roster,
most notably Hall of Famers Ernie Banks and Billy Williams.

Cubs fans had put up with a lot as the team struggled for years
under owner Philip K. Wrigley, the gum magnate who had inherited the team in 1932. Once, for example, Wrigley traded his team
manager for another team's broadcaster.

But that was nothing compared to what Wrigley concocted
in 1961. Scrambling for a new strategy, he unveiled not one new
manager that season, but eight. Instead of a single face in the
dugout, Wrigley had devised a bizarre new system he called "The
College of Coaches."

Coaching Carousel

Here's how it worked: From a pool of coaches, Wrigley would
select one to be the head coach, or manager, for an unspecified
period of time. Then, whenever he felt like it, Wrigley would pick
a new head coach from the pool.

The concept behind the College of Coaches was that instead
of firing the manager if the team played poorly, Wrigley could
merely demote him and immediately choose a replacement from
seven others rather than spend long hours searching for a new
manager.

He also intended for the coaches, during the times they were not the head coach, to work with the players to instill a cohesive system and style. Therefore, whenever a new head coach was appointed, the players would already know the system.

The idea received a storm of ridicule. "The Cubs have been playing without players for years," said one critic. "Now, they're going to try it without a manager."

The Ship of Fools

Undeterred, Wrigley and the Cubs sailed into the 1961 season on the good ship College of Coaches—and promptly began listing to one side. The experiment violated a cardinal rule of successful sports teams: Consistency is vital. Under the College of Coaches, the players never knew who was going to be in charge, or for how long. The comfort and security a player felt under one manager might be yanked away the next day when a new man took over.

In addition, the other coaches weren't always inclined to help the existing head coach if things went bad, preferring to wait until they got their own shot at the top job. With each head coach set in his own way of doing things, chaos reigned in the Cubs dugout.

Report Card

In 1961, the first year of the College of Coaches, the team finished four games better than they had the previous year. But in 1962, the Cubs' ship really sank as the team went 59–103, finishing the season ahead of only the hapless New York Mets, who lost a record 120 games that year.

In 1963 and 1964, Wrigley kept up the pretense of rotating coaches, although he kept one man in charge all year. In November 1965, the system mercifully came to an end.

Although Wrigley Field was famous for its ivy-covered outfield walls, Wrigley's experimental "college" was anything but Ivy League.

The College of Coaches had flunked out.

Odd Ordinances

- Kissing a woman while she's asleep is a crime in Logan County, Colorado.

- Any man with a moustache is not allowed to kiss women in Eureka, Nevada.

- Flirting in public is against the law in Little Rock, Arkansas.

- Michigan law states that a woman's hair is technically owned by her husband.

- It's illegal for kids under the age of seven to attend college in Winston-Salem, North Carolina (sorry, Doogie).

- Talking on the phone without a parent on the line is a crime in Blue Earth, Minnesota.

- You can't buy a lollipop without a doctor's note while church services are in session if you live in Kalispell, Montana.

- Any man who comes face-to-face with a cow has to remove his hat in Fruithill, Kentucky.

- It's illegal to eat chicken with a fork in Gainesville, Georgia.

- You could go to jail for making an ugly face at a dog in the state of Oklahoma.

- A frog—yes, a frog—can be arrested for keeping a person awake with its "ribbit" noises in Memphis, Tennessee.

- Eating nuts on a city bus in Charleston, South Carolina, could cost you a $500 fine or even 60 days in jail.

- Don't get too friendly at happy hour in Nyala, Nevada—buying drinks for more than three people in a single round is against the law.

- North Dakota has outlawed the serving of beer with pretzels at public restaurants and bars.

Domestic Daredevils

*Extreme ironing: serious sport or tongue-in-cheek
response to the "extreme" sports of the '90s?*

Board to be Wild

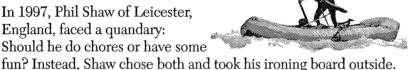

In 1997, Phil Shaw of Leicester,
England, faced a quandary:
Should he do chores or have some
fun? Instead, Shaw chose both and took his ironing board outside.

A new sport was born. According to Shaw's Web site, extreme
ironing is a "danger sport that combines the thrills of an extreme
outdoor activity with the satisfaction of a well pressed shirt." With
a bit of bravery and tongue firmly in cheek, athletes are required
to take an ironing board and iron to an extreme location, such as a
mountain cliff or deep underwater, and press a few items of clothing.

Go, Crease Lightning!

Shaw, who calls himself Steam, has toured America, Fiji, New
Zealand, Australia, and South Africa in a worldwide recruitment
campaign. Enthusiasm for the sport spread, and the 2002 Extreme
Ironing World Championship took place near Munich, Germany.
Since then, enthusiasts have been setting extreme-ironing records,
which require a board that's at least 1 meter long and 30 centimeters
wide, a recognizable landmark, visual proof of your feat, and a garment that is at least the size of a tea towel.

Extreme ironers, who go by nicknames like Perfectly Pressed and
Crease Lightning, have ironed in the back of taxi cabs; underwater
off the coast of Dahab, Egypt; in the Antarctic tundra; and while suspended from a crane in a transparent box. While early practitioners
used extension cords to power their irons, serious contenders use
battery-powered gear to reach the most extreme locations.

Whether these domestic daredevils are serious or merely poking
fun at the absurdity of extreme sports remains to be seen. For those
interested in taking their ironing outside, however, the Extreme
Ironing Bureau recommends simply starting in your own backyard.

Fast Facts

- *The Bible contains 32 references to dogs, but none to cats.*

- *A mouse only takes 35 days to reach its adult sexual maturity.*

- *In 1843, the first commercial Christmas card was printed in England, using illustrations by John Calcott Horsley, a noted London artist of the time. The press run was 1,000 cards. Today, in the United States alone, two billion cards are sent every Christmas—something of a hallmark.*

- *The average snail lives six years.*

- *Every single U.S. president has worn glasses at least some of the time.*

- *Before Popeye, Olive Oyl's boyfriend was named Ham Gravy.*

- *Three presidents died on the Fourth of July: Thomas Jefferson, John Adams, and James Monroe.*

- *Prior to his presidential career, Gerald Ford spent some time as a male model.*

- *The most commonly used letter in the English language is "e." The most common consonant is "t," and the most common second letter in a word is "h." (No surprise—the most popular word in the English language is "the"!)*

- *There are pink dolphins in the Amazon River.*

- *The world's largest bagel weighed 868 pounds and was a full six feet in diameter. It was made at Bruegger's Bagels in Syracuse, New York.*

Spoken For: Commitment Customs

❖ ❖ ❖ ❖

*First comes love, then comes marriage . . . or so
the saying goes. However, some couples prefer to stretch
the period of time between love's first blush and the
culminating bonds of marriage by "engaging" in practices
that publicly express their commitment without
taking it all the way to the altar.*

Rings . . .

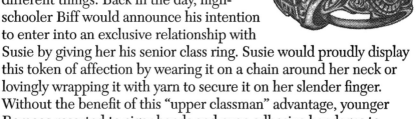

Precious metals that are forged into circular
shapes without beginning or end, rings are
a time-honored symbol of love and commitment. However, different rings signify
different things. Back in the day, high-
schooler Biff would announce his intention
to enter into an exclusive relationship with
Susie by giving her his senior class ring. Susie would proudly display
this token of affection by wearing it on a chain around her neck or
lovingly wrapping it with yarn to secure it on her slender finger.
Without the benefit of this "upper classman" advantage, younger
Romeos resorted to cigar bands and even adhesive bandages to
express their ardor.

A promise ring was the next stop on the love train. More feminine and mature than a class ring—not to mention custom-fit—
a promise ring held the pledge of a future engagement and signified
the first tentative step toward the aisle.

. . . and Things

Rings are not the only items used to express commitment. Letter
sweaters, jackets, and ID bracelets also symbolize a "going steady"
status. Some college men present their sweethearts with lavalieres,
necklaces with their fraternity letters, to signify the seriousness of
their relationship. But the ultimate Greek act of commitment occurs
when a frat boy "pins" his intended life partner.

The Catholic Church took a dim view of the monogamous trend
that began among youth in the 1950s. In 1957, *TIME* magazine

reported a Catholic high school in Connecticut that expelled four students for going steady. An article in a Paulist Fathers publication warned it was "impossible" for a young boy and girl in an exclusive relationship to be alone together "without serious sin." (Amen.)

Gestures of Love

Exchanging trinkets is not the only way to express commitment. Some couples feel the need to memorialize their undying affection for each other by publicly linking their names for all to see. Whether scrawling their names on trees, water towers, bathroom stalls, or their own skins via tattooing, the whole world is a canvas for young lovers.

In Rome, the Eternal City, couples often express their commitment in a "novel" way. In life-imitates-art fashion, recently young lovers have been mimicking a scene from *I Want You*, a best-selling-book-turned-movie in which the protagonist padlocks a chain around a lamppost on a bridge; he then tosses the key into the Tiber river to signify his ever-lasting love. Since then, so many love locks have been wrapped around lampposts over Rome's Ponte Milvio bridge that the authorities have had to install special steel posts to preserve the light posts.

Commitment Ceremonies

Ceremonies are sometimes used to signal commitment without entering into a ball-and-chain contract. Handfasting, an ancient Celtic ritual where the couples' wrists were symbolically tied together, was practiced by the upper class as an engagement of sorts, to signify a promise of marriage before the dowry details were worked out. For the peasant class, for whom dowries often weren't an issue, handfasting was kind of a trial marriage signifying that the couple would stay together for a predetermined length of time, generally a year, and then reevaluate their relationship. The phrase "tying the knot" reportedly originated from handfasting.

"Jumping the broom," in which couples literally jump over a broom, is another non-wedding commitment ceremony, although today many African weddings incorporate this practice into the traditional rites. The origins of this ceremony are thought to have begun during America's slavery era. Since slaves were not allowed to marry, the broom-jumping ritual was a way for the couple to publicly vow their fidelity.

ANAGRAMS

*An anagram is a word or phrase that exactly reproduces
the letters in another word or phrase. The most interesting of them
reflect or comment on the subject of the first.*

An old shoe—Had no sole

The countryside—No city dust here

Punishment—Nine thumps

Southern California—Hot sun, or life in a car

The cockroach—Cook, catch her

Norwegians—Swen or Inga

On any screen—Sean Connery

The best things in life are free—Nail-biting refreshes the feet

Contaminated—No admittance

School cafeteria—Hot cereal fiasco

Semolina—Is no meal

The nudist colony—No untidy clothes

Alien forms—Life on Mars

Dormitory—Dirty room

Thug ponders—Drops the gun

I love you—You, Olive

The piano bench—Beneath Chopin

Ulysses S. Grant—Try sunglasses

Funeral—Real fun

Roast turkey—Try our steak

Halitosis—Lois has it

A psychiatrist—Sit, chat, pay, sir

Feel the Burn:
The Active Denial System

The U.S. Air Force and the Department of Defense, paired with corporate weapons contractors, have developed a new non-lethal weapon called the Active Denial System (ADS).

While this weapon has the potential to save lives, some worry about the potential for abuse.

The Pain Ray

The story behind the Active Denial System reads like a sci-fi thriller: Academics discover the power of invisible rays, and the government harnesses that technology for the forces of good *and* evil, all against the backdrop of a controversial war.

In the 1980s, scientists discovered that a wavelength of energy called a "millimeter wave," which registers somewhere between an X-ray and a microwave, causes intense pain when directed on human skin. At a frequency of 94 to 95 gigahertz, the energy penetrates 1/64 of an inch below the skin, causing the water molecules located there to heat rapidly. This technology was named "Active Denial" for its potential to actively deny potential intrusions or assaults—in this case, "active denial" is a euphemism for "causes perpetrator to retreat in spasms of pain." In fact, the media sometimes refers to ADS as the "pain ray."

Beginning in 2000, the Air Force Research Laboratory, in partnership with the Department of Defense's Joint Non-Lethal Weapons Directorate, created prototype weapons that harnessed this technology. Large-scale tests were done on human subjects, and the weapon was used in simulated military scenarios. The ADS looks like a satellite dish with a long arm that directs the invisible beam of millimeter energy onto a target. The device is operated by software that controls the strength of the beam, the duration of the beam's shot, and the distance the beam travels to reach the target. Ideally, when the beam hits a person, they'll run away in pain.

Putting ADS to Use

Now that ADS technology has been tested and developed, the question remains about its use. In 2003, generals in the Iraq war requested ADS units in hopes that its crowd-dispersal potential would limit Iraqi civilian deaths, but ADS testing wasn't complete until 2007. The government's goal is to use ADS units in military operations as early as 2010.

Generals in Iraq are not the only anticipated buyers. Another version of ADS technology is being developed by the Justice Department in the hope that one day these painful beams will emit from small handheld devices, sort of like high-tech mace. The weapons contractor corporation Raytheon, which was involved with the military's development of ADS, is developing and marketing the technology for law enforcement and private security use.

Potential Problems

While ADS technology certainly doesn't have the apocalyptic potentials of past developments like the atomic bomb, some red flags have been raised. During trials, a small number of subjects sustained burn blisters after exposure; one test subject suffered from second-degree burns. The trial tests were ambiguous concerning how the intensity of the beam is calibrated to the distance of the target. Another issue is whether victims will really get out of the way before they are seriously injured. This concern was referred to in a 2007 report as the "safety margin between the repel response and injury." Another worry is that the method's "crowd dispersal" potential will be used to limit civil liberties and peaceful protests.

While most information on ADS testing has been released to the public, some information still remains classified, including the system's operational range (i.e., how far the beam can shoot), and its potential use for "unconventional countermeasures" (whatever that means). As ADS technology continues to proliferate, one can only hope that it will be used for its stated purposes of saving, rather than taking, human lives.

The Cottingley Fairy Hoax

❖ ❖ ❖ ❖

It was a story so seemingly real that even the creator of the world's most intelligent literary detective was convinced it was true.

Pixie Party

It was summertime in the English village of Cottingley in 1917 when cousins Elsie Wright and Frances Griffiths borrowed Elsie's father's new camera. When he later developed the glass plate negatives, he saw a photo of Frances with a group of four tiny, winged fairies. A prank, he figured. Two months later, the girls took another photo. This one showed Elsie with a gnome. At that point, her father banned them from using the camera again.

But a few years later, Wright's wife mentioned her daughter's fairy photos within earshot of theosophist Edward Gardner, who was so taken with them that he showed them to a leading photographic expert. After studying them extensively, this man declared the photos genuine. They caught the attention of spiritual believer Sir Arthur Conan Doyle, author of the Sherlock Holmes series, who published a magazine article announcing the Cottingley fairies to the world.

A Delusional Doyle

In 1922, Doyle published *The Coming of the Fairies*. The book argued for the existence of fairies and contained the original photos along with three new pictures that Elsie and Frances had produced. Both the article and book ignited a pitched battle between believers and doubters. Many thought Doyle's fertile imagination had finally gotten the better of him.

Fairy Tale?

As years passed, people remained fascinated by the story. In 1981, Elsie admitted that the whole thing was a hoax taken too far, and that the fairies were actually paper cutouts held up by hatpins. Frances, however, maintained the fairies were authentic even up to her death.

Talk to the Expert

CIRCUS ARTIST

Q: You prefer to be called a "circus artist," rather than a "trapeze artist," because you've done a little bit of everything.
A: I consider myself an "aerialist," because I've done trapeze and Spanish web and aerial fabrics—what they call "the silks." I used to be an acrobat, and I'd fly through the air and somersault.

Q: I can't resist: Did you fly through the air with the greatest of ease?
A: I would have to say that I did. When you do it as much as I did growing up—I started training when I was five—it actually becomes second nature. Like being a musician: Your muscles remember where the chords are; your body remembers how to do it.

Q: You grew up in a circus family, which is unusual.
A: Not to me! All of my friends grew up in a circus family. My dad joined the circus in his 20s and wanted his family to be a part of it. My mother was a second-generation circus family.

Q: You make it look so easy up there, but it really takes amazing strength. How do you achieve that?
A: What I tell my students is that if you keep doing it, you build up the strength for it. A lot of people come in and get really frustrated. They say, "I'm gonna go work out and come back stronger." But the strength that you develop is really specific for aerial. You can work out; you can do Pilates every day of your life. You still wouldn't have the skills or level of strength for these specific apparatuses.

Q: Is it true what they say about not looking down?
A: Yes! I've never really been scared of falling. I mean, everybody should be scared of falling, because that's natural. But if you focus on the fear, you're not going to do anything.

Crime and Punishment

This tale of greed and mass murder
ushered in a new era of forensic science.

Love's Labor Lost

Jack Graham's mother, Daisie King, knew her only son was no angel, but she must have hoped he'd change his ways: Barely into his 20s, Graham had little patience for lawful employment, and he'd already been convicted of running illegal booze and check forgery. It's thought that King paid for her son's lawyer and anted up $2,500 in court-ordered restitution on the forgery convictions.

By 1953, however, it seemed that Graham was settling down. He married and by 1955 had two children. His mother, a successful businesswoman, bought a house in Colorado for the young couple, built a drive-in restaurant, and installed Graham as its manager.

But the drive-in lost money. Graham blamed his mother's meddling in the management for the loss, but he later admitted he had skimmed receipts. He also confessed to vandalizing the place twice, once by smashing the front window and the second time by rigging a gas explosion to destroy equipment he'd used as security for a personal loan. A new pickup truck Graham bought himself mysteriously stalled on a railway track with predictable results. This too proved to be an attempt at insurance fraud.

Flight to Doom

In the fall of 1955, King wanted to see her daughter in Alaska, and she prepared for her trip there via Portland and Seattle. On November 1, Graham saw her off on United Air Flight 629. Eleven minutes after takeoff, the plane exploded in the sky. Forty-four people died, including King.

Within 24 hours FBI fingerprint experts were at the crash site to help identify bodies. The painstaking task of gathering wreckage from over a three-mile trail of scraps started. By November 7, Civil Aeronautics investigators concluded sabotage was the probable cause of the disaster.

Criminal investigators joined the FBI technical teams. Families of passengers and crew members were interviewed while technicians reassembled the plane's midsection where the explosion likely occurred. In the course of sifting through wreckage, bomb fragments and explosives residue were identified.

Avalanche of Evidence

Inevitably, investigators took an interest in Graham. Not only would he receive a substantial inheritance from his mother's estate, he had also taken out a $37,500 travel insurance policy on her. Moreover, he had a criminal record, and according to witnesses, a history of heated arguments with his mother.

Graham was first interviewed on November 10, and again over the following two days. In a search of his property on November 12, agents discovered a roll of primer cord in a shirt pocket and a copy of the travel insurance policy secreted in a small box. Circumstantial evidence contradicted his statements, including that provided by his wife, half-sister, and acquaintances.

Finally, Graham admitted he'd built a bomb and placed it in his mother's luggage. On November 14, he was arraigned on charges of sabotage. At the time the charge did not carry a death penalty, so he was brought back into court on November 17 and charged with first-degree murder.

A Case of Firsts

Notwithstanding the confession, investigators continued to gather forensic evidence, putting together what may have been the most scientifically detailed case in U.S. history up to that date. The case had other firsts as well. It was the first case of mass murder in the United States via airplane explosion. Graham's trial, which began on April 16, 1956, also marked the first time TV cameras were permitted to air a live broadcast of a courtroom trial.

On May 5, 1956, the jury needed only 69 minutes to find Graham guilty. On January 11, 1957, he was executed at Colorado State Penitentiary, remorseless to the end.

Behind the Music of Our Time

- The catchphrase from Metallica's '90s smash hit "Enter Sandman" almost didn't happen. Singer James Hetfield originally wrote the lyric "disrupt the perfect family" in place of the catchy "we're off to never-never land." The band decided it was too dark for the song to succeed and convinced Hetfield to change it.

- The inspiration for Duran Duran's "Hungry like the Wolf" came from Little Red Riding Hood.

- Blondie singer Deborah Harry worked as a Playboy bunny before becoming a full-fledged pop star.

- The Beatles' "I Want to Hold Your Hand" was the top-selling single of the 1960s.

- Elvis Presley's "Don't Be Cruel/Hound Dog" was the best-selling single in the 1950s.

- Elvis scored an unimpressive grade of C in his junior high music class.

- John Lennon's "(Just Like) Starting Over" is considered the best-selling posthumous hit of all time.

- Both pre-fame Elvis Presley and Buddy Holly didn't make the cut when they tried out for *Arthur Godfrey's Talent Scouts,* a '50s-era talent show.

- The Righteous Brothers' "You've Lost That Lovin' Feeling," written by Phil Spector, Barry Mann, and Cynthia Weil, is considered the most-performed rock song of all time.

- One of the women in the group of background singers on "You've Lost That Lovin' Feeling" was none other than a then-unknown Cher.

- The Dire Straits' *Brothers in Arms* has the honor of being the first CD to sell a million copies.

- Thanks to a copyright ruling in the mid-'90s, every child who sang in the chorus of Pink Floyd's 1979 hit "Another Brick in the Wall (part II)" earned a rumored $850 in royalties—nearly two decades after the recording.

Camelot 9-1-1:
JFK's Secret Ailments

❖ ❖ ❖ ❖

*The universal image of President John F. Kennedy is a young,
athletic one: playing touch football, swimming a great
distance after his PT boat was attacked, and rough-housing on
the White House lawn with his children. But the popular
image is false—in reality, Kennedy was a very sick man.*

State Secrets

The status of presidential health is as zealously guarded as the
formula for Coca-Cola. The image of a vigorous president is considered vital to the health of the nation, even if in reality he is incapacitated (Woodrow Wilson's debilitating stroke), seriously ill (Grover
Cleveland had cancer surgery on his mouth), or just plain unhealthy
(William Howard Taft weighed in at more than 300 pounds). To this
day, many people still don't know that Franklin Roosevelt needed
braces to stand because he and his staff hid his disability so well.

Kennedy was different. The youngest man ever elected a U.S.
president, he projected an image of strength and vitality. Yet the
further one gets from the idealistic façade of Camelot, the more one
learns about it.

A Lifetime of Medicating

Kennedy was a sickly child. He suffered from scarlet fever, bronchitis, measles, whooping cough, chicken pox, and ear infections—all
before age 13. He had an operation for appendicitis in the early
1930s, and he was rushed to the hospital in the winter of 1936 where
doctors feared he had leukemia. He also went to the Mayo Clinic
that year to be treated for colitis, and repeatedly complained of
abdominal pain.

Kennedy took steroids for his ailments, possibly as early as
1937 but certainly by 1947. When he ran for a seat in the House of
Representatives in 1946, he was described as looking "like a skeleton." Due to his many and varied illnesses, he received the Last

Rites twice between 1947 and 1955. Robert Kennedy later said, "When we were growing up together we used to laugh about the great risk a mosquito took in biting Jack Kennedy—with some of his blood the mosquito was almost sure to die."

When Kennedy ran for president in 1960, an aide carrying a bag filled with medical supplies always followed him. Once the bag was misplaced in Connecticut. Kennedy frantically telephoned the state's governor to find the bag.

Patient-in-Chief

After he was elected president, Kennedy felt it more important than ever to maintain the fiction that he was in good, robust health. Reporters who tried to pursue stories of his Addison's disease (a rare disorder that affects the adrenal gland's production of steroid hormones) were told that he had a mild adrenal deficiency, which was being handled by oral medication.

As Chief Executive, Kennedy outwardly portrayed a picture of tanned vitality. However, the truth was that he had numerous doctors available at any given time. Among the physicians caring for the president were an allergist, an endocrinologist, a gastroenterologist, an orthopedist, a urologist, and an internist.

Kennedy's medical problems during his first six months in office read like the script for a melodramatic medical movie: high fevers; problems with his colon, stomach, and prostate; abscesses; back troubles; adrenal ailments; periodic dehydration; high cholesterol; and sleeplessness. During this time, Kennedy took so many medications that Dr. Janet Travell, the internist, kept a list called the "Medicine Administration Record" to keep straight all the drugs he was receiving.

In addition, Kennedy also kept Dr. Max Jacobson close at hand. A German doctor known as "Dr. Feelgood" and "Miracle Max," Jacobson treated celebrities for depression and fatigue with injections laced with amphetamines, steroids, multivitamins, and other substances. In 1961, Jacobson accompanied the president on a trip to France, flying there on a chartered jet so that he could continue treating him. Kennedy dismissed questions about Jacobson's dubious injections with a curt, "I don't care if it's horse piss. It works."

Long-term Effects

One long-term effect of steroids (unknown when Kennedy began taking them) is that they cause osteoporosis in the lower backbones. That, and several back surgeries, kept Kennedy in almost constant back pain for years. In the autumn of 1961, one of Kennedy's physicians, Admiral George Burkley, decided that the injections the president had been getting for his back, along with braces and other devices that he wore, were hurting rather than helping him. Burkley feared that Kennedy would soon be wheelchair-bound. He brought in orthopedic surgeon Hans Kraus, who warned Kennedy that he must begin immediate exercise to strengthen the muscles. Kennedy began exercising three times a week. By the spring of 1962, the president was doing better than he had in several years.

The million-dollar question is whether or not Kennedy's many medications affected his performance as president. Historians agree that it doesn't seem to be the case. While president, Kennedy was taking antibiotics (urinary tract infections), anti-spasmodics (colitis), steroids (Addison's disease), antihistamines (allergies), and painkillers (back pain). Yet these medications probably helped him function at times when he otherwise could not have.

The Great What-If

History is filled with conjecture; one of the most intriguing theories concern the stiff back brace Kennedy was wearing the day of his assassination in Dallas, Texas, on November 22, 1963. If he had not been wearing the brace, which was designed to hold him upright, perhaps he might have moved or slumped sideways when the first shot hit him. Perhaps he would have been able to avoid the fatal second shot. But that's the funny thing about conjecture: We'll never know for sure.

FROM THE VAULTS OF HISTORY

Navel Novelties
During the 1960s, women weren't allowed to show much skin on television. Decades before Janet Jackson's infamous "wardrobe malfunction," TV censors barred actress Mariette Hartley from exposing her belly button on a 1969 episode of *Star Trek* (for all you Trekkers out there, it was episode 78, "All Our Yesterdays"). But Gene Roddenberry, creator of the successful sci-fi series, decided to get back at the censors. When he released the 1973 science fiction TV movie, *Genesis II,* he gave Hartley *two* belly buttons.

Starring: Napoleon
As far as powerful people featured in movies go, Jesus Christ doesn't compare to Napoleon Bonaparte. The "little general" is the most-often played historical figure, with over 194 movies to his credit. Jesus comes in second with 152, and the 16th president of the United States, Abraham Lincoln, is a distant third with 137 appearances.

Masses for the *Messiah*
The Irish love their music and always have. So on April 13, 1742, when the New Music Hall on Fishamble Street in Dublin hosted the first performance of Handel's now-famous *Messiah,* it was standing room only. In fact, so many music lovers were squeezed into the hall that management asked men not to wear their swords and women to leave their hoop skirts at home.

Cerf's Challenge
In addition to being a panel member on the popular 1950s television show, *What's My Line,* Bennett Cerf co-founded the Random House publishing company. One of Cerf's earliest authors was Theodor Geisel, who wrote under the pen name of Dr. Seuss. Cerf bet Geisel that he couldn't write a book using exactly 50 words—no more, no less. Geisel stunned the publisher when he rose to the challenge and produced one of the best-selling children's books of all time, *Green Eggs & Ham.*

Hallelujah!: Celebrities Who Found God

These famous folks got the call—and answered it.

Sam Kinison: It may be hard to believe that this loudmouth (and often vulgar) comedian once commanded a pulpit, but before he graced the stages of the late night TV shows, he was an evangelical preacher (just like his Dad).

Kirk Cameron: He started out as lovable Mike Seaver on the TV show *Growing Pains.* But at age 18, the teen heartthrob did a little soul searching and became a part of the Christian evangelical ministry, The Way of the Master. Now he focuses his acting efforts on Christian productions such as the *Left Behind* series.

Run (from Run-DMC): This rap superstar asked us to "Walk This Way" with Aerosmith in 1986. Now the Reverend Joseph "Run" Simmons dispenses spiritual wisdom as a Pentecostal preacher.

Reggie White: The football star came by his nickname honestly— the NFL's "Minister of Defense" was an ordained evangelical minister.

Ralph Waldo Emerson: This famed poet graduated from Harvard University in 1821 and began his studies at Harvard Divinity School. Although he didn't graduate, he became a Unitarian minister in 1829. He resigned a few years later over a dispute with church officials but went on to publish a number of well-known essays and poems, including "Nature," which laid the foundation for the philosophy of Transcendentalism.

Mister Rogers: This kind neighbor with a closet full of cardigans was the real deal. Fred Rogers was a graduate of the Pittsburgh Theological Seminary and a Presbyterian minister before he followed the trolley to the Neighborhood of Make Believe in *Mister Rogers' Neighborhood.*

He Said, She Said

"Age is strictly a case of mind over matter. If you don't mind, it doesn't matter."

—*Jack Benny*

"At my age flowers scare me."

—*George Burns*

"Everything we do in life is based on fear, especially love."

—*Mel Brooks*

"To me, there is no greater act of courage than being the one who kisses first."

—*Janeane Garofalo*

"I drink too much. The last time I gave a urine sample it had an olive in it."

—*Rodney Dangerfield*

"Giving up smoking is the easiest thing in the world. I know because I've done it thousands of times."

—*Mark Twain*

"I don't worry about terrorism. I was married for two years."

—*Sam Kinison*

"Middle age is when you still believe you'll feel better in the morning."

—*Bob Hope*

"Doing nothing is very hard to do...you never know when you're finished."

—*Leslie Nielsen*

"The secret to staying young is to live honestly, eat slowly and lie about your age."

—*Lucille Ball*

"If the world comes to an end, I want to be in Cincinnati. Everything comes there ten years later."

—*Will Rogers*

"You know you're getting old when you get that one candle on the cake. It's like, 'See if you can blow this out.'"

—*Jerry Seinfeld*

Alex Was No Birdbrain

Alex was an African Grey parrot who could talk, count, and follow orders from his trainers. Alex died in 2007, but the knowledge he lent to science about animal cognition ensures his legacy.

The Avian Learning Experiment

There was once a time when Dr. Irene Pepperberg was not particularly interested in parrots. Sure, she had a parakeet as a child, but that was about it. In 1973, she was working toward a PhD in theoretical chemistry when she saw a television documentary about animal communication and intelligence. Inspired, Pepperberg continued working toward her doctorate while studying birds on the side, in an attempt to understand how animals think.

Pepperberg decided to test animal intelligence by working closely with a single animal from a young age. She picked an African Grey parrot because they live a long time (upwards of 70 years), they are known for their intelligence, and they possess the anatomy required to imitate human sounds and syllables. Pepperberg went to a pet shop and chose a one-year-old parrot. She named him Alex, an acronym for her project, the Avian Learning Experiment.

A Nutty Way of Learning

The scientific community questioned whether animals learn through simple operant conditioning, or whether some animals are capable of a more nuanced associative learning. The former involves simple input and output. If you want to teach a bird how to say "hello," you teach them through repetition—a person's entrance will coincide with a positive stimulus, but only if the word "hello" is also spoken. Previous researchers had failed to teach parrots a high vocabulary by training them in this manner.

Pepperberg suspected the problem was that researchers assumed birds are incapable of associative learning. In the wild, an associative learning scenario might go something like this: A parrot encounters a large variety of berries. Over time, the parrot learns that some berries are like or different than other berries, and should be eaten at different times of the year and in different quantities. This leads to mental categorization. From this comes *representation,* or the ability to represent objects within these categories through social interaction. One bird pecking another bird's head might mean "macadamia nuts." This is linked to functionality, so that interaction might mean, "let's go find macadamia nuts." This implies the ability to have abstract thoughts about desire, intention, and future activities.

We may never know how birds think—the abstract thoughts and representations in avian brains may work in ways we can never fully conceive. But one path to understanding is to teach them *our* mode of representational communication: words. How parrots use these words might indicate whether they have abstract thought.

Alex's Abilities

Scientists commonly believe that intelligence and learning is rooted in social interaction, so Pepperberg taught Alex in a social manner. Alex competed with his trainers for rewards, and learned words in their social context so that the word was not disjointed from its meaning. Alex learned quickly; soon he knew over 150 words and could accurately label objects according to their color, shape, and material. He also answered questions about relative size and quantity. According to reports, when he was tired of testing, he said, "I'm going to go away." If a trainer got annoyed, Alex replied, "I'm sorry."

Some argue that Alex was not really capable of representational thought. When he says, "I want nut," he might not know what the words "want" and "nut" mean. However, many instances suggested he understood what the words communicated. For example, Alex was once shown an apple, for which he did not have a word. He did, however, know the words "banana" and "cherry." Alex spontaneously said "banerry," which suggests he understood the words represented categories and items. When he was taught a new color, he immediately labeled objects accurately according to his new word. Unfortunately, Pepperberg's experiment was cut short by Alex's early death; another parrot, Griffin, is his successor.

Fast Facts

- *Airlines in America buy 20 million barf bags a year.*

- *More car crashes happen on Saturday than on any other day.*

- *Lettuce is named for milk. The word is derived from the Latin word* lactuca, *which means milk. It's believed the term was used because of a white liquid that can come out of a lettuce stalk when it's snapped in two.*

- *The same person who came up with the comic book character Wonder Woman also came up with the polygraph.*

- *"Heroin" was once trademarked as a brand name. Bayer bought the rights to the word in 1898.*

- *The restaurant Denny's was originally named Danny's.*

- *Draft dodging between the United States and Canada has a long tradition. So many U.S. draft dodgers came to Canada during the Civil War that locals began to worry about competition for jobs. During the Vietnam War, Canada was still the draft dodger's destination of choice when as many as 80,000 men crossed the border northward. But the practice was no one-way street. Canadian draft dodgers often headed south to escape entering WWI; that is, until the United States entered the conflict in 1917.*

- *There are 21 moons orbiting Uranus.*

- *Traces of peanuts can be found in dynamite.*

- *JELL-O once tried to market a celery flavor. It also tried coffee and cola with equally poor success.*

- *The number of calories burned while eating celery surpasses the number of calories actually contained in celery.*

The Baddest of the Bad Boys

❖ ❖ ❖ ❖

What is it about bad boys that women find so appealing? And what about those infamous guys who, despite their horrible deeds, still seem to attract the ladies? Maybe it's as poet Sylvia Plath once wrote, "Every woman adores a fascist."

Adolf Hitler reportedly had a relationship with his 20-year-old half-niece, Geli Raubal, who eventually shot herself. He went on to have several more girlfriends: Fran Hoffman, Jenny Hang, and Helene Hanfstaengl (who prevented Hitler from killing himself). Of course, the gal who would go down in Hitler history was teenager Eva Braun, whom he met in 1929. She became Frau Hitler on April 29, 1945; less than 24 hours later, however, the couple celebrated their honeymoon with a double suicide as the Allies were coming for them.

Hitler contemporary and cohort **Joseph Stalin** was married to Ekaterina Svanidze, who passed away. Nadezhda Alliluyeva was wife number two, but she later committed suicide (although some allege Stalin murdered her). It was speculated that Stalin was secretly married a third time to his mistress, Rosa Kaganovich.

Commune leader **Charles Manson** first moved in with UC Berkeley librarian Mary Brunner. Soon he convinced Brunner to allow more women to move in with them—more than a dozen in all. Later, Manson moved to "Spahn Ranch" with his infamous "Manson family," most of who were female lovers. The infamous 1969 Tate-LaBianca murders were committed by some of these female followers, under Manson's instruction.

After being convicted of the 1989 murders of their parents, brothers **Lyle** and **Erik Menendez** both married pen pals that they met while serving life sentences. Although Erik and wife Tammi have been married since 1998, the only contact they have is in the prison's public visiting area.

Some women waste no time: **Scott Peterson**, convicted in 2005 of murdering his wife and unborn child, had barely been on death row an hour when he got his first proposal!

Fumbling Felons

Hold Up 101
There are beginner books for knitting, marketing, and just about any other hobby or profession. Perhaps there should be one for criminality as well.

Two would-be robbers from Palm Beach, Florida, could have certainly used such a primer to learn whom *not* to rob. They walked into a local police station and demanded cash from the receptionist. To complete their tough-guy illusion, they held their hands in their pockets to indicate that they were holding guns. The crooks—finger guns and all—were quickly apprehended.

A Matter of Perspective
An obviously drunk man was driving a van that had already sustained considerable damage. The Georgia police officer that stopped the van discovered several outstanding warrants on the driver. When the drunk-ard was brought in to the police station, he told the cops he didn't even have change for a phone call. Incredibly, the man had won $3 million in a lottery five months ago!

As the man told it, he had so far received an initial payment of $94,000. First he dropped $30,000 in the Atlantic City casinos. Next he spent another $30,000 on the van, which he later rolled because he had drunk copious amounts of expensive French wine (approximately $10,000 worth). Curious, the cop asked what had happened to the other $24,000. "Oh," the guy replied. "I spent the other $24,000 foolishly."

The Not-So-Great Escape
Some criminals need a really big wall calendar. This was certainly the case with the Rhode Island man who was sentenced to 90 days in jail. Determined to show that no Big House could hold him, he labored on an elaborate escape scheme. He finally put his plan into action—on the 89th day of his sentence. Initially, everything went according to plan; he actually escaped for all of five minutes. After his recapture, he was sentenced to 18 months in prison, which gave him more than enough time to learn how to keep an accurate tally of the passing of days.

I Now Pronounce You
Man and Dog

This Indian farmer took an odd path to release a curse.
At least the reception must have been interesting!

The Happy Couple

In November 2007, a 33-year-old Indian farm laborer named
P. Selvakumar married a four-year-old female dog named Selvi.
There's no word as to where the couple registered for gifts.

The family of the groom had selected Selvi from an array of
strays, then bathed the bride-to-be and dressed her in an orange sari
and garland of flowers. In the style of a traditional Hindu marriage
ceremony, the betrothed strolled at the head of a celebratory procession toward the Hindu temple in Manamadurai, a town in the
Sivaganga District. There, Selvakumar formalized the marriage by
tying the *mangal sutra,* or sacred string, around Selvi's furry neck.

Nearly 200 guests attended the reception—enough of a crowd
to spook the bride into making a run for it. Selvi was later captured
and placated with a bun and some milk. After all, making arranged
marriages work can be difficult, and the ways of the heart are often a
mystery.

Star-Crossed

Selvakumar actually wed Selvi on the advice of his astrologer in an
attempt to rid Selvakumar of a curse that had followed him for more
than a decade and a half, ever since he had stoned two mating dogs
to death and hung their bodies from a tree. The contrite farmer
claimed that ever since the incident he suffered from hearing loss
in one ear, paralysis of his legs and hands, and speech impairment.
Medical doctors were unable to help him.

Such unions are not uncommon in the more rural areas of India,
particularly to banish bad luck or evil spirits. After the curse is lifted,
Selvakumar will be free to marry a human bride without the inconvenience of a divorce lawyer or Animal Control.

Behind the TV Shows of Our Time

- Oprah Winfrey's name was supposed to be "Orpah"—based on a biblical character—but someone made a mistake on her birth certificate. She stuck with the switched-around version.

- According to the show, *Sesame Street* favorite Kermit the Frog is left-handed.

- *ER* holds the honor of the most Emmy nominations for a single television program, with a whopping 122 nods.

- *Cheers* star Ted Danson might not have made it onto the program if not for his sweet start in the industry: The sitcom star got one of his early breaks selling pie mix in a TV commercial.

- In an average year of *Jeopardy!* approximately 14,000 questions are asked by contestants.

- The TV series *Flipper* featured three different dolphins as the title character over the years.

- The same horse played Mr. Ed all throughout the show's duration.

- Mister Rogers' trolley choo-chooed its way across more than 100 miles during *Mister Rogers' Neighborhood* 33-season run.

- The globe that used to appear in the background of *NBC Nightly News* actually spun the wrong way for years before someone caught on.

- Johnny Carson's brother, Dick, was the man behind *The Merv Griffin Show:* He directed the program.

- The first and last line ever spoken in *Seinfeld* contained the same exact words. Jerry tells George: "See, now to me, that button is in the worst possible spot. The second button literally makes or breaks the shirt. Look at it. It's too high, it's in no-man's land."

- Jerry Seinfeld was offered $5 million an episode to continue his series after the ninth (and final) season.

- Kramer could have played the role of Al Bundy in *Married with Children—Seinfeld's* Michael Richards auditioned for the part.

ross-Dressing
cross History

❖ ❖ ❖ ❖

as the opposite gender, whether for fun
is nothing new. In fact, cross-dressing
reds, if not thousands of years. Here are
—and often surprising—cross-dressers.

.a. Francis Clalin) was a Minnesota woman
f as a man named Jack Williams. Along with
L. Clayton, the disguised Clayton enlisted in
;iment in the Civil War in 1861. She learned
:hew tobacco, to better hide her true iden-
n for many months, and the couple fought
attles until Elmer was killed in the Battle of
.essee on December 31, 1862.

Georgia-born daughter of a slave woman and
rn into slavery, Craft was light-complected
able to escape in 1848 by disguising herself as
r husband William acted as her black servant.
; daring getaway, Craft had to pretend to be
time no white woman would have traveled
t a servant. Eight days after their departure
:afts arrived in Philadelphia as a free man and
t in men's clothing.

Duchamp was one of the leaders in the Dada
ovements of the early 20th century. Under
ose) Sélavy (thought to be a pun on the
vie"), Duchamp made several photographic
:n's clothing for photographer Man Ray.
Rose as attribution for a number of written
e of his sculptures, *Why Not Sneeze, Rose*

Plastic Panic:
What's Killing India's Cows?

❖ ❖ ❖ ❖

Plastic shopping bags: they're not eco-friendly, but who
knew they weren't e-cow-friendly? In India, where
the cow is sacred, plastic bags are more than just a
whole lotta mess—they're a holy health hazard.

Sick Cows

In India, it's pretty typical to see herds of cattle, fresh from their
morning milkings, roaming the streets to feed on the city's garbage.
But in 2000, a police officer in the city of Lucknow noticed a strange
phenomenon: skeletal cows with engorged bellies, dropping dead in
the street, sometimes as many as 100 a day. Other sick-looking cows
were seen staggering over to dumpsters, but walking away instead of
eating as usual.

A group of these sick cows was corralled to the vet, where they
were anesthetized and their stomachs surgically examined. Inside,
they found plastic bags—up to 60 pounds of them. Apparently, the
cows had eaten the bags along with whatever food was tucked inside.
The cows' stomachs (a cow has four of them) were so full of plastic that they could no longer eat. The cows were starving to death
as a result. What's more, India's Animal Husbandry Department
found that drinking milk from the sick cows could cause cancer and
tuberculosis.

Plastic Boom

Plastic bags have only been in India since the mid-1980s, when the
government authorized plastic production to help the nation compete in the global market. More than 50 percent of the plastic is
used for packaging, and nearly all of it is thrown away, which creates
a major waste problem in a country otherwise known for its recycling efforts. No joke: In India, glass bottles are used over and over
again and repaired if broken; "plastics mechanics" make house calls
to fix broken items with heat fusion; and anything broken or worn

beyond repair is picked up by "ragpickers," a low caste of people who scavenge and sell garbage for whatever they can get.

Aye, There's the Rub(bish)

In the trash-selling game, plastic usually sells for 12 rupees a kilo (about 14 cents a pound). But plastic bags are so thin that even a bunch of them don't weigh enough to be worth much. Hence, plastic-bag pollution.

Although a few local governments tried to ban plastic bags in the late 1990s, it wasn't until 2000—with the lives of sacred cows suddenly at risk—that a national solution was sought.

Thicker Bags

Why ban the bags, asked the plastics industry, when we can just make them thicker? This way, ragpickers would take the bags, keeping them off the streets and out of the cows' bellies.

Both the government (making a pretty penny selling milk and liquor in plastic pouches) and the plastics industry agreed this was a win-win solution. A new rule was made: All plastic bags must be thicker than 20 microns (that's about 78/100,000 of an inch).

Unfortunately, the plastics industry also continued to make the thinner bags, which shopkeepers unwittingly continued to use—after all, who can tell the difference between 19 microns and 21 microns? Rumor had it that government officials, equipped with special bag-thickness-testing instruments, were stopping by stores to enforce the new rule. But for the most part, the situation didn't, and hasn't, changed.

Still, hope hasn't been bagged entirely: the Polythene Agony Campaign, launched in 2000, has been dedicated to educating people about the dangers of plastic bags and how to dispose of them properly. As for the afflicted cows, India's Animal Husbandry Department provides rumenotomies, or "plastic-bag-ectomies," to restore the cows to health.

- *India is home to more than 200 million cows.*

- *Some Hindus consider it good luck to feed a cow before breakfast.*

The T[...]

- After ten years [...]
  York City on Fe[...]
  44 platforms a[...]

- The "Armory S[...]
  shocked Amer[...]
  cago, where s[...]

- On March 3, t[...]
  the right to vo[...]
  Crowds of jee[...]
  and finally, ph[...]
  the marchers.[...]

- In May, the Fir[...]
  Empire's Euro[...]
  and Monteneg[...]
  War, setting t[...]
  a Serbian nati[...]

- Henry Ford op[...]
  build a car fro[...]

- Mohandas Ga[...]
  citizens in pro[...]
  with the techr[...]
  fight for India[...]

- Bengali poet [...]
  win the Nobel[...]

- The first-ever [...]

- B'Nai B'rith, t[...]
  founds the Ar[...]

People dressin[...]
or for necessit[...]
dates back hun[...]
some famous—[...]

- Frances Clayton (a.[...]
  who disguised herse[...]
  her husband, Elmer[...]
  a Union Missouri re[...]
  to swear, drink, and [...]
  tity. The ruse went [...]
  together in several [...]
  Stones River in Ten[...]

- Ellen Craft was the [...]
  her white master. B[...]
  enough that she was[...]
  a white man while h[...]
  In order to make th[...]
  a man because at th[...]
  alone, with or witho[...]
  from Georgia, the C[...]
  a free woman—albe[...]

- French artist Marce[...]
  and Surrealism art r[...]
  the name Rrose (or [...]
  phrase, *"Eros, c'est [...]*
  appearances in wom[...]
  Duchamp later used[...]
  works and at least o[...]
  Sélavy?

- Fifteenth-century French heroine Joan of Arc wore men's clothing while she traveled, as well as armor when she went into battle. Unfortunately, this fact was noted many times during her trial for heresy, of which she was ultimately convicted and burned at the stake.

- Dorothy Lawrence, an English reporter living in Paris at the outbreak of World War I, hoped to report on the conflict, but was aware that as a woman she would be unable to access the front lines. So Lawrence got a military-style haircut and a soldier's uniform and enlisted with the British Expeditionary Force. After ten days of service, she revealed her identity and was promptly arrested. Upon release, she promised not to tell or write of her experiences in the army—the original intent of her pretending to be a man. Sadly, she was eventually institutionalized and remained so far the rest of her life.

- Edward Hyde, the Third Earl of Clarendon, served as governor of both New York and New Jersey from 1701 to 1708. Hyde, whose governorship was tainted by charges of corruption, is remembered as one of the worst American colonial governors. He is also noted for his reported penchant for wearing women's clothing. It is said that he opened the 1702 New York General Assembly dressed as Queen Anne of Great Britain.

- Ed Wood, the man behind cult-schlock favorites such as *Plan 9 from Outer Space* and *Bride of the Monster,* is often considered the worst motion picture director of all time. While that distinction alone guarantees him a place in the history books, it turns out that in addition to directing ghastly movies, he also enjoyed dressing like a woman. In fact, he wrote, directed, and starred in *Glen or Glenda,* a semiautobiographical movie about transvestitism, in which Wood appeared in a blonde wig and fuzzy angora sweater. "If you want to know me, see *Glen or Glenda,* that's me, that's my story. No question," said Wood. "But *Plan 9* is my pride and joy. We used Cadillac hubcaps for flying saucers in that."

He Said, She Said

"If God did not intend for us to eat animals, then why did he make them out of meat?"

—*John Cleese*

"An onion can make people cry but there's never been a vegetable that can make people laugh."

—*Will Rogers*

"I don't like to commit myself about heaven and hell—you see, I have friends in both places."

—*Mark Twain*

"Being with a woman never hurt no professional ball player. It's staying up all night looking for a woman that does him in."

—*Casey Stengel*

"Nobody in football should be called a genius. A genius is a guy like Norman Einstein."

—*Joe Theismann*

"Get-well cards have become so humorous that if you don't get sick you're missing half the fun."

—*Flip Wilson*

"When Thomas Edison worked late into the night on the electric light, he had to do it by gas lamp or candle. I'm sure it made the work seem that much more urgent."

—*George Carlin*

"Childbirth, as a strictly physical phenomenon, is comparable to driving a United Parcel truck through an inner tube."

—*Dave Barry*

"Be careful about reading health books. You may die of a misprint."

—*Mark Twain*

"The guy who invented the first wheel was an idiot. The guy who invented the other three, he was a genius."

—*Sid Caesar*

INSPIRATION STATION

"Hi, I'm Alice. As in 'Wonderland.'"

Charles Dodgson, more commonly known by his pen name, Lewis Carroll, wrote *Alice's Adventures in Wonderland* in 1865. The story, as most people know, is a fantastical one, full of talking animals, bizarre circumstances, and one special little girl named Alice. The pipe-smoking caterpillar might have come from the recesses of Carroll's imagination, but the story's heroine was actually inspired by a real girl named Alice Liddell. Carroll was a friend of the Liddell family, and he met Alice when she was about four years old. Carroll often entertained the Liddell children with his wild tales. One day in 1862, Carroll was on a boating day trip with a reverend and the Liddell girls. Little Alice asked him for a story "with lots of nonsense in it." Carroll began making up a tale on the spot, and he placed Alice at the center of the story. Alice liked it so much, she asked Carroll to write it down; the rest is English literature history.

You Know You Love It: The Scoop on the Macarena

When Spanish singing duo Los Del Rio went to Caracas, Venezuela, in the early 1990s, they had no idea that the trip would result in a song that would soon be on the lips (and hips) of millions. According to the band, Antonio Romero and his singing partner Rafael Ruiz were watching an exceptionally talented flamenco dancer perform in a club in Caracas; the woman, whose name was Macarena, was so gifted that Romero was moved to blurt out, "Give your body joy, Macarena, that your body is to give joy and good things!" The duo put the words to music, added some backstory for their character, and called the piece "The Macarena."

The song was released in 1993 and became a hit in South America and on cruise ships. Then a couple of DJs known as The Bayside Boys got a hold of the track and made a club remix. The infectious song, with its Latin beat and unintelligible (for many people) lyrics, spread like wildfire across the United States and around the world. These days, no office Christmas party, wedding reception, or bar mitzvah is complete without a rousing group dance to "The Macarena."

Fast Facts

- *The cucumber is considered a fruit, not a vegetable.*

- *M&Ms are named after the candy's two creators: Forrest Mars Sr. and Bruce Murrie.*

- *Armadillos are able to walk underwater.*

- *Couples married in the first three months of the year tend to have higher divorce rates than those married in the later months.*

- *The founder of Kodak, George Eastman, is said to have hated having his photo taken.*

- *Fish sometimes cough under water.*

- *Over a lifetime, an average human spends about six months on the toilet.*

- *A typical toilet flushes in the key of E flat.*

- *The game Simon Says was originally set to be called Do This, Do That.*

- *The spots on dice are called "pips."*

- *Chinese households used to set off firecrackers as a form of fire alarms.*

- *A typical American buys 17 yards of dental floss every year of his or her life.*

- *The world goes through about 1.75 billion candy canes every year.*

- *There was once a coffee-scented postage stamp in Brazil.*

One Reptile to Rule Them All

*Some people are ruled by their pets; others are ruled
by their work. Conspiracy theorist David Icke believes
that we're all being ruled by reptilian humanoids.*

Worldwide Domination

David Icke has worn many hats: journalist, news anchor for the BBC,
spokesman for the British Green Party, and professional soccer player.
But after a spiritual experience in Peru in 1991, he took on another
role: famed conspiracy theorist.

Like many other conspiracy theorists, Icke believes that a group
called the Illuminati, or "global elite," controls the world. According
to these theorists, the group manipulates the economy and uses mind
control to usher humanity into a submissive state. Icke also believes
that the group is responsible for organizing such tragedies as the
Holocaust and the Oklahoma City bombings.

Some of the most powerful people in the world are members,
claims Icke, including ex-British Prime Minister Tony Blair and former U.S. President George H. W. Bush, as well as leaders of financial
institutions and major media outlets. However, not all members are
human. According to Icke, those at the top of the Illuminati bloodlines
are vehicles for a reptilian entity from the constellation Draco. These
shape-shifters can change from human to reptile and back again, and
they are essentially controlling humanity.

Is Icke Onto Something?

In the documentary *David Icke: Was He Right?*, Icke claims that
many of his earlier predictions, including a hurricane in New Orleans
and a "major attack on a large city" between the years 2000 and 2002,
have come true. But are we really being ruled by reptilian humanoids or is Icke's theory a bunch of snake oil? Icke was nearly laughed
off the stage in a 1991 appearance on a BBC talk show. But with
16 published books, thousands attending his speaking engagements,
and nearly 200,000 weekly hits to his Web site, perhaps it's Icke who's
having the last laugh.

Sin Eating:
A Strange Profession

❖ ❖ ❖ ❖

*An ancient custom of "eating" a dying person's sins has
made its way into contemporary culture—and brought with
it a wave of questions about the unusual approach.*

To Die Without Sin

If you think you've had a rough lunch, wait until you hear about
these guys: The so-called sin eaters were a group of people who
would perform intricate eating rituals to cleanse dying people of
their sins. The idea was to absolve the soon-to-be-deceased of any
wrongdoing so they could die peacefully, without guilt or sin.

Much of the history of sin eating is based on folklore, particularly
from Wales. Historians, however, have traced mentions of the practice back to early Egyptian and Greek civilizations, and references
to sin eating can be found elsewhere in England as recently as the
mid-1800s. *Funeral Customs,* a book published in 1926 by Bertram
S. Puckle, refers to an English professor who claims he encountered
a sin eater as late as 1825.

The sin-eating ritual is believed to have typically taken place
either at the bedside of someone who was dying or at the funeral
of one who had already died. Legend has it that for a small fee, the
sin eater would sit on a low stool next to the person. Then, a loaf of
bread and a bowl of beer would be passed to them over the body.
Sometimes the meal would be placed directly
on the body, so that the food would absorb
the deceased's sin and guilt. The sin eater
would eat and drink, then pronounce the person free from
any sins with a speech: "I
give easement and rest
now to thee, dear man.
Come not down the lanes

or in our meadows. And for thy peace I pawn my own soul. Amen." Family members, it is believed, would burn the bowl and platter after the sin eater left.

Odd Job

Sin eating wasn't the most lucrative profession, nor were sin eaters highly regarded among their peers. Many of them were beggars to begin with, and most were considered scapegoats and social outcasts. They would live alone in a remote area of a village and have little or no contact with the community outside of their work. Some accounts say they were treated like lepers and avoided at all costs because of their association with evil spirits and wicked practices. It was also widely believed that sin eaters were doomed to spend eternity in hell because of the many burdens they adopted. The Roman Catholic Church allegedly excommunicated the sin eaters, casting them out of the Church.

Sin Eating Today

Interestingly enough, sin eating lives on—at least in spirit. The idea of the sin eater saw its most recent resurgence with the 2003 movie *The Order.* The film (titled *The Sin Eater* in Australia) starred Heath Ledger and focused largely on a sin eater who was discovered after the death of an excommunicated priest.

In 2007, Hollywood revisited sin eating with *The Last Sin Eater.* That movie, based on the 1998 novel of the same name by Francine Rivers, tells the tale of a young girl whose grandmother has just died. At the funeral, the girl makes eye contact with the sin eater— something suggested as a forbidden act. The girl then spends most of the story trying to figure out how to absolve herself of this act. Sin eating has also made its way into several comic book storylines, most often as the name of villainous characters. These characters have been featured in numerous Spider-Man storylines as well as in some of the Marvel Ghost Rider creations.

While the custom may have died out in modern society, one thing's for certain: The archaic legend of the sin eater is just too delicious to pass up.

HOW IT ALL BEGAN

No Bending, Folding, or Stapling

When the U.S. Postal Service introduced Parcel Post in 1913, some thrifty parents of small children saw a bargain they couldn't pass up. Comparing the price of a train ticket to that of a few postage stamps, they realized mailing Junior to Grandma's house for a visit was cheaper than buying him a train ticket.

On February 19, 1914, four-year-old May Pierstorff was mailed from Grangeville to Grandma's house in Lewiston, Idaho, riding in a mail car with 53 cents in stamps pasted to her coat. Grandma was delighted to see her granddaughter. The railway mail clerk found his "parcel" to be a cheerful diversion from the tedium of sorting mail. However, the head office went postal, especially as more parents caught on to the deal.

Finally, in 1920, a head-office bureaucrat stepped in and put an end to the practice. He ruled that "children clearly do not come within the classification of harmless live animals, which do not require food or water while in transit."

Spun Sugar Story

Cotton candy has been a staple of fairs, circuses, and expositions for well over a century. Of the four men recognized to have commercialized this spun sugar into the manner we know it today, Josef Lascaux of Louisiana may have been the most enterprising.

Lascaux called his version of cotton candy "fairy floss," and he freely gave it away to clients of his main business. For any other businessman, this may have been a legitimate, ethical marketing ploy. Indeed, Lascaux probably thought so. He became a big success in both endeavors; possibly due to the fairy floss, he received a lot of repeat business. After all, Lascaux's main occupation was dentistry.

Soupy Sales

Chicken noodle soup was first placed on grocery store shelves 75 years ago. Today, the Campbell Soup Company needs nearly a million miles of noodles yearly to meet demand. As to how many chickens they need, that's classified information.

The Impossible 'Possum

Let's face it: Opossums are weird. But here are some interesting facts that might change your mind about the unique opossum.

- Opossums are the only marsupial (i.e., a mammal that carries its young in a pouch) found in North America.

- The word "opossum" comes from the Algonquin word *apasum*, meaning "white animal." Captain John Smith used "opossum" around 1612, when he described it as a cross between a pig, a cat, and a rat.

- Although it is often colloquially called the " 'possum," the opossum is completely different from a possum, an Australian marsupial.

- The opossum's nickname is "the living fossil," as it dates back to the dinosaurs and the Cretaceous Period, 70 million years ago. It is the oldest surviving mammal family on Earth.

- When cornered, opossums vocalize ferociously and show all 50 of their teeth, which they have more of than any other mammal. But they are lovers, not fighters, and prefer to run from danger.

- If trapped, they will "play 'possum," an involuntary response in which their bodies go rigid, and they fall to the ground in a state of shock. Their breathing slows, they drool a bit, and they release smelly green liquid from their anal sacs. This is enough to convince most predators the opossum is already dead, leaving it alone.

- Despite their predilection for eating anything—including rotting flesh—opossums are fastidious about hygiene. They bathe themselves frequently, including several times during each meal.

- Opossums are extremely resistant to most forms of disease and toxins, including rabies and snake venom, the latter probably due to their low metabolism.

- The idea that opossums mate through the female's nostrils is a myth. Although the male opossum has a forked (bifid) penis, he mates with the female in the normal manner. Conveniently, she has two uteri, so he deposits sperm into both of them at once.

Odd Ordinances

- In the 1930s, it was a crime to serve apple pie without a cheese topping in Wisconsin.

- Throwing pickle juice on a trolley is illegal in Rhode Island.

- Firemen aren't allowed to rescue women wearing nightgowns in Saint Louis.

- The city of Pasadena, California, made it illegal for secretaries to be alone with their bosses.

- Bathing without clothes is not allowed in the state of Florida.

- Women are not allowed to bathe in business offices in Carmel, California.

- It's illegal to fall asleep in a bathtub in Detroit.

- In Brooklyn, people can sleep in tubs—but donkeys cannot.

- Not taking a bath on a Saturday night is against the law in Barre, Vermont.

- Driving a car while asleep is a crime anywhere in Tennessee.

- It's illegal to drive a car if you're blind in New York.

- In Cleveland, the law prohibits you from driving if you are sitting in someone else's lap.

- Husbands, listen up: It's illegal for a mother-in-law to visit her kids more than 30 days out of any given year at California's Paiute Indian Reservation.

- Throwing banana peels on the streets will get you in trouble in Waco, Texas. The reason? They could cause a horse to slip.

- Riding an ugly horse on a public street in Wilbur, Washington, is a crime.

- Horses in Fort Lauderdale, Florida, are required to wear horns and headlights.

Benjamin Franklin: Secret Agent Man?

❖ ❖ ❖ ❖

*Benjamin Franklin was a man of many roles:
inventor, scientist, publisher, philosopher, diplomat,
and one of America's founding fathers.
But could he also have been a spy?*

French Connection

Rumors abound that Franklin was involved in French espionage activities during the American Revolution. While most say that Benjamin Franklin was spying for the Americans, some claim that Franklin was in league with the British.

In September 1776, Congress appointed Franklin, Silas Deane, and Thomas Jefferson commissioners to France to plead the American cause in its war against Great Britain. Jefferson declined, but Franklin (despite the fact that he was 70 years old) and Deane agreed.

One of the most celebrated people on the planet, Franklin could hardly slip into France unnoticed. Almost from the moment he arrived, he was involved in a web of intrigue. Spies surrounded Franklin at every turn. French police chief Jean-Charles Lenoir ran an organized and efficient spying operation in Paris, which was so riddled with spies that it was said when two Parisians talked, a third inevitably listened. In addition to being tailed by the French, the British ambassador to France was also following Franklin's every move.

The Spy Who Stayed Cold

Every week, like clockwork, secret messages were sent from Franklin's residence to British intelligence, keeping them abreast of everything Franklin was planning, doing, or talking about. While Franklin was certainly involved in this undercover war, was he aware of these notes? Was he the source of them? Or was this all part of Franklin's master plan?

Franklin could hardly have been unaware of the situation. Soon after he arrived in France, a Philadelphian living in Paris had warned Franklin to be wary. In a letter she wrote, "You are surrounded with spies who watch your every movement."

His reply has become legendary. "I have long observed one rule... to be concerned in no affairs I should blush to have made public, and to do nothing but what spies may see and welcome." He did nothing to tighten security, which led John Adams to believe that Franklin was, at best, senile, and at worst, criminally careless. Franklin even claimed that he would not dismiss his valet, Edward Bancroft, even if he were "a spy, as probably he is."

Double-Aught-Seven

If Franklin wasn't a British spy, was he spying for America? Biographer James Srodes calls this a more plausible scenario, and notes that mid-20th century CIA director Allen Dulles concluded that Franklin had set up a spy network inside the British government. However, his assumption lacks documentation. As Srodes notes, Franklin hardly needed a ring of secret informants in London; he had many friends inside the British government, any of whom could feed him valuable information.

"The important thing about intelligence is not how it is obtained but how it is used," says Srodes. Franklin used information obtained from England to force the French to move quickly to the aid of American rebel forces. He then turned around and casually let it be known how much France was aiding America, which disturbed the British.

This much we know: Franklin had indeed been close to someone who was a spy. Decades later it was revealed that his valet was indeed spying for America—and for England.

We may never know whether or not Bancroft's boss, Benjamin Franklin, was also a spy, or even for what side. However, what we do know is that Benjamin Franklin was certainly a cagey American.

Sweet Lemons? It's a Miracle!

"When life gives you lemons, make lemonade." A great maxim made even easier if you have a supply of miracle fruit.

Change Your Taste

Miracle fruit *(Synsepalum dulcificum)* is a small berry that can literally change the way common foods taste. After eating a miracle berry, stout beer tastes like a chocolate milkshake and cheese tastes like cake frosting. It can make hot sauce taste like a glazed donut, vinegar taste like apple juice, and oysters taste like chewing gum.

Miracle fruit is indigenous to West Africa and grows on trees that can reach 20 feet high. Although the trees produce crops only twice a year, the berries can be freeze dried or refrigerated indefinitely. The fruit can also be ordered online in tablet or granulated form. After eating one small berry, its glycoproteins bind to the tongue's taste buds, producing miraculin, which makes bitter and sour foods taste sweet. The effects last from 30 minutes to 2 hours.

Miracle fruit first gained popularity in the United States during the 1970s when it was marketed as a dieting aid, so that people could enjoy low-calorie menus without feeling deprived. So why aren't we all eating the fruit? Allegedly, the Food and Drug Administration folded to pressure exerted by the sugar industry and stopped allowing its import.

Miracle Fruit for the Masses

If you would like to have your own miracle fruit, you can order berries or seeds from vendors online. There are five steps to enjoying miracle fruit:

1. Buy a selection of foods like citrus fruits, rhubarb, bleu cheese, stout beer, and cheap tequila.
2. Wash the miracle fruit and put a berry into your mouth. Swirl it around for about a minute.
3. Bite into the berry, liberally coating your tongue with the juice.
4. Taste a lemon wedge—it should taste like sweetened lemonade.
5. Proceed with the other foods, throwing caution to the wind.

🎥 Behind the Films of Our Time

Tarzan, the Ape Man
The oft-quoted words "me Tarzan, you Jane" never actually are spoken in the 1930s classic film *Tarzan, the Ape Man*. Tarzan simply speaks his name, then taps Jane and says hers.

Lord of the Rings
Sean Connery turned down the role of Gandalf in the *Lord of the Rings* trilogy, which was given to Ian McKellen. Connery said he didn't want to devote the time to filming the movie in New Zealand, and he also didn't understand all the strange characters in the script.

Seabiscuit
Blow-up dolls provided much of the background crowds in *Seabiscuit*. Original plans called for 7,000 extras—a number too expensive for its budget—so a production assistant came up with the idea of having inflatable people fill the void. Computer effects helped them look a little livelier.

Gone with the Wind
Bette Davis decided not to accept the lead role of Scarlett O'Hara in *Gone with the Wind*. At the time, she thought the male lead was going to be Errol Flynn, and she said she wouldn't work with him again after their experience making *The Private Lives of Elizabeth and Essex*.

Silence of the Lambs
Gene Hackman was originally set to play the part of Hannibal Lecter in *Silence of the Lambs,* but he left the project before it ever got off the ground. Michelle Pfeiffer was first approached about playing Clarice Starling but supposedly thought the movie was too dark.

The Matrix
Keanu Reeves wasn't the top choice for the star of *The Matrix;* Ewan McGregor and Will Smith were both approached first. Smith has since said he felt he wouldn't have played the part as well as Reeves did.

The Graduate
Robert Redford opted out of playing the starring role of *The Graduate* in 1967, leading to Dustin Hoffman's first big break as Ben Braddock.

Buried Alive!

*Death is the most natural thing in the world, yet
it inspires the most fear. And there are few things that
horrify people more than the idea of being buried alive.
Meet some people who, to paraphrase the poet Dylan
Thomas, did not go gentle into that good night.*

Can't Keep a Good Person Down

Throughout history, urban legends have circulated about people being buried alive—whether voluntarily or not. The first recorded case of a burial gone wrong occurred during the first century, when a magician named Simon Magus buried himself alive, hoping that a miracle would save him. It didn't. When Thomas Kempis, the 13th-century author of *The Imitation of Christ* was dug up for reinterrment and potential canonization, they found the inner coffin lid striated with scratch marks and wood embedded underneath his fingernails. Unfortunately, since he did not willingly embrace his fate, he was denied sainthood.

In 1674, Marjorie Halcrow supposedly died and was buried. Soon after, grave robbers attempted to steal a ring by cutting off one of her fingers, but Halcrow scared them off when she reacted with a moan. After being rescued, she went on to raise two sons and outlive her husband by six years until her second, more permanent burial. And in 1996, a missionary named Reverend Schwartz reentered the land of the living when he heard his favorite hymn being played at his funeral. As mourners passed by his closed coffin, they could hear the good Reverend singing along with them.

Avoiding the Inevitable

The alarming incidence of premature burials has concerned some people so much that they began taking drastic steps to ensure that it didn't happen to them or their loved ones. "Waking the dead," the practice of sitting next to the deceased for several days until their burial, usually fell to friends and family, particularly in the 19th century. Many terminally ill patients have specified in their wills that after death, they be subjected to surgical incisions, scalded with boiling-hot water, stabbed through the heart, branded with red-hot irons, and even decapitated to insure that they were genuinely departed before being interred. Others have requested that they be buried with guns, knives, or poison inside their coffins in the event that they needed to finish the job themselves.

If you think that premature burials can be solved with embalming, consider the unfortunate demise of Cardinal Somaglia in 1837. After the Cardinal passed out and was pronounced dead, plans were made to immediately embalm his body. After the embalmer made the initial incision into his chest, he noticed that the Cardinal's heart was still beating. The Cardinal reached up and batted the scalpel away to prevent further damage but ultimately died from his wounds.

A newspaper article reported on an incident in 1984, in which a pathologist assigned to conduct a post-mortem examination was stunned when the corpse sat up and grabbed him by the throat. The victim continued to live a few more years but the pathologist died immediately from shock.

What's a Body to Do?

One surefire way to avoid being buried alive is to purchase a specially outfitted Italian coffin that's been available since 1995. The $5,000 casket comes equipped with a two-way microphone and speaker to enable the questionably deceased to communicate with their loved ones. A flashlight, small oxygen tank, heartbeat sensor, and cardiac stimulator are available at an additional charge.

Of course, for those who are really concerned with being buried alive, there are other solutions. According to a pamphlet published in 2003 by the Cremation Society of Australia, the number ten reason why you should consider their services: "Cremation eliminates all danger of being buried alive."

Fast Facts

- *Ever wonder why Chicago O'Hare Airport is abbreviated ORD? It used to be called Orchard Field, and the shorthand stuck.*

- *Talk about irony: The official motto of New Hampshire, printed on its license plates, is "Live Free or Die"—and those license plates are made at a state prison.*

- *The oldest university in America is Harvard.*

- *It cost nearly $41 million to build the Empire State Building. The New York City landmark has more than 10 million bricks.*

- *Ever wonder what NERF actually stands for? Although some people have claimed it stands for "Non-Expanding Recreational Foam," NERF actually means absolutely nothing.*

- *An American baseball uses 108 stitches.*

- *An American football has only four seams.*

- *Babe Ruth used an unusual cooling system: He kept a cabbage leaf under his hat, which he swapped out for a new one every few innings.*

- *Soccer is considered the most globally popular sport.*

- *Golf balls were originally made of leather and stuffed with feathers. That didn't change until the mid-1800s.*

- *Boxing rings actually used to be round, hence the term "boxing ring."*

- *Men blink half as much as women.*

Word Histories

Slogan:

Now the banal realm of advertising companies and political parties, the word originally referred to the Gaelic battle cry *sluagh-ghairm*, which invoked the name of their clan leader as they marched into the fray.

Antifogmatic:

Though not commonly heard today, early 18th-century American imbibers of alcoholic beverages would refer thusly to a drink taken in the morning as a bracer against dampness or fog.

Bellwether:

An Anglo-Saxon word that originally referred to a bell-wearing, castrated male sheep that served as leader of a flock.

Sawbuck:

Slang for an American ten-dollar bill. This term originally referred to cross supports used to hold wood for sawing, also called a "sawhorse." The use of the term to reference a ten-dollar bill most likely derives from the Roman numeral X, which appears on the currency.

Robot:

Derived from the Czech word for "slave," robot was first used by the playwright Karel Capek in his 1921 work *R.U.R.*

Pretzel:

Though some have ascribed the twisted shape of these snacks to resemble the arms of praying children, nobody knows for sure why pretzels are twisted—though the term itself is from the German word for "branch."

Ignoramus:

Commonly applied to fools, the term derives from the plural Latin for "we don't know." Until the 17th century, it was used in British courts when juries could not decide a case due to lack of evidence. The 1615 George Ruggle play *Ignoramus*, about a clueless attorney, gave the term its current meaning.

The Golden Era of Cigarette Ads

When Sir Walter Raleigh helped popularize tobacco during the 16th century, he probably had no idea that he would be responsible for one of the largest and most profitable advertising campaigns in the history of Madison Avenue. These campaigns saw a single product go from lifestyle enhancer to pariah of the medical community within a matter of years.

Give Me Your Young at Heart

Before their negative association with health, cigarettes were marketed to successful young men and women as a way to relax and get more out of life. One mid-century ad for Lucky cigarettes featured virile, athletic men and women prancing around tennis courts in snow-white shorts exclaiming, "WHAT A DAY...what a game... what a cigarette! Why is Lucky so much a part of moments like this?"

Like any other product that clamored for the consumer's attention, the multi-million dollar tobacco industry embarked on a constantly evolving campaign. Advertising executives spoke to savvy young men and women about exactly how cigarettes enhanced the good life: "She swims...she rides...she's typically modern in her zest for the active life. Typically modern, too, in wanting to know the scientific facts about the cigarette she smokes," read one ad.

Showbiz Gets into the Act

Hollywood got into the action by glorifying the romance of cigarette smoking in films. A full-page advertisement in *LIFE* magazine showed a voluptuous actress draped in front of a roaring fire in her evening wear. The ad purred, "As lovely Maureen O'Hara knows, it's wise to choose a cigarette for the pleasure it gives." Even John Wayne got into the game when promoting his 1952 film, *Big Jim McClain,* boasting, "Mild and good tasting pack after pack. And I know. I've been smokin' em for twenty years."

Ironically, "The Duke" battled stomach and lung cancer, the latter of which he blamed on his six-pack-a-day habit.

About the same time, the young television industry found that Big Tobacco was only too happy to contribute millions of advertising dollars to a burgeoning industry that hadn't quite figured out how to pay for itself. One ad featuring a up-and-coming actor with political aspirations promised, "Want to be the next President? Just do what Ronald Reagan does, smoke lots and LOTS of Pall Mall Brand cigarettes! The sooner you start, the faster you'll rise to political success!"

Public Reaction

By the late 1960s, the tobacco industry became concerned with the negative association between their consumers' health and cigarette smoking. Advertisers countered these complaints with advertisements that reasoned, "Should you CUT DOWN now? Why cut down on the relief and enjoyment of extra smoking now, when you feel you need it most? Even chain-smokers find that new Julep Cigarettes banish unpleasant over-smoking symptoms. Unlike ordinary cigarettes, Juleps sparkle up your mouth, refresh your throat and keep your breath clean and inviting."

Everyone got on the bandwagon by promising that their products would minimize the unsavory side effects of inhaling hot, burning leaves: "No 'stale-tasting' mouth: Even if you chain-smoke, your mouth feels clean and sparkling all day long." Another ad ran: "No raw 'burned-out' throat: Miracle mint stays in the smoke of Juleps, and refreshes the throat. No 'dry-as-dust' rawness, even if you smoke 20–40–60 Juleps a day."

As pressure continued to rise, advertisers mounted concentrated campaigns and even managed to draw the medical community into their web. Doctors (who, of course, smoked) went before television cameras and claimed, "More doctors smoke Camels than any other cigarette!" and "After all, doctors are human too. Like you, they smoke for pleasure. Their taste, like yours, enjoys the pleasing flavor of costlier tobaccos. Their throats too appreciate a cool mildness."

After all, who's going to argue with a doctor?

Fast Facts

- The "57" on Heinz products is actually just an arbitrary number.

- The king of diamonds in a standard card deck is designed after Julius Caesar. The king of spades is for King David; clubs for Alexander the Great; and hearts for Charlemagne.

- More Americans choke on toothpicks than on any other item. Ballpoint pens are blamed for a good amount of choking as well.

- A third of people say they flush while still sitting on the john.

- Two dozen U.S. states consider impotence legal grounds for divorce.

- In ancient Egypt, people would shave off their eyebrows when their pet cats died.

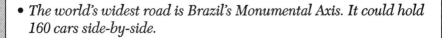

- It took more than 1,700 years to build the Great Wall of China.

- The world's widest road is Brazil's Monumental Axis. It could hold 160 cars side-by-side.

- Ever wonder why there are always so many mirrors in lobbies? Designers say it's no mistake: The mirrors are there because visitors tend to be less bothered by slow elevators while they're absorbed in their own reflections.

- There are more than 600 rooms in England's Buckingham Palace.

- The complete name of Los Angeles is technically El Pueblo de Nuestra Señora la Reina de los Ángeles de Porciúncula. Try that, Mr. Hollywood!

- At any time, 0.7 percent of the world's population is drunk.

Sunny Days Around the World

Sesame Street isn't just an American address. The iconic kids' show now reaches more than 100 other countries.

Sunny days are sweeping clouds away in neighborhoods far from our familiar Muppet-filled street. The makers of *Sesame Street* have brought their award-winning antics to countries all across the globe, and each production has its own unique twist.

Sesame now airs in more than 120 nations. Some just show overdubbed versions of the American program, but others have their own original characters and concepts. So grab on to Grover and get ready—we're taking a ride around the world.

First Stop: South Africa

South Africa's *Takalani Sesame* tackles some of the toughest issues of all. With millions of HIV-positive children in the South African audience, the folks at Sesame Workshop felt AIDS was something they could not ignore. Thus came the introduction of an HIV-positive Muppet Kami. The creature (who is supposed to be a five-year-old) is said to be shy but friendly and serves as a strong influence for children living with the deadly virus.

Other characters include Moshe, a four-year-old Muppet who likes to dance, but who also has heavy concerns for the environment. Moshe allows the show's creators to address difficult ideas related to government policy.

Next Up: China

Bet you didn't know Big Bird had an identical Chinese cousin. Meet Da Niao, the Asian counterpart to America's giant yellow-feathered friend. Da Niao shares more than just his looks with our Big Bird; he, too, is friendly and chipper but sometimes a little slow to catch on. His friends include Hu Hu Zhu, a fuzzy blue pig descended from famous philosophers, and Little Plum, a messy-haired girl with a loud snore.

Moving on to Bangladesh

Tuktuki is only five, but she plays an important role in Bangladesh's *Sisimpur.* Tuktuki's story is just one of many serious issues covered in India's take on *Sesame Street,* which cleverly includes political and social issues. The purple Muppet with braided pigtails and a bright green dress represents the ideal of gender equality in India. Her storylines show young viewers how girls can be given the same kinds of opportunities and treatment as boys.

Fourth Stop: Kosovo

Calling it a challenge to create a children's show in the war-torn nation of Kosovo would be an understatement. But *Sesame* shines through with two locally produced programs, *Rruga Sesam* and *Ulica Sezam.*

Here, the familiar faces of Bert, Ernie, and Elmo focus on messages of unity, and segments showcase similarities among children of different ethnic backgrounds. Storylines might include different groups of kids playing the same sorts of games or singing similar songs.

Turning to the Netherlands

In the Dutch rendition, known as *Sesamstraat,* Big Bird's avatar is the blue, silly-looking Pino. As a cousin of our yellow avian pal, Pino shares Big Bird's orange beak and sense of curiosity. His friends include Tommie, the teddy bear/dog mix; Purk, the messy baby pig; and Ieniemienie, the precocious, giant-eared mouse.

Last Stop: Germany

We'll end our tour in Germany, with its grouch-infested *Sesamstrasse.* Here Oscar's relative, Rumpel, revels in all things dirty, smelly, and grumpy. Rumpel hangs out with his caterpillar friend Gustav, snail Finchen, and brown bear friend Samson.

That's just the beginning of the multicultural versions of *Sesame* that can be found around the world. From Mexico's giant green parrot, Abelardo, to Palestine's Internet-savvy rooster, Kareem, there's a Muppet for nearly every place and purpose. All you need to know is how to get there—and odds are, you can find a child who can tell you.

Got Goose, Will Travel

❖ ❖ ❖ ❖

Geese may look like docile creatures, but these quackers can get territorial and downright cranky when provoked. Here's a look at some surprising uses for the common goose.

Beware the Roused Goose

An incensed goose is a frightful thing, with a nearly five-foot-wide wingspan; a serrated beak capable of biting a hole in a metal bucket; and a loud, piercing war-honk. If attacked by a goose, one should never break eye contact with it—this will be perceived as a sign of weakness and will only encourage the aggressor. It's best to back away slowly, and try to position yourself so that there is a fence between you and the angry goose; although they are marvelous flyers, geese hate to go over a fence.

Guardians of Western Civilization and Whiskey

For most of recorded history, man has kept geese. We know that the ancient Egyptians practiced goose husbandry, as did the Romans, who valued the animal so highly that they regularly offered the bird as a sacrifice to the god Juno. These noble beasts had uses far beyond that of supplicating the gods, however; in 390 B.C., the holy geese in the Roman temple roused the sleeping guards in time to fend off attacking Gallic hordes. Indeed, geese are still used as watch animals throughout the world. For instance, at the Ballantine's whiskey-aging facility in Glasgow, Scotland, geese guard 240 million liters of alcohol. Farmers have also learned that geese are capable of looking after a flock of smaller waterfowl and will protect them from foxes and other predators.

A far more quotidian employment for the goose, however, is that of gardener; they will eat weeds and regrowth without disturbing crops. It takes only two geese to keep an acre of row crops free of weeds. Best of all, a goose gardener works for just a bit more than what it can eat on the job and leaves behind nothing but webprints and fertilizer.

FROM THE VAULTS OF HISTORY

Superstition Everywhere

Superstition is a common phenomenon among both ordinary folk as well as the rich and famous. Queen Elizabeth II of England was so afraid of severing the "ties of friendship" that she insisted on paying a halfpenny after being presented with a gift of cutlery. According to lore at the time, there was a superstition that said that to accept a knife without some form of payment risked cutting the bonds of friendship with those who are close to you.

Franklin Roosevelt

Writer Somerset Maugham warded off bad vibes by having the "evil eye" symbol carved into his fireplace mantel. Although British Prime Minister Winston Churchill was brilliant, he also struggled with his share of superstitions. He believed that Fridays were unlucky and avoided traveling on those days. Another famous figure who avoided traveling on Fridays was U.S. President Franklin D. Roosevelt. Also, if asked to sit at a table that accommodated 13 people, he would move to another table. To ensure a successful event, entertainer Al Jolson wore old clothes to open a new show. Grammy Award-winning singer and songwriter Missy "Misdemeanor" Elliott will actually turn around and go back home if a black cat crosses her path, regardless of her destination or purpose.

Wagons Ho!

If you were a child addicted to spending Saturday afternoon munching on popcorn and watching westerns, you probably thrilled at the scenes of wagon trains laboring across the open prairie. There would be an Indian attack, and the wagon master would scream at the top of his lungs, "Circle the wagons!" In reality, circling the wagons to defend against attacking Indians never really happened, and it was largely the invention of 20th-century movie directors. The act of slowing down the horses and turning the wagons inward into a circle took far too long to be a defensive tactic. While it's true that travelers did circle their wagons at night when they camped, it was usually designed to corral the animals—not to guard against travelers getting scalped.

Hot Ice

*Antediluvian is highly pressurized carbon that began as dead
plant and animal matter—hardly the stuff of romance, right? Yet
that's precisely what diamonds have become, after a lot of buffing,
cutting, and polishing… and, oh yes, a business plan driven by
more than a century of relentless promotion and market control.*

Have a De Beers

Diamond mines were established near Kimberley, South Africa,
around 1870, and soon after, British colonialist Cecil Rhodes began
to poke around the area. He purchased various diamond claims, and
in 1888 Rhodes merged his company with another, creating De Beers
Consolidated Mines, Ltd.

From the outset, De Beers aimed for complete
dominance of the African diamond trade. This
was a very ambitious goal, not simply because of
Africa's challenging geological and political nature, but
because for years a diamond was considered just another gemstone,
found only in riverbeds in Brazil and India. The very few diamonds
that were cultivated and sold justified a high price, but speculators
were more interested in rarities such as gold and jade.

De Beers was nothing if not visionary. The company forged connections with miners, sellers, buyers, and cutters who were allowed to
deal in diamonds from De Beers and its affiliates, and from nowhere
else. In structure and in practice, this was a cartel, which eventually
had almost complete control over the trade. The key was manipulation
of supply and demand. De Beers maintained a stockpiled inventory
of unsold diamonds and purchased stones from other producers. By
periodically withholding diamonds from the market, demand—and
prices—escalated.

Sweet Romance

Meanwhile, Westerners fell prey to an ingenious marketing scheme
that maintained diamonds were an ego-boosting signifier of discre-
tionary income. Diamonds were also marketed as the only way a fella

could hope to get his gal to blurt, "Yes! I'll marry you!" A copywriter named Frances Gerety devised the familiar ad line "A Diamond Is Forever" in 1947. By the second half of the 20th century, about 80 percent of the world's diamond supply was under De Beers's control. Almost all of those gems were mined in African colonies under shabby European control; the vast majority was sold in the United States.

An amusing irony to all this "commerce of romance" is that most raw diamonds are purchased cheaply by industry, because the real, practical value of diamonds is tied to the gems' extraordinary hardness and durability. Relatively simple contouring makes a diamond sharp, and ideally suited for the grimy, dusty chores of cutting, drilling, grinding, and polishing.

Blood Diamonds

Western wholesalers, retailers, and everyday buyers weren't concerned about where their pricey rocks came from until the "blood diamond" scandal of 1998. The controversy began to brew in 1992, when a rebel group mixed up in the Angolan civil war created a complex diamond-smuggling network to finance arms deals. The strategy worked well and was adopted throughout the '90s by other troubled African nations, including Sierra Leone, Liberia, the Republic of Cote d'Ivoire (Ivory Coast), and the Democratic Republic of the Congo. The armies and militias that abused the populace of these countries, and stole boys and young men for duty as soldiers, would barely have been possible if not for the mining and sale of rough diamonds.

The United Nations undertook an investigation of blood diamonds (also known as "conflict diamonds") in 1998. Lurid news stories about torture and slaughter financed by the West's desire for the gems were damaging embarrassments to De Beers and others in the diamond trade. The industry quickly distanced itself from the miserable nations that had become so topical. De Beers didn't have direct ownership of mines in any of the war-torn countries, but it did buy rough diamonds from war zones. The UN noted this and other facts, and initiated resolutions that prohibited the purchase of diamonds mined in conflict zones. In 1998, Angola was the first nation to be hit with UN sanctions on the diamond trade.

A Snag in the Process

By 2000, representatives of De Beers, other diamond concerns, and nonprofits formed the World Diamond Council. This body introduced the Kimberley Process Certification Scheme, to ensure that all rough diamonds are bought and sold in non-conflict zones. De Beers now claims that all of its diamonds are conflict-free.

The snag in the Kimberley Process is that while diamonds can be called conflict-free, to accurately trace the origins of many African diamonds is very difficult. It's a step in the right direction, but it may not be enough. Some observers are skeptical because the Kimberley Process is run from Kimberley, the very location of De Beers's earliest jackpot mines, and the home of De Beers-affiliated offices, mines, and distribution centers. Defenders of the Process may call the setup "practical." Others may call it "cozy."

Once the Kimberley Process was set in motion, an enormous number of diamonds were churned from mines that had supposedly been worked dry years before. The industry's toughest critics claim that the town is a way station that launders diamonds from questionable sources.

Is the Diamond Market Forever?

Very recent years have seen increased diamond-mining activity in Canada, Russia, and Australia. Diamonds from these nations are certifiably conflict-free, and are a growing presence on the world market. As for De Beers, its presence isn't as monolithic as before, but the company (and its many subsidiaries) still controls about 40 percent of the world's diamond trade. However, the global economic recession that began to take hold in the fall of 2008 prompted De Beers to suspend mining operations in South Africa at the end of that year. In March 2009, De Beers temporarily shut down mines in Botswana, the most prolific of the company's African sources. As one diamond dealer in Johannesburg, South Africa, explained to *The Times* of London, "The bottom has fallen out of the market."

No market for high-end diamonds? Now that's a conflict.

INSPIRATION STATION

The Chocolate Chip Cookie: Accidental Inspiration

Okay, maybe it's a stretch to call a cookie a "work of art," but there are millions of people who would argue that a great chocolate chip cookie gives any masterpiece a run for its money. The inspiration behind the beloved sweet was born out of necessity. Ruth Graves Wakefield was a dietician and co-owner of a Massachusetts tourist lodge in the 1930s along with her husband. Their lodge was dubbed the Tollhouse Inn, and it quickly gained a reputation for serving fantastic homemade desserts.

One day, Wakefield was making a batch of chocolate cookies when she realized she was out of her usual baker's chocolate. She substituted chunks of semi-sweet chocolate instead; rather than melting into the cookie, the chocolate stayed in chunks after baking. Lo, the chocolate chip cookie was born. Handily, the chocolate she used had been a gift from her friend Andrew Nestlé. Nestlé's chocolate manufacturing company bought Wakefield's recipe and supplied her with a lifetime supply of chocolate chips. The Tollhouse recipe can still be found on the back of every bag of Nestlé chocolate morsels.

Cookie Monster: Proust's Madeleine

Leave it to Marcel Proust to make a mountain out of a molehill—or a seven-book, six-volume, 4,300-page story out of a cookie. *In Search of Lost Time* is a loosely autobiographical account of Proust's life that took him 13 years to write. The story begins when the protagonist bites into a madeleine, a pound-cakelike cookie in the shape of a seashell that was popular in France. The taste of the madeleine dipped in a cup of tea instantly sends the author back to the halcyon days of his childhood. From there, it's a bonanza of time, space, memory, and decidedly Proustian motifs—all from an afternoon snack.

In Search of Immortality

❖ ❖ ❖ ❖

*Meet Gene Savoy, the "real Indiana Jones," who set
off to discover cities and a whole lot more.*

Born in Bellingham, Washington on May 11, 1927, Douglas Eugene "Gene" Savoy had no formal training as an archaeologist. But that didn't stop him from heading deep into the jungles of Peru. Once dubbed "the real Indiana Jones" by *People* magazine, Savoy discovered more than 40 lost cities in his career, including Vilcabamba, the last refuge of the Incas from the Spanish conquistadors.

Like movie-hero Indiana Jones, Savoy's expeditions weren't entirely driven by archaeology. Savoy had grander plans—including finding the legendary city of El Dorado, where it was rumored that one could delve into the "ancient roots of universal religion" and the fabled fountain of youth.

In 1969, Savoy left the jungle to search the sea. He captained a research ship and sailed around the world gathering information on sea routes used by ancient civilizations to prove that they could have been in contact with one another.

In 1984, Savoy returned to Peru, where he discovered Gran Vilaya, the largest pre-Columbian city in South America. On one of his last trips to Gran Vilaya, he unearthed a tablet with inscriptions alluding to King Solomon's ships that were sent to the biblical land of Ophir to gather gold for his temple. This tablet sent Savoy on what was perhaps his most ambitious adventure: to find the exact location of Ophir, find proof that the gold in Solomon's Jerusalem temple came from South America, and to learn the secret to immortality. Throughout his career, however, scholars scoffed at his theories and were skeptical of his findings.

But immortality alluded Savoy, and he died in 2007 in Reno, Nevada, where he was known as The Most Right Reverend Douglas Eugene Savoy, head of the International Community of Christ. Members of the church believed that staring at the sun would allow them to take in God's energy and become immortal (albeit damage their eyes)—a secret Savoy said was revealed to him in the jungles of Peru.

Canucks of Comedy

Canadians have a reputation for politeness and modesty, no matter how unseemly the issue. Perhaps this is why Canadian comics are so funny—they have to work twice as hard!

Serious About Comedy

Comedians learn their craft from their environment, and Canadian comics are no exception. Perhaps it's their upbringing, their country's wide-open spaces, or the extreme cold, but Canadians manage to take their surroundings and give it an "ah well" shrug. Toronto, a cornerstone of Canada's industry, is known to the rest of the country as "Toronto, the Good" because of its ever-proper image. Among the golden triangle's native sons are **Jim Carrey, Mike Myers,** the late **John Candy, Eugene Levy, Martin Short,** and **Howie Mandel.**

Collectively, these six comics have a heap of awards, including two Emmys, a Tony, a Grammy, two Golden Globes, two People's Choice Awards, and a whopping 16 MTV Awards. Sure, there are a few Golden Raspberry nominations (for Hollywood's worst movies) as well, but in Jim Carrey's case, his Razzie nomination was for Worst New Actor in *Ace Ventura: Pet Detective,* a movie that still made a ton of money. When asked in interviews where Canadians get their sense of humor, Carrey has (jokingly) pointed to a single reason: repression.

Nature vs. Nuture

Perhaps the most improbable spawning ground for comedic talent is Canada's capital city, Ottawa, which has grown from a brawling lumber town into a staid bureaucratic nirvana. As Canadian writer Alan Fotheringham once remarked, "Ottawa is the town fun forgot." Early on, Ottawa native **Dan Akroyd** belied that view during his Catholic school years when he dressed a pig as the pope for his classroom show-and-tell. Akroyd was expelled, but his outrageous brand of humor later made him a *Saturday Night Live* star.

Rich Little, known as "The Man of a Thousand Voices," is as much a Las Vegas fixture as Wayne Newton. Born in Ottawa, Little's first impressions were of Canadian politicians—perhaps because they work so hard to be righteously serious. The late U.S. President Richard Nixon also remains one of Little's most popular imitations.

Hey Ladies!

There are plenty of hilarious Canadian women as well. **Catherine O'Hara** got her start on the wacky Canadian sketch comedy show *SCTV,* but she's more known to U.S. fans for her movie roles. O'Hara steals the stage with her funny and fine-tuned characters, from her turn as Winona Ryder's uptight mother in *Beetlejuice* to her affectionately odd ducks in the Christopher Guest series of mockumentaries, including *Waiting For Guffman, Best in Show,* and *A Mighty Wind.*

Tackling tough topics is hard work—even if it's for a fake news program. Just ask **Samantha Bee,** who for years was the sole female reporter on Comedy Central's *The Daily Show With Jon Stewart.* As a comedic reporter, Bee, who was born in Toronto, has delved into such intricate topics as hunters and gas and oil executives who claim to be environmentalists, to an in-depth look at championship-level poker players. "Last year people won more than one billion dollars playing poker," Bee reported. "And casinos made $27 billion just by being around those people."

Canucks on Canada

"Wherever you go in the world, you just have to say you're Canadian and people laugh."

—*John Candy*

"Canada is the essence of not being. Not English, not American, it is the mathematic of not being. And a subtle flavour—we're more like celery as a flavor."

—*Mike Myers*

"Canadians have been so busy explaining to the Americans that we aren't British, and to the British that we aren't Americans, that we haven't had time to become Canadians."

—*writer Helen Gordon McPherson*

"Americans know as much about Canada as straight people do about gays. Americans arrive at the border with skis in July, and straight people think that being gay is just a phase. A very long phase."

—*Kids in the Hall cast member Scott Thompson*

Perfect: Sculptures

❖ ❖

on may be a centuries-old art, still a complicated process.

most obvious sign that someone
t of wax sculpting has been around
known Madame Tussaud made her
tatue slides its way into a museum,
gins with weeks of research.
nission a particular person's model,
s of photographs and measure-
d person. But before they even
rts and putting the pieces together,
w the end product should appear.
il, ranging from the facial
robe and setting. They'll even go
entists to get a better feel of the
e those decisions have been made
time to start sculpting.

measurements and sometimes
sts work on creating a plaster
. Next, they pour hot wax into this
with manufactured petroleum-
rtificial coloring and chemicals to
heat. After everything is in place,

is removed and the assembly
l to best match the person's gaze.

PALINDROMES

A palindrome is a phrase that reads the same in both directions. The word is derived from the Greek palíndromos, which means running back again (palín = again; drom-, drameîn = to run).

Salt an atlas

Star rats

Yo! Bozo boy

Last egg gets Al

A car, a man, a maraca

Yell alley

Lion oil

Ed is on no side

Drowsy sword

Slap my gym pals

So, Ida, adios

Yawn way

Taboo bat

Put Eliot's toilet up

Go, dog!

Stack cats

Tell Abe to vote ballet

Harass Sarah

Sue us

Lee has a racecar as a heel

Step on no pets

Darn ocelots stole Conrad

Anarchy and Peace:
The Dutch Provo Movement

❖ ❖ ❖ ❖

In the summer of 1965, Holland's media were preoccupied with the activities of the Provos, a self-described anarchist group whose witty prank-like "happenings" appealed to the country's politically minded youth—and bothered the hell out of the Dutch police, who often were the unwitting victims of Provo mischief.

Where Ideals Converge

Provo pranksterism traces back to the late 1950s, beginning with Robert Jasper Grootveld, a young performance artist seemingly impervious to embarrassment. In one prank, Grootveld wrote "cancer" across cigarette billboards. It wasn't subtle, but it did have an impact.

Grootveld's early activities coincided with those of the Nozems, a group of disaffected, unemployed Dutch teens who got a kick out of mild, aimless troublemaking. By 1965, an intellectual named Roel Van Duyn realized that the Nozems' aggression could be channeled into "revolutionary consciousness." Together, Van Duyn and Grootveld became the nexus of a new, performance-oriented sort of social protest: The Provos.

The Provo agenda was rife with fascinating contradictions: Laziness and action. Protest and peace. Intellect and ignorance. The Provos were fueled by the power of those contradictions and embraced the opposite pillars of protest movements: the educated intellectuals who criticize society from behind ivory towers, and the uneducated punk riffraff who protest society by refusing to participate in it.

Provo political activities played like cleverly planned comedic farces that were almost too absurd to be true. One plot was designed to reveal the police force's ineptitude when it came to marijuana laws. To do so, the Provos continuously called the police on themselves and got arrested for possession, though the *faux* pot would prove to be tea and legal herbs. With this Trojan horse, the police were made to appear foolish time and time again; eventually they became afraid to arrest anyone for cannabis for fear they would be victim of another Provo plot.

Picture
Making Wax

❖ ❖

*Making a wax likeness of a per
but this sort of portraiture i*

The First Stages

Ah, the wax sculpture—perhaps the
has made it as a cultural icon. The a
since the 1700s, when the now well
first figures. These days, before the
it has to make a long journey that be

Once a museum decides to com
a team of artists begins to collect pi
ments of the soon-to-be-immortaliz
think about building the separate p
the museum must decide exactly ho

Curators consider every last de
expression and posture to the war
as far as interviewing barbers and
person's most intimate details. On
and the data has been collected, it

Building the Face

Using a combination of photos and
even a real-life impression, the art
mold of the head using regular cla
mold. Beeswax is often used along
based waxes, mixed together with
help the goo stay strong and resist
it's time to let the magic happen.

The Fine Details

Once the mold has cooled, the wa
begins. Prosthetic eyes are selecte

1

Porcelain teeth, similar to dentures, are used to fill the kisser. And real human hair is brought in to be inserted, one strand at a time, into every spot where it's needed: the head, the eyebrows and eyelashes, and even the arms and chest. Specially trained workers use a tiny needle to painstakingly place every last hair perfectly. This process alone takes up to 60 hours. One can imagine that, in the case of hirsute comedian Robin Williams's model, it could take 60 days.

Next, painters use translucent paint to even out the skin tone and add in any blemishes or distinguishing features. The paint is put on in thin layers, allowing the wax to shine through and look more lifelike. The crew then puts all the pieces together and passes the final figure off to the next team.

The Big Picture

Now that the model is done, the rest of the work begins. Seamstresses and costuming consultants come in to create the figure's wardrobe and fit it onto the body. Designers then assemble the full set, including backgrounds, props, and furnishings to match the moment frozen in time. At long last, the model is ready to be placed into the scene. After final touch-ups, engineers are hired to design lighting that will play up the sculpture's features. Finally, the journey is done, and the show is ready to open.

All together, the entire process usually takes a minimum of six months. Some cases have been more extreme: Royal London Wax Museum's model of former U.S. President Bill Clinton took eight months, and its sculpture of former Canadian Prime Minister Jean Chretien took just over a year. Museums say the creations can cost anywhere from $10,000 to $25,000, not including the various furnishings. Kind of makes the salon's $25 wax special seem a little more reasonable, doesn't it?

• *Madame Tussaud, born in 1761, was involved in the French Revolution, and was even scheduled to meet her fate at the guillotine for her supposed royalist sympathies. It was her talent with wax that saved her—she was hired to create death masks of those felled by the guillotine, including some of her friends.*

Bad Ad Grab Bag

"Advanced Products Inc., 10% Satisfaction Guaranteed."

"Wanted: Looking for someone to do yard work. Must have hoolahoop."

"1 man, 7 woman hot tub—$850/offer."

"Amana washer $100. Owned by clean bachelor who seldom washed."

"Snow blower for sale...only used on snowy days."

"Free puppies...part German shepherd, part dog."

"2 wire mesh butchering gloves, 1 5-finger, 1 3-finger, pair: $15."

"Tickle me Elmo, still in box, comes with its own 1988 mustang, auto, excellent condition $6,800."

"'83 Toyota hunchback—$2,000."

"Free puppies: ½ cocker spaniel, ½ sneaky neighbor's dog."

"Full sized mattress. 20 yr warranty. like new. slight urine smell."

"Free 1 can of pork & beans with purchase of 3 br 2 bth home."

"German shepherd. 85 lbs. neutered. speaks German. free."

Bill's Septic Cleaning: "We haul American made products."

"24 Hour Service Animal Control...Removal of Nuisance Wild Animals, Chimney Caps, Rats & Bats." *In an ad with images of "nuisance wild animals," including raccoons, bats, skunks—and a baby boy.*

"If you had no idea what to get her for Valentine's Day...Imagine how overwhelming arranging her funeral would be. Give her the perfect gift, make pre-arrangements as a couple with the affordable funeral home. By the way did we tell you we were affordable?"

"Tough Glass Cutting Board—Easily Cleaned, Hygienic—Warning: Not Suitable for Chopping Food On."

Would You Like Fried Worms With That?

Granted, to some people a Twinkie probably looks pretty weird. But at least Twinkies don't slither or smell like poo. Here's a sampling of some of the weirdest foods in the world.

Nutria

The nutria is a semi-aquatic rodent about the size of a cat with bright orange teeth. After World War II, they were sold in the United States as "Hoover Hogs." Since the animals chew up crops and cause erosion, in 2002 Louisiana officials offered $4 for every nutria killed. Still, their meat is rumored to be lean and tasty.

Uok

The coconut: Without it, the piña colada and macaroons wouldn't exist. Neither would the Uok, a golf ball-size, coconut-dwelling, bitter-tasting worm enjoyed by some Filipinos. Just pull one down from a mangrove tree, salt, and sauté!

Balut

If you're craving a midnight snack, skip the cheesecake and enjoy a boiled duck embryo. Folks in Cambodia will let eggs develop until the bird inside is close to hatching, and then they boil it and enjoy the egg with a cold beer.

Frog Smoothies

In Bolivia and Peru, Lake Titicaca frogs are harvested for a beverage affectionately referred to as "Peruvian Viagra." The frogs go into a blender with some spices and the resulting brown goo is served up in a tall glass. Turn on the Barry White...

Duck Blood Soup

Bright red goose blood is the main ingredient in this Vietnamese soup. A few veggies and spices round out the frothy meal.

Doin' the Duck and Cover

*Growing up as an American child during the 1950s
and '60s with the Cold War looming made for an
interesting, and often surreal, childhood.*

Only a Sunburn

If you can remember hiding under your school desk with your hands
over your head, then you are most likely a "Cold War survivor."
Growing up in America during the 1950s, this "Duck and Cover"
drill would have been part of your education. Intended to teach kids
what they should do in the event of a nuclear blast, the drill even
had its own mascot, Bert, an astute turtle who happened to carry his
shelter on his back. Newsreels featuring Bert the Turtle warned children that the explosion of a nuclear bomb could "knock you down
hard." But, if you only managed to "duck and cover" under a table or
desk, you would be protected from the "sunburn" of the explosion.

Head in the Sand

These films were created by the Federal Civil Defense Administration, which had been given the responsibility of educating and
protecting American citizens in the event of nuclear war. In effect,
they were responsible for much of the American Cold War propaganda produced during this time. One of their newsreels assured
Americans that they would fare much better than the Japanese had
in Hiroshima. After all, they reasoned, unlike the Japanese, Americans were being given the information they needed to survive: If
they just remembered to "clean under their fingernails, and wash
their hair thoroughly," Americans were sure to be spared the effects
of radiation.

A Culture of Fear

Fear had enormous impact on those growing up during the '50s and
'60s. Many mid-century suburban towns had been built, in part, with

the fear of Soviet attack in mind. Since it was expected that cities would be obliterated from falling bombs, the government encouraged suburban development as a way to scatter the population. Did you share a room with your brothers or sisters? During the Cold War, large families were encouraged as a way to fight the virus of communism—what better way to fight Soviet domination than to arm the country with a bursting population of wholesome capitalist American children? Birthrates soared to the highest levels of the century, with 29 million "baby boomers" born during the '50s.

The Cold War paranoia escalated after October 4, 1957, the day the Soviets launched *Sputnik I*, the world's first satellite. Suddenly, the nuclear threat emanating from Russia felt tangible. U.S. leaders decided the nation's best weapon against it was the youth of America, and so money was poured into schools and universities. No longer eggheads, scientists and engineers suddenly became the new elite.

Americans' response to the very real danger of nuclear war was sometimes surreal. In 1959, *LIFE* magazine ran a story featuring a couple planning to spend their honeymoon in a bomb shelter. The young couple was pictured surrounded by tin can provisions, which they took with them into their concrete "hotel." Children played with Sputnik toys and dressed as rockets for Halloween. Teenagers sported the latest swimsuit fashion, the bikini, named for the Bikini Island H-Bomb test site because its daring style was equally "dangerous."

On the Other Side

Since the fall of the Soviet Union it has been possible to learn how these years were experienced behind the Iron Curtain. Interestingly, many Soviet people did not fear impending nuclear war nearly as much as Americans did. For a child in the Soviet Union, *Sputnik's* flight was a celebration of scientific progress, and America was the source of pop songs—not total destruction.

Fumbling Felons

It's Not Easy Being Pink

Picking a good hiding place is like shooting dice: Sometimes you roll lucky sevens, and sometimes you crap out.

When police raided the house of a suspected drug dealer, the guy decided to hide inside a large roll of fiberglass insulation to elude the search. A cop spotted him in his pink cave; the officer decided that the distinctive sound of a shotgun being loaded would force him out of hiding.

The cop loaded the gun, and the suspect quickly scrambled out of the insulation. But it wasn't the sound of the shotgun loading that drew him out. Lying in the fiberglass material had irritated his skin, making him itch like mad. The scratching suspect was hauled off to the police station, desperately wishing for some hydrocortisone cream.

Animal Passion

Some criminals are hard cases. Then there are some that are just hard-shelled.

After an Indiana man and woman met, the attraction wasn't mutual: He had fallen in love big-time, but the sparks just weren't there for her. She tried to let him down easy, but he didn't want to hear it. He burst out of her home and into the night, but moments later he was back, brandishing...a snapping turtle.

Yes, somewhere he had found a snapping turtle, and now he proceeded to chase his former flame around her kitchen with the creature, trying to make the turtle bite her. But the turtle was no fool. It wanted nothing to do with this domestic disturbance and wouldn't cooperate. Finally the woman managed to call the police, who arrived and were able to separate the man from his reptilian weapon.

The man was charged with assault. The turtle was let off with a warning not to engage in any more shell games.

Earth Sense

❖ ❖ ❖ ❖

Ask anyone what they'd like to accomplish in their lifetime—
chances are they'll say that they'd like to make an impact on the
world, that they'd like to be remembered for their contributions.
No one says, "I'd like to leave behind 67 million tons of trash."

An Enduring Legacy

It's easy to forget about garbage: Out of sight, out of mind, right? But
during the course of producing consumer products such as plastic
bottles, newspapers, disposable diapers, and aluminum soda cans, we
create a veritable ocean of waste for future generations to contend
with. The sheer amount of garbage being thrown away is mind-bog-
gling: The average American family consumes more than 182 gallons
of soda, 104 gallons of milk, and 26 gallons of bottled water, with most
of the empty containers being tossed in landfills or the ocean. One-
third of the water Americans use is literally flushed down the toilet.
Meanwhile, rainforests are being destroyed at a rate of 100 acres per
minute, and 20 species of plants and wildlife are disappearing every
week due to the impact of human waste on the environment. Nice
legacy, huh?

Paper or Plastic? How About Neither?

Despite the fact that we can get our news in various ways, including
television, radio, or online, many Americans still have a daily newspaper habit: Each day, more than 44 million newspapers are tossed!
Although we now have more acres of forest than we did in 1920, it's
still wise to keep in mind that more than 25 million trees a year are
used to create these newspapers—valuable trees that eliminate carbon
dioxide. By dispensing with a single run of just one major metropolitan Sunday paper, more than 75,000 trees could be saved. If all else,
recycling the newspapers is the next best thing.

Junk mail is a pain to receive, but it's also a massive waste: The
average U.S. household discards more than 13,000 pieces of junk
mail per year—44 percent of which goes into the trash without ever
being opened.

Another source of trash is the supermarket. Before we've wheeled our grocery cart to the car, we've loaded up with dozens of paper and plastic bags that are destined for landfills. Even with the shift to plastic bags, each supermarket could go through more than 700 paper bags an hour—more than 60 million bags across the United States. The plastic bags that don't make it to the recycling bin often end up in the ocean where they kill as many as 1 million creatures a year. Bringing your own grocery bags is clearly the way to go. And those plastic rings that come with a six-pack of soda? They certainly don't make good necklaces for curious otters and other water-dwelling creatures, yet many birds and animals die from strangulation or drowning as a result of those plastic rings. Simply cut up the rings before throwing them away—look at that, you just saved an otter!

Add It Up

Consider this: Every year, the U.S. goes through 16 billion disposable diapers, 2 billion pens, enough car tires for 220 million vehicles, and 2 billion razor blades. Americans constitute only 5 percent of the world's population but generate more than 40 percent of the planet's trash, creating two to three times the waste of other industrialized countries with comparable or higher standards of living.

The answer, of course, is recycling. Surprisingly, recycling is nothing new: New York City introduced recycling programs back in 1890, and the city built its first recycling plant in 1898. By 1924, 83 percent of American cities were making at least minimal efforts to separate and recycle trash.

Although there's been some progress, it's estimated that more than 90 percent of what's in our trash bins could still be recycled. The energy saved from recycling a single glass bottle could run a 100-watt light bulb for over four hours. If each person recycled one aluminum can, they could save the equivalent of half a gallon of gasoline—or enough energy to run a television for three hours. Now that's a legacy to leave to the next generation!

Fast Facts

- It's been rumored that SPAM stands for "SPiced hAM." Not so, says Hormel, the company that makes the canned meat. Their official stance on the topic: "In the end, SPAM means SPAM."

- An umpire at the first professional baseball game was given a six-cent fine for using profanity.

- Vincent Van Gogh didn't die until two days after he shot himself.

- An average human eats about 60,000 pounds of food in his or her lifetime.

- Ketchup was first created in China.

- The world's largest Kentucky Fried Chicken is located in the Chinese city of Beijing.

- Americans spend more cash on cat food than on baby food each year.

- Croissants are a bit of a mystery. No one is sure when they were invented or where. One story goes that croissants were invented in 1680, after the people of Vienna defeated the invading Turks. A local baker made pastries in the shape of the crescent moon on the Turkish flag as a reminder that the Viennese had "devoured" the Turks.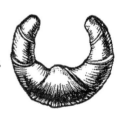

- Israel's postage stamps use kosher adhesive.

- Passing gas in a NASA spacesuit can damage it.

- Dieters, beware: The adhesive on a lickable U.S. postage stamp contains 1/10 of a calorie.

- A mole is capable of tunneling 15 feet an hour; the most diligent can do 300 feet in a night.

Con Talk

❖ ❖ ❖ ❖

*As long as there has been greed, there have
been con artists. In fact, these games cons play
have a language all of their own.*

- The **shill** is important to many con schemes because he's the confederate who draws the sucker to the bait. The shill is also called the **roper** or **stooge.**

- **Cooling the mark**—This remains the most important part of any confidence game, as it allows the victim, or **mark**, to depart the scene feeling like he got lucky, when in fact, he's been taken.

- The **Big Store con** made famous in the movie *The Sting* was based on reality. Involving high overheads and multiple confederates, this con is directed at a single mark—often another con man—for a big payoff. One Chicago-based con man, Yellow Kid Weil, staffed a fake bank with prostitutes and fellow con artists in order to take a corrupt businessman. Most cons aren't that elaborate.

Smaller Scale Cons

Short cons come in all sizes and flavors. They're the bread and butter for many con artists because they can be carried out quickly and inexpensively. Among these are:

- **Chugging**—Hustling donations to a fictitious charity. Currently used for fake disaster relief donations.

- **The Gypsy Switch**—Involves switching something valuable for something worthless. This con is probably the origin of the adage, "If it seems too good to be true, it probably is."

- **True Believer Syndrome**—Fake swamis, palm readers, and psychics love naïve marks afflicted with this "syndrome," because it means they keep coming back for more. Repeat business is always better than a one-time con.

The Times They Are-A-Changin'

1923

- On January 1, the constitution of the newly established Union of Soviet Socialist Republics goes into effect.

- "King" Oliver's Creole Jazz Band makes the first commercial recording by an African American band.

- Unidentified gunmen assassinate Mexican revolutionary Pancho Villa on June 23, three years after he negotiated peace with the government of President Victoriano Huerto.

- The Walt Disney Company is founded.

- On August 2, U.S. President Warren G. Harding dies from heart failure while in office.

Walt Disney

- The National Women's Party endorses an Equal Rights Amendment on the 75th anniversary of the Seneca Falls Convention. Sen. Charles Curtis and Rep. Daniel R. Anthony Jr. introduce the amendment to Congress as a joint resolution. The amendment is introduced in every session of Congress from 1923 to 1972.

- On November 6, the USSR adopts an experimental calendar, featuring five-day "weeks."

- Adolf Hitler seizes Munich's Bürgerbraükeller as the first step in a National Socialist Party revolution. The "Beer Hall Putsch" fails and Hitler is imprisoned for eight months.

- The second Ku Klux Klan, founded in 1915, is at the height of its membership. Two hundred thousand Klan members attend a three-state conclave in Kokomo, Indiana. Oklahoma declares martial law to protect people and property from Klan attacks.

- *TIME* magazine debuts.

Move Over, Rosa:
The Ida B. Wells Story

❖ ❖ ❖ ❖

Almost a century before Rosa Parks refused to give up
her seat on a bus in Montgomery, Alabama, activist
Ida B. Wells made a similar point on a train in Tennessee.

Emerging Strength

Our culture's pantheon of fame may only have room for a limited number of individuals, but Ida B. Wells should certainly be
included among this honorable group. She was born in 1862 to
slave parents who were freed along with the rest of America's
slaves in 1865. When Wells was 16, her parents and youngest
sibling died during a yellow fever epidemic. In order to keep her
family together, Wells showed her budding strength as she took a
job as a schoolteacher and raised her younger siblings.

Wells moved her family to Memphis, Tennessee; it was here
that she experienced the act of racism that launched her career.
Wells had bought a first-class train ticket for a "ladies'" car, but
the conductor told her to move to the "colored" car to make room
for a white man. When Wells refused, the conductor attempted to
forcibly move her. As Wells explained in her autobiography, "the
moment he caught hold of my arm I fastened my teeth in the back
of his hand." It took two more men to drag her off the conductor
and off the train.

Lashing Out Against Lynching

Wells sued the railroad company; she won the case in lower courts
but lost the case when it was appealed to the Supreme Court of
Tennessee. But the case served to instigate the fight for equality.
Wells became the co-owner and editor of *Free Speech*, an anti-
segregationist newspaper in Memphis. She focused her energies on
revealing the widespread horrors of lynching. In her landmark book,
A Red Record: Tabulated Statistics and Alleged Cause of Lynching
in the United States, she showed how horrifyingly common the

practice of lynching was, picking apart one popular excuse used to justify it: A black man's rape of a white woman. "Somebody must show that the Afro-American race is more sinned against than sinning, and it seems to have fallen upon me to do so," Wells said.

Wells argued that whenever the rape defense was brought into a lynching case, the truth was that it usually was a voluntary act between a white woman and a black man. Wells traced the history of this rape defense, and pointed out that white slave owners would often leave for months at a time, leaving their wives under the care of their black male slaves. In fact, she argued, white-black sexual liaisons were typically the other way around, with white owners sleeping with or raping female slaves.

Wells was the first scholar of note to unearth the hypocrisy behind the white man's so-called protection of white women's honor through lynching: "To justify their own barbarism," Wells wrote, "they assume a chivalry they do not possess...no one who reads the record, as it is written in the faces of the million mulattoes in the South, will for a minute conceive that the southern white man had a very chivalrous regard for the honor due the women of his own race, or respect for the womanhood which circumstances placed in his power." Wells concluded that the brutal lynching epidemic was really the result of fear for economic competition, combined with white men's anger at voluntary liaisons between white women and black men and a large helping of racism.

Continuing the Fight

Wells' work for civil rights continued until her death in 1931. She married fellow activist and writer F. L. Barnett in 1895. Together the couple had four children and worked to help the African American community in Chicago. Wells also was a founding member of the NAACP and the first president of The Negro Fellowship League. In 1930, shortly before her death, she ran for the Illinois Senate. Wells's resume is extensive and her activism was effective, and she certainly earned her right to the hall of fame of civil rights leaders.

FROM THE VAULTS OF HISTORY

Fürher Facts

By now, most students of history have read about the seamy side of Adolf Hitler—his bad breath, irritable bowel syndrome, skin lesions, syphilis, gastritis, and Parkinson's disease. And those who have delved further into Hitler's life probably also discovered that he was an illegitimate child, had a Jewish great-grandmother, and was probably addicted to methamphetamines. His third-grade report card remarked that he was "bad tempered and fancied himself a leader"—a prediction that was realized years later when he was voted *TIME* magazine's man of the year in 1938.

Being a devout nonsmoker, Hitler heavily promoted antismoking campaigns during World War II, and he promised a gold watch to any of his associates who successfully quit smoking. Ironically, when word spread of his suicide, the first thing that many of his officers, aides, and secretaries did was light up. Hitler was also fascinated by hands and collected hundreds of well-thumbed books that contained pictures of hands that belonged to famous people in history. He bragged to guests that his hands resembled those of his hero, Frederick the Great.

Entwistle's Irony

If you're looking for an ironic story with a Hollywood ending, consider the life and death of Lillian "Peg" Entwistle. Peg was a blue-eyed, blonde actress who made her start in show business doing bit parts in London theaters. After leaving England at age 14 to pursue a career in the United States, she eventually landed in Beachwood Canyon, an upperclass neighborhood in the shadows of the famous Hollywood sign.

Entwistle was a RKO contract player and starred in films with Billie Burke and Humphrey Bogart, although most of her scenes ended up on the cutting room floor. After years of unemployment and unsuccessful auditions, in 1932 Entwistle told her uncle that she was going out to the drugstore; instead, she climbed to the top of the "H" in the Hollywood sign and did a swan dive to end her life. As fate would have it, the next morning a letter arrived for her from the Beverly Hills Playhouse, offering her a lead role in a play—about a woman who is driven to suicide.

Body Talk: Anthropometrics and Human Engineering

❖ ❖ ❖ ❖

Every day, anthropometry and its related fields, ergonomics and biomechanics, directly affect your life. In fact, you'd be hard pressed to name one modern man-made device that isn't preceded by years of research regarding its size, shape, function, color, and how marketable it is to its consumers.

The Measurement of Body Parts

Anthropometry is the science of measuring human body parts. It's typically done for the fields of architectural, industrial, and clothing design—in short, any field that can benefit from understanding how a body moves through space. Alphonse Bertillon, born in 1853, was one forerunner in the field of anthropometry. His system, measuring and cataloguing facial and bodily characteristics to help identify criminals, was being used by 1883. Eventually, his methods were replaced by modern fingerprinting. In the 1940s, William Sheldon took Bertillon's work one step further by identifying three *somatotypes* or basic human body types: the ectomorph, mesomorph, and endomorph. According to Sheldon, every human fits into one of these basic body types.

In the early 20th century, anthropometry was used to characterize the nuances between various human races to identify those deemed "inferior." It also played an important role in so-called human intelligence testing, in which physical measurements such as height, width of the head, foot length, and width of the cheekbones were taken using crude measuring devices.

Today, anthropometric measurements are taken using computerized 3-D scanners. General Dynamics Advanced Information Systems (GD-AIS) has used 3-D scanning to improve products such as clothing. By scanning the human body, the scan can show how it fills a garment and how a jacket or blouse effectively moves with its wearer. GD-AIS also invented the "Faro Arm" to analyze how commercial and military pilots move within their cockpits and what happens to a pilot's concentration when their eyes wander from one instrument to another. This data affects where the controls need to be placed.

Biomechanics: The Body Moving Through Space

Another area of study concerned with the physical characteristics of the human body is *biomechanics,* or how the body moves in the home, workplace, and in everyday activities. Have you ever wondered how they came up with the cupholders that hold your drink while you're driving? How about the weight-training equipment at the gym? All of these were developed after years of painstaking research using biomechanics.

A number of new inventions that make our lives more comfortable are also based on biomechanical principles. Take the Reach toothbrush: The toothbrush existed for thousands of years as a series of fibers glued to a straight spine. It wasn't until recently that someone took a look at the design of the human mouth and determined through biomechanical and anthropometrical measurements that the back teeth could be cleaned more efficiently by tilting the end of the toothbrush.

Making Life Easier

If you've ever seen one of the new, curved ergonomic computer keyboards used to eliminate long-term stress effects that result in carpal tunnel syndrome, then you've seen an example of how science can work with medicine. *Ergonomics* is the science that determines how man-made objects "fit" human beings. Ergonomists evaluate specific tasks in the home or workplace and determine the demands they put on the worker, the equipment being used, and how they are performed.

Ergonomists look at the safety, comfort, performance, and aesthetics of commonly used products. Their ratings directly imply how well the product will sell. For instance, medicine bottles must come with labels that are easy to read by people with limited vision. Alarm clocks use "contrast principles" that make them easy to read in the dark without keeping the owner awake, and poorly designed VCRs spend years blinking "12:00" because their owners can't figure out how to set the time.

The Art of Gurning

*An untold number of mothers have warned their children,
"If you keep twisting your face, it will stay that way
permanently!" Little did Mom know that making ugly faces
could be viewed as training for a gurning competition.*

Gurning is a contest that pits challengers vying to contort their faces
into unbelievable displays of anatomical distortions. The mother of
all gurning contests is held each year at the Egremont Crab Fair
in Cumbria, England. Contestants come from every corner of the
globe to see who can pull the "world's ugliest face." But, unlike other
natural advantages in life, being ugly to begin with doesn't necessarily mean that you'll win.

"Just because you're oogly doesn't mean to say that ya [gonna]
win it," says gurning champion Peter Jackman in the book *True
Brits.* "Because gurnin' means the art of pullin' faces, not oogli-
ness." On the other hand, points are awarded to contestants who can
accentuate what they do or don't naturally have to work with. "You
get fellows like Peter," says Egremont organizer Alan Clements.
"He's a good-lookin' guy, but he can make himself into a monster—
that's what you're lookin' for."

Winning a gurning championship doesn't come easy. Champs like
Gordon Mattinson practice day in and day out until they can accom-
plish with their faces what you can only imagine in your nightmares.
The most successful gurners even come up with names for their
faces. Mattinson perfected his "Quasimodo," while the late Ron
Looney became famous for his "Popeye."

And, just in case you're thinking about stopping by Egremont
on your next vacation to capture the prize, be advised that gurning is a sport for professionals. Amateurs rarely make it to the final
round. "They don't really know what gurnin's about," says Jackman.
The Egremont Gurning Championship is held every year during the
third week of September.

PALINDROMES

A palindrome is a phrase that reads the same in both directions. The word is derived from the Greek palíndromos, *which means* running back again *(palín = again; drom-, drameîn = to run).*

Some men interpret nine memos

Ed is loopy poolside

Do geese see God?

Detach cat, Ed

Neptune nut pen

Desserts stress Ed

Elite tile

Bald elf fled lab

We panic in a pew

Pooch coop

Ed, a crab arcade

Sit on a potato pan, Otis

See bees

Rise to vote, sir

Stacy, must I jujitsu my cats?

Borrow or rob

Boston did not sob

Liar trail

Too hot to hoot

Rats live on no evil star

A nut for a jar of tuna

May a moody baby doom a yam?

Lucy the Beached Elephant

❖ ❖ ❖ ❖

Imagine this exchange between a ship's lookout and his captain as the vessel closed in on the New Jersey coastline near Atlantic City during the 1880s:

Captain: *"Tell me, what do you see?"*

Lookout: *"Elephant!"*

Captain: *"Elephant? I told you to stay out of the rum!"*

But it was true. From the coast rose a six-story, white wooden elephant standing serenely on the beach in South Atlantic City.

Real Estate Agent

The iconic elephant (later named Lucy) was built as a real estate gimmick in the early 1880s by James Lafferty Jr. Now, Lafferty had acquired overgrown, bramble-filled beachfront lots in South Atlantic City, and he needed to sell them. He figured a 65-foot-high wooden elephant standing on the beach near the lots was just the thing to attract attention. Sure enough, the people came. Tourists were suitably impressed by the elephant, climbed the stairs inside her leg to her hollow center, stood on top of her to enjoy the gorgeous ocean view—and then went home, money in hand. As it turned out, Lucy was a dismal failure as a real estate agent, and Lafferty was forced to sell her to Anton Gertzen.

Extraordinary Attraction

Gertzen didn't put Lucy to work. He didn't have to, because enough people (including U.S. President Woodrow Wilson and inventor Henry Ford) came to see the wooden pachyderm that she did just fine for decades as an oddity attraction. Occasionally, Lucy pursued other careers, serving as a rooming house and tavern.

But by 1963, Lucy was aging, and she was rapidly falling apart. Margate (formerly South Atlantic City) officials wanted to demolish the elderly elephant. For several years the fight raged between preservationists and officials, but in the eleventh hour, the elephant was restored. In 1976, Lucy was named a National Historic Landmark. More than 100 years later, Lucy is still Queen of the Beach.

HOW IT ALL BEGAN

Barnum's Biscuits

Master showman P. T. Barnum may have inspired more creativity in other people than any other entrepreneur in the past century. One item still keeps bakery ovens hot, not because of the thing itself, but because of its packaging: animal cracker boxes.

These tiny, tasty biscuits were around long before Barnum arrived on the scene. However, his traveling circuses stirred a pioneering success in packaging small boxes colorfully illustrated as animal circus wagons —large enough to hold a good portion of cookies and small enough to use as an ornament or toy.

Fatal Attraction

The term "painted lady" goes as far back as 3500 B.C., when Queen Shubad of Sumeria was reported to have coated her lips with a poultice of ground red rocks and lead. Centuries passed before the toxicity of certain ingredients in ladies' "paint" was understood. For example, in addition to lead, mercury was used in manufacturing rouge and eye shadow for many years.

A Crackerjack Idea

Pre-Columbian peoples likely discovered popcorn when someone over-cooked corn kernels. Confectioners mixing popcorn with molasses or melted marshmallows produced popcorn balls. However, Cracker Jack was the snack that stormed the North American market in 1900. Movie-house buttered popcorn came much later.

Cracker Jack, featuring sweet-meets-salty caramel-coated popcorn, was a wild success—even beyond the tiny free prizes found in every box. First, the creators, Fred and Louis Rueckheim, figured out a way to prevent all the components from sticking together in a big gooey ball. They went for bite-size pieces, and then added peanuts. Their real coup over the competition came when they packaged it all in a sealed box that preserved their product.

Of course, their crackerjack of a name helped too. The branding was so successful that Cracker Jack was listed in the Sears Catalogue without even a line of product description.

Fast Facts

- *The sport of badminton was once called "poona."*

- *The world's largest bowling alley is the 156-lane Nagoya Grand Bowl in Japan.*

- *Legend has it the man who invented the light bulb, Thomas Edison, was quite scared of the dark.*

- *Astronaut Buzz Aldrin, the second man to walk on the moon, has a second connection to the giant circle in the sky: His mother's maiden name was, fittingly, Moon.*

- *Bamboo is the world's tallest grass, growing as much as 90 centimeters in a single day.*

- *Australian toilets are designed to flush counterclockwise.*

- *Barbie has a full name that many people don't know: Barbara Millicent Roberts. Not quite as catchy.*

- *An airplane mechanic came up with the idea for the Slinky toy while working with engine springs.*

- *Mr. Potato Head holds the honor of being the first toy featured in a television commercial.*

- *In Tennessee, it's apparently all right to shoot whales from a moving car, but in landlocked Oklahoma, hunting whales is forbidden.*

- *Pac-Man was originally going to be called Puck Man. The name was changed because of a fear that troublemaking teens would change the "P" to another, less-appropriate letter on arcade machines.*

- *Most women work through six pounds of lipstick in their lives.*

Heads Up: The Study of Phrenology

❖ ❖ ❖ ❖

Sure, someone may look like a nice enough guy,
but a phrenologist might just diagnose the
same fella as a potential axe murderer.

He Had the Gall

There are bumps in the road and bumps in life. Then there are the bumps on our heads. In the last half of the 19th century, the bumps and lumps and shapes of the human skull became an area of scientific study known as *phrenology.*

Early in the century, an Austrian physicist named Franz Joseph Gall theorized that the shape of the head followed the shape of the brain. Moreover, he wrote, the skull's shape was determined by the development of the brain's various parts. He described 27 separate parts of the brain and attributed to each one specific personality traits.

Gall's phrenological theories reached the public at a time of widespread optimism in Europe and North America. New and startling inventions seemed to appear every week. No problem was insurmountable, no hope unattainable. Physical science prevailed.

By mid-century, Gall's theories had spread favorably throughout industrialized society. What was particularly attractive about phrenology was its value as both an indicator and predictor of psychological traits. If these traits could be identified—and phrenology presumably could do this—they could be re-engineered through "moral counseling" before they became entrenched as bad habits, which could result in socially unacceptable behavior. On the other hand, latent goodness, intellect, and rectitude could also be identified and nurtured.

As it grew in popularity, phrenology found its way into literature as diverse as the Brontë family's writings and those of Edgar Allen

Poe. It also influenced the work of philosopher William James. Famed poet Walt Whitman was so proud of his phrenological chart that he published it five times. Thomas Edison was also a vocal supporter. "I never knew I had an inventive talent until phrenology told me so," he said. "I was a stranger to myself until then."

Criminal Minds

Early criminologists such as Cesare Lombroso and Èmile Durkheim (the latter considered to be the founder of the academic discipline of sociology) saw remarkable possibilities for phrenology's use in the study of criminal behavior. Indeed, according to one tale, the legendary Old West figure Bat Masterson invited a phrenologist to Dodge City to identify horse thieves and cattle rustlers. A lecture before an audience of gun-toting citizenry ended with the audience shooting out the lights and the lecturer hastily departing through the back exit.

In 1847, Orson Fowler, a leading American phrenologist, conducted an analysis of a Massachusetts wool trader and found him "to go the whole figure or nothing," a man who would "often find (his) motives are not understood." Sure enough, years later Fowler was proven to be on the money. The man was noted slavery abolitionist John Brown, and he definitely went the "whole figure."

Bumpology Booms

By the turn of the century, the famous and not so famous were flocking to have their skulls analyzed. Phrenology had become a fad and, like all fads, it attracted a number of charlatans. Death masks and cranial molds also became popular sideshow exhibits. By the 1920s, the science had degenerated into a parlor game. Disrepute and discredit followed, but not before new expressions slipped into the language. Among these: "low brow" and "high brow" describe varying intellectual capacity, as well as the offhand remark, "You should have your head examined."

Nevertheless, phrenology did figure in the early development of American psychiatry, and it helped point medical scientists in new directions: neurology for one and, more recently, genomics—the study of the human genome.

Who's Afraid of the Dark?

❖ ❖ ❖ ❖

Well, Keanu Reeves is, for one. But he's not the only celebrity with a phobia. Read on to find out what scares the stars.

Acrophobia (fear of heights): Sure, he scaled tall buildings in the *Spider-Man* movies, but Tobey Maguire would rather keep his feet on the ground.

Ataxophobia (fear of disorder): Soccer pro David Beckham likes to have things in order, matching, and in even numbers. In fact, his wife Victoria told *People* magazine, "If there are three cans of Diet Coke he'd throw one away rather than having three because it's uneven."

Aviophobia (fear of flying): This common fear keeps many stars on the ground, including John Madden, Colin Farrell, Aretha Franklin, and Jennifer Aniston.

Claustrophobia (fear of enclosed spaces): Uma Thurman can handle a lot of things, but tight spaces aren't among them. "There was no acting required. Real screams available," said the actress about a scene in *Kill Bill: Vol. 2* where she is buried alive in a coffin.

Clourophobia (fear of clowns): Though he's a natural-born entertainer, you're not likely to find actor Johnny Depp anywhere near a circus. "Something must have happened when I was a kid," he told *Entertainment Weekly.*

Coimetrophobia (fear of graveyards): When filming *Buffy the Vampire Slayer,* Sarah Michelle Geller requested a fake cemetery be built because of her phobia.

Hoblophobia (fear of guns): Although he has played super spy James Bond, Roger Moore is not a fan of guns, fake or not.

Hydrophobia (fear of water): With all the time she spent frolicking in the water on *Baywatch,* it's hard to believe that Carmen Electra has a fear of it.

Ovophobia (fear of eggs): You'd think that nothing could scare master of suspense Alfred Hitchcock. But the sight of eggs made him squirm.

Fast Facts

- *If you need something super fast, ask for it in a yoctosecond. That's the smallest unit of time.*

- *A female ferret can die from going into heat and not mating.*

- *For passengers who may not quite get it, American Airlines printed instructions on their peanut packages. "Open packet, eat nuts." Ever helpful advice.*

- *Cockroaches like eating the adhesive off the back of postage stamps.*

- *A typical shark can swim as fast as 40 miles per hour.*

- *An adult's shower takes an average of five to ten minutes.*

- *More than half of Americans wake up before 7 A.M.*

- *Three-quarters of Americans say they make their beds on a daily basis.*

- *Smokers have less frequent dreams compared to nonsmokers.*

- *The word "nicotine" comes from a man named Jean Nicot de Villemain. He was the French ambassador to Portugal and was the first to write about tobacco's "medicine-like" qualities.*

- *The Statue of Liberty's foundation alone weighs 54 million pounds.*

- *Onions are technically a type of lily.*

- *Throughout Germany and Austria, post boxes are available where mothers can deposit unwanted newborns, which are quickly picked up by childcare service workers for adoption. The boxes hit the news in 2007, when a drunk managed to squirm into one of them, smoke a cigarette, and then peacefully go to sleep. Presumably he was unadoptable; childcare services returned him to his family.*

Dino Mix-Ups

❖ ❖ ❖ ❖

The field of paleontology, once the realm of dusty fossils displayed in museums, has in recent years become a hot field of study. New methods of testing, using DNA analysis, CAT scans, and MRI imaging, allow researchers to study fossil findings in new ways. However, one result of this current wave of research is the unearthing of mixed-up fossils, scientific wrong turns, and mistaken identities.

You Say *Brontosaurus*, I say *Apatosaurus*

One of the earliest dino-bloopers was the case of the *Brontosaurus.* In 1877, paleontologist O. C. Marsh identified a specimen as being of the species type, *Apatosaurus ajax.* A few years later, he found a more complete sample of the same dinosaur. In the paper following this find, Marsh called the beast a Brontosaurus, setting off decades of confusion. The two names actually mean the same thing, but over time they began to be thought of as two different dinosaurs. According to the rules for naming new species, the older name takes precedence; to put a halt to the confusion, Brontosaurus was officially dropped as the dino's name. Despite this, the Brontosaurus is still one of the most recognized names of dinosaurs.

Big, Bigger, Much Bigger

At an estimated 90 feet long and weighing 11 tons, the long-necked, plant-eating *Diplodocus* was considered to be the largest animal ever to have lived. It enjoyed that distinction for nearly a century until someone discovered the 100- to 130-foot-long *Supersaurus* in 1972. Then the *Seismosaurus*, at 150 feet long and weighing 85 tons, was uncovered in 1979. As more research emerges, museums around the world continue to rewrite the identification cards for these

100- to 130-foot-long *Supersaurus* in 1972. Then the *Seismosaurus,* at 150 feet long and weighing 85 tons, was uncovered in 1979. As more research emerges, museums around the world continue to rewrite the identification cards for these long-necked beasts. It is now thought that while the Seismosaurus probably made tremor-like sounds when stamping through the forest, and the Supersaurus was without question very, very big, they were not separate species. In fact, both were just large specimens of the Diplodocus.

Plateosaurus Puzzler

It is remarkable that scientists can make any sense out of the jumble of bones that they discover. It's something like putting together a puzzle—one that is sure to have missing pieces, broken parts, and no picture on the box to show how it should look in the end. It is not surprising that the pieces would get mixed up at times, as in the case of the *Plateosaurus.* In the late 1800s, German fossil hunters found the skeleton of a dinosaur that had the razor teeth of a meat eater. This was named *Teratosaurus* ("monster reptile") and was thought of as a slow-moving, long-necked carnivore. It took almost 100 years for paleontologists to sort out the fact that the Teratosaurus was actually the remains of a plant-eating Plateosaurus, whose skull was mixed up with that of the crocodile-like creature that ate it. This beast, one of the top predators of the time, was actually not a dinosaur at all. Even so, it got to keep the name Teratosaurus.

Oviraptor: Falsely Accused

When the first *Oviraptor* specimens were discovered in Mongolia, they were found near fossilized eggs. It was assumed at the time that the eggs were from the *Protoceratops,* and since the new dinosaur was found to be toothless, it made sense to assume the eggs were a part of its diet. This theory led to its name: Oviraptor ("egg thief"). However, it was not until the 1990s when excavations in China cleared the Oviraptor's name. At the site, Oviraptor specimens were found, as they had been in the past, near eggs. Thanks to new technologies, this time scientists were able to examine the inside of the fossilized eggs. What they found was the embryo of an Oviraptor—the "egg thieves" were actually very good parents, protecting their nests and their young with their lives.

No Little Feat

Even the batting average for 3'7" Eddie Gaedel in his only game is short: a solid .000. But while he was up at the plate waving his miniature bat, Gaedel was as big as Babe Ruth.

Go For the Gimmick

St. Louis Browns owner, Bill Veeck, loved a good show. Having a Little Person up at bat was Veeck's brainchild, as was exploding scoreboards, outlandish giveaways, and other promotions.

The Browns provided Veeck with a great challenge. The team was the perennial sad sack of the American League, and was constantly outdrawn by the rival St. Louis Cardinals. As the public's interest waned for the losing team, Veeck tried every trick he could think of to boost attendance.

Double the Fun

For the August 19, 1951, doubleheader between the Browns and Detroit Tigers, Veeck promised team sponsor Falstaff Brewery something "spectacular" in honor of Falstaff Brewery Day. The first game was routine, but in the bottom of the first inning of the second game, it was announced, "[Batting] for the Browns, number ⅛, Eddie Gaedel." Armed with his miniature bat, 65-pound Gaedel was at the plate.

The park erupted in laughter, and photographers scrambled to get pictures. The Tiger's catcher got down on his knees to offer his pitcher a target. Veeck had worked with Gaedel on a crouch that made his strike zone 1½ inches high, but the excited Gaedel stood straighter. No matter—the Tiger pitcher was laughing so hard, four straight throws whizzed over Gaedel's head. By the time Gaedel trotted to first base and was taken out for a pinch runner, he was a sensation.

Outraged, the American League immediately banned Gaedel from ever playing pro ball again. Veeck (with tongue firmly in cheek) threatened to investigate whether diminutive New York Yankee shortstop Phil Rizzuto was a short ballplayer or a tall Little Person.

Eddie Gaedel, meanwhile, just enjoyed his 15 minutes of fame.

FLUBBED HEADLINES

"Hamlet Shaken by Murder Then Suicide"

"Fried Chicken Cooked In Microwave Wins Trip"

"Skywalkers in Korea Cross Han Solo"

"Lawyer Says Client Is Not That Guilty"

"Alzheimer's Center Prepares For an Affair to Remember"

"Gas Cloud Clears Out Taco Bell"

"Harrisburg Postal Employees Gun Club Members Meet"

"Have You Driven a Fjord Lately?"

"After Detour to California Shuttle Returns to Earth"

"Woman Improving After Fatal Crash"

"New Study of Obesity Looks for Larger Test Group"

"A-Rod Goes Deep, Wang Hurt"

"Study Reveals Those Without Insurance Die More Often"

"Man Found Dead in Cemetery"

"Red Tape Holds Up New Bridge"

"Typhoon Rips Through Cemetery—Hundreds Dead"

"Gators to Face Seminoles With Peters Out"

"Man Struck by Lightning Faces Battery Charge"

"Astronaut Takes Blame for Gas in Spacecraft"

"Kids Make Nutritious Snacks"

"British Union Finds Dwarfs in Short Supply"

"Local High School Dropouts Cut in Half"

"Health Officials Say Flammable Water is OK to Drink"

"Bladder Control Causes Sunset Beach Flooding"

"Alton Attorney Accidentally Sues Himself"

Dem Bones: X-ray Shoe Fitting Machines

During the 1940s, people were particularly concerned about their feet—mothers, fathers, even the U.S. Army. As a result, the guardian of modern foot care was created: the Adrian X-ray Shoe Fitting Machine.

A Star is Born

Although there are conflicting stories about its origin, the first X-ray shoe-fitting machine has generally been attributed to Dr. Jacob Lowe, a Boston physician who was looking for a fast and efficient way to analyze soldiers' feet during World War I. Dr. Lowe was concerned with the poorly fitting boots worn by many military recruits and was interested in a way to reduce their foot-related injuries. In addition to providing the doctor with a superior view of the foot, the X-ray shoe-fitting machine allowed Dr. Lowe to speed up production, since soldiers didn't have to remove their boots.

The machine was a simple design: A fluoroscope was mounted on the base of a wooden platform, which sent X-rays upward toward a fluorescent screen. The client placed their foot inside and the image would be directed up to a reflector, where three viewing scopes displayed the foot's image. The entire area was sealed within a lead-shielded area for protection of the client. Unlike X-rays that are captured on film, the machine displayed a real-time image of the client's foot, shoes and all.

After the war, Dr. Lowe starting making the rounds to retail shoe stores, and in 1927 he sold the patent to the Adrian Company of Milwaukee. About the same time, a similar patent was granted in Great Britain for the Pedoscope, although the Pedoscope Company claimed that their instrument had already been in use for more than five years.

Better Shoe Fitting Through Science

The public went wild over this new way to be "scientifically" fitted for shoes. Concerned mothers were grateful that someone had finally come up with a method for accurately fitting their children's shoes; the manufacturer claimed that by being able to view the foot inside the shoe, a child's shoe would last longer and promote the child's foot health and comfort. By the 1950s, more than 10,000 Adrian X-ray Shoe Fitting Machines had been installed all over the country.

As the machines gained in popularity, however, so did the government's concern over their safety. When the machines were first introduced, little was known about continued exposure to radiation. As a result, children and adults were repeatedly exposed to X-ray radiation, with little concern over its ill effects. The average shoe salesman might expose himself to 20 to 30 doses in a single shift. In 1946, the American Standards Association defined a "safe and tolerable dosage" of radiation and began regulating how the X-ray machines were to be used. Ultimately, the American Conference of Governmental Industrial Hygienists issued uniform guidance standards.

The Adrian Company assured parents that the new machines were safe and could "just as easily be operated by 'old timers' with more than 20 years of shoe fitting experience as 'Saturday extras' who only had their jobs for a few weeks."

The End of an (X-ray) Era

By the early '50s, a number of medical societies became concerned that nonmedical personnel were operating the fluoroscopes. Eventually they issued warnings that only licensed physiotherapists should operate the machines. A number of states began enforcing even stricter rules, requiring that licensed physicians only use the X-ray fitting machines. In 1957, Pennsylvania became the first state to ban the use of the shoe-fitting fluoroscopes. It didn't take long for the rest of the country to follow suit.

Fumbling Felons

Whipped and Witless

Some criminals consider themselves masters of disguise. Not this guy.

A Louisiana man decided that he had devised the perfect way to mask his features while robbing a bank. He would cover his entire head in whipped cream. After all, the topping was easy to apply, quickly wiped off, and covered his face beautifully. Never mind that he resembled a walking marshmallow.

One spring day, the man, looking like a small cloud with feet, strode into a Louisiana bank. The laughter among the employees erupted almost as soon as he entered the building. In fact, by the time he walked up to a teller and demanded money, the bankers could barely stand up from laughing so hard.

And what of the robber's brilliant disguise? Unfortunately, he had neglected to consider the fact that whipped cream needs to stay cold to stay solid. With the combination of warm weather and jittery nerves, the cream was beginning to melt and run down his body. The police, having been summoned by a silent alarm, quickly arrested the gooey criminal.

Return to Sender

It seemed to be the perfect crime: A man had walked into a crowded Florida liquor store and handed the busy clerk a note demanding money. The clerk complied, and in the confusion of the hold-up, the man managed to slip away virtually unnoticed. When police arrived, it seemed they had no evidence and no clues to help them find the robber.

That is, until they looked at the robber's note. In his haste, the criminal had scrawled his stick-up note onto the back of a letter he had received from his probation officer. Neatly printed on the front of the letter was the man's name and home address.

The case quickly went from perfect crime to laughable attempt as the cops cruised to the listed address and nabbed the unthinking crook, who by then probably wished his probation officer had simply used e-mail.

A Tangled Web

❖ ❖ ❖ ❖

*So-called "black widows"—women who marry and then
kill their spouses and sometimes families for profit—stand
out for their sheer unlikelihood as perpetrators. The black
widows that follow got caught up in their own webs.*

Artiste of Arsenic

Norwegian immigrant Belle Poulsdatter, known as the Black Widow
of the Heartland, was married for 17 years before her husband died
and she collected $8,000 in life insurance. Belle moved her family
to LaPorte, Indiana, where she later married wealthy widower Peter
Gunness, who died when a meat grinder tumbled from a high shelf
and landed on his head. His death was ruled accidental, and Belle
collected Peter's insurance money and his estate.

Belle advertised for farmhands in a newspaper that catered
to incoming Norwegian immigrants. Of those who responded,
Belle hired the ones who came with a sturdy bank account as
well as a sturdy back. Laborers came and went—and some simply
disappeared.

When the Gunness farmhouse burned to the ground in 1908, the
bodies of Belle's children and an unidentified headless female were
found in the cellar. A search of the property revealed the bodies of
Belle's suitors and laborers buried in the hog pen, some killed by
arsenic, some by skull trauma. The widow was nowhere to be found.
Belle's remaining beau-cum-farmhand was convicted of murdering
Belle and her family. However, the identity of the headless corpse
was never conclusive, leading some to believe that Belle staged the
entire thing and escaped.

The Giggling Grandmother

From the mid-1920s to the mid-'50s, Nannie Doss left a trail of
corpses: her mother, two sisters, a nephew, and a grandson. A
mother of four trapped in an unhappy marriage, Nannie also murdered two of her children with rat poison before her first husband

left her. She collected on the children's life insurance policies. Nannie married three more times, but each husband contracted a mysterious stomach ailment and died, leaving his widow his insurance settlement, home, and estate.

Coincidentally, Nannie's fifth husband also died of a stomach ailment. His physician ordered an autopsy, which showed a significant amount of rat poison. After her arrest, the bodies of her former spouses were exhumed for examination; all showed traces of poison. Nannie giggled as she confessed her crimes to the police, earning her the nickname, "The Giggling Grandmother."

Nobody Buys the Doppelgänger Bit

Frank Hilley had been married to Marie for more than 20 years when he was admitted to the hospital with stomach pain and diagnosed with acute infectious hepatitis in 1975. He died within the month, and Marie collected on his life insurance policy. Three years later, she took out a life insurance policy on her daughter Carol, whereupon Carol developed a strange illness with symptoms of nausea and numbness in her extremities. Physicians detected an abnormal level of arsenic in Carol's system and suspected foul play. Frank's body was exhumed and tests revealed that he had died of arsenic poisoning.

Marie was arrested in October 1979 for the attempted murder of her daughter, but was released on bond a month later. She promptly disappeared. Despite her indictment for murder, Marie remained a fugitive for more than three years before marrying John Homan in Florida under the alias Robbi Hannon.

In a bizarre turn of events, Marie invented a twin sister, "Teri," staged "Robbi's"death, and then returned to her husband pretending to be her grief-stricken twin, Teri. The ruse was discovered, and Marie was sent to Alabama, where she was wanted on other charges. The house of cards fell apart, and she was convicted of murder and attempted murder and sentenced to life in prison. Marie served four years of her sentence before she escaped during a furlough. She was found days later, freezing and wandering in the woods near Anniston, Alabama. Marie was admitted to the hospital, where she died of hypothermia.

He Said, She Said

"Often it does seem a pity that Noah and his party did not miss the boat."
—*Mark Twain*

"I feel like Zsa Zsa Gabor's sixth husband. I know what I'm supposed to do, but I don't know how to make it interesting."
—*Milton Berle*

"Human beings are the only creatures on earth that allow their children to come back home."
—*Bill Cosby*

"I looked up my family tree and found three dogs using it."
—*Rodney Dangerfield*

"Let's face it; God has a big ego problem. Why do we always have to worship him?"
—*Bill Maher*

"It ain't those parts of the Bible that I can't understand that bother me, it is the parts that I do understand."
—*Mark Twain*

"The good people sleep much better at night than the bad people. Of course, the bad people enjoy the waking hours much more."
—*Woody Allen*

"People say that money is not the key to happiness, but I always figured if you have enough money, you can have a key made."
—*Joan Rivers*

"A man who views the world the same at 50 as he did at 20 has wasted 30 years of his life."
—*Muhammad Ali*

"If you think you have it tough, read history books."
—*Bill Maher*

"Eighty percent of married men cheat in America. The rest cheat in Europe."
—*Jackie Mason*

Down in the Dumps

*Sorry, E.T. can't phone home—he's
buried in a landfill in New Mexico.*

A Lovable Alien

In 1982, the world was introduced to a lovable alien named E.T.:
The Extra-Terrestrial in an exceedingly successful movie of the same
name. The film went on to win four Oscars and two Golden Globes,
which led to a flurry of international movie merchandising. One
success story was found in Hershey's ability to boost the sales of its
struggling brand Reese's Pieces, the candy that in the movie entices
E.T. out of hiding and into Elliot's bedroom. Not all merchandising
is created equal, however; thus begins the sad tale of Atari and the
first video game based on a movie.

At the time, video game arcades were extremely popular in the
United States. In 1981, Americans spent $5 billion playing more
than 75,000 hours on arcade games, out-grossing both movies and
the recording industry. Atari's VCS (Video Computer System), more
commonly known as the Atari 2600, was a new but successful player in
the home video game market. Atari's goal, along with other companies
such as Coleco and Mattel, was to bring the arcade into consumer's
homes with game cartridge versions of their favorite games.

Dumped

What Atari didn't take into consideration, as they rushed their most
hyped new game to market in time for Christmas 1982, was that the
consumer wasn't necessarily excited to play a game about a movie
involving a boy and his alien friend. It didn't help that the game
was so rushed into production that it proved dull and difficult to
play, and it simply didn't hold the player's attention. Stores returned
millions of E.T. game cartridges, while many games were just never
shipped out from Atari's plant in Texas. In the end, 14 truckloads
of the unsold games were driven to a landfill in Alamogordo, New
Mexico. There they were dumped, crushed, and covered in a layer of
concrete to discourage scavengers.

INSPIRATION STATION

A (Really) Big Idea: Stan Lee's Incredible Hulk

Everyone's favorite green superhero, the Incredible Hulk, was inspired by two of literature's most famous monsters: Frankenstein and the dualistic personality of Dr. Jekyll and Mr. Hyde. By combining the two characters, says creator Stan Lee, "I got myself the monster I wanted, who was really good, but nobody knew it"—much like the monster in Mary Shelly's classic novel, *Frankenstein.* "He was also somebody who could change from a normal man into a monster," Lee said, which was the case for Dr. Jekyll in the famous story by Robert Louis Stevenson. The whole green skin thing was less an inspired idea and more of a fluke, however; the printer of the comic couldn't achieve the shade of gray that Lee had originally desired. Lee okayed the Hulk's color change to green.

Inspiration, Muppet Style

Genius entertainer and puppeteer Jim Henson dreamed up a Muppet rock band as far back as 1951. The inspiration for what would become The Electric Mayhem came directly from musicians in the world of rock 'n' roll. Muppet bass guitarist Sgt. Floyd Pepper is an obvious reference to the Beatles album, *Sgt. Pepper's Lonely Hearts Club Band.* Pepper is also a nod to Pink Floyd, since he's pink in color, and well, named Floyd. Janice, the lanky-haired sometime vocalist and lead guitar player is named after Janis Joplin, although rumors abound that both her appearance and character were inspired by Joni Mitchell. Blues musician Dr. John directly inspired Mayhem bandleader Dr. Teeth. And although Henson never confirmed it, manic drummer Animal is said to have been inspired by Keith Moon of The Who. Some say the rumor is substantiated by the fact that Henson named one of his *Fraggle Rock* characters Wembley, which happens to be the town in which Moon was born.

"Life's like a movie, write your own ending. Keep believing, keep pretending."

—*Jim Henson*

A Diner-English Glossary

From the mid-1800s through the 1970s, diner slang
helped hash-slingers avoid confusion, entertain
customers, and add a bit of local flavor to the food.

Birdseed and Hope—Breakfast

- Cackleberries, Hen Fruit: eggs
- Wreck 'Em, Shipwreck: scrambled eggs
- Wrecked and Crying: scrambled eggs with onions
- Drown the Kids: boiled eggs
- Flop Two: two fried eggs, over easy
- Dough Well Done With Cow to Cover: buttered toast
- Burn the British: toasted English muffin
- Blowout Patches: pancakes
- Birdseed: cereal

Slop and Splash—Soups

- Bowl of Red, Red Bull: chili
- Bossy in a Bowl: beef stew
- Guess Water: soup of the day
- Let the Chicken Wade Through It: chicken soup

Down the Hatch—Beverages

- Adam's Ale, City Juice: water
- Boiled Leaves: tea
- Canned Cow: evaporated milk
- Cup of Mud: black coffee
- Hot Blonde With Sand: coffee with cream and sugar
- Hail: ice

Cutting the Fat

❖ ❖ ❖ ❖

*From "snack taxes" to federally mandated student fitness
standards, and from "skinny lattes" to healthy fast food
alternatives, Americans are striving to overcome an epidemic
of obesity—sometimes with humorous consequences.*

The National Crises

Whether you blame fast food, video games, or
automobiles, the simple fact is that Americans are
consuming more while doing less, and it's starting to
show. In fact, two of every three Americans are now
overweight, and nearly 70 million Americans are considered obese; that is, they have exceeded their optimal
body mass by more than 30 percent. It's estimated that
the resulting health crises will lower the national life-
expectancy average, possibly by as much as five years, for
the first time in American history.

Certainly the obesity crisis in America is a serious
matter; but given the increased media coverage and
resulting awareness in recent years there is good cause
for hope. In the meantime, consider two illustrative
events in the quest for good health that are, if not
cause for laughter, then perhaps a polite smile.

Mississippi Leads the Way (to the Buffet)

West Virginia, Indiana, Alabama, and Mississippi have consistently
ranked among the states with the highest rates of obesity in the
United States, with Alabama and Mississippi usually within a hairs-
breadth of each other for first place. Recently, Mississippi received
the dubious honor of being the fattest state in the nation for three
years in a row.

This alarming state of affairs was not lost on Mississippi State
Representatives Ted Mayhall, John Read, and Bobby Shows, who
decided to take action. In 2008, the three reps cosponsored House
Bill 282, making it illegal for a restaurant to serve an obese person.

Besides pointing out the impossibility of enforcing the proposed law, critics claimed that the measure amounted to cruel punishment of obese individuals. The executive director of the Obesity Society called the proposed law "the most ill-conceived plan to address public health crisis ever proposed," and the chairman of the state House Public Health and Human Services Committee publicly announced that he would veto the measure when it reached his desk.

Chew on This: Rep. John Read claimed that the measure was simply meant to raise public awareness of the obesity crises. In this he succeeded: House Bill 282 received national attention, and it reminded everyone that Mississippi was still the fattest state in the nation.

Chew on This: At the time he introduced the bill, the 5'11" Read weighed 230 pounds—if his own bill had passed, he would have been unable to eat in restaurants.

It's a Not-So-Small World

In 2007, representatives of the Disneyland resort in Anaheim, California announced that the popular "It's a Small World" ride would close for the first time in four decades. It seems that the boats, which carried groups through Walt Disney's singsong tour of the world's cultures, were bottoming out and getting stuck in Canada and Scandinavia. Disney representatives were quick to blame the problem on "fiberglass buildup," but most observers concluded that it was simply the result of the average national weight increasing by 25 pounds since the ride was built in 1964.

When the work is completed, the channels will be an inch deeper and the boats will be more buoyant. Certainly the cast members who work on the ride will be relieved by the improvements, as they were often put in the awkward position of having to leave empty seats on boats containing larger people or faced the task of retrieving stranded patrons after their boats ran aground.

Chew on This: As the stoppages became more frequent, passengers whose rides were cut short by a grounded boat were compensated with a ticket for free food.

The Iroquois Theater Fire of 1903

❖ ❖ ❖ ❖

We're often told not to yell "Fire!" in a crowded theater. Wise advice, unless, of course, the theater happens to actually be on fire. In the 21st century, it's easy to take for granted safety measures such as well-lit exits, unlocked doors, and fire escapes. But these precautions weren't always available—even when they were most sorely needed.

A Spooky Premonition

Twenty-eight years prior to the fateful 1903 fire, a *Chicago Times* article titled "Burned Alive" spoke of the state of the current poorly designed buildings and predicted that because of the unsafe conditions, a building fire would take the lives of hundreds of people. Years later, an event occurred at Chicago's Iroquois Theater that would eerily mirror the article.

A "Completely Fire-Proof Theatre"

Advertisements and playbills for the Iroquois Theater, which opened on November 23, 1903, claimed the building was impervious to fire. Much like the infamous "unsinkable" *Titanic,* the theory was untested. Sure, it was easy to think all was well while sitting underneath the ornate, 60-foot-high ceiling and among the white marbled walls and grand staircases. The owners even planned 30 exits, which they claimed would help evacuate the entire building in five minutes. (They only built 27 exits, however.) They also had a special glass skylight built over the stage that could vent flames upward and out of the building instead of inward and toward the audience.

But, before the theater's opening, Chicago fire inspectors found exit signs were either missing or obscured by thick drapes, there were no backstage phones, no fire alarm system was in place, no sprinklers or fire buckets, and there lacked a sufficient number of hoses. In fact, the only fire-fighting equipment in the theater was six metal canisters containing a dry chemical product called Kilfyre. Little did the inspectors know that the owners had even skimped on the stage's asbestos safety curtain, which was only part asbestos—the rest was made of wood pulp. Other sources say the curtain jammed on its rod, rendering it ineffective.

The Inferno

A little after 3 P.M. on December 30, an overfilled theater of nearly 2,000 patrons was enjoying a matinee of the comedy *Mr. Bluebeard.* During the performance of the song "Pale Moon Light," the main spotlight began burning. Bits of curtain and the front of the stage caught on fire first, and embers fell onto the increasingly nervous singers below. Initially, the audience wasn't aware of any trouble, but in moments, flames began to lick the stage curtain. Finally, the audience was alarmed.

To avoid a rush of panicked patrons, the orchestra, as well as performer and Chicago-native Eddie Foy, came out onstage and tried to calm the crowd. But the fire was out of control; hundreds leapt up and headed for what they thought were exits. In some corners, large mirrors were hung, which disoriented the crowd. In other corners, they were met with locked accordion gates (to prevent people from sneaking to better seats on other levels), doors that opened inward, or even gaping holes where unfinished fire escapes forced person after person to fall to their death as the crowd rushed in from behind. Then, the theatre went black; hundreds were trampled on the grand staircases as they tried to escape. All told, 602 people were killed that day at the Iroquois Theater, and all within only 20 minutes.

One for the Record Books

As a direct result of the Iroquois Theater fire, the self-releasing fire exit bolt, or "panic bar," was invented and installed as a mandatory safety improvement. As of 2008, according to National Fire Protection Association records, it is still the worst single-building fire in U.S. history in terms of fatalities. In comparison, the New York City Triangle Shirtwaist Factory fire claimed 148 lives, the Great Chicago Fire killed 250, and the Boston Cocoanut Grove fire killed 492.

Talk to the Expert

WAITRESS AT A 24-HOUR DINER

Q: What's your shift?
A: My shift is from 4:30 in the afternoon 'til 2:00 in the morning.

Q: Your internal clock must be reversed from working these hours.
A: I'm used to it. I've been doing this for 15 years.

Q: It's 12:30 A.M. on a Thursday, and it's actually really busy right now.
A: It's quiet right now. Usually we're busier. But it's about that time when people start taking their vacations, right before the kids go back to school. It goes up and down.

Q: I bet you've got some crazy stories to tell about working this shift.
A: There are a lot of crazy things. Sometimes people have been out drinking, they're demanding. You say, "OK, I'll get it to you immediately." If they hear the word "immediately," it pacifies them. And then there are people who don't want to talk. They just want to eat and be left alone. When you do this job, you learn to read people.

Q: What's the secret to doing this job well?
A: You have to have patience, and you have to be able to take control of a table.

Q: How do you do that?
A: You do that by approaching the table in a professional way. Sometimes if I'm busy and can't get to the table right away, I'll say, "Hi, how are you. I'll be with you in a few minutes. Can I get you something to drink?" The important thing is to acknowledge them. I don't care if it's waitressing or in an office or anything—you have to acknowledge people.

Haunting the Sea: Oregon's Ghost Forests

The gnarled, twisted shapes rising up from Oregon's coastline are macabre memorials to the magnificent forests that stood here ages ago. Like a ghost town eerily preserved in time, these "ghost forests" are shrouded in mystery: What caused the mighty trees to fall? Why are they still here? And where are they going?

An Eerie Appearance

These groves of ancient tree stumps—called "ghost forests" because of their age (approximately 1,000 to 4,000 years old) and bleak appearance—emerge along the 46-mile stretch between Lincoln City and Tillamook. For years, tourists and scientists alike have been perplexed by the forests' strange beauty. Some trees extend out of the sand like angular sculptures; others look like floating chunks of brown; others are just visible as tiny tips poking through the water.

All are remnants of the giant Sitka spruce forests, which towered 200 feet above Oregon's coastline for years. That is, until something knocked them down.

A Cataclysmic Collapse

No one knows for sure just what that "something" was, but experts agree that for such forests to be preserved, the trees must have been very suddenly submerged in sand, clay, or mud. This submersion would not only kill the trees but also keep them frozen in time by shutting off their oxygen.

The original (and still widely held) belief is that a giant earthquake, which suddenly dropped the ground 25 feet below sea level and immersed the trees in sand and water, toppled the forests. Another theory is that it wasn't an earthquake but a tsunami that struck, drowning the trees under a massive tidal wave. A third theory suggests that it was a combination of the two—an earthquake buried the trees and then caused a tsunami that lopped off the tree tops, leaving only stumps behind.

A newer theory is that the trees died as a result of sudden landscape changes, with sand levels rising over the course of a few decades (that's "sudden" when you're speaking in geologic terms) to eventually overwhelm the forest.

Seasonal Specters

For decades, ghost forests were seen only occasionally during the harsh winter months, when violent waves strip away layers of sand, exposing the tree stumps just briefly before the calmer waves of spring and summer carry sand back to the shores and bury them once again.

But lately, the ghost forests have become less of a rarity. Since 1998, more and more spooky spruces have been popping up—the result of a decade of rough winters, washing away as much as 17 feet of sand in some areas, combined with less sand recovery in the spring and summer.

In 2007, Arch Cape saw stumps for the first time in 40 years, along with the mud-cliff remains of a forest floor, and in the winter of 2008, an unprecedented ten-foot drop in sand level revealed a new forest at Cape Kiwanda.

Just a few miles away at Hug Point, the waves uncovered stumps that could date back 80,000 years to the Pleistocene era, when woolly mammoths and saber-toothed tigers roamed the earth. And the remains of roots marred by saws at Moolack Beach show that early European settlers harvested the trees for fire and shelter. Oregon's most impressive and most famous ghost forest is found at Neskowin, where 100 twisted shapes can be seen poking through the water year-round.

Grim Tide-ings

But the erosion that has newly exposed these phantom forests may also be destroying them. The stumps at Neskowin and Cape Lookout are reportedly showing so much that waves are ripping them out by the roots.

Some experts believe this increased erosion means the coastline is gradually disappearing—and taking the ghost forests with it. Perhaps soon, the ghost forests of Oregon will haunt only our memories.

The Amazing Ackermonster

❖ ❖ ❖ ❖

*"If Forrest J Ackerman had not existed, it would have
been necessary to invent him."*
—Anthony Boucher

For Forrest J Ackerman, life has been simply monstrous...and that's
a good thing. Ackerman has spent his entire life passionately pursuing and promoting horror films. Not the modern ones, where buckets
of blood substitute for terror, but the classics like *Frankenstein* and
Dracula, where every creaky stair sends a chill down the spine.

Early Acker
Born in 1916, Ackerman saw his first fantasy film, *One Glorious Day*,
at the tender age of five. He was immediately hooked. In 1926, Ackerman attained his first fantasy magazine *(Amazing Stories)* and became
involved in the genre for the rest of his life, serving as literary agent
for some of the greatest writers in the fantasy genre. He even coined
the genre-forming term, "sci-fi," in 1954.

Monstrous Fame
But it was as the irreverent editor of the magazine *Famous Monsters
of Filmland* that Ackerman (dubbed "Ackermonster") was to shine. It
was first published in 1958, just as the classic horror films were beginning to reach television. The magazine influenced a generation of
future filmmakers, including Steven Spielberg, who devoured Ackerman's slightly off-kilter accounts of the actors, films, and makeup
secrets of popular horror films.

While in his 90s, Ackerman continued to give tours of his home
in Los Angeles, dubbed "Son of Ackermansion" (he moved from the
original 18-room Ackermansion in 2002), showing off his museum-
worthy collection of movie monster memorabilia and sharing stories
about the spooky side of the silver screen.

Alas, the Ackermonster passed on in December 2008. From those
who share an appreciation for things that go bump in the black-and-
white night, only one thing can be said for Ackerman: "Fangs for the
memories, Forrest."

Behind the Music of Our Time

- Pop group ABBA turned down a $1 billion offer to reunite.

- Singer Farrah Franklin, best known for her stint in the hit group Destiny's Child, actually has the middle name Destiny.

- The most popular song for the first dance at weddings is Bryan Adams's "Everything I Do (I Do It For You)," which was featured in the 1991 movie, *Robin Hood: Prince of Thieves.*

- The Alicia Keys hit "Fallin'" has been banned from *American Idol* auditions because the judges were sick of hearing people butcher it.

- Legend has it that Ringo Starr nearly missed his cue during the recording of "Hey Jude." The Beatles' drummer left the studio to go to the restroom right before his part was to begin.

- The Beatles' classic "Yesterday" initially had the words "scrambled eggs" in its chorus until Paul McCartney came up with the magic word.

- The Beatles' "Lovely Rita Meter Maid" got its inspiration from a parking ticket Paul McCartney received from a female officer—fittingly enough, while on London's Abbey Road.

- The Beatles' anthem "A Day In The Life" ends with a high-pitched whistle that no human could possibly hear (although a dog could).

- Pink Floyd has put out many albums, but only one band member has played on every single one: drummer Nick Mason.

- The '80s Toto hit "Rosanna" was written for actress Rosanna Arquette (sister of Patricia and David), who was rumored to have had a relationship with keyboardist Steve Porcaro.

- The rock classic "Johnny B. Goode," written by Chuck Berry, was once a controversial tune. The lyric "that little country boy can play" was originally written as "that little colored boy can play." Berry, as the tale is told, realized he'd have to change the word for the song to see any success.

Fast Facts

- The Sabino, *a steamship in Mystic, Connecticut, and the San Francisco cable car are the only two moving National Historic Landmarks in the United States.*

- *The turkey is said to be the least intelligent of all farm animals.*

- *"Auld Lang Syne" translates to "times gone by."*

- *Contrary to popular belief, karate was actually invented in India.*

- *Pumpkin is the most favored holiday pie for American families.*

- *You can form the number 12,345,678,987,654,321 by multiplying 111,111,111 by 111,111,111.*

- *Chicago's O'Hare airport sells more hot dogs than any other airport in the world.*

- *The "WD" in WD-40 stands for Water Displacement. The "40" came about because it took the creators that many attempts to get the formula right.*

- *A U.S. Green Card is actually yellow.*

- *North Carolina has both a city named Republican and a city named Democrat.*

- *The U.S. government owns about a third of all American land.*

- *The official medical name for earwax is "cerumen."*

- *Your nose is capable of smelling 10,000 different distinct scents.*

- *Checkers was a sport in the 1900 Olympic Games.*

Beauty: The Long and Short of It

❖ ❖ ❖ ❖

If beauty is in the eye of the beholder, apparently, most beholders are dissatisfied with the status quo. Throughout history, women have felt obligated to alter what Mother Nature dealt them by plucking, waxing, dying, painting, injecting, cinching, and lifting their natural assets to attract a mate.

Head Binding

The practice of reshaping the head was popular on several continents, although in distinctly different forms. In Africa, the Mangbetu people bound their babies' heads with raffia to create an elongated shape. The women exaggerated their profile by coiffing their hair around baskets to achieve an even more elongated look.

In the South Pacific island nation of Vanuatu, head binding is still practiced. Oil is used to soften babies' skulls, which are then tightly wrapped in a soft bandage made from banana bark and topped with a basket bonnet. Vanuatans prefer cone-shaped noggins and believe that this skull silhouette is not only beautiful, but also helps to increase the brain's capacity for memory. A 17th-century French textbook also reportedly advocated head binding as a memory enhancer.

Lip Stretching

Collagen-injected lips seem tame by comparison to the beauty regimens of some African tribes. When a young Mursi girl reaches age 15 or 16, she begins the lip-stretching process that will make her fetching enough to attract a mate.

The process begins by puncturing the girl's lower lip and inserting a wooden plug into the cut. Increasingly, larger plugs are inserted until the lip can accommodate a disc with a diameter up to five inches. Sometimes the lower teeth are removed to allow room for a larger plate. A woman reportedly has the right to decide when she has been stretched to her limit.

Neck Elongation

Swan-like necks are prized in many cultures, but a tribe who lives along the Thai-Burma border called the Padong (a subsect of the larger Karen group) has carried this ideal to the extreme. Going for a look more akin to a giraffe than a swan, their women begin their beautification routine around age six by having brass rings clasped around their necks. Each year brings a new ring or two, until the women eventually are adorned from chin to clavicle with 20-some neck rings. The more the better—one woman is known to boast 37 rings!

This practice appears to stretch the neck, but in reality the heavy brass rings press down on the collarbones to create this illusion. Since the rings are worn continuously, the neck muscles become too weak to support the women's heads if the rings are removed. However, on her wedding night, a Karen Padong woman takes off her rings for a neck-washing ritual.

Foot Binding

For the Chinese, less was considered more. There, teeny-tiny feet were treasured for many centuries. Foot binding is said to date as far back as the Shang dynasty (1700–1027 B.C.), when a club-footed Empress ordered that her court was to be hobbled like her. Another tale attributes the origin of foot binding to the Song dynasty, around A.D. 960, when a Chinese concubine seduced a ruler with her bound "lotus" feet.

The foot binding procedure generally began before age six, when a young girl's bones were still flexible and her arch was not yet fully developed. The process began soothingly, with a sort of pedicure, but ended with eight of the girl's smaller toes broken; the toes were then secured tightly to the heel with long strips of bandages.

The binding process was repeated for many years until the young woman's feet were permanently contorted to a length of four inches or less. This disfigurement was appealing to men because it rendered the woman frail, dependent, and less likely to stray from home. Apparently, it was also a turn-on, since tiny feet feature prominently in ancient Chinese erotica.

High Tide: Tales of Survival

❖ ❖ ❖ ❖

Humankind has been subjected to every imaginable hostile condition, but very little beats the grueling stories of survival for days, weeks—even months—lost at sea.

Hold On Tight

Ocean-going tales of survival have a certain mythic status. They bring to mind epic travels; age-old yarns of sea monsters, mermaids; and nourishment via filtered water and the sucked bones of fish. Yet legend aside, even factually verified survival stories seem implausible. To be stranded on the sea (and to live to tell the tale) seems, well, unreal.

A hierarchy applies when gauging the relative extremity of a sea survival story. Those in cold water are the worst off, since hypothermia sets in within minutes. Survival time also depends on whether there's something to hold onto, or the person is simply treading water. Survival time is also cut short by solitude—humans have a difficult time being alone for extended periods. The best-case scenario, if such a scenario exists, is to be stranded on a boat, in warm water, along with some comrades. What follows are some recent record breakers that run the gauntlet of these hapless scenarios:

Juan Jesus Caamano
Survived 13 hours with no boat in cold waters

In 2001, a fishing boat capsized off the coast of Spain. Nine of the 16 men made it into a lifeboat, another two jumped into the frigid waters without putting on their bodysuits (and died immediately), while five others managed to get their suits on before the boat sank.

Two of those five were 36-year-old Juan Jesus Caamano and his brother-in-law. Their boat had sent out a mayday signal before sinking, so planes, helicopters, and ships from several countries were sent to look for the victims. After only four hours, the nine men in the lifeboat were saved. Experts, who estimated a man in Caamano's circumstances could survive a maximum of 3½ hours, were surprised when, after 13 hours, Caamano was found alive, afloat in the stormy waters, tied to his dead brother-in-law. In all, six men died.

Laura Isabel Arriola de Guity
Survived six days; found clinging to driftwood in warm waters

In 1998, Hurricane Mitch ravished Central and Latin America, killing more than 7,000 people in Honduras alone. Isabella Arriola, 32, lived in a small coastal Honduran village that was literally swept away by the ocean. She survived for six days with no life jacket, drifting in and out of consciousness, while clinging to pieces of driftwood. Somehow, she survived through high waves and winds that climbed to 185 mph. Arriola was eventually spotted by a coastguard aircraft and was rescued by helicopter. Unfortunately, she found that her husband, children, and half her village had perished in the storm.

Steven Callahan
Survived 76 days on a small raft

In 1982, Steven Callahan, a naval architect, was participating in a sailing race when his boat was damaged during a storm and sank in the Atlantic Ocean. Callahan managed to salvage a tiny amount of food before setting off in an inflatable rubber raft. He survived for 76 days on rainwater, fish, and seabirds before being rescued by a fishing boat. Callahan's extensive background and experience with the high seas helped him survive the ordeal. He holds the longest known record for surviving alone on a raft.

Maralyn and Maurice Bailey
Survived 117 days on a small raft

In 1973, British couple Maralyn and Maurice Bailey set out on an ambitious voyage from England to New Zealand on their yacht, which was struck by a large whale and capsized off the coast of Guatemala. Maurice happened to be an expert on maritime survival skills; before they boarded their rubber raft, they collected a small amount of food, a compass, a map, an oil burner, water containers, and glue. When the Baileys ran out of food, they caught sea animals with safety pins fashioned into hooks. After two months, the raft started to disintegrate, and it needed constant care. Finally, 117 days later, a small Korean fishing boat rescued them.

Odd Ordinances

- It's illegal for horses to eat fire hydrants in Marshalltown, Iowa.

- Presumably, it's all right to drink beer from a bucket in St. Louis. Just don't do it while sitting on the curb—that's against city law.

- Better wear shoes if you're getting behind the wheel in Alabama. Driving barefoot or in slippers is illegal.

- Youngstown, Ohio, has made it a crime to run out of gas.

- Wiping your car with used underwear within San Francisco city limits is a crime.

- In Memphis, a law was passed to prohibit women from driving unless they have a man walking in front of the car while waving a red flag.

- Walking with your shoelaces undone could get you arrested in Maine.

- You aren't allowed to ride public transportation in Atlanta if you have bad body odor.

- Putting salt on a railroad track could get you the death penalty in Alabama.

- Having an unusual haircut is against the law in Mesquite, Texas.

- The state of Washington has made it illegal to pretend your parents are rich.

- Don't give a baby coffee in Lynn, Massachusetts—it's illegal.

- No one other than a baby is allowed to ride in a baby carriage in Roderfield, West Virginia.

- Drunken men and women cannot be married in Pennsylvania. Good thing that's not the case in Las Vegas.

- Playing Scrabble in the moments before a politician's speech is against the law in Atwoodville, Connecticut.

The Narwhal: Mother Nature's 35 Million-Year-Old Joke

❖ ❖ ❖ ❖

Perhaps if Herman Melville had made Moby Dick a narwhal instead of a boring old white whale, we'd all have a little more love for this bizarre-looking (but lovable) aquatic animal.

- A typical narwhal averages somewhere between 11.5 and 16.4 feet, and weighs in at around 3,500 pounds.

- Narwhals swim upside down! Researchers are still trying to figure out exactly why narwhals spend 80 percent of their time inverted, but they think it's because the animals send sonar signals underwater to detect prey. Swimming upside down may direct the sonar beam downwards, where lunch is likely to be most abundant.

- Narwhal enemies include polar bears and killer whales, but human poachers pose the biggest threat.

- The most distinguishing characteristic of a narwhal is its long, unicornlike tusk. The tusk points slightly downward, which is another reason narwhals may swim on their backs—while looking for food on the sea floor, they don't want to bust their horns on a rock.

- Over 10 million tiny nerve endings are found on the surface of a narwhal tusk, making it an essential tool for sensory perception.

- Narwhals lack a dorsal fin, which is unusual in underwater creatures of their kind. Scientists believe the narwhal evolved without a dorsal fin as an adaptation to navigate beneath ice-covered waters.

- Newborn narwhals are called "calves." Calves are weaned after a year or so, and then they move on to a regular diet of fish, squid, and shrimp.

- If you see a group of narwhals above water, rubbing their tusks together, they're "tusking." This activity helps the narwhals clean their tusks—kind of like when humans brush their teeth.

Booze, Broads, and Busted Careers: Hollywood's Bundy Drive Boys

Before Sinatra's Rat Pack hit the scene, another group of legendary bad boys made a name for itself. Amid the glitz and glamour of Hollywood's Gilded Age, the Bundy Drive Boys lived hard, drank hard, and died hard.

Six Degrees of Barrymore

The lynchpin of the Bundy Drive Boys was legendary stage and screen actor John Barrymore. Already an established star in the 1920s and '30s—when the other Boys were just beginning their careers in New York—Barrymore befriended bulbous-nosed comedian W. C. Fields; writer Sadakichi Hartmann; writer Gene Fowler; and John Decker, a caricature artist who sketched actors for the *New York Evening World.*

In Hollywood, Barrymore partied with Errol Flynn and John Carradine who, as a college student, had shown up unannounced at Barrymore's house just to meet the actor. Barrymore also ran with Anthony Quinn, who got his start spoofing Barrymore in a Hollywood play (while Barrymore sat in the audience); and screenwriter Ben Hecht, who famously boycotted the first Academy Awards in 1929—and used his award for Best Original Screenplay as a doorstop. But the Bundy Drive Boys had more than Barrymore in common. They also battled the same demons.

The Drinking

When Barrymore died in 1942 at age 60, doctors estimated the actor had drunk hundreds of gallons of alcohol. One estimate puts the number at about 640 gallons over a 40-year period—about 16 gallons of booze each year.

To keep Barrymore from drinking on film productions, his managers often hired prostitutes to keep him company. His drinking got him fired from the 1933 film *Romeo and Juliet,* but the director hired him back on one condition: Barrymore must spend each night in an insane asylum to keep from drinking. But the Boys had Barrymore's back: One night, Fowler and Decker visited the asylum, distracted a guard, and hoisted booze up to Barrymore's window.

Barrymore wasn't the only one whose life and career was afflicted by alcohol. Decker arrived in New York in 1921 and made a name for himself with his witty caricatures and portraits—most notably a painting of Fields as Queen Victoria. But for all of his success as a painter (and sometimes art forger), he would immediately blow any money he made on parties and alcohol. Hartmann won a role opposite Douglas Fairbanks in the 1924 film *The Thief of Baghdad*—for a rumored fee of $250 a week and a case of whiskey. Several weeks into the project, Hartmann abandoned the set. As legend has it, he complained that the whiskey was "inferior." And Flynn was allegedly so drunk on the 1958 set of *Too Much, Too Soon* (in which he portrayed his late friend Barrymore) that it required 17 takes for him to say "parole" instead of "patrol."

Barrymore, Decker, and Flynn, as well as W. C. Fields, would all die from cirrhosis of the liver, caused by chronic alcoholism. Fields would be the oldest at 66 years old, although Flynn, who died at age 50, was said to have had the "body of a 75-year-old."

The Dames

Barrymore and Carradine each had four wives, while Hecht had two. Fowler had only one wife, and so did Fields, but only because his Catholic wife wouldn't divorce him. Instead, Fields had a mistress for most of his adult life. Hartmann also married only once, but fathered children (as many as 12 or 13) with other women. Flynn, Decker, and Quinn had three wives apiece.

Divorced from his first wife, Flynn was acquitted of statutory rape in 1943. During the trial, he fell for the teenage girl working the cigar stand at the courthouse, whom he soon married (and divorced). He remarried again in 1950, but died in the arms of his 15-year-old mistress in 1959.

Decker also went to court over a woman—namely his first wife, whom he forgot to divorce before marrying the other two.

Quinn left his first wife of 27 years when his mistress (and later wife) gave birth to their son. Thirty years later, the nearly 80-year-old Quinn fathered a daughter with his secretary (50 years his junior) and divorced wife number two to marry her. Quinn's last child was born just after the actor's 81st birthday in 1996. All in all, he fathered 13 children with a rumored five women.

The Distant Dads

Beyond the drinks and the dames, many of the Bundy Drive Boys were haunted by a darker secret: their fathers. Barrymore feared going insane, as his father had. Decker was abandoned by his parents when he was a teenager, and Hartmann was left by his father when he was just an infant. Fowler's father left his family; Quinn's died when the actor was nine years old. Fields had been physically abused by his father, while Flynn, on the other hand, suffered from a verbally abusive mother.

The Clubhouse

If Barrymore was the president of this self-destructive club, in 1940, Decker's new Bundy Drive home became its official hangout. Group members regularly arrived unannounced to drink, smoke, sword fight, trade insults, and deliver monologues. Hartmann occasionally wet his pants as he sat drinking at the bar. But the good times were short lived: In less than a decade, most of the club's founding fathers would be dead.

In January 1944, shortly after Barrymore's death, Hartmann gathered with the remaining men at Decker's home and gave an ominous prediction: He himself would be dead in less than a year; Decker in three; Fields in two; Fowler in four—although Hartmann jokingly agreed to give him 16 years if Fowler would pay for his trip to the East Coast. On all counts, Hartmann was right. Quinn, the youngest of the Boys, outlived them all—dying at the age of 86 in 2001.

Behind the TV Shows of Our Time

Frasier

- Many of the celebrities who voiced phone call-ins for Frasier Crane's radio show on *Frasier* literally phoned it in, recording their parts without ever going to the studio.

- The role of Roz on *Frasier* was originally given to Lisa Kudrow, who was later cast as Phoebe on *Friends.* Producers decided to replace her with Peri Gilpin before filming began.

- *Frasier* was originally written without the role of Niles. It was actor David Hyde Pierce's resemblance to star Kelsey Grammer that is said to have sparked the idea for the character.

Seinfeld

- Jerry Stiller didn't originally play the part of Frank Costanza on *Seinfeld;* instead, an actor named John Randolph appeared as George's dad in an early episode. That episode only aired once. Producer and co-creator Larry David later reshot it with Stiller before the show went into syndication.

- Barney Martin also didn't play Jerry's dad, Morty Seinfeld, from the start. Actor Phil Bruns played the part in the second episode, but again, Larry David decided he wasn't the right fit. Bruns's scenes were never reshot.

- Co-creator Larry David provided the voice of Yankees owner (and George Costanza's boss in *Seinfeld)* George Steinbrenner, whose face was never seen. David returned to do the voice even after leaving his managerial role on the show.

Friends

- Courteney Cox was initially cast as Rachel in *Friends.* Producers switched her to Monica after hearing her read both parts.

- The role of Monica on *Friends* was offered to Janeane Garofalo, who turned it down. Leah Remini, later cast in *King of Queens,* also tried out.

- The part of *Friends'* wiseacre Chandler Bing was offered to Jon Cryer and Jon Favreau before being given to Matthew Perry.

A-'Changin'

cellor of Germany, a
, the Reichstag building
sts and uses the resulting

office as president of
for 12 years. Congress
ith the economic crisis.

cing a nationwide bank
March 9. The next day,
t, the first in a series
tes recover from the

at Dachau.

entury of Progress" in
he Depression, more than
visit the fair.

unties remain dry.

oyce's *Ulysses* is not por-
ropriate in context.

oncession to explore for oil
Arabia. The wasteland is
erve.

nden, New Jersey.

aign of political repres-
irected against "enemies
nsolidate his control of the
are expelled from the Party
beria.

A Fungus Among Us

❖ ❖ ❖ ❖

*The world's largest living organism has been
growing underground for thousands of years.*

State Celebrity

Sure, a blue whale can reach lengths of up to 80 feet and can weigh
up to 110 tons, but that's small potatoes compared to the *Armillaria
ostoyae*. Otherwise known as the Honey Mushroom, the fungus has
the honor of being the world's largest living organism.

If you've never heard of this monstrous mushroom, it's probably
because it has only recently been discovered. In 1992, researchers in
Michigan used DNA techniques to study a fungus that was infecting
the state's forests. While above ground one might see various collections of small, honey-colored mushrooms, underground there is
a vast network of stringlike tendrils, which would invade the tree's
root systems. The researchers found that all of the samples they
were collecting were actually genetic clones of each other: They had
stumbled upon an enormous spreading fungus estimated to be at
least 1,500 years old and weigh nearly 100 tons.

The discovery caused a media sensation. The *New York Times* ran
a front-page story heralding the discovery of "the largest and oldest
living organism on Earth." The town of Crystal Springs, Michigan,
near where the fungus was found, began hosting "Humongous
Fungus" festivals. The fungus was even featured as a Michigan tourist attraction on U-Haul moving vans.

A Rival Appears

However, it didn't take long for researchers to find other *Armillaria*
to rival Michigan's favorite fungus. In 2000, an *Armillaria* was identified in Oregon's Blue Mountains and is now officially considered the
world's largest living thing. Covering an area of over 2,200 acres—an
expanse larger than 1,600 football fields—it is estimated to be at
least 2,400 years old. Oregon's most recently discovered attraction
has a lot of scientists interested in its secrets, but as of yet, there's no
festival in its honor.

Odd Ordinances

- The town of Rumford, Maine, has made it illegal to bite under any circumstances.

- Slurping soup is against the law in New Jersey.

- Mixing cornmeal with wheat flour is frowned upon in M

- Barbers aren't allowed to eat onions in Waterloo, Nebr 7 A.M. and 7 P.M.

- No one can go to a theater within four hours of eating Indiana.

- Wearing a hat in a theater could cost you in Wyoming, happens to block anyone else's view of the show.

- It's illegal to offer someone a glass of water without a Walden, New York.

- Peeling an orange in a hotel room in California is a crir

- Bristow, Oklahoma, mandates that all restaurants serv one peanut per every glass of water.

- Serving wine in a teacup is against the law in Topeka, I

- Restaurant owners can't offer margarine in Vermont un a public notice posted.

- Eating in a restaurant that is on fire is a crime in Chica

- It's illegal for a girl to ask a guy out on the phone in Dy Tennessee.

- In Whitesville, Delaware, women aren't allowed to prop

- Portland, Maine, has outlawed any tickling of girls unde a feather duster.

- Kissing without first wiping your lips is not allowed in Ri nia. You also have to use carbonated rose water for the

The Times They Are

1933

- On January 30, Adolf Hitler is appointed Cha position he will hold for 12 years. In Februar burns. Hitler blames the fire on the Commur crisis to seize absolute authority.

- On March 4, Franklin Delano Roosevelt take the United States, a position he, too, will ho grants Roosevelt broad powers for dealing \

- Roosevelt launches the New Deal by announ holiday to begin on March 6 and continue to Congress passes the Emergency Banking A of legislation designed to help the United St Depression.

- The first Nazi concentration camp is opene

- The Chicago World's Fair opens, named "A celebration of the city's centennial. Despite 48 million Americans pay 50 cents each to

- Prohibition is repealed. Still, hundreds of co

- Justice John M. Woolsley rules that James nography because the "obscenities" are ap

- Standard Oil receives a 60-year exclusive c on 320,000 square miles of desert in Sauc discovered to hold the world's largest oil re

- The first drive-in movie theater opens in Ca

- Soviet leader Joseph Stalin begins the can sion known as the "Great Purge." Officially of the people," Stalin uses the purges to c Communist Party. In 1933 alone, 400,00C and executed or exiled to labor camps in

Beatrix Potter's Scientific Side

❖ ❖ ❖ ❖

Although the name Beatrix Potter brings to mind bunnies and briar patches more than it does algae and Agaricineae, this iconic children's author was much more than just the creator of Flopsy, Mopsy, Cottontail, and Peter Rabbit.

A Victorian Upbringing

Call it a case of living in the wrong place at the wrong time. If not for the strict Victorian society of her upbringing, Beatrix Potter might have been too busy conducting breakthrough scientific research to introduce readers worldwide to the tale of Peter Rabbit. Born in 1866 to a wealthy family in London, her parents left her upbringing to a string of tutors and governesses. In fact, Potter was so sharp that most of her teachers could not keep up with her. At one point, she learned six of Shakespeare's plays by heart in less than a year.

Potter the Scientific Illustrator

The Victorian era was a time when it was not considered necessary, or even appropriate, to send girls away for a proper education. Instead, Potter's teachers were to instruct her in so-called "womanly" subjects such as French and drawing. Certainly, the study of mushrooms and lichen were not part of Potter's formal curriculum.

But Potter had been fascinated by nature since childhood. She kept all sorts of animals as pets, and she drew beautiful and accurate pictures of them. This interest continued to manifest itself in her botanical drawings, particularly of mushrooms. In her late 20s, unmarried and increasingly at odds with her parents who expected their daughter to take on the domestic responsibilities of their household, Potter found a much-needed escape in her drawings and nature studies.

Potter began visiting the Royal Botanical Gardens at Kew to learn more about the fungi that were being researched there. In a journal (in which she wrote in code to keep her studies a secret from her mother), Potter expressed her excitement over recent scientific findings such as that of scientist Louis Pasteur. She grew her own spores, observed them under a microscope, and carefully recorded her findings. Entirely self-taught, Potter began developing theories of her own.

A Dream Denied

At the time, the British scientific community deemed the notion that lichen could actually be made up of two organisms—an algae and a fungus—absurd. However, Potter's readings of recent findings from Continental Europe contradicted this. In her studies, she had observed firsthand how the algae and fungus found in lichen did, in fact, need each other to survive. She wrote her findings in an 1897 paper, *On the Germination of the Spores of Agaricineae*. Unfortunately, because she was a woman, she was not allowed to be present when it was read at a meeting of a society of naturalists. Her work had little impact on the biologists of her time; decades later, however, her findings would be accepted as pioneering work in the understanding of symbiotic relationships in biology.

Potter also tried to gain acceptance as a student at the Kew Gardens in order to formalize her research and gain credentials as a scientist. When she went to meet the director, however, botanical drawings in hand, it was immediately clear to her that he did not take her application seriously. The director would not even look at her drawings. The visit was great humiliation for the shy Potter; afterward, she gave up what she called "grown-up science" altogether.

The Birth of a Bunny

The same year her paper was rejected, Potter began throwing her energies into the writing and illustration of children's books. With her 25 little books, she would eventually achieve what few women of her era managed: financial and intellectual independence. She may have given up her formal studies, but she never stopped drawing with scientific accuracy. After all, even if her rabbits are wearing sweaters, the trees and flowers in the background are drawn with a biologist's eye for detail.

Word Histories

Jazz: This was first used in the early 20th century in reference to an energetic baseball player or game.

Martini: Though you can use Martini & Rossi–brand vermouth to make this cocktail, its name actually derives from the place where it was allegedly invented: Martinez, California. The drink was originally called a "Martinez cocktail."

Hello: Though it is one of the most commonly used words in the English language, the greeting didn't come into use until late in the 19th century. Its ancient predecessor *hallow* was used as early as the 1300s. "Hello" replaced the popular "hullo" after the invention of the telephone.

Gull: Indicative of the sea bird's plaintive cries, the word comes from the Breton word *goelaff* meaning, "to weep."

Guillotine: Contrary to popular belief, the French physician Dr. Joseph Ignace Guillotin did not invent, nor did he die from, this deadly device. Rather, he passionately entreated the French government to develop a more merciful manner of carrying out executions than the swords and ropes used at the time. The device was actually invented by Dr. Antoine Louisette but "La Louisette" never caught on, and a host of popular songs calling the new execution machine "La Guillotine" cemented the name with the public. After his death, Guillotin's family unsuccessfully tried to have the French government officially change the name of the device.

Gourmet: This term originally referred to a horse groom, then to minor household servants who tasted the wine for quality. In time, this position at a wine shop was used to refer to a connoisseur of fine wines. This led to the modern meaning of one who prefers, can distinguish, or can create fine food and drink.

Addict: Originally, an *addict* was a slave given as a reward to a victorious Roman soldier.

Fast Facts

- A typical child laughs 26.67 times more per day than a typical adult.

- Ever hear someone say she wears her heart on her sleeve? Of course, that's just an expression. For a shrimp, though, it'd be literal and accurate to say it wears its heart on its head—the shrimp's blood-pumping organ is actually located there.

- The average lifespan of a goldfish living in the wild is 25 years.

- Male lions are able to mate 50 or more times in a single day. Tell your husband.

- A baby hippo weighs around 100 pounds.

- The first step on the moon by astronaut Neil Armstrong was with his left foot.

- Fingernails grow faster on your dominant hand.

- Sportscaster Foster Hewitt is credited with being the first person to say, "He shoots! He scores!" It happened at a hockey game between 1931 and 1935.

- It is against pro table tennis regulations for a player to wear a white shirt while playing with white balls. The visibility is considered too difficult.

- Legend has it the striped barber pole has a bloody past. Barbers were evidently also surgeons in the old days, and tales say that they would hang up blood-soaked towels to dry on poles outside their shops, thereby creating the red-and-white stripe design still replicated today.

Hawaii's Upside-Down Waterfall

❖ ❖ ❖ ❖

Hawaii's third largest island, Oahu, touts the state's
most unusual waterfall—one that defies gravity.

Tears in the Mist

The lush Nu'uanu Valley on the eastern coast of Oahu stretches from
Honolulu to the Ko'olau Range and ends quite suddenly in steep cliffs,
called the Pali.

Here, on only the rainiest and windiest of days, visitors can see the
famous Upside-Down Waterfall, so called because water cascading
from the 3,150-foot summit of Mount Konahuanui falls only a few feet
before strong trade winds blow it back up in the air. The water dissi-
pates into mist, creating the illusion of water slowly falling upward.

Natives call the waterfall *Waipuhia,* or "blown water." According to
one legend, Waipuhia was named for a young girl who lived in the hills
of the Nu'uanu Valley and whose bright eyes pleased the gods. One
tragic day, the girl's true love was lost in a storm, and when she wept
for him, her tears were caught halfway down the cliff by the god of
wind and tossed into the spray by the god of mist.

Lookout Lore

Weather permitting, the best view of the waterfall is from the 1,186-
foot Nu'uanu Pali Lookout, itself an infamous spot in Hawaiian lore.
As the legend goes, in 1795, King Kamehameha I drove the Oahu warriors up the Nu'uanu Valley to the Pali, where thousands of them were
driven over the cliffs to their deaths.

While scholars pooh-pooh the story, natives say that at night the
cries of long-dead warriors can be heard echoing through the valley.
Others tell of seeing a ghostly white figure—perhaps the king—on the
Pali Highway leading up to the Lookout, as well as ghost warriors falling from cliffs.

What eventually became the Pali Highway was built in 1898 by
Honolulu native (and future mayor) John Wilson. Apparently, Wilson's
workers encountered several bones during the project—and simply
laid the road right over them.

Misheard Lyrics

Beck, "Loser"
Correct: "In the time of chimpanzees I was a monkey"
Wrong: "In the time of ham and cheese I was bologna"

Duran Duran, "Hungry Like a Wolf"
Correct: "Smell like I sound, I'm lost in a crowd"
Wrong: "Smell like a clown, I'm lost and I'm found"

Barry Manilow, "Mandy"
Correct: "Oh Mandy, well you kissed me and stopped me from shaking"
Wrong: "Oh Mandy, will you get me a pizza from Shakey's?"

Til Tuesday, "Voices Carry"
Correct: "Hush, hush, keep it down now. Voices carry"
Wrong: "Oh John, keep it on now, you're so hairy"

R.E.M., "Losing My Religion"
Correct: "That's me in the corner, that's me in the spotlight"
Wrong: "Let's pee in the corner, let's pee in the spotlight"

Creedence Clearwater Revival, "Bad Moon Rising"
Correct: "There's a bad moon on the rise"
Wrong: "There's a bathroom on the right"

The Beatles, "Get Back"
Correct: "Jo Jo was a man who thought he was a loner"
Wrong: "Jo Jo was a man before he was a woman"

Madonna, "Like a Virgin"
Correct: "Like a virgin touched for the very first time"
Wrong: "Like a virgin touched for the thirty-first time"

Jimi Hendrix, "Purple Haze"
Correct: "'Scuse me, while I kiss the sky"
Wrong: "'Scuse me, while I kiss this guy"

U2, "Mysterious Ways"
Correct: "She moves in mysterious ways"
Wrong: "Shamu the mysterious whale"

How Does It End?:
Real Alternate Movie Endings

*Think you know everything about your
favorite films? Think again.*

Movie studios often preview new movies with test audiences who
can help producers and directors predict whether or not they've got
a hit on their hands. After getting feedback, changes to the film are
made—anything from small tweaks to total overhauls. An organization
called The National Research Group is responsible for the majority of
audience testing in Hollywood; they often quietly make or break the
direction of a movie. Read on for some cases of big changes that were
made at the eleventh hour. Consider this your official spoiler alert.

Little Shop of Horrors
The Broadway version of this story goes something like this: Boy
meets girl, boy and girl fall in love, boy and girl get eaten by carnivorous plant. Audiences were traumatized by Frank Oz's movie version
of *Little Shop,* however, so the boy and girl live happily ever after on
the big screen.

I Am Legend
This film adaptation, starring Will Smith in Richard Matheson's classic
horror novella, is all about role reversals. Well, that and vampires. In
the book, the mean, nasty vampires are actually revealed to be com-
passionate creatures only out to protect their own. It becomes clear
that Smith's character is *their* enemy, just as much as they seem to
be *his.* Well, this cautionary tale didn't fly with test audiences, so the
main theme of Matheson's book was scrapped. Instead, Smith's character in the movie pretty much just blows everybody up.

The Wizard of Oz
The first audiences for this ultra-classic film thought Dorothy's classic
"Over the Rainbow" number slowed down the story. It was kept in at
the last minute.

Blade Runner

Ridley Scott, the Oscar-winning director who adapted Philip K. Dick's sci-fi classic to film, loved the dark tone of the story. The studio, however, didn't love it as much. In the original version of the film, the intense protagonist (played by heartthrob Harrison Ford) decides to harbor the renegade android he loves, even though she's doomed to short-circuit any second. Throughout the film, there are also allusions to the notion that Ford's character himself might be an android. The studio thought all this was a little too bleak, though, and decided to let the man and his android live happily ever after.

Pretty Woman

In the original version, Vivian, the prostitute with a heart of gold and legs for miles (played by Julia Roberts), rejects Richard Gere's character and goes on to seek her fortune. Test audiences cried foul and the film ends with the couple together.

Fatal Attraction

Crazy Alex Forrest, the jilted lover brilliantly played by Glenn Close, was originally supposed to commit suicide and frame Michael Douglas's character for it. Test audiences didn't want the nasty lady to get off so easy, though; instead, Close's character was shot by Douglas's wife.

E.T.: The Extra-Terrestrial

In the original script, the lovable alien E.T. dies. This didn't sit well with children, so director Steven Spielberg gave in and allowed the little guy to make it home.

Butch Cassidy and the Sundance Kid

At the end of this timeless Western, Butch and Sundance are surrounded by what seems to be the entire Bolivian army. The film ends before the final gunfight, a clever way to leave it up to the audience to decide if the duo dies or manages to survive. The original version of the film showed their death, but test audiences preferred the alternate, more ambiguous (and less bloody) ending.

The World's Most Toxic Places

❖ ❖ ❖ ❖

Toxic chemicals and radioactive materials are putting
human health in serious danger in many parts of the world.

Environmentalists have tracked down the ten most toxic sites on the
planet, and what they've found paints a startling picture of problems left unsolved. Experts say living in one of these cities is like
"living under a death sentence." The statement, as you can see, is no
exaggeration.

Sumgayit, Azerbaijan
This former Soviet industrial center is now home to countless con-
taminants. Untreated sewage and mercury-laden sludge are among
the chief concerns, leading to unusually high cancer and death
rates. Scientists have also found a large number of premature births
or babies born with defects as extreme as clubbed feet and extra
fingers.

Linfen, China
More than three million people are at risk in Linfen, a city in the
Shanxi province known for its place as a leader in Chinese coal production. Families say they actually choke from the thick dust in the
air. Bronchitis, pneumonia, and lung cancer are common diseases.

Tianying, China
Lead production leaves this region with up to ten times the air pollution that national health standards allow. Even worse, crops at local
farms have been found to have almost 25 times the recommended
maximum levels of lead. Children suffer the worst effects, with rampant learning disabilities, low IQ, and other physical ailments.

Sukinda, India
Chromium's the issue in this mine-heavy region of India. Untreated
water has been found to have more than twice the amount national
and international standards allow. Side effects range from internal
bleeding to widespread tuberculosis and infertility.

Vapi, India
In this town in southern India, chemical manufacturing plants produce pesticides, pharmaceuticals, and fertilizers, but with no safe disposal system, the waste runs right into the groundwater. The pollution is so severe that some areas are now devoid of biological life.

La Oroya, Peru
In this city, toxic emissions from mining result in food filled with high levels of lead. In fact, inspectors found only one percent of children have normal amounts of lead in their blood. Hospitals say many babies are never even born because of prenatal damage.

Dzerzhinsk, Russia
Pollution in Dzerzhinsk dates back to the Cold War era, named by the *Guinness Book of World Records* as the most chemically polluted city in the world. The average life expectancy for humans here is only 44 years.

Norilsk, Russia
Russia's second largest city above the Arctic Circle has hundreds of tons of copper and nickel oxides in the air, thanks to metal mining and processing plants in the area. Scientists report that the snow there is black and the air tastes of sulfur. Life expectancy is low in Norilsk, and the rate of illness among children is alarming.

Chernobyl, Ukraine
More than 20 years after the world's worst nuclear disaster, much of Chernobyl is still unlivable. The meltdown of a nuclear plant reactor's core sent unfathomable amounts of radiation into the city. Thousands of cases of cancer have been detected in young adults, and millions still suffer from various health-related problems.

Kabwe, Zambia
Children bathe in contaminated water in this African nation, once home to intensive lead mining operations. Lead saturates the city's water and soil and there are no health restrictions to keep the community safe. Many children have blood-lead levels just barely under the amount considered deadly.

INSPIRATION STATION

Napoleon Dynamite: Based On a True Story?

For all you liger-loving folks out there who connected with the painfully nerdy hero of the 2004 indie blockbuster *Napoleon Dynamite,* take heart: Truth is just as strange as fiction. Many of the eccentric details that made *Napoleon* so endearingly weird was inspired by the experience of director Jared Hess. The llama, the martial-arts obsession, the uncle's online purchase of a time machine—those details came straight from the life of either Hess or his friends and family, many of whom live in small-town Idaho. The film was originally a short feature, filmed on a budget of $200,000. Fox Searchlight pictures picked up the story for $4 million and a bespectacled legend was born.

V.I.P. Muse: Francesca da Rimini

Should you ever find yourself forced into an arranged marriage, here's a silver lining: If your story is tragic enough, you might become the subject of artistic masterpieces for centuries to come. Anyway, that's how it went for Francesca da Rimini, a young Italian woman in the 13th century. Her father wanted to marry Francesca off to Giovanni Malatesta, the lame and disfigured son of an ex-rival. Knowing that Francesca would never agree to it, her father arranged for a switcheroo, thus "marrying" his clueless daughter to the handsome younger son Paolo (but really to Giovanni). Once Francesca figured out that she'd been fooled into marrying Giovanni, she began a steamy affair with Paolo. Giovanni found out, however, and murdered the pair.

The story has inspired countless artists, including Dante, who included the couple in parts of his *Divine Comedy;* Auguste Rodin, who sculpted *The Kiss* in 1888–89, used the lovers as his subject; Tchaikovsky wrote a poem about Francesca and Paolo; and Rachmaninoff dedicated an entire opera to the couple, called simply, *Francesca.*

Less Is Bore: Way-Out Architecture

❖ ❖ ❖ ❖

Architect Mies van der Rohe once defined modern architecture with the famous dictum "less is more." But not everyone agrees.

Casa Milà–Barcelona, Spain

Casa Milà, known informally as *La Pedrera* (or, "The Quarry"), is the most extreme expression of Antoni Gaudí's very personal architectural style. The façade of the apartment building was built without flat surfaces, straight lines, or symmetry. The roofline undulates, punctuated by chimneys that look like they were squeezed from a pastry tube. The interior is equally eccentric, with rounded walls and ceiling and floor heights that differ from room to room.

The Longaberger Basket Building–Newark, Ohio

This office building is built in the shape of the Longaberger Basket Company's most popular product, complete with handles that arch over the roof. It is a late example of Mimetic architecture, which flourished in the United States in the 1920s and '30s. The Longaberger building is billed as the "largest basket building in the world," which begs the question: How many other basket buildings are there?

The Crooked House–Sopot, Poland

The Crooked House, part of the Centrum Rezydent shopping center, was inspired by the work of Polish illustrator Jan Marcin Szancer and Swedish artist Per Dahlberg. With its bent lines and distorted walls and doors, the Crooked House sort of looks as if Salvador Dali illustrated Grimm's fairy tales. Unlike Casa Milà, the eccentricity is only skin-deep; the commercial spaces inside hold no surprises.

Burj al Arab–Dubai, United Arab Emirates

Currently holding the title of tallest hotel in the world at 1,053 feet, this luxury hotel moves Mimetic architecture beyond kitsch. Built in the shape of the billowing sail of an Arabian *dhow* ship on a man-made island off the coast, the hotel seems to sail past the city.

Fast Facts

- Not even acid can dissolve a diamond.

- An ant has five different noses, each for different scents.

- Honeybees can lay as many as 1,500 eggs in a single day.

- Congratulations: You have just practiced neology. (The study of new words.)

- A standard pencil could draw a 35-mile-long line before it runs out of lead.

- Hot water is lighter in weight than cold water.

- Finland is considered the country with the best water quality. Canada comes in second.

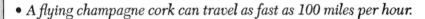

- An average penguin can run as fast as an average man.

- A flying champagne cork can travel as fast as 100 miles per hour.

- Mayonnaise used to be considered a delicacy and was used only for fine dining. It wasn't until 1912, when Richard Hellmann began selling it in jars in his New York deli, that the condiment became commonplace.

- The stuff in Play-Doh was first used for cleaning wallpaper.

- Vatican City claims the honor of having both the lowest divorce rate and the lowest birth rate of anywhere in the world.

- Peanut butter soup used to be popular in the 1920s.

- Graceland reports getting daily calls from people asking to speak with Elvis—still.

Prince Edward:
Nazi Sympathizer?

❖ ❖ ❖ ❖

Romance in high places can lead to lofty regal
fantasies—even when lifted by Nazi schemes.

Absolute Ruler? Absolutely Not!

Members of Britain's Royal Family are taught from birth how to be
regal, with the pomp, public works, privilege, and all that it entails.
If the family member is next in line to the throne, learning these
skills is vital. So it was in the 1930s for Edward, eldest son of King
George V.

Even before George's death in 1936, Edward's behavior was
raising royal eyebrows. He was great on the pomp. His public works
were passable, though critics said he sometimes lacked the proper
enthusiasm. As for privilege, to him it meant that anything he might
want, including setting policy for the country's governance, was his
as a birthright. That simply could not work in a democratic country.
Then there was the problem of his having fallen in love with Wallis
Simpson, a divorced American socialite.

Whether Wallis truly loved him or loved the notion of becoming
the Queen of England is moot. Edward VIII gave up the throne for
her, and she left her second husband for him; their marriage was
lauded as the Romance of the 20th Century. However, Edward still
held on to the delusion that his subjects would eventually welcome
him back to the throne. It was something that only Edward, Wallis,
and Adolf Hitler believed.

Loose Lips

Nazi Germany was re-arming, ostensibly to defend itself against (if
not crush) Communist Russia. That worked well for Edward, who
believed Hitler had exactly the right aggressive anti-Communist
plan. He also believed Britain should support Germany as an active
ally. Moreover, Edward expounded his views to anyone within hearing, including Nazi officials, their spies, and collaborators.

Perhaps Edward felt vindictive; after all, he was distantly related to the Romanovs, who had been executed by the Communists. In Edward's opinion, one simply did not go about executing royalty. Edward must have asked himself where the Communist onslaught would end. He was related to most of the crowned heads of Europe, and his German ties ran particularly deep.

From his abdication in 1936 until 1940, when he accepted the governorship of the Bahamas, Edward and Wallis lived in France until its fall to Hitler and then in pro-Nazi Spain. In 1937, the loving couple toured Germany where they were lionized by Hitler and senior officials such as Goering, Goebbels, and von Ribbentrop. The Nazi leaders treated Edward and Wallis as royalty.

Close Ties

Among Edward's closest confidantes during this period was Charles Bedaux, a man suspected to be a high-ranking Nazi espionage operative. Edward and Wallis married in Bedaux's French chateau, and Bedaux was an almost daily visitor to Edward's household. But from there, things become a little murky. Circumstantial evidence suggests Bedaux was a go-between for Edward and Hitler. By accident or design, Edward provided Hitler valuable intelligence in the days leading up to the blitzkrieg through the Low Countries and France.

While in Spain and, briefly, in Lisbon, Edward was being actively courted by the Nazis to become their quisling King of England. Moreover, Edward may have been the originator of the idea.

Shut Up, Cover Up

Having had to keep Edward out of Britain because of his outspoken appeasement policies, Prime Minister Winston Churchill had to figure out how to keep him out of Europe. Ever the diplomat, Churchill finessed Edward into shipping out to the Bahamas.

The most intriguing evidence of Edward's potentially traitorous relationship with the Nazis is the lengths the Royal Family went in the immediate postwar years to locate and destroy any documents that defined that relationship. The king, it seems, could condone the Romance of the 20th Century, but definitely not what may have been the Betrayal of the 20th Century.

♞ Behind the Films of Our Time

- John Wayne died in seven movies: *Reap the Wild Wind*, *The Fighting Seabees*, *Wake of the Red Witch*, *Sands of Iwo Jima*, *The Alamo*, *The Cowboys*, and *The Shootist*.

- *King Kong*, filmed in 1933, has a handful of scenes never seen by most. One features the gorilla taking off actress Fay Wray's clothes. Another involves Kong shaking a group of sailors off a bridge and into a spider-infested valley. The producer said the scene was so disturbing to the preview audience that he decided to remove it the next day.

- A chariot scene in the historical epic *Ben-Hur* has a small red car moving through the background.

- Film execs removed one song from the final cut of *The Wizard of Oz:* "The Jitter Bug." In the sequence, Dorothy and her friends were attacked by "jitter bugs" on their way to the witch's castle. Even though the song took five weeks and $80,000 worth of effects to create, MGM decided it wasn't crucial to the storyline and worried the reference could make the movie seem dated because of the similarly named "jitter bug" dance that was popular that year.

- Liza Minelli, daughter of Judy Garland (*The Wizard of Oz*'s Dorothy), ended up marrying Jack Haley Jr., whose father played the film's Tin Man.

- The mega hit *Titanic* originally had a less dramatic ending. In the first version, the final scene featuring the aged Rose dropping her "Heart of the Ocean" necklace into the water wasn't so simple. Instead of the poetic tossing, several of the ship's crewmembers see the woman and go over to talk to her, thinking she was going to commit suicide. Once they realized that Rose was just throwing her necklace overboard, they try to talk her out of it.

- The movie *Clue* was created with three endings; viewers saw different ones depending on where they saw the film. The endings were randomly selected for movie theaters across America. The DVD, however, features all three.

Pen Names and Pulp

As Vin Packer, Ann Aldrich, M. E. Kerr, and Mary James, this author has sold millions of books. Will the real Marijane Meaker please stand up?

Vin Packer and the Paperback Revolution

In the early 1950s, young college graduate Marijane Meaker was doing entry-level work as a proofreader for Fawcett Publishing's new paperback line, Gold Medal Books. Although Meaker had literary aspirations, she never imagined that her work would sell millions of books.

Before World War II, most books published in the United States were hardcover and were sold mainly in urban bookstores and department stores. But after the war, readers embraced the value and convenience of 25- and 35-cent paperbacks. The little books found success on spinner racks in bus stations, newsstands, supermarkets, candy stores, drugstores, and other nontraditional book outlets.

The paperback revolution produced a new literary genre: lesbian pulp. Ironically, these novels were originally written by and for straight males. Yet with paperbacks widely available outside of big cities, small-town women—many of whom could barely believe there were others out there who felt as they did—avidly consumed the lesbian pulps as well. Gold Medal caught on more quickly than other publishers; in 1952, Meaker was invited to write a lesbian-plot paperback original. Whether or not Gold Medal knew that she happened to be a real-life lesbian is unclear. At any rate, Meaker and the publisher agreed on the (faintly androgynous) pen name "Vin Packer." A publishing star was born.

Introducing Ann Archer

The first Packer novel, *Spring Fire*, sold nearly 1.5 million copies over the course of three wildly successful printings. And, sensational theme aside, it turned out Packer could really write! *Spring Fire* is propelled by complex, believable female characters whose longings and emotions are sensitively portrayed. Although federal and local censorship boards prevented the books from offering a happy ending that might validate lesbianism, Packer did suggest that the lifestyle had as much potential for joy as the straight life.

After Meaker retired the pseudonym in the early 1960s, she redebuted as "Ann Archer," whose nonfiction books about lesbianism are as unblushingly bold as their titles: *We Walk Alone, We Too Must Love,* and *Take a Lesbian to Lunch.* The Archer books naturally attracted the interest of lesbian and general readers, as well as feminists. By about 1970, Meaker/Archer was well respected within the burgeoning women's movement.

Meet M. E. Kerr

In 1972, Meaker reinvented herself yet again, this time as "M. E. Kerr," author of thoughtful teen novels. As is the case with the Packer titles, not every Kerr book includes homosexual characters (like 1994's Deliver Us from Evie), but the stories' central figures are psychologically complex and often at odds with "polite" society. More importantly, Kerr wrote about issues that were typically absent in teen books, such as serious illness, gay romance, divorce, death, and social-class tensions. Kerr often trafficked in endings that were less than completely happy—something teenagers could relate to. Meaker has said that whatever the genre or pen name she uses, she seeks to "write about people who struggle, who try to overcome obstacles, who usually do, but sometimes not. People who have all the answers and few problems have never interested me." For her boldness and quality of prose in books for young adults, Meaker was given a lifetime achievement award by Young Adult Library Services in 1993.

Meaker Moving Onward

While some observers have speculated that Meaker's pen names are part of an attempt to hide her own lesbian identity, the author has never denied her sexual orientation. And Meaker's fans can't be pigeonholed, either: young, old; male, female; straight, gay. Meaker understands the importance she holds for many readers, and the significance of her pen names to various groups of readers. This awareness helped prompt her to resurrect Vin Packer in 2007 for *Scott Free,* a provocative kidnap thriller featuring a new character, Scotti House—a male-to-female transgender insurance investigator!

He Said, She Said

"I told my dentist my teeth are going yellow. He told me to wear a brown tie."

—Rodney Dangerfield

"A day without sunshine is like, you know, night."

—Steve Martin

"Giving money and power to government is like giving whiskey and car keys to teenage boys."

—P. J. O'Rourke

"You don't pay taxes—they take taxes."

—Chris Rock

"Giving birth is like taking your lower lip and forcing it over your head."

—Carol Burnett

"I'm not offended by all the dumb blonde jokes because I know I'm not dumb, and I also know that I'm not blonde."

—Dolly Parton

"Changing a diaper is a lot like getting a present from your grandmother—you're not sure what you've got but you're pretty sure you're not going to like it."

—Jeff Foxworthy

"I never drink water because of the disgusting things that fish do in it."

—W. C. Fields

"Sometimes that light at the end of the tunnel is a train."

—Charles Barkley

"Women might be able to fake orgasms. But men can fake a whole relationship."

—Sharon Stone

"Love is the answer, but while you are waiting for the answer, sex raises some pretty good questions."

—Woody Allen

"Don't let yesterday use up too much of today."

—Will Rogers

Odd Ordinances

- It's illegal for infants to dance in a public hall in Los Angeles.

- In Kentucky, remarrying the same man four times is a crime.

- Breaking more than three dishes a day isn't allowed in Florida.

- Women can't drink coffee after 6 P.M. in Corvallis, Oregon.

- Women in Kentucky aren't allowed to be in swimsuits while on highways—unless they are either being escorted by two officers or are carrying clubs.

- Men are required to grow beards in Brainerd, Minnesota.

- Birds have the right-of-way on highways in Utah.

- The town of Tryon, North Carolina, has made it illegal to play the piccolo between 11 P.M. and 7:30 A.M.

- Tying a giraffe to a telephone pole is against the law in Atlanta.

- Carrying a bear on a Missouri highway is illegal, unless it's in a cage.

- Galveston, Texas, doesn't allow camels to wander the streets unattended.

- Blindfolding cows on highways in Arkansas is illegal.

- In Arizona, you can't shoot a camel.

- Punching a bull in the nose is illegal in Washington, D.C.

- Milking someone else's cow is a crime anywhere in Texas.

- It's a crime to swim with a deer in water higher than its knees in North Carolina.

- Giving booze to fish is illegal in Oklahoma.

- It is illegal to go "underneath a sidewalk" while in the state of Florida.

Bounced by the System

*In New York City's reassignment centers, a.k.a. "rubber rooms,"
schoolteachers who have committed an offense have to spend what
time would normally be used for teaching doing, well, nothing. Many
consider these salaried teachers' time spent inside to be an advance
trip to purgatory—not to mention a waste of taxpayer money.*

Clock In, Hang Out

Every morning, hundreds of New York City schoolteachers clock in
and take their places—but not in a classroom. While other teachers are preparing to spend the day lecturing about Shakespeare or
demonstrating long division, these teachers are expected to simply
sit around and wait out their time in one of the many "reassignment
centers" run by New York City's school systems. Otherwise known
as "rubber rooms," it is in these large, sometimes windowless rooms
that teachers (who have been taken off-duty for an offense and are
waiting to find out their fate) spend the school day playing games,
sleeping, knitting, reading, or watching DVDs. Not one of them is
ever found doing what they were hired to do: *teaching*.

A Divisive Situation

As of 2007, 12 such rubber rooms existed, with more than 750 teachers doing time. The thing is, nobody's really quite sure what the
endgame is supposed to be, or exactly what offenses qualify as
actionable.

The Board of Education will tell you that the rubber rooms are
a necessary evil—due to tenure and a strong teachers' union, bad or
subpar teachers are almost impossible to fire. In addition, a teacher's
contract requires a hearing before any actions are taken.

Jeanne Allen, president of Washington, D.C.'s, Center for Education Reform sums up this divisive issue. According to Allen, the rubber room exists "because of worn-out and, quite frankly, irrelevant
union contracts that do more to protect people's jobs than they do to
protect kids."

Teachers, however, would probably respond that the rubber rooms are a heavy-handed tactic devised to break their will, push them out the door for political reasons, or punish them for infractions, slight, severe, or sometimes even imagined.

In 2008, David Pakter completed a full year of rubber-room "duty" for purchasing an unauthorized plant for his school and giving students gifts for getting good grades. Now he's taken a stand as one of the more outspoken opponents of the rubber room system. Previously named an NYC "teacher of the year," Pakter used his salary from his stay in the rubber room—doing nothing—to purchase a Jaguar automobile. In a *New York Post* interview, he took the opportunity to rail against a system sorely in need of overhaul. "It's a present from [Schools Chancellor] Joel Klein," said Pakter. "I want to teach, they won't let me teach, but they'll pay me enough to buy a car. Can someone explain this to me?"

Nobody Wins

With New York City teaching salaries running between $42,500 and $93,400 in 2007, it's the taxpayers who lose. Throw in the exorbitant cost of hiring substitute teachers to replace those stuck in the rubber rooms, and the leasing of 12 rooms, and the problem only gets worse. According to the *Post,* the current rubber-room policy costs about $40 million dollars a year, based on the median teacher salary. For their part, the offending teachers speak of depression brought on by the dehumanizing effects of this "guilty until proven innocent" scenario and the boring downtime that awaits them each weekday.

In the end, it's the schoolchildren who are getting the rawest deal of all. With regular teachers being held indefinitely and substitute teachers coming and going, the children's progress is prohibited by bureaucratic red tape. New Yorkers hope their kids' education can bounce back from the effects of the rubber room.

A Diner-English Glossary, Part II

Between the Bread—Sandwiches and Burgers

- Bun Pup, Bow Wow, Coney Island Chicken: hot dog
- Noah's Boy on Bread: ham sandwich
- Wimpy: hamburger
- Wimpy and Drag It Through Wisconsin: burger with cheddar cheese
- Melting Snow: melted Swiss cheese
- Wax: American cheese
- Cremate It: toasted bread (usually white)

Blue Plate Specials—Main Dishes

- First Ladies: spare ribs
- Foreign Entanglements: spaghetti
- Hounds on an Island: franks and beans
- Stars and Stripes: pork and beans
- St. Pats, Irish Turkey: corned beef and cabbage
- Zeppelins in a Fog: sausage and mashed potatoes
- Cluck: chicken

How Sweet It Is—Desserts

- Chicago: pineapple sundae
- Houseboat: banana split
- Life Preservers, Sinkers: doughnuts
- Nervous Pudding: Jell-O
- Pink Stick: strawberry ice cream
- Put a Hat on It: top with ice cream
- Shake One in the Hay: strawberry milkshake
- Fluff It: add whipped cream
- Bucket of Cold Mud: chocolate ice cream

Fast Facts

- It is possible for a whale to get lice.

- A baby elephant seal is called a "weaner."

- Tickets to the first Super Bowl went for $12—and that was for the most expensive seat.

- The exclamation point is short for the Latin word "io," which means "exclamation of joy." It used to be written with a lowercase "i" over a lowercase "o." That eventually gave way to the abbreviation (!) we use today.

- The dollar sign abbreviation started as a "P," to match the shorthand for the peso. It then morphed into a "P" with an "S" over it, which then gave way to the symbol ($) we use now.

- The idea for Wheaties cereal came from a health spa owner in Minneapolis who used bran gruel to help patients lose weight. Then one day, some of it spilled onto the stove and hardened. Voila!—Wheaties were born.

- Dancing the tango was considered a sin in Paris during the early 1900s.

- Kissing was once a crime in England. In the mid-1400s, King Henry VI declared it to be a disease-spreader.

- The letters "SOS" don't actually stand for "Save Our Ship." In fact, they were only selected because they translate into a simple Morse code message of three dots, three dashes, and three dots. The letters never meant anything more.

- The U.S. Department of Agriculture says there are likely 1,000 cockroaches in your home for every one that you see.

Cold Case:
The Cadaver Synod

*The Cadaver Synod—or Cadaver Trial—is considered the
lowest point in papal history. How low? Try six feet under.*

V as in Vengeance (and Stephen VII)

The mastermind behind what became known as the Cadaver Synod
was Italy's King Lambert, who sought revenge for Pope Formosus's
actions against his father, Guido, the duke of Spoleto. Previously,
Formosus's predecessor Pope Stephen VI had crowned Guido and
Lambert co-Holy Roman Emperors in A.D. 892. But Formosus
favored the German king Arnulf, and he convinced Arnulf to invade
Italy and usurp the crown. Guido died before he was forcibly removed
from office, and in February 896, Arnulf was crowned emperor.

Physical paralysis ultimately cut short Arnulf's reign; he returned
to Germany, leaving Lambert to take over and exact his revenge on
Formosus. The pope died before Lambert got a chance to strike, but
that didn't stop Lambert: He ordered Formosus's successor Pope
Stephen VII—himself a Spoletian sympathizer—to dig up the pope's
body and put it on trial for perjury, violating church canons, and
coveting the papacy.

A Trial of the Grotesque

No transcript of the Cadaver Synod exists, but historians agree as to
how it probably went down: In January 897, the rotting corpse (it was
only nine months after Formosus's death) was exhumed, carried into
the courtroom, dressed in elaborate papal vestments, and propped in
a chair, behind which cowered a teenage deacon, who was in charge
of speaking for the dead pope. Stephen ranted and screamed at
Formosus's body, who, of course, was found guilty of all charges.

As punishment, Stephen ordered that all of Formosus's papal
ordinances be overturned, that the three fingers on his right hand
used to give papal blessings be hacked off, and that his body be
stripped of its papal vestments, dressed in peasant's clothes, and

reburied in a common grave. After the sentence was carried out, the pope's body was dug up yet again and tossed in the Tiber River, from which a monk retrieved it and buried it. Again.

The Cadaver Synod caused a public rebellion and within a few months, Stephen was deposed, stripped of his vestments, and sent to prison where he was strangled to death in 897.

Return of the Synod

In 897, Pope Theodore II held a synod to annul the Cadaver Synod—one his few actions as pope, since his pontificate lasted only 20 days. Formosus's body was dug up once more and carried back to St. Peter's Basilica, where it was redressed in papal vestments and returned to its tomb. The next pope, John IX, held another synod to confirm Theodore II's decision. He also declared it illegal to put a dead body on trial.

But John's successor, Pope Sergio III, who participated in the Cadaver Synod and was a "violent hater of Formosus," held his own synod to reverse the decisions made by the previous two popes. Maybe because it was finally illegal to dig up and put dead bodies on trial, he simply had an epitaph made for Stephen's tomb that heaped insults on Formosus. Sergio's ruling was never overturned, however; it was just ignored.

- *Formosus means "good-looking" in Latin.*

- *From A.D. 896 to 904, there were nine popes—the same number of popes throughout the entire 20th century.*

- *Pope Sergio III was quite the controversial figure. His papacy has been called "The Rule of the Harlots."*

- *Though Formosus has been unanimously vindicated and cleared of all charges, there has never been a Pope Formosus II. Cardinal Pietro Barbo apparently thought about taking the name in 1464 but was talked out of it. He took Paul II instead.*

HOW IT ALL BEGAN

Eye of the Beholder

Unless you manufacture them or wear them, it's sort of easy to forget about artificial eyes. The ancient Egyptians even wore them, beginning around the fifth century B.C. Since then, artificial eyes have had a slow but steady evolution.

First came gold and painted enamel eyes, followed by glass, and, finally, acrylic. During the evolution other materials were tried in search of realism: aluminum, sponge, asbestos, rubber, and paraffin, to name a few. Researchers in Toronto have rocketed the science of artificial eyes into the realm of high technology, developing a robotic eye that mimics natural movements by using electrodes implanted in the wearer's head. That takes the development a long way from the Egyptians who simply painted an eye on a piece of cloth, which hung over the eye socket.

The First Alaska Highway

The 1,500-mile Alaska Highway, which runs from Dawson Creek in Canada's Yukon to Fairbanks, Alaska, was not the first Alaskan highway. Sure, it got the name and fame, but it was a highway-come-lately compared to the 1,150-mile Iditarod Trail between Seward and Nome. The Iditarod opened in 1915; the Alaska Highway in 1942. Granted, the Alaska Highway is open year-round and is paved, while the decidedly more rustic Iditarod Trail is just, well, a trail, navigable only in winter and only by dogsled.

Still, the Iditarod has an international claim to fame. Each winter since 1973, dog mushers from every snowy corner of the world gather to race over the trail in the "Last Great Race on Earth," an annual tribute the history and contributions of the dog sleds, from the gold prospectors who opened Alaska's interior (the dogs would haul the gold), to the dogs that ran serum vaccines to isolated Nome to prevent a diphtheria epidemic in 1925.

So, what exactly is an "Iditarod"? It's a ghost town that was once the midpoint on the trail.

Arf! Dog-Men in History

❖ ❖ ❖ ❖

*Dog may be man's best friend, but he's also been invoked
to explain the unexplainable, and even to denigrate
enemies—reasons why tales of men with the heads of dogs
are not uncommon throughout the historical record.*

Dog-Headed Foreigners

Ancient stories about dog-headed men unwittingly reveal an appre-
hensiveness about the power of canines. We love our pooches, but let's
face it: They have claws and sharp teeth, they run faster than we do,
and they can eat our faces if they feel like it. Historically, this small bit
of disquiet bubbling beneath our adoration has encouraged cultures
to invoke doglike creatures for diverse purposes, sometimes as gods,
such as Egypt's Anubis, and frequently to belittle other cultures.

Whatever the motives, the eventual effect of these pervasive tales
was to make fantastical dog-men seem very real. Most imaginative of
all, though, were ancient writers from China, India, and Europe, who
relayed purportedly true stories of human beings who literally had the
heads of dogs.

Sit, Cynocephali!

Dog-headed peoples are often referred to as *Cynocephali,* Greek
for "dog-head." In the fifth century B.C., Greek historian Herodotus described a distant country inhabited by "huge snakes and the
lions, and the elephants and bears and asps, the Kunokephaloi (Dog-
headed) and the Headless Men that have their eyes in their chests."

Herodotus was not alone in his testimony about dog-headed peoples. Fellow Greek historian Ctesias claimed that on the mountains in
distant India, "there live men with the head of a dog, whose clothing is
the skin of wild beasts."

In accounts of this nature, it's difficult to sort out myth from fact.
Like many of today's bloggers, ancient historians made implausible
claims based on hearsay rather than direct observation. Writers played
so fast and loose with the available facts that many believed—and
made their readers believe—that some foreign societies barked rather
than spoke.

Some historians tried to legitimize their claims by skipping down the road of pseudo-science. The second-century Greek historian Aelian included the Cynocephali in his book of animals. He declared that beyond Egypt one encounters the "human Kynoprosopoi (Dog faces) . . . they are black in appearance, and they have the head and teeth of a dog. And since they resemble this animal, it is very natural that I should mention them here [in a book about Animals]."

Racism Collides with Legend

Many present-day historians charge that these accounts of dog-headed tribes aren't simply reflections of a fear of foreigners, but racist ignorance. Repeated accounts of dog-headed groups in northern Africa suggest that race did indeed help encourage some dog-driven tales. These African groups were often referred to as the Marmaritae, who engaged in on-again off-again warfare with the Romans. Legend has it that St. Christopher was a captured dog-headed slave from a Marmaritae tribe—paintings that depict the saint with the head of a brown dog still exist. According to lore, Christopher's dog head was replaced with a normal human head after he was baptized.

Modern scholars believe that historical references to dog-headed tribes derived from the lore created by many tribes in Central Asia, who described their own origins as having roots in the progeny of a human female who mated with a male dog. Biology this startling certainly would have tickled the imaginations of outsiders, and reinforced the notion that dog-headedness signified a profound and culturally expedient "otherness" of foreigners.

Baffling Baboons

And then there's the issue of *Papio cynocephalus,* central Africa's yellow baboon, whose head is curiously doglike. Foreigners' accounts of Africa often remarked on this intriguing animal with zeal. In fact, during the mad European scramble to colonize the African continent in the 19th century, baboons were shipped to the West for exhibition in circuses and freak shows as exotic dog-men. One such circus claimed that its baboon-man had been captured from an ancient African tribe. Marveling audiences failed to see the baboon face on the baboon, just as people failed to see the legitimate uniqueness of persons who didn't look or act as they did.

Salvador Dalí and Harpo Marx: A Match Made in Surrealist Heaven

The great 20th-century surrealist artist Salvadore Dalí knew how to put a brush to canvas, but after making fast friends with Harpo Marx of the Marx Brothers, Dalí was inspired to try his hand at writing comedy. Thus was born a surrealist comedy script that was deemed unmarketable—even by Hollywood standards.

Dalí the Filmmaker

Salvador Dalí was never one to paint a dull picture. From melting watches to roses that float in the middle of the desert, Dalí painted the world as he imagined it, not as it was. And Dalí did not limit this dreamlike vision to painting—he designed clothing, furniture, and stage settings in Broadway productions. In effect, Dalí transferred his unique vision to whatever media would hold it. "Painting is an infinitely minute part of my personality," he said.

From a young age, Dalí had a particular interest in the surrealist potential of film. He grew up watching silent film comedic greats such as Charlie Chaplin and Buster Keaton. Slapstick comedic acts often had a distinct surrealist slant—after all, how many pie fights can a person encounter in a day? Dalí saw the potential inherent in cinema's ability to place one image right on top of another in time, thus allowing for the juxtaposition of bizarrely disconnected images, such as, say, a slashed human eye followed by a pink teddy bear. Dalí once described the epitome of film as "a succession of wonders."

At age 25, Dalí set to work making his imagined succession of wonders a sur-reality. He paired with friend and famed surrealist filmmaker Luis Bunuel to make a short film called *Un Chien Andalous* (1929), which is now considered a groundbreaking first in avant-garde cinema. His film career may have begun with this bang, but *Un Chien Andalous* and *Âge d'or, L'* (1930) proved to be the only Dalí films to make it into production. In 1946, he collaborated with Walt Disney on a short six-minute animated film, *Destino,* that was abandoned as too strange and unmarketable. Eventually, *Destino* was released in 2003 after Dalí's death. He also made a short dream sequence for Hitchcock's *Spellbound,* but for the most part Dalí's film projects were nipped in the bud.

Dalí the Comedian

The inspiration behind Dalí's wackiest unmade film script was his friendship with Harpo, the Marx brother who consistently hid crazy gags up his sleeve. Harpo's very persona was surreal: His character refused to speak, instead relying on the art of pantomime, whistles, and props to communicate. He wore outrageous outfits topped by his wild mat of curly clown hair and was a self-taught virtuoso harpist.

Dalí was enthralled with Harpo. After the two met in Paris in the summer of 1936, they strummed up an appropriately peculiar friendship. Dalí sent Harpo a gift: A gilded harp with barbed-wire strings and teaspoon tuning knobs. Delighted, Harpo returned the favor by sending Dalí a photograph of himself playing the harp with cut-up, bandaged fingers.

The following year, Dalí traveled to California to see Harpo. As he noted in a postcard, "I'm in Hollywood, where I've made contact with the three American Surrealists: Harpo Marx, Disney, and Cecil B. DeMille." According to the always-dramatic Dali, upon arrival, he found Harpo lying "naked, crowned with roses, and in the center of a veritable forest of harps." During their vacation, Dalí drew sketches of Harpo at his harp, grinning with a lobster on his head. The two also began collaboration on a surrealistic Marx Brothers film called *Giraffes on Horseback Salad.* The film followed the misadventures of a Spanish businessman who comes to America and falls in love with a woman, to be played by Dalí's wife, Gala. The script also calls for burning giraffes wearing gas masks and Harpo catching Little People with a butterfly net. The film was never realized as MGM, the Marx Brothers's studio, refused to make it. The script does, however, still exist in a private collection—perhaps someday Dalí and Harpo's inimitable dream will come to fruition.

Fast Facts

- In an ironic twist, Mel Blanc, best known as the voice of Bugs Bunny, had an aversion to raw carrots.

- The Guinness Book of World Records *holds a record of its own. The hefty book is considered the most commonly stolen volume from libraries around the world.*

- When it comes to bookstores, however, the Bible is actually considered the most commonly shoplifted book in America.

- If you order "white tea" in China, you'll end up with a cup of plain boiling water.

- About 500 pounds of Silly Putty are produced every day.

- There are more horses than people in the country of Mongolia.

- In Hebrew, dogs are quoted as saying "hav hav" instead of "bow wow."

- November 19 is considered by many to be "Have a Bad Day Day."

- An average of 900 million Valentine's Day cards go out across America every February.

- An average porcupine has 30,000 quills.

- Every male warthog has four warts, while every female has two.

- Television master chef Antony Thompson hastily had to rewrite his recipe for an organic salad after recommending that a dash or two of henbane would perk up the flavor. Henbane, however, is a toxic poison.

Ant-ics

❖ ❖ ❖ ❖

*Considered more of a pest than a pet, getting positive
PR is no picnic for an ant. But despite their perceived
lowly status, ants are anything but common.*

Ants outnumber humans a million to
one. Their combined weight outweighs
the combined weight of all the humans
in the world. Possessing the largest of
insect brains, an ant's intellect report-
edly rivals the processing power of a Macintosh II computer. Yet,
despite these distinctions, ants are stepped on the world over.
Respect is due!

Long Live the Queen
In the ant world, males are superfluous. During the queen's brief
courtship, she mates with several "kings," extracting and storing
enough sperm to last her 10- to 30-year reign. No longer necessary,
the male ants soon die. The queen then gives birth to thousands
of subjects, populating her empire. Her fertilized eggs become
females; unfertilized eggs become males. Most females are born
sterile, consigned to be workers.

Ants pass through four life stages: egg, larvae, pupae, and adult.
The tiny ant eggs are sticky, allowing them to bond together for ease
of care. Since eggs and larvae are susceptible to cold temperatures,
worker ants must ferry them back and forth from deep within the
nest to the nest's surface to control their climate.

Models of Civility
Most ants live in organized, industrious harmony. Young workers
care for their queen mother and larvae, then graduate to nest duties
such as engineering, digging, and sanitation. Finally, when they are
older (and closer to death), they advance to the dangerous positions
of foraging and security. By frequently switching jobs, ants remain
cross-trained and ready for emergencies.

However, such civility is not universal. Members of the barbarous *Polyergus rufescens* species, or slave-maker ants, raid neighboring nests to steal their young. Sir John Lubbock, an acclaimed chronicler of ant behavior, reported that certain slave-making ants were so dependent on their minions that they would starve to death if the slaves failed to feed them.

Agricultural Innovators

Only four of the world's species engage in agriculture: humans, termites, bark beetles, and ants. But ants were the first. Leaf-cutter ants carefully cultivate subterranean fungus gardens by spraying their crops with self-produced antibiotics to ward off disease, then fertilizing them with their protease-laced anal secretions.

Ants also engage in livestock farming. They domesticate and raise aphids, which they milk for honeydew like a farmer would a cow for its milk. The honeydew provides important nourishment for ants, which are incapable of chewing or swallowing solids.

Some ants are also accomplished hunters. Marching in long processions while carrying their eggs and larvae on their backs, nomadic South American army ants attack everything in their path. Though blind, they fearlessly swarm on reptiles, birds, small mammals, and other insects (which they kill but don't eat). Up to 700,000 members strong, an army ant colony can make thousands of kills each day.

Comrades Extraordinaire

Lubbock theorized that ants possess the innate ability to detect and defend their own even under duress. To test his hypothesis, he selected two groups of subjects from different colonies and then scrambled their senses with whiskey. (He had to dunk the ants in the liquor since they refused to imbibe on their own.)

Lubbock dropped the inebriated ants onto an island inhabited by the nest mates of half his subjects. Momentarily stunned by this puzzling development, the sober ants quickly assessed the situation, then took action. Identifying their intoxicated sisters, the sober ants culled them from the crowd and carried them home to recuperate. Then they rounded up the drunken intruders and tossed them into the moat. Apparently, an ant's love extends only to her immediate family.

Modern Rocketry
and the Moonchild

*American rocket scientist Jack Parsons wielded
the power to bring about mass devastation—
though not in the way he anticipated.*

A Flight of Fancy

In 1936, 22-year-old Jack Parsons was the epitome of "tall, dark, and handsome." Parsons's natural charisma and fierce intellect, however, did not prevent him from leaving his chemistry studies at Caltech, where he drew criticism for his abiding interest in rocketry, specifically the quest to develop a workable rocket fuel. In Depression-era America, rocketry was seen as nothing more than a flight of fancy. Exiled from campus for their explosive experiments, Parsons and his fellow enthusiasts trekked out to the isolated Arroyo Seco Canyon. On October 31, they conducted a test that, instead of resulting in an explosion, led to a successful launch. Soon thereafter, they formed the Jet Propulsion Laboratory (JPL).

So Far, So...Bad

With the advent of the Second World War, Parsons's talents were suddenly very much in demand. Thanks to Parsons's intuitive understanding of chemistry, the company was able to produce a working jet-assisted take-off (JATO) rocket for aircraft. The military found the JATO particularly useful on the short runways that dotted the South Pacific islands.

Parsons soon started another successful enterprise—AeroJet Corporation. The founding of AeroJet seemed like just another chapter in Parsons's successful life. But then everything seemed to take a much darker turn. Jack sold his AeroJet shares to finance his other abiding interest—the occult.

British writer, hedonist, and self-proclaimed master of the occult Aleister Crowley led a religious organization called Ordo Templi Orientis, through which he spread his mystical life philosophy of

Thelema, dictating "Do what thou wilt." This pagan, power-based religion of the individual appealed to Parsons, who had regularly invoked the Greek god Pan when conducting rocket tests for JPL. Jack joined the West Coast chapter in 1941 and was quickly recognized as a likely successor to Crowley himself. A year later, Parsons was made the leader of the West Coast church and began conducting "sex magick" rituals intended to bring about the end of the world.

Then things got really weird.

Enter (and Exit) L. Ron Hubbard

Parsons's first wife, Helen Parsons Smith, left him shortly after he joined Crowley's church. And no wonder—Parsons and his new friend, fellow church member L. Ron Hubbard, were busy conducting lewd rituals intended to call forth an "elemental" partner to sire a "moonchild," who was to be the harbinger of the apocalypse. After a particularly vigorous ritual, a young woman knocked on the door. Redheaded (a prerequisite for the elemental), she was willing to carry Parsons's moonchild. Despite many attempts at conception, it was to no avail. Finally, Hubbard absconded with all of Parsons's money, as well as his girlfriend. Soon thereafter, Hubbard used the money to finance his first book, and lo, Scientology was born.

But, Getting Back to Jack

Parsons's life began to unravel. The moonchild didn't materialize, his friend had stolen his money, and he was under investigation by the FBI. For a time he worked at a gas station; later he remarried and began making special effects for movies. He was reportedly hard at work on a new kind of artificial fog when an explosion in his apartment took his life on June 17, 1952.

By then, the Cold War was new and fear was rampant. Soon both the Soviet Union and the United States developed intercontinental ballistic missiles, and the threat of global nuclear apocalypse grew increasingly real. Parsons may not have conceived a magical moonchild to bring about the apocalypse, but he had created the technology needed to hurl atomic weapons through space—enabling a possible apocalypse in itself.

Fumbling Felons

Helping Hands

A robber in England broke into a local supermarket, but the police arrived quickly and apprehended him. Despite the handcuffs, however, the man somehow managed to break free before the cops could bundle him off to the station.

The crook had pulled off a near-miraculous escape and should have thanked his lucky stars. But there was still something that didn't feel right to him—he was still wearing the handcuffs.

The dim-witted robber went to the nearest police station, hoping that the cops would help him get the hand-cuffs off. After all, they were the only things marring a perfect escape. Not surprisingly, the cops didn't see it his way and quickly rearrested him.

The Flasher

Kids love those sneakers with the lights in the heels, because every time they put their foot down, the lights flash. Good for kids; bad for crooks.

A Kansas criminal found this out after he robbed a convenience store at night. Fleet of foot, he knew the area well and was confident in his ability to elude the cops that were chasing him. But to the bandit's dismay, every time he darted down another dark alley to elude a cop, more would show up right behind him to continue the pursuit. No matter how much he juked and jived, hopped fences, and cut through darkened yards, there was always an officer hot on his trail.

All good things come to an end, and ultimately, so did the crook's stamina. The cops corralled their man, who was amazed that all of his fancy footwork had gone for naught. It was then he learned how the cops had always been able to find him: They had merely followed the flashing lights in the heels of his athletic shoes, which gave them clear pursuit in the dark. Unfortunately for the crook, the next red flashing lights he saw were on the police car he rode in to the station.

Curse of the (Polish) Mummy

❖ ❖ ❖ ❖

*In 1973, a group of research scientists entered the tomb of
King Casimir IV, a member of the Jagiellon dynasty that
once ruled throughout central Europe. Within weeks of
entering the tomb, only two scientists remained alive.*

The Jagiellon Curse

Indiana Jones didn't have it easy, but as archaeologist work hazards
go, there are worse fates than snake pits and big rolling boulders.
For example, there are strains of mold fungi that eat your body
from the inside out. This was the inauspicious fate of several scientists who opened a tomb that had been shut for centuries, thereby
unleashing a powerful mummy's curse—or, more realistically and
less fantastically—powerful microorganisms.

   The tomb of King Casimir IV of Poland and his wife, Elizabeth
of Habsburg, is located in the chapel of Wawel Castle in Krakow,
Poland. Casimir served as king for more than 40 years in the 13th
century. He left behind 13 children, many of whom went on to positions of great power. In 1973, Cardinal Wojtyla (who later went on
to become Pope John Paul II) gave a group of scientists permission
to open King Casimir's tomb and examine its contents. Within the
tomb, the unlucky group found a heavily rotted wooden coffin—not
so surprising, given the box had been decaying for nearly 500 years.
However, within a few days, four of the twelve researchers were
dead; six more died soon after.

Killer Fungi

While sensationalists blamed the tragedy on a mummy's curse,
the scientific-minded questioned whether the sudden deaths were
related to the icky molds, fungi, and parasites that would linger in a
room that had been sealed off for centuries. This was precisely the
suspicion of Dr. Boleslaw Smyk, one of the two surviving scientists.
He set out to discover what exactly had killed his colleagues, and he
came up with three species of fungi mold that had lingered in King

Casimir's tomb: *Aspergillus flavus, Penicillim rubrum,* and *Penicillim rugulosum.*

Not a Mummy, But No Less Scary

These are not the kindest of specimens. *Aspergillus flavus* is toxic to the liver, while *Penicillim rubrum* causes, among a host of other afflictions, pulmonary emphysema. These toxins grow on decaying wood and lime mortar, both of which were in Casimir's tomb. The toxins remained in the tomb in the form of mold spores, which can survive for thousands of years in closed environments. It is likely the researchers breathed in the spores immediately upon entering the coffin, since the sudden flow of fresh air into a closed tomb would blow the spores about. Toxic spores that are inhaled in this fashion can lead to organ failure and death in a very short time.

It's therefore unsurprising that whisperings of a "mummy's curse" abound. The more famous legend came from the 1922 Egyptian excavation of Pharaoh Tutankhamun's tomb. Lord Carnarvon, one of the main financiers of the King Tut excavation, died a few months after he entered the fungi-laden tomb—the same fungi spores that were identified in King Casimir's tomb were also present in King Tut's. Stories of a mummy's curse followed, although it's unclear whether Carnarvon's death actually was related to his archaeological pursuits: Carnarvon had a cut on his cheek that became infected weeks after the excavation. He fell ill and eventually died of pneumonia and septicemia from the cut.

Whether or not Carnarvon died of natural causes, rumors of the supernatural took on a life of their own. After news of his death spread, fantastical stories grew regarding the grisly deaths of anyone who had entered King Tut's tomb. Today, even modern archaeologists are warned of their potential exposure to the dreaded Mummy's Curse.

Diamonds Are Forever

Most diamonds have had a peaceful existence. Still, there are others awash in blood or are even rumored to be cursed. Read on for some gem-studded legends.

The Good, the Bad, and the Pretty

The **Cullinan Diamond,** discovered in 1905 and weighing in at 1.3 pounds, is still the largest rough-cut gem-quality diamond that has ever been found. Some gemologists hypothesize that it may be part of a much larger diamond.

Although it is rumored that the **Koh-i-noor Diamond** was originally found 5,000 years ago, historians definitely know that it was a British prize of war in the 1849 bloody conquest of the Punjab. It later ended up in Britain's Crown Jewel collection. Still, many of the diamond's previous owners suffered terribly, and stories of lootings of kingdoms, torture, and the like prevail. In one battle, 20,000 people died—not for the Koh-i-noor itself, but because of the power, pride, and rapaciousness of its owner, symbolized by the gem.

The **Orlov Diamond** is another gem with an allegedly bloody history. At one point, the diamond was stolen from a Hindu statue by a soldier, who then offered it to an Armenian merchant. When a price could not be reached, the soldier sold it to someone else. The Armenian killed the soldier and the purchaser; later, when he and his brothers could not agree on the division of spoils, he killed them too.

As the story goes, Russian Count Grigoryevich Orlov later bought the diamond in 1775 and gave it to Czarina Catherine the Great in order to win her favor. His ploy didn't work—though she did keep the diamond.

Perhaps it is the **Hope Diamond** that carries the most baggage. However, most of the curses surrounding the fabled diamond— insanity, disease, violent death, and suicide—appear to be stories invented in 1910 by the renowned jeweler Cartier to pique a potential buyer. Since then, any curse seems to have dissipated.

Pawned, You Say?

The famous **Sancy Diamond** spent much of its early history in pawnshops that catered to European royal families. Its owner, a mercenary named Nicholas de Sancy, first used it as collateral to finance several military campaigns on behalf of monarchs. Later, the exiled queen of Charles I used the gem for a loan to support her lifestyle, but she blew her bankroll and failed to redeem it. The diamond was sold again, this time to the French King Louis XIV. Later, in the aftermath of the French Revolution, it was again pawned to finance military operations.

The **Regent Diamond** was part of the French Crown Jewels collection, pawned by Napoleon Bonaparte to pay for the cavalry and supply horses he needed to win the pivotal Battle of Marengo. That win opened the door to his historic empire-building military initiatives.

All About Harry

Harry Winston was not your average storefront jeweler. In fact, his name still comes up when some of the world's most famous diamonds are discussed, including the **Hope, Idol's Eye, Jonkers,** and the **Lesotho.** Here are some other Winston-related facts:

- When Winston donated the Hope Diamond to the Smithsonian Institution in 1958, he trusted its delivery to the U.S. Postal Service.

- Winston's firm also cut the diamond that became known as the **Taylor-Burton Diamond** when actor Richard Burton gave it to actress Elizabeth Taylor.

- In 1974, Winston negotiated a deal with DeBeers Consolidated Mining for $24.5 million—the largest single diamond purchase in the world. As negotiations were being finalized, he casually asked for and received a "deal sweetener" of a 181-carat rough diamond. When cut, this gem provided several stones, the largest of which was 45.31 carats. Appropriately, Harry named that one the **Deal Sweetener.**

He Said, She Said

"Hearing nuns' confessions is like being stoned to death with popcorn."
—*Fulton J. Sheen*

"The only difference between this game and Custer's last stand was Custer didn't have to look at the tape afterwards."
—*Terry Crisp (coach of the Tampa Bay Lightning)*

"It is better to keep your mouth closed and let people think you are a fool than to open it and remove all doubt."
—*Mark Twain*

"When I played drunks I had to remain sober because I didn't know how to play them when I was drunk."
—*Richard Burton*

"Money doesn't make you happy. I now have $50 million, but I was just as happy when I had $48 million."
—*Arnold Schwarzenegger*

"Advertising is the art of convincing people to spend money they don't have for something they don't need."
—*Will Rogers*

"On the plus side, death is one of the few things that can be done just as easily lying down."
—*Woody Allen*

"Behind every successful man is a woman, behind her is his wife."
—*Groucho Marx*

"I know a baseball star who wouldn't report the theft of his wife's credit cards because the thief spends less than she does."
—*Joe Garagiola*

"It isn't necessary to be rich and famous to be happy. It's only necessary to be rich."
—*Alan Alda*

"I think men who have a pierced ear are better prepared for marriage. They've experienced pain and bought jewelry."
—*Rita Rudner*

So You Want to Swallow Swords

With time, patience, and a tolerance for physical discomfort, you too can learn how to swallow a sword. But should you just because you can? Here's a look at what goes into the art of sword swallowing.

Gag Me With a Sword

Billed as the most dangerous form of performance art, sword swallowing relies on mental and physical concentration. The act requires controlling more than 50 pairs of muscles. In fact, "sword sucking" is a more accurate description. Performers swallow a wide variety of potentially lethal objects, including neon tubes, umbrellas, and pool cues, but most stick to steel blades. The "industry standards" stipulate that swords must be non-retractable and non-collapsible, 15 to 24 inches long, and ½ to 1 inch wide.

First, the performer suppresses his or her gag reflex, relaxing the throat to allow the blade into the esophagus. Passing the heart, lungs, and other organs, the sword moves through the lower esophageal sphincter to the bottom of the stomach. (The distance between a person's teeth and stomach is approximately 16 inches.) The performer holds the blade for a few seconds, before carefully sliding it out.

Professional Hazards

As of 2006, there are approximately 110 people worldwide who have swallowed swords; however, there are only a few dozen who currently do so. The act is always physically unpleasant, and it is dangerous enough to make many reconsider. On average, there are four to eight serious injuries reported every year. Even when all goes well, it has nasty side effects, including throat pain, sinus infections, esophageal or pharynx perforations, and a persistent metallic taste in the mouth.

If you're thinking that sword swallowing is for you, find a mentor. This is not a skill to learn from books or online. Controlling your gag reflex can take months; making the leap to swallowing swords could take a decade. But even after years of work, experienced swallowers know that each performance could be their last

Unusual Medical Maladies

❖ ❖ ❖ ❖

The human body is able to play some nasty tricks on its owner. While none of them are considered life-threatening, the six syndromes and disorders described below are documented cases of unusual medical maladies.

Who Is That?

Take the interesting and perplexing diagnosis of **Capgras Syndrome,** a rare psychological disorder that makes sufferers suspicious of their loved ones or even their own reflections. For a number of reasons, including schizophrenia, epilepsy, and malformed temporal lobes of the brain, Capgras victims have difficulty making physical and emotional connections with the people, places, and things they see, even ones that have been a part of their lives for years. Sufferers see themselves in a mirror or other shiny surfaces and wonder who the stranger is that's peering back at them. According to Dr. V. S. Ramachandran, director of the Center for Brain and Cognition at the University of California, San Diego, people diagnosed with this disorder can also find themselves suspicious of animals or other objects, such as a pair of running shoes. In such cases, they convince themselves that someone has broken into their home and replaced familiar objects with imposters.

Can You Direct Me to the Loo?

Foreign Accent Syndrome is even more rare: a disorder that causes the afflicted to suddenly and unexplainably speak in an unfamiliar dialect. One of the first cases of FAS was discovered in 1941 after a young Norwegian woman sustained a shrapnel injury to her head during a wartime air raid. Although she had never been out of her home country, she suddenly began speaking with a German accent, which resulted in her being shunned by her family and friends. In Indiana, a 57-year-old woman suffered a stroke in 1999 and began speaking with a British accent, including colloquialisms like "bloody" and "loo."

Get Your Hands Off of Me!

If there was ever a malady that a high-school boy might envy, it's **Alien Hand Syndrome,** also known as **Dr. Strangelove Syndrome.** Alien Hand Syndrome is caused by damage to the parietal or occipital lobe of the brain. Those afflicted often find one of their hands operating independently from the rest of their body and sometimes completely against their conscious will. AHS sufferers often report incidences of a "rogue hand" getting involved in disobedient behavior such as undoing buttons or removing clothing. One patient reported a bizarre incident in which her right hand put a cigarette into her mouth. Before she could light it, her left hand yanked the cigarette out and crushed it in an ashtray.

Please Pass the Dirt

At one time or another all kids will experiment by eating an occasional handful of dirt. The good news is that it's a passing phase for the majority of youngsters. The bad news is that if this fascination with eating nonfood items persists longer than a month, your child could be afflicted with **Pica.** Associated with developmental disabilities such as autism or mental retardation, Pica typically affects children younger than 24 months. It can also appear in people with epilepsy and pregnant women.

Pica sufferers find themselves craving and consuming a wide variety of nonfood items such as dirt, sand, hair, glue, buttons, paint chips, plaster, laundry starch, cigarette butts, paper, soap, and even feces. There was even one documented case of "cutlery craving," in which a 47-year-old Englishman underwent more than 30 operations to remove various items from his stomach—including eight dinner forks.

Another form of Pica, called **Geophagia,** is practiced by cultures that eat earth substances such as dirt and clay to relieve nausea, morning sickness, diarrhea, and to remove toxins from their bodies.

Something Smells Fishy Around Here

Bad breath, body odor, and the occasional flatulence—we've all had to deal with them in one way or another. But how would you like to live with someone who constantly smelled of pungent fish?

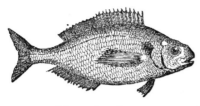

A rare metabolic disorder called **Fish Odor Syndrome** (also known as trimethylaminuria or TMAU) results in the afflicted releasing an enzyme called trimethylamine through their sweat, urine, and breath. This enzyme also happens to give off a strong "fishy" odor. The condition appears to be more common in women than men, and researchers suspect that female sex hormones such as estrogen or progesterone may be at fault.

While there is no cure for Fish Odor Syndrome, people afflicted can control the disease by avoiding eggs, certain meats, fish, legumes, and foods that contain choline, nitrogen, and sulfur. And, of course, showering regularly.

A Permanent Bad Hair Day

If you've suffered from the occasional bad hair day, consider yourself lucky—you could be afflicted with **Uncombable Hair Syndrome.** UHS is a rare disease that affects boys and girls before puberty. In fact, it's so rare that there have only been 60 cases reported in medical literature between 1973 and 1998.

UHS is an inherited disease with subtle hair changes noted in several preceding generations. It begins with a hair follicle that produces triangular hair shafts with several longitudinal grooves that also has very little pigment and is exceptionally dry and brittle. Because the hair is so dry, it rarely lies down; instead, the hair grows straight out from the scalp.

So what should you do if you are diagnosed with UHS? First, cancel your appointment with your hairdresser. People afflicted with UHS typically experience alopecia, or periodic baldness. The hair that does grow frequently breaks off before it has time to mature. And there is hope: There has been some success with medication, and some cases have recovered spontaneously several years after the first outbreak.

Myth and Truth

In the early 12th century, Christian Crusaders returned to Europe with hair-raising descriptions of the hashshashin as drug-crazed, wanton killers for hire. The reference to "drug-crazed" was false but was probably assumed from the sect's name—at the time, hashish and its mind-altering effects were known in the Middle East and Europe. However, the sect's purported connection to drug use was spurious. To the contrary, the group was meticulous, efficient, and focused.

The Crusaders were relatively safe; after all, the hashshashin's quarrel was with the Sunni and a particular Sunni ally, the Turkish Seljuk, who had reached a power-sharing agreement with the Sunni in 1092. Despite the limited nature of hashshashin reach and ambition, their terrifying reputation had wide impact. Many political assassinations across Europe, for instance, were conveniently blamed on the hashshashin, although the group never operated in that part of the world.

The Ultimate Sacrifice

Within the Middle East, though, Ismaili and hashshashin strength was such that the Seljuk sent an army against them. The action turned out to be ill considered, for not only was the Seljuk Vizier Nizam al-Mulk assassinated by stabbing, the army was defeated in its attempt to destroy the hashshashin fortress at Alamut. Although those who murdered the vizier were killed on the spot, the incident reiterated two key points—death by dagger and the immediate death of the assassins—that were trademarks of the hashshashin, who gladly gave their mortal lives in order to ensure their entry into Paradise.

Of course, soldiers have died "for the cause" throughout history. The difference is that the hashshashin not only did so systematically, but also to rid themselves of enemies and inspire fear in the enemies' followers. Particularly intimidating was the hashshashin belief that to survive in the commission of the crime was profoundly shameful. One way or another, a lot of blood was going to be spilled.

Toward the middle of the 13th century, hashshashin and particularly Ismaili power dwindled due to deadly inter-group disputes. There was also a new enemy, the Mongols, who attacked and finally destroyed the hashshashin fortress at Alamut in 1256. Although the hashshashin have faded into history, their unnerving brand of religiously ideological murder lives on.

Fast Facts

- Bears do not urinate while they are hibernating.

- Less than 1 percent of the poems written by Emily Dickinson were published during her lifetime.

- Insomnia is the top health complaint reported to American doctors.

- Lower back pain is the top physical problem.

- In 1900, the average white woman's life expectancy was only 48.7 years. For women of color, the life expectancy was 33.5 years.

- Brussels sprouts are ranked as the most hated vegetable in America.

- Your stomach creates a new mucus layer every two weeks.

- Your body produces 300 billion new cells every day.

- America goes through 12 billion bananas in a typical year.

- Humans are among only 3 percent of mammals that practice monogamy.

- Breast reduction is the fifth most popular plastic surgery procedure for men.

- Thomas Edison preferred to do his reading in Braille, and he proposed to his wife in Morse code.

- The rock band Jethro Tull was given the improbable name by its agent in 1968, who perhaps had a penchant for the history of farm mechanization: In 1701, an English farmer named Jethro Tull invented the revolutionary horse-drawn seed drill.

The Times They Are-A-Changin'

1943

- Wartime rationing continues in the United States.

- In January, Franklin Roosevelt and Winston Churchill plan an Allied war strategy at the Casablanca Conference. They agree that the ultimate goal is "unconditional surrender" by Germany and Japan.

- Rodgers and Hammerstein's *Oklahoma!* opens on Broadway. The first musical to treat music, dance, and story as an integrated unit, *Oklahoma!* runs for an unprecedented 2,000 performances and transforms American musical theater.

- From April 19 to May 16, inhabitants of the Warsaw Ghetto revolt against the occupying German troops. Although the Jewish resistance is poorly armed and malnourished, it takes the German garrison more than a month to subdue, and finally massacre, the ghetto's 56,000 residents.

- The Supreme Court rules that U.S. children do not have to salute the flag in school if it is against their religion.

- On October 30, the one and only time Bugs Bunny is outwitted is released in the Merrie Melodies animated short, "Falling Hare."

- The Pentagon is built in Arlington, Virginia. It is the largest office building in the world.

- W. E. B. DuBois becomes the first African American member of the National Institute of Letters.

- On September 21, Congress adopts a "one-world" resolution drafted by J. William Fulbright, the freshman representative from Arkansas. The Fulbright Resolution is the first step toward U.S. participation in what would become the United Nations.

- Dr. George Nicholas Papanicolaou publishes his study on the use of the vaginal smear test (now known as the Pap smear) to diagnose cervical cancer, then the leading cause of death among American women.

You Live *Where?*

❖ ❖ ❖ ❖

*Ever hear of Boring, Maryland? How about Nimrod,
Minnesota, or Boogertown, North Carolina? Many of the
small towns that dot the United States have interesting
stories (true or not) behind the oddball names. Here are a
few stops to put on your next cross-country road trip.*

- **Peculiar, Missouri**—As the story goes, 30 miles south of Kansas
City was a small community needing a name. The folk put off
naming their town—they didn't want to name it until their post
office actually required it. The postmaster wrote the U.S. government requesting the regal-sounding name "Excelsior." Unfortunately, the name was already taken. The postmaster wrote time
and time again for permission, using different names each time.
Finally, in his exasperation he told them, "We'll take any name you
have available as long as it's peculiar." Apparently it stuck!

- **Wide Awake, Colorado**—One night when a group of miners
were sitting around a campfire, they were trying to come up with a
good name for their new settlement. After passing a bottle around
late into the night, someone finally said, "Let's just turn in and talk
about it more when we're wide awake." "That's it!" shouted one of
the miners. "Let's call it Wide Awake!"

- **Toad Suck, Arkansas**—Before the Army Corps of Engineers
completed a highway bridge over the Arkansas River in 1973, the
most reliable way over the river was by barge. Next to the river
stood an old tavern where many of the bargemen would pull over
to drink rum and moonshine. As one version of the story has it,
it was at this tavern that they would "suck on bottles until they
swelled up like toads."

- **Accident, Maryland**—The town of Accident traces its history
to 1750 when a local named George Deakins accepted 600 acres
from King George II of England in relief of a debt. Deakins sent
out two independent surveying parties to find the best 600 acres

in the county—neither of which was aware of the other. By coincidence, they both surveyed the same plot, beginning at the same tree. Confident that no one else owned the property, Deakins named the tract the "Accident Tract."

- **Hell, Michigan**—There are several competing stories as to how Hell got its name. One story suggests that two traveling Germans stepped out of a stagecoach and remarked, *"So schön und hell!"* which loosely translates to "So beautiful and bright!" Hearing this, the neighbors focused on the latter part of the statement. Another story is that one of the early settlers, George Reeves, was asked what they should call the town. Ever the eloquent gentleman, Reeves replied, "For all I care, you can name it Hell!"

- **Ding Dong, Texas**—Despite evidence to the contrary, the town of Ding Dong was not named because it's located in Bell County. Nor was it named after Peter Hansborough Bell, the third Governor of Texas, nor for the Hostess snack cake. Back in the 1930s, Zulis and Bert Bell owned a country store, and they hired a creative sign painter named C. C. Hoover to put up a new sign. Hoover suggested that he dress up the sign by painting two bells on it with the words, "Ding Dong." The surrounding community quickly took to the name.

- **Tightwad, Missouri**—During the town's early days, a local store owner cheated a customer (who just happened to be a postman) by charging him an extra 50 cents for a watermelon. To get back at the proprietor, the postman started delivering mail to the newly dubbed town of Tightwad, Missouri.

Other Oddball Town Names:

- Hot Coffee, Missouri

- Truth or Consequences, New Mexico

- Embarrass, Wisconsin *and* Minnesota

- Knockenstiff, Ohio

Talk to the Expert

ABRAHAM LINCOLN IMPERSONATOR

Q: May I ask how tall you are?
A: I am 6′3″, almost. Mr. Lincoln was closer to 6′4″.

Q: Was this something you always wanted to do, or was it more like, "Hey, I'm an actor. I'm tall. This could be a good job for me."
A: I was actually cast as Lincoln in a play back in 1987. Fortunately for me, it turned into a part-time job/avocation; now this is how I earn a living.

Q: You are a former vice president of the National Association of Lincoln Presenters. How many Lincoln impersonators are there?
A: We have about 75, maybe 80 Lincolns, at least two dozen [of Lincoln's wife] Marys, and half a dozen of what we call "teams"—Abraham and Mary. Plus we have some other characters from history, like Frederick Douglass and Ward Hill Lamon, who was Lincoln's bodyguard in Washington, D.C. So the association now has roughly 200 members.

Q: Are there really enough jobs to keep you all busy full-time?
A: There are about six or eight of us that actually do this as a living. The rest do parades and things on Lincoln's birthday.

Q: So do you have to keep the Abe beard going all year, or with enough notice, can you grow it before a gig?
A: Well, I haven't shaved in close to 30 years, so I guess the answer is I keep it going. Plus I have enough events that I couldn't if I wanted to.

Q: What's the toughest thing about being Lincoln?
A: I think it's getting to know the history of the United States up to and around the Civil War. When I'm asked a question, sometimes I have to stop and think, "I can't answer that because that hasn't happened yet."

The *Really* Secret Service

Backroom swamis may have given fortune telling a bad name, but powerful people still seek ways to consult with dead relatives and discover future happenings.

Spiritual Speed Dating

Just when you think you know somebody: William Lyon Mackenzie King was Canada's prime minister for 22 years, but it wasn't until after his death in 1950 that his interest in the supernatural was revealed. With the help of mediums, King was able to contact the spirits of Leonardo da Vinci, Florence Nightingale, Robert Louis Stevenson, Anne Boleyn, Queen Victoria, his favorite dog, and, of course, his late mother. King was hooked. After starting with direct-voice mediums, he moved on to table-tapping, automatic writing, numerology, and tea-leaf reading. Lucky is the man who has a full-service seer.

King eventually gave up on mediums—not because they were a money drain, but because he believed he was a psychic himself. He did, however, swear off prognostications during World War II. Still, it was very likely that he followed the stories the British generated about Adolf Hitler's astrology readings—which appear never to have happened.

The Doubting Dutch

Since the time humans realized there was a tomorrow, they have been searching for ways to foretell what that tomorrow would bring. But as long as there have been seers and swamis, there have also been skeptics and scoffers who are quick to jump on the miscues and ambitions of people with possible extrasensory power. When you're a high-profile head of state, discretion is key—and that's where Queen Juliana of the Netherlands erred.

In 1956, skeptics were delighted when the queen was forced by public pressure to dispense with the services of her faith healer, Greet Hofmans, whom she had moved into the royal palace. The fear was that Hofmans was meddling in Dutch foreign policy and had far too much influence on the queen.

Stars Over the Rose Garden

American presidents have also sought the wisdom of psychics and astrologers, though it must be said their First Ladies were more often the ones to spearhead this interest. Among the believers were Mary Todd Lincoln, Florence Harding, and Nancy Reagan.

Nancy's involvement with astrologers such as Joan Quigley and Jeane Dixon are well documented in tell-all books, and Ronald admitted he was superstitious and regularly read newspaper astrology columns. In fact, as California's governor, he signed legislation that removed astrologers from the state criminal code, thus making them more legitimate. Their beliefs made the Reagans the butt of many jokes. In 1976, psychic Jeane Dixon missed a Reagan prediction, and Nancy fired her—showing that psychics, like musicians, are only as good as their last gig. Dixon was replaced by Quigley, who would boldly brag that she'd helped end the Cold War. Maybe yes, maybe no, but she certainly sold a lot of books.

While Calvin Coolidge, Franklin D. Roosevelt, and Richard Nixon were also rumored to be pro-astrology, Teddy Roosevelt let it all hang out when he signed on as a founding member of the American Society for Psychic Research.

Corporate Due Diligence

The ancient Romans would not go into battle without approval from their College of Augurs. The Greeks relied on the Oracle of Delphi. In our hip, sophisticated age it seems some of our high-flying moguls won't cut their mega-million dollar corporate deals without a thumbs-up from their "intuitionists" or "mentalists" whom the companies keep on retainer. Don't know what an intuitionist is? Basically, it's a psychic—minus the embarassing connotations of head scarves and gypsy tents.

One of these intuitionists is Laura Day, a New York City mother who averages five clients monthly, typically corporate businesses, law firms, and entertainment honchos. Her going rate is $10,000 a month per client. Granted, Day has to be on call around the clock, and she isn't paid overtime, but every job has a downside. It seems the business of fortune telling has come a long way from sideshow crystal ball readings.

High Demand

❖ ❖ ❖ ❖

This flowering poppy-plant-turned-addictive-narcotic shaped China and, along with it, much of the Western world.

Think the war on drugs is a recent phenomenon? Think again. The ancient Sumerians used opium and, if Greek and Roman texts are to be believed, so did Homer, Hesiod, and Hippocrates. And although many of us associate opium with China, it's very likely opium did not reach China until Muslim traders introduced it in the eighth century A.D. Read on for some more poppy-related facts.

The Real Demon Weed

When tobacco was introduced to China in the 17th century, it became an instant fad. Some bright person thought to combine tobacco—already an addictive substance—with opium. Soon opium's medicinal properties were replaced by its recreational uses. It became fashionable to enjoy tea accompanied by an opium pipe or two, much the way British gentry savored an after-dinner brandy and cigar.

Poppies for Presidents

While George Washington was growing marijuana (granted, for hemp), other important Americans were growing poppies. Thomas Jefferson grew the little red flowers at Monticello. For a time, visitors could purchase a packet of seeds descended from Jefferson's poppy plants at the Thomas Jefferson Center for Historic Plants gift shop. That is, until the University of Virginia ordered the plants be ripped up and the seeds destroyed after an unrelated 1991 campus drug bust made the Board of Directors jumpy.

Just a Spoonful of Sugar

In Victorian Britain, opium was a common ingredient in many medicines. Parents purchased concoctions to administer to their colicky, sick, or just plain fussy children. One of the most popular was Godfrey's Cordial, which contained a good bit of opium. But because of the era's cavalier attitude toward opium, many children ended up addicted to the drug or dead from opium poisoning.

He Said, She Said

"There are only three things women need in life: food, water, and compliments."

—Chris Rock

"My wife Mary and I have been married for 47 years and not once have we had an argument serious enough to consider divorce; murder, yes, but divorce, never."

—Jack Benny

"Never go to bed mad. Stay up and fight."

—Phyllis Diller

"If you want to read about love and marriage, you've got to buy two separate books."

—Alan King

"Show me where Stalin is buried and I'll show you a Communist Plot."

—Edgar Bergen

"Sex education may be a good idea in the schools, but I don't believe the kids should be given homework."

—Bill Cosby

"I went to a bookstore and asked the saleswoman, 'Where's the self-help section?' She said if she told me, it would defeat the purpose."

—George Carlin

"All men make mistakes, but married men find out about them sooner."

—Red Skelton

"The difference between divorce and legal separation is that a legal separation gives a husband time to hide his money."

—Johnny Carson

"Happiness is having a large, loving, caring, close-knit family— in another city."

—George Burns

"A man's true character comes out when he's drunk."

—Charlie Chaplin

Extreme Pet Pampering

❖ ❖ ❖ ❖

*When does pet pampering go too far? Some people are taking
the idea of luxury with their furry friends to new extremes.*

They're man's best friend, sure—but $12 million for a dog? Hotel
heiress Leona Helmsley made her priorities clear when she left a
large chunk of her family fortune to her pooch. A court ultimately
intervened, reducing the canine's inheritence to a measly $2 million
and redistributing the rest to Helmsley's charitable foundation. Still, a
nearly $200,000 annual budget isn't bad for an animal. As it turns out,
dogs living, well, high on the dog is not as unusual as one might think.

The Fashion
Plenty of pet owners are providing the high life for Fido. America's
pet spending tops $40 billion a year—double what we're shelling out
for children's toys. Some dogs are even amassing enormous acces-
sory collections. Designer carriers made by companies such as Juicy
Couture can go for nearly $300 a pop. Jewelers are marketing pricey
dog-collar charms made of real sapphires and pearls. There are per-
fume-scented leashes, fashionable doggy shoes, and specially designed
dog sunglasses. Add the fabulous outfits—complete with sweaters,
pajamas, and even hats—and Fido is one must-see pup. But it doesn't
stop at material possessions.

The Relaxation
Animal spas all over the country offer services such as facials for
cats and dogs. There are massages, acupuncture, and even cosmetic
surgeries on the menu. Hotels such as Manhattan's Ritzy Canine
Carriage House offer animal suites at $80 a night for large dogs. They
can also get an hour-long massage for $60, and the hotel also offers
grooming, training, a designer gift boutique, and room service. Other
centers, such as the Inn's Naples Dog Center in Florida, provide
special treatments that purportedly soothe an animal's emotional and
spiritual state. Some spas even have pet herbal rinses, mud baths,
swimming sessions, and surfing lessons for owners willing to splurge
on their furry friend.

The Drinks

Tired of drinking alone? Now your four-legged friend can cozy up to the bar with you. Happy Tail Ale is a nonalcoholic brew made for dogs. It's noncarbonated and boasts all-natural beef drippings. Yum.

Perhaps your pet isn't bent on beer. How about fine wine? Bark Vineyards has built a business out of gourmet wine for cats and dogs. Also alcohol-free, the popular drink includes such flavors as "Barkundy," "Sauvignon Bark," "Pino Leasheo," and "White Sniff 'N' Tail." Really.

The Food

What good are all the drinkable delights without some fancy food to accompany them? Companies such as Evanger's offer up organic meal creations that seem fit for a five-star restaurant. For an extra fee, your pet can opt for kosher meals instead.

Sounds pretty good, doesn't it? Well, don't be jealous: You can share your dog's dishes. Dick Van Patten's Natural Balance Dog Food is made for both dog and human consumption. Just think: Now you can enjoy chili or a Chinese entrée right alongside your precious widdle snookums.

The Electronics

People aren't the only ones who can enjoy electronics. Gadgets such as the Talking Bone allow you to record messages for your pet that it can play when you aren't around. Meanwhile, the Pet Spa Grooming Machine gives them a spa treatment at home, complete with aromatherapy. You can also buy CDs to expose your animals to foreign languages. Perhaps best of all, though, Edible Greeting Cards creates holiday messages for animals that can be eaten. Creative and convenient!

One thing's for sure: The pet-pampering industry is a booming business, and many pet owners are more than willing to dish out the dough. Heck, if people are spending more on their Chihuahuas than their children, then maybe the hotel heiress wasn't as crazy as she seemed.

On second thought...

The Intriguing Life of Lady Randy

❖ ❖ ❖ ❖

Wife of a British aristocrat and the mother of Sir Winston Churchill, Lady Randolph Churchill was an American-born socialite who both scandalized and fascinated British society with her lust for life—and her life of lust. Vivacious, flirtatious, charming, and disarming, she used her beauty and wit not only to advance her own social status, but also to further the legendary political careers of her husband and son.

An Early Influence

Jennie Jerome was an American princess long before she married into the British upper crust. The second daughter of Clara and "Wall Street King" Leonard Jerome was born in upstate New York on January 9, 1854, with a silver spoon firmly entrenched in her mouth.

Her father's leisure pursuits ranged from opera to horse racing and he was instrumental in founding the American Academy of Music and the American Jockey Club. Jerome also had an eye for the ladies: Jennie is rumored to have been named for Swedish nightingale Jenny Lind, who sang at the Jeromes's private theatre in their Madison Square residence.

Although Jennie moved to Paris with her mother and sisters in 1867, her father's philanthropic and philandering ways may have strongly influenced her character. A champion of countless charitable causes and staple of the London social scene, Jennie was also noted for her parade of paramours—possibly numbering up to 200.

Romance with Randolph

Lord Randolph Churchill, the third son of the 7th Duke of Marlborough, fell madly in love with the young, raven-haired American beauty he met at the Cowes Regatta in August 1873. Jennie accepted his proposal, but it took time for both sets of parents to acquiesce. They married the following April.

Seven and a half months later, their son, Winston Churchill, was born—with various justifications for his premature birth. Lord Randolph recalled Jennie's labor was hastened by a fall; her sister explained her nephew's early arrival as triggered by spirited dancing at the St. Andrew's ball. Sir Winston later quipped, "Although present on that occasion, I have no clear recollection of the events leading up to it."

Roller Coaster Social Status

Displaying a lively wit, a keen political intellect, and a talent for the piano, Lady Randolph was accepted into London's society, forgiven of her unfortunate American breeding. Dubbed "Lady Randy," her popularity soared when she was branded a "professional beauty," or P. B., a status equivalent to today's supermodel. A fashion icon, Jennie was noted for cinching her waist to a remarkable 19 inches.

Lady Randy's popularity with highly placed political figures reportedly extended beyond the parlor into pillow talk. She is reputed to have dallied with kings and counts, which some historians credit as the impetus for her husband's (and later, Winston's) political successes.

The Churchills were included in the Prince of Wales' inner circle until an unfortunate attempt by Lord Randolph to blackmail the prince backfired, and the couple and Winston were exiled to Ireland for seven years. During this time, Jennie gave birth to a second son, John Strange Spencer Churchill. Six years Winston's junior, he was reputed to be the lovechild of Irish nobleman Colonel John Strange Jocelyn.

Maternal Misfit to Political Manager

Restored to the prince's favor, the Churchills resumed their A-list social life, which left little time for parenting. Winston and Jack were raised by a nanny, then packed off to boarding school. Although Jennie's mothering skills are often disparaged, young Winston appears to have felt a bond with her. In an 1887 letter imploring her to spring him from school to attend the Queen's jubilee, Winston addresses her "My dear Mamma" and writes, "I love you so much dear Mummy and I know you love me too much to disappoint me."

Fast Facts

- *Your right lung is bigger than your left lung.*

- *Most people take about 23,000 breaths a day.*

- *A skin cell doesn't live for more than a day.*

- *Air Canada banned smoking before any other North American airline.*

- *Modern-day "tightie whities" derived from the European-style bathing suit.*

- *The first paper towel came from defective toilet paper. Someone at the Scott company saw a crumpled, seemingly ruined roll of TP and decided it should be sold as a kind of disposable hand towel.*

- *The first modern (and recorded) vending machine was used to sell tobacco in England during the 17th century.*

- *The yo-yo has been used as an actual weapon for hunting in the Philippines.*

- *Women's hearts beat faster than men's hearts.*

- *Men get hiccups more often than women.*

- *Tijuana, Mexico, is the most common foreign city visited by Americans.*

- *If you ever need to wake a penguin in a hurry, try stepping on its foot. That's said to be the quickest way to wake them up.*

- *The 50,000-word novel* Gadsby, *written by Ernest Wright, does not contain a single "e."*

Sea-Monkey See, Sea-Monkey Do

In the past 50 years, millions of people have ordered Sea-Monkeys. Alas, these people were disappointed to find their microscopic pets don't wear tiaras or even live very long. Here's a look at the PR machine that turned a homely crustacean into a generation-spanning fad.

The Man Behind the Monkey

In 1957, mail-order marketer Harold von Braunhut had already given the world Invisible Goldfish and X-Ray Spex. Upon encountering brine shrimp, he saw potential for his next great venture, which he called "Instant Life."

Brine shrimp, or *artemia salina,* are the perfect pet for someone who doesn't have a lot of space and doesn't mind if their pet has zero personality. Fully grown, they are only ¾ inch long. The official Web site says the name stems from their monkey-like "funny behavior and long tail," but any simian resemblance is questionable. What appealed to von Braunhut was their cost-effectiveness: Brine shrimp eggs can exist out of water for years, dormant and seemingly lifeless. But just add water and the eggs hatch, making them perfect for warehouse storage and mail-order shipping.

A Shrimp by Any Other Name...

Alas, initial sales were lackluster. In 1962, von Braunhut renamed his product "Sea-Monkeys," marketing them through colorful ads in comic books that depicted them as a family of smiling, playful merfolk. Despite fine-print warnings that these were not accurate representations, people were smitten. Von Braunhut began selling other products that people could buy to show their Sea-Monkeys affection, such as special desserts and aphrodisiac elixirs. Soon, competing toy companies began carrying Sea-Monkey accessories such as racetracks, ski lodges, and elaborately themed aquariums.

Sea-Monkey ads are still ubiquitous. The first generations of Sea-Monkey owners have since wised up, but each year another generation begs to order them.

ESCAPE!

QUICKSAND

In countless adventure movies, people fall prey to quicksand. They're unable to get out, and soon they're in over their heads in the goopy stuff. But most of quicksand's properties is pure hype. You don't have to be Houdini to escape this natural pitfall.

Quicksand is a unique substance made of fine sand, clay, and salt water. Stress causes the compound to become more fluid, which is why people struggling tend to sink lower down. But it's impossible for a human to be pulled all the way under; our bodies aren't dense enough to have that happen. Still, one errant step and you'll find yourself stuck—unless you know how to beat the trap.

- **Avoid Moving:** Because of the sand's stress factor, struggling and writhing around will only hurt your chances of escape. Relax and remain as still as possible. In fact, the people who have drowned in quicksand only did so because they panicked and were flailing about.

- **Don't Get Pulled:** Having friends pull on you will not do any good; in fact, it will make matters worse. That kind of pressure may actually injure you. The best way they can help is by spreading wooden boards across the ground until they can reach you and give you a solid surface to climb up on.

- **Use Leg Power:** Scientists suggest gently pumping your legs as if you were riding a bicycle. This creates open space in the sand where water can flow in and help loosen the stuff.

- **Plan in Advance:** The leg movements can work, but your best bet is to carry a thick wooden pole, or walking stick, with you while in an area known for having quicksand. Then, the second you start to sink, lay the pole flat on the ground, horizontally across the surface of the quicksand. Move your body so the pole is under your back. This will stop you from sinking. Then, one leg at a time, pull yourself out and slowly move to stable ground.

FROM THE VAULTS OF HISTORY

Our Thoughts Eggs-actly

As foods go, eggs fill a rather mundane but important part of diets around the world. But they have also been at the center of many cultural beliefs. Long thought of as a symbol of life and rebirth, the Greeks and Romans revered eggs and buried them in tombs along with the dead. The Maoris also held eggs in high esteem and would place them in the hands of the dead before burial. Many other egg customs still exist: Eggs that are laid on Good Friday and eaten on Easter Sunday are believed to protect their consumer throughout the entire year. In Germany, eggs that are hung in evergreen trees represent powerful symbols of rebirth and renewal.

How Eastre Became Easter

Along with eggs, the Easter Bunny is the featured guest when celebrating the annual holiday. But why not a cow, goat, or pig? When Christian Crusaders attempted to convert pagans to their religion, they found that the pagan festivals of Eastre (or Eostre, the Germanic goddess of fertility and growth) often coincided with the celebration of the resurrection of Christ. Eastre, meaning "spring," represented the goddess of fertility and was symbolically represented in the form of a rabbit.

Egg Fight!

In one wild story from the so-called "Easter Wars" circa A.D. 975, a light-hearted battle broke out, pitting the Bishop and Dean of Chester, England, against the cathedral choir. As legend has it, an egg fight began during the Easter service and lasted for more than an hour until all combatants ran out of "ammunition."

Fabulous Fabergé

In the 19th century, Carl Fabergé, the court jeweler to the Czar of Russia, took the plain old egg to dizzyingly new heights by creating beautiful, hand-decorated eggs out of porcelain, gold, and crystal. The incredibly intricate Fabergé eggs are still coveted and sold as priceless works of art around the world.

Road Trip:
Pakistan's M2 Highway

❖ ❖ ❖ ❖

On Pakistan's paradoxical M2 highway, law and order is
exactly what you'll get when you get behind the wheel.

Sharif's Dream

In 1991, Pakistan's Prime Minister Nawaz Sharif decided that his
country needed a new highway. It took him more than six years to
get the job done, but in 1997, the M2 was officially open for business. The road begins in the city of Lahore and runs 367 miles
through the hills, valleys, and over the rivers of the Punjab province
until it reaches Islamabad, the capital of Pakistan.

One of the most extraordinary characteristics of the M2 is its
perfectly manicured appearance—it's probably the only road in
the world that is swept by hand. Crews work diligently to keep the
pride and joy of the Pakistani roadways neat and tidy, actually using
brooms to brush away the grit.

The Changing Landscape

A trip that used to take six hours on the older roads now takes three
hours on the M2. There are six lanes to choose from, but that doesn't
mean it's an *über*-fast highway like Germany's Autobahn. The speed
limits are strictly enforced, especially near the hairpin turns that
occur in the northwest Salt Ranges. In that area, going over 20 miles
per hour is extremely dangerous.

In some areas of Pakistan, police have been known to take a bribe
from time to time, but that behavior won't fly on the M2. Impecca-
bly dressed highway police watch the highway with radar guns at the
ready and aren't shy about pulling over those with a lead foot.

For as proud as Pakistan is of its meticulously maintained highway, there aren't too many people using it. High fuel costs, civil
unrest, a poor economy, and a relatively low number of drivers mean
that the M2 is a pretty lonely, empty road.

ANAGRAMS

An anagram is a word or phrase that exactly reproduces the letters in another word or phrase. The most interesting of them reflect or comment on the subject of the first.

Pub's motto—Bottoms up

Life's aim—Families

A sentence of death—Faces one at the end

Rest in Peace—A sincere pet

Elvis—Lives

William Shakespeare—I'll make a wise phrase

Jay Leno—Enjoy L.A.

The Morse Code—Here come dots

Microsoft Windows—Sown in discomfort

The eyes—They see

Barbie doll—Liberal bod

The Titanic disaster—Death, it starts in ice

Western Union—No wire unsent

Bruce Springsteen—Creep brings tunes

Tom Cruise—So I'm cuter

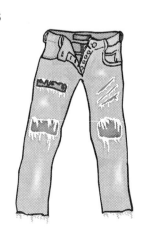

Dick Cheney—Needy chick

Debit card—Bad credit

A decimal point—I'm a dot in place

Jennifer Aniston—Fine in torn jeans

Clothespins—So let's pinch

Spice Girls—Pig slicers

Christmas—Trims cash

Whip It!: Roller Derby Names

❖ ❖ ❖ ❖

Roller derby is back on the scene in a big way. Check
out this fun list of derby girls' nom de skate.

In 2004, the Women's Flat Track Roller Derby Association was
founded, bringing women's competitive roller derby back to the
masses. With roots going as far back as the 1930s, derby bouts are
rowdy, risky, fun, and imbued with a special brand of gallows humor,
as evidenced by the names of the players, referees, and support staff.

There are multiple reasons derby girls skate under an alias. For
one, the fake names are a lot of fun, which is basically derby's MO.
Alter egos also allow derby girls to show their ferocious sides: mild-
mannered working girls and stay-at-home moms by day can be
competitive, outrageous skaters by night. Below is just an example
of names in a list of derby girls, referees, and staff members past and
present numbering well over 13,000 worldwide and growing.

Name and League
Tequila Mockingbird—Windy City Rollers
Bone Crawford—Jersey Shore Roller Girls
Gefilte Fists—Philly Roller Girls
Midwife Crisis—Arch Rival Roller Girls
Genghis Connie—Assassination City Roller Derby
Grrrilla—Sonoma County Roller Derby
Graceless Kelly—Maine Roller Derby
Doris Day of the Dead (referee)—Windy City Rollers
Skatie Couric—Boston Derby Dames
Cruisin' B. Anthony—Ithaca Roller Derby
Grudge Judy—Texas Rollergirls
Abbey Rogue—Denver Roller Dolls
Raggedy Animal—Gotham Girls Roller Derby
Tall Drinka Slaughter—Windy City Rollers
Ella Mental—Rollers Syndicate
Count Smacula—Pikes Peak Derby Dames
Bloody Holly—L.A. Derby Dolls
Octopushy—Mad Rollin' Dolls

Welcome to the Kalakuta Republic

❖ ❖ ❖ ❖

*Fela Kuti is an internationally known Afropop musician. He was
also the leader of a Nigerian anti-government movement. Read
on to discover one man's trials and tribulations, as seen from
his compound, otherwise known as the "Kalakuta Republic."*

A Corrupt Country

In the mid-1970s, Nigeria, with more than 100 million citizens, was
the most populous country in Africa; as a new member of OPEC, it
was also one of the world's leading oil exporters. Although enormous
amounts of foreign money flowed into the government's coffers,
it quickly flowed into the hands of the ruling class. But life for the
vast majority of Nigerians was as hard as ever. Crime was rampant,
poverty widespread, and all forms of dissention were violently sup-
pressed. Yet one man in Lagos continued to publicly criticize the
rulers and their backers: the musician, Fela Kuti.

From Lagos to London to Los Angeles

Afropop is a hypnotic, compelling blend of American funk arrangements, European classical compositional technique, jazz, and
African tribal rhythms. Kuti, the genre's originator, was the son
of a decidedly left-wing, middle-class family from Lagos. His jazz
highlife band, Koola Lobitos, attracted sufficient notoriety to justify a 1969 tour of the United States. Kuti would later say that the
ten months he spent in America galvanized all of his later political
thinking.

Africa 70 Is Born

While in the United States, Kuti was exposed to the black power
movement. A Black Panther friend gave him a copy of Malcolm X's
autobiography; Kuti was an instant convert. He returned to
Nigeria and formed Africa 70, a huge ensemble complete with
horns, saxophonists, guitarists, dancers, singers, and entourage.
Kuti and his band established themselves at the local club Shrine.

Although his songs frequently attacked the status quo, the country's leaders were generally content to leave the "crazy" musician alone.

An Independent Republic

Kuti established the area around his Lagos home as a commune, complete with medical facilities, farm animals, and a recording studio. Kuti went a step further and had the compound fenced with electrified barbed wire and proclaimed it a sovereign nation—the Kalakuta Republic. With Africa 70 selling millions of albums, Kuti's political and social diatribes became increasingly brazen. Military leaders hated him for his flagrant criticism, and the bourgeoisie hated him because of his free lifestyle.

Tensions between Kuti and the military reached a breaking point in 1976, following the second World Black and African Festival of the Arts and Culture. Kuti withdrew Africa 70 from the official lineup and staged a counter festival at Shrine, where he debuted "Zombie," a song mocking government soldiers. "Zombie" became an overnight sensation, but for the military, it was the last straw.

The Raid and Its Aftermath

On February 18, 1977, more than 1,000 soldiers amassed outside the Kalakuta Republic compound. They barricaded the building, set fire to the generator, and attacked the building with savage ferocity. Soldiers beat people, raped women, and smashed equipment. Kuti's aging mother, herself a renowned political activist, was thrown through a window and later died from her injuries. Kuti was dragged from the building and severely beaten, suffering a fractured skull and broken bones. The rest of the residents were carted to jail or the hospital. A government-sponsored committee later found no wrongdoing on the part of the soldiers.

Kuti and his music survived the raid. He established a new Kalakuta Republic and one year later defiantly married 27 women in a Yoruba ceremony. Though he was often jailed and beaten, he continued to reside in Lagos where he performed and preached against the ruling power. Kuti's persistence earned him the name *Abami Eda,* or "Chief Priest," among his fans. He remained a vibrant force in Nigeria and in world music until his death from AIDS in 1997. More than one million people attended his funeral procession.

HOW IT ALL BEGAN

Banning the Rays

Sunglasses have been around a lot longer than you'd think. The Arctic-dwelling Inuit found more functional uses for whalebones than merely as stays in women's corsets. Among these innovations was what may be the first pair of sunglasses: whalebone with narrow slits, designed to reduce snow and ice glare, thus preventing snow blindness.

Inscrutable 14th-century Chinese judges made themselves even more enigmatic by wearing smoked quartz glasses to hide their facial expressions while in the courtroom.

In the 20th century, "shades" became popular. Movie stars wore them. So did pilots, musicians, and gangsters—the latter notably when appearing as witnesses in front of Senate subcommittees.

Bee-ing Sensible

In the category of "you can never be too safe," Californian Virginia Buttes has come up with a self-contained plastic enclosure for protection against killer bees. Not only that, it folds up and stores in a compact pouch that fits nicely into a pocket, purse, or knapsack. Now we need something for people who accidentally sit on a hill of fire ants.

What's Hot, Corny, and Cool?

Anyone who walks into a ballpark or a 7-Eleven store knows about hot dogs. In fact, the convenience-store chain sells 100 million a year, and the United States has officially declared July National Hot Dog Month.

Since 1938, people have also been treated to corn dogs, a cornmeal-coated wiener on a stick. Then, in 2002, along came a new product. On Red Sox Opening Day in Fenway Park, concessionaires put Cool Dogs on offer.

Cool Dogs look sort of like hot dogs: wiener-shape ice cream in a hot dog bun-shape sponge cake. As for condiments, buyers can choose from whipped cream, hot fudge, cherries, candy—just about anything other than mustard, relish, ketchup, or sauerkraut.

Cool Dogs kept a low profile until 2005 when they turned up at the Super Bowl. Suddenly, the treat was making its mark and began to be available in dairy cases throughout the country.

Daily Life in England, A.D. 1100

❖ ❖ ❖ ❖

Think it's rough nowadays? Step back 900 years, and you'd see a whole new definition of hard living. Life was completely different in A.D. 1100: People believed the earth was flat; serfs were tied to the land, not quite slaves and not quite free; and the first Crusaders had sailed for the Holy Lands, but had not yet returned with new knowledge from the Islamic world. It wasn't obvious, but the Dark Ages were coming to an end. Here's a look at what daily life was like back then.

There was little room for social climbing.

From king to serf, everyone was born into a set position in society, and every rung of the feudal social ladder was defined by a complicated exchange of rights and services. The only possibility for social mobility was in the church. Men and women from all walks of life could join a religious order and be trained for a position based on ability rather than birth. Even the poorest country priest could usually read and write—skills the local lord might not have.

Living conditions were, well, *rustic.*

Most people lived in small rural settlements and never went more than a few miles from where they were born. With the exception of the local manor, houses were no sturdier than those built by the Three Little Pigs: made of turf, or straw-reinforced mud, with thatched roofs. Floors were beaten earth that were covered with rushes. Instead of a fireplace, open fires burned on a raised hearth in the middle of the room; smoke found its way out a hole in the ceiling that also let in wind and rain. Furniture was at most a rough table and some stools. People slept on straw pallets on the floor.

Basically, everyone smelled horrible.

The only way to wash yourself, or anything else, was to carry water inside and heat it over the fire. Even nobility, who had servants to haul and heat water, did not bathe regularly. Clothing was not designed to be washed. Peasants often had only one set of rough wool garments, while nobles' clothing was embroidered with jewels and trimmed with fur. The rich hung their most expensive clothing on hooks in the privies (basically, the bathroom) that were built into the walls of manors and castles, believing the fumes would kill lice and other vermin. However, doing so did nothing to improve the smell of unwashed velvet.

Sanitation was primitive, especially in the towns. London had only 16 public latrines for a population of 30,000. People emptied slop jars into the streets, even though it was illegal. Many private homes had cesspits underneath the floorboards; when the pit filled up, the householder paid a "gong farmer" to dig it out. (Part of his pay was anything valuable that he found in the pit as well as the right to use the sewage as fertilizer.)

The food was a bit bland.

The potato, which later became the staple diet of the poor, would not reach Europe from the New World for another 400 years. Instead, peasants relied on grain for both food and drink: bread, porridge, and home-brewed ale. Most peasants lived on barley and oats, supplemented with vegetables from the garden and roots, nuts, and berries from the woods. Honey was the only sweetener. Most families could afford to keep chickens and a pig, but animals often had to be sold for cash to pay rent or taxes. Only the wealthiest could afford pepper or other spices, which came overland from the East—a trip that took more than a year. It was a hungry time, made hungrier by frequent crop failures and a growing population.

- *Ale wasn't all that alcoholic, and was drunk in large quantities because the ingredients were boiled, which usually made it safer to drink than water.*

- *The flour used to bake and cook was so gritty it would wear down tooth enamel over time.*

William Shakespeare, Screenwriter

❖ ❖ ❖ ❖

Does that big-screen storyline seem familiar? You may have actually read it in a book. The following movies are all based on plays from the original storyteller himself, William Shakespeare.

She's the Man *(Twelfth Night):* This modern version of Shakespeare's cross-dressing comedy stars teen actress Amanda Bynes as Viola.

Forbidden Planet *(The Tempest):* Many fans draw parallels between Shakespeare's classic story and this 1956 sci-fi flick, which features a stranded spaceship, a robot, and Oscar-nominated special effects.

O *(Othello):* Set in a high school, this adaptation is about a black basketball star in a mostly white world who is driven to murder his girlfriend Desi after being deceived by a jealous teammate.

Scotland, PA *(MacBeth):* This dark comedy transports the tragedy to 1975 as Joe and Pat McBeth scheme to take over the hamburger stand where they work.

My Own Private Idaho *(Henry IV, Part 1):* Directed by Gus Van Sant, this indie film about a pair of young male hustlers features sections of Shakespeare's script.

Ran *(King Lear):* A 1985 Japanese film with a $12 million budget, *Ran* follows the demise of Lord Hidetora Ichimonji and his three sons who are battling for power.

10 Things I Hate About You *(Taming of the Shrew):* This late-'90s adaptation features a twisted plot in which teenage sisters Bianca and Kat face the tribulations of dating.

Angoor *(Comedy of Errors):* This Bollywood slapstick comedy tells the tale of two sets of identical twins separated at birth. Come to think of it, so does *Big Business*, starring Bette Midler and Lily Tomlin.

West Side Story *(Romeo & Juliet):* This Broadway-phenom-turned-movie-musical retells the classic love story on the streets of New York City. However, instead of the Montagues and the Capulets, it's the Jets versus the Sharks.

Fast Facts

- *The human big toe has fewer bones than its smaller neighboring toes.*

- *The sound of a Harley motorcycle could have been trademarked: Harley-Davidson tried to buy the rights to the vrooming noise, as well as to the word "hog." Both attempts were denied.*

- *Ben & Jerry's gives its employees three free pints of ice cream every day.*

- *Rod Stewart once dug graves for a living.*

- *Sean Connery once polished coffins for cash.*

- *Danny DeVito almost became a professional hairdresser.*

- *A watermelon contains 92 percent water.*

- *A pound of peanut butter is made up of 720 peanuts.*

- *Stephen King's first story, "I Was a Teenage Grave Robber" was published in a fanzine when he was 18 years old.*

- *A hummingbird can dive at up to 60 miles per hour.*

- *A greyhound runs about 41 miles per hour.*

- *Before James Madison, U.S. presidents wore knee breeches instead of long pants.*

- *Zip codes didn't exist until 1963.*

- *Schenectady, New York, has the honor of having the Zip code 12345.*

The Mystery of the Fortune Cookie

❖ ❖ ❖ ❖

*The fortune cookie may be the most famous
symbol of Chinese food in America. But venture over to China and
you won't find an advice-filled twist of dough anywhere in sight.*

A fortune cookie is to Chinese food as a stomachache is to a greasy-spoon joint: There's no question it'll follow the meal. It turns out, though, that the former is far from common in the actual country of China; in fact, you might be hard-pressed to find anyone there who's even heard of one. So where did this crunchy cookie come from? It seems there's no single proverb that holds the answer.

The Chinese Theories

Some theories trace the cookie's creation to the early Chinese immigrants in America as a means to carry on traditions from their homeland. One story says the cookie's roots originated as far back as 12th-century China, during the rule of the Yuan Dynasty.

According to that tale, rebel monks started making a special kind of mooncake, into which they'd slip secret messages to their comrades without the invading Mongols finding out. Legend has it the men baked the cakes, messages and all, then sold them to Chinese families to spread their plans for upcoming rebellions.

Another theory traces the first fortune back to ancient Chinese parlor games. In these sessions, men would write proverbs on paper and then place them inside twisted pastries.

Yet another hypothesis puts the cookie credit in the hands of George Jung, founder of Los Angeles's Hong Kong Noodle Company. Jung is believed by many to have cooked up the first fortune cookies as a way to add some happiness in the dreary post–World War I era. However, some speculate the cookies may have also served as a simple distraction for Jung's guests while their food was being prepared.

The Japanese Alternative

The other school of thought claims the Japanese actually invented the fortune cookie. Researchers have found family bakeries in the city of Kyoto that have been making similarly shaped fortune crackers since the late 1800s, long before the treat first surfaced in America around 1907.

Called *tsujiura senbei* (fortune crackers) or *omikuji senbei* (written fortune crackers), the Japanese cookies do have some differences: They are larger, darker in color, and have more of a sesame-miso flavor than the vanilla-butter combo of the Chinese variety. The fortunes are also presented within the fold rather than inside the cavity. Even so, fortune-cookie devotees insist the similarities are too great to ignore.

Some Japanese families theorize that the cookies first came over to the United States around 1890, when a man named Makoto Hagiwara helped build the Japanese Tea Garden in San Francisco's Golden Gate Park. A nearby bakery called Benkyodo, Makoto's family claims, served the cookies to visitors. It was from there, they say, that other Asian restaurants in California picked up the idea, leading to its nationwide explosion.

Fortune Resistance

Wherever it began, years later the fortune cookie still hasn't taken off within the nation of China. An American importer named Nancy Anderson is trying to change that, but the work isn't coming easy. Anderson imports fortune cookies from California to Hong Kong to sell to restaurants, mainly ones that cater to—surprise, surprise—foreign tourists.

With added packaging requirements, translation costs, and international taxes, the cookies end up costing more than double their worth. All factors considered, Anderson has found most restaurant owners wary of the desserts and hesitant to make an investment; her efforts have yielded little success.

International disdain aside, though, the beloved little cookie doesn't seem to be in any danger of disappearing from Chinese custom in America—and that's one fortune you can count on.

Fumbling Felons

Hands Up! This Is a Confession!

Sometimes it just doesn't pay to volunteer—just ask the two crooks who were on trial for armed robbery and assault. In the courtroom, the female victim took the stand, and in a quavering voice, proceeded to tell her story. Then the prosecutor asked her the jackpot question: "Are the two men who committed this horrible crime in the courtroom today?"

Before she could say anything, the two defendants helpfully raised their hands. Even the judge cracked up at the sight of the two crooks aiding their own conviction.

It's Always Something

We've all had one of *those* days—a flat tire, kids late for school, boss yelling for no good reason, grocery bag shreds on the way out of the supermarket. Even criminals have bad days.

An Ohio crook walked into a local café, waved a gun, and demanded money from the proprietors. The waitress obligingly filled a paper bag with cash. So far, so good, right? But as the thief was escaping across the parking lot toward his pick-up truck, the bag ripped open, and the money spilled out onto the concrete. The crook grabbed as much money as he could with his hands. Then, fists stuffed with greenbacks, he got to his pick-up, fished his keys out of his pocket, and thrust them into the door lock.

The key broke off in the lock.

Not wanting to admit defeat, the criminal still tried desperately to open the door. He twisted, turned, jiggled, and rattled the lock, but to no avail. However, his gyrations did accomplish something—he shot himself in the foot with his gun.

Finally realizing that this wasn't his day, the thief gave up and limped from the parking lot. But when he hobbled into a hospital emergency room a few minutes later, the staff notified police, who took him to the station without further mishap.

Trudeaumania

❖ ❖ ❖ ❖

Canadians called him PET, but this prime minister could bite.

The Man for All Seasons

Pierre Elliot Trudeau, Canada's prime minister during the 1970s, was no rock star, but rock stars might well envy his ability to enthrall a crowd. Prior to his election, the usually reserved country was awash in "Trudeaumania." So much so that his swooning electorate familiarly knew Trudeau by his initials, PET.

A Renaissance man, Trudeau was as quick to quote Plato as paddle a canoe down the Amazon or shepherd legislation through a lupine Parliament. While he had the dashing charisma of former American president John F. Kennedy, he wasn't so easily tied down: Throughout his first campaign for leadership he was an eligible bachelor. When he married in 1971, it was to a 22-year-old beauty he'd met in Tahiti. He was 51.

Trudeau's background included University of Montreal Law School, the Sorbonne, the London School of Economics, and Harvard, all the while using his downtime to wander around the world. He savored life, and let Canadians know it. The nation ate it up, even relishing Trudeau's occasional outbursts of temper. On one occasion, an annoyed Trudeau gave the finger to the entire Opposition party in Parliament. In 1969, he chastised a boy throwing grain at him while he was giving a speech in Saskatchewan: "If you don't stop that, I'll kick you right in the ass."

The End of an Era

Trudeau often showed his fun side, notably during the most solemn of ceremonies. When he did a pirouette behind the back of the Queen of England while she was signing Canada's new Constitution, all but Canada's staunchest royalists and rabid Anglophobes were delighted. PET was their guy, and he served for three terms, formally retiring in June 1984. When his term ended, he opted to whisk himself over the hill in his Mercedes sports car rather than ride in the official black limo.

Gotta Dance

*What do wild, maniacal dancing, a strange disease,
and patron saints have in common with each other?
If you guessed the medieval epidemic called
"dancing mania," you'd be right!*

Taking the Fun Out of "Fungus"

"Dancing mania" is often associated with several diseases: St. Anthony's Fire, St. Vitus's Dance, and St. John's Dance. All three describe bizarre neurological diseases that hit Europe between the 13th and 18th centuries. The first outbreak of dancing mania affected the majority of the inhabitants of Aachen, Germany, in 1374, and it reached its pinnacle 100 years later in Strasbourg, France. While there are a number of plausible theories about how the disease took hold of nearly an entire population, the most widely accepted hypothesis 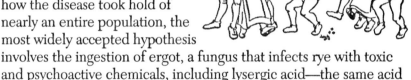 involves the ingestion of ergot, a fungus that infects rye with toxic and psychoactive chemicals, including lysergic acid—the same acid that would ultimately be synthesized into LSD.

The symptoms of dancing mania were as peculiar as their origin. Those affected exhibited uncontrolled and painful seizures, diarrhea, paresthesias (a pins-and-needles feeling), itching, foaming at the mouth, maniacal laughter, erratic gyrations, jerking movements, nausea, hallucinations, headaches, and vomiting. But the most appalling symptoms were involuntary muscular contortions of the face and extremities that appeared to resemble dancing. That's where the bizarre treatments came in.

Take Two Tunes and Call Me in the Morning

Medicine, being as primitive as it was, had no plausible theories or cures for the diseases; the "science" often took as much from medieval witchcraft as it did from the Catholic Church. And because the diseases affected thousands of people, physicians needed to come up with an effective treatment for the masses, and fast. After a number of unsuccessful treatments, the medical community finally agreed on a solution: music.

In the 14th century, music was considered a "magic bullet" for just about everything and was used extensively to drive demons from anyone with an inexplicable malady. So, the town's elders gathered the afflicted and marched them through the center of town to the accompaniment of upbeat music in hopes that it—coupled with copious amounts of sweat generated from the movement—would exorcise the demons. Being under the spell of the gyrating rhythms (and the ingredients of LSD), many of the afflicted ended up tearing off their clothes and dancing through the streets naked until they fell to the ground, exhausted. The few who weren't immediately cured were eventually hauled off to the nearest cathedral where they offered themselves in prayer—that's where the saints come in.

The Saints Come Marching In

St. Vitus was the only son of a well-to-do Sicilian senator who went on to perform a number of documented miracles. The Sicilian administrator (think mayor) was fed up with Vitus's antics and sentenced him to martyrdom. Just before losing his head—literally—Vitus prayed to God that those afflicted by the dance mania be cured.

Dancing mania also came to be known as St. John's disease because one of the first major outbreaks arose in St. Johannestanz, Germany.

A continent away, St. Anthony was an Egyptian monk who lived between A.D. 251 and 356. Withdrawing into an abstemious life at an early age, he finally emerged from years of solitary confinement to establish one of the first monasteries. During his self-imposed confinement, it is said that he battled with the devil, who attacked him with wild beasts and temptations of exotic feasts and naked women. But Anthony's prayers and penitence prevailed over evil. During the 12th century, the Order of Hospitallers of St. Anthony in Grenoble, France, became the destination of those afflicted with dancing mania, which is also called St. Anthony's Fire.

Word Histories

Abracadabra: The magical word of magicians is one of the few words completely without meaning. Thought to invoke the mystical powers of infinity, the word was first recorded in the second century A.D. by the poet Quintus Severus Sammonicus. Many scholars believe it is a corruption of the Hebrew words for Father *(Ab)*, Son *(Ben)* and Holy Spirit *(Ruach Acadsch)*.

Acre: At one point in its history, this word referred to a measurement of the amount of land a yoke of oxen could plow from sunrise to sunset.

Slapstick: This term once referred to sticks that were tied together and used by early vaudeville performers to strike one another, producing a loud, sharp sound. The term later came to mean any production involving rough but comedic behavior.

Explode: Though the term now refers to a destructive force, its original meaning was from the Latin *ex-* and *plaudere* (to applaud). It referred to the clapping and heckling that poor actors received from disgruntled audiences.

Jackpot: This word comes from the pot of cash accumulated by gamblers playing a type of draw poker that does not end until one of the players has a hand containing two jacks or better.

Scofflaw: During the Prohibition era, Massachusetts's millionaire and prohibitionist Delcevare King offered a prize of $200 to whoever could come up with the best word to describe those who ignored the 18th Amendment. King received more than 25,000 entries; among them, Henry Irving Shaw and Kate Butler came up with the winning term, "scofflaw." Although the word wasn't very popular in the 1920s, it returned to usage in the '50s when New York City's Chief Magistrate John Murtagh used it repeatedly to refer to those who refused to pay their traffic fines.

Villain: If you used this word in feudal England you would have been referring to a poor but honest person who worked as a serf on a noble's estate. The name comes from the Latin *villanus* ("farm servant") and evolved to mean a person capable of base acts. Its first recorded use to refer to a dastardly character is in an 1822 play by Charles Lamb.

Cracked Despots

They say it's lonely at the top—perhaps that's why certain world leaders have wandered over the fine line separating genius from insanity. Or maybe it is the nature of power itself that strips some men of their humanity. As Lord Acton succinctly stated in 1887, "Power tends to corrupt, and absolute power corrupts absolutely." Whatever the explanation, the following dictators displayed some absolutely abominable personality traits.

Nero

Legend has it this Roman ruler fiddled while Rome burned. While technically incorrect (the violin hadn't been invented yet), figuratively speaking Nero may have somehow fiddled with the great fire of A.D. 64. Although he was out of town when the blaze began, it was widely rumored that Nero wanted to raze Rome's slums and rebuild the city into a shiny-new Neropolis.

Whether he ordered the arson or his enemies did in an attempt to frame him, Nero turned the situation to his advantage by blaming an obscure new sect called the Christians. In return, Nero had their leader Peter crucified upside down on Vatican Hill and had Paul beheaded. He turned the persecution of Christians into public entertainment by throwing them in with wild beasts at his circus. Some he used as human torches to light his gardens, smearing their bodies with pitch and setting them ablaze.

But this wasn't necessarily new to the people of Rome: Nero certainly was no hero, and his immoral activities shocked even the most sexually liberated Romans. He took his own mother for a mistress and then had her murdered. He also trumped up charges of adultery against his wife Octavia, then later had her killed so he could marry his mistress Poppaea Sabina, who also happened to be his friend's wife.

When not indulging his lusts, Nero entertained himself by entertaining others—whether they wanted to be entertained or not. Performing before captive audiences, Nero sang songs, recited poetry, and played the lyre. No one was allowed to leave the building while the Emperor was on stage, including women giving birth. It is rumored that some men pretended to die in order to escape.

However, as Nero's popularity waned, his enemies grew stronger. When his imperial guard refused to serve him, Nero realized the writing was on the wall. At age 31, he stabbed himself in the neck and died on June 9, A.D. 68, the anniversary of his wife's murder.

Kim Jong-il

Although the actions and anecdotes of North Korea's "Dear Leader" make a pretty compelling argument for insanity, some people warn that he is crazy like a fox. In a BBC interview, Kim claims to have been born on a sacred Korean mountaintop with his arrival eliciting thunder, lightning, and a double rainbow. It is said that he wrote six operas in two years, and he brags that the first time he golfed he made 11 holes in one.

Much like the Wizard of Oz, Kim is rarely seen but omnipresent. Despite his cartoonish appearance—short (standing 5′3″) and pudgy stature, pompadour-styled hair, elevator shoes, and oversized glasses—his likeness appears everywhere throughout North Korea. He has been abroad only three known times, and he rarely entertains outsiders, yet he commands the world's attention because he has his finger on the button of a nuclear bomb.

Kim led a privileged life as the son of North Korea's founder Kim Il-sung. He has had many diversions in his lifetime, including yachts, Harley-Davidson motorcycles, horses, fast women, and liquor, but he has only two great passions: film and food. Kim reportedly has a collection of more than 20,000 movies; in 1973, he wrote an instruction manual on filmmaking.

While still a dictator-in-training, Kim kidnapped a legendary South Korean film director and his wife. After a four-year imprisonment subsisting on a diet of grass and rice, the director agreed to make movies for the leader, including one featuring Pulgasari, a communist-style Godzilla.

Millions of North Koreans starved to death between 1989 and 2001, with CNN.com reporting that about ⅓ of the people are dependent on food aid coming from outside the country, which may not last much longer. Still, Kim's personal chef reports that Kim would dispatch him all over the world in search of the finest foods. He traveled to China for melons, Denmark for pork, and Uzbekistan for caviar. The chef, meanwhile, escaped from North Korea in 2001 while on a seafood-hunting quest to Japan.

Turkmenbashi

Born Saparmurat Niyazov, the Turkmenistan head of state adopted the name of Turkmenbashi, meaning "Leader of All Ethnic Turkmen." In 1999, he became ruler for life of this former Soviet republic situated north of Iran and Afghanistan.

Picking up the pieces after the collapse of socialism, Turkmenbashi rebuilt Turkmenistan in his own image—literally. His face was everywhere and could be found on posters, statues, currency, and vodka bottles. Streets and airports were named after him, and in 1998, a meteorite found in Turkmenistan was named Turkmenbashi. The head of state even renamed the calendar months to honor himself and his family. Turkmenbashi also ordered government officials and students to devotedly study the Ruhnama, a book he wrote combining poetry, philosophy, and revisionist history, to guide his citizens to a higher life through better living.

In addition to his megalomania, Turkmenbashi also was a control freak. He controlled the media, the universities, and the country's borders. He controlled the appearance and habits of his people by banning beards, long hair, and gold teeth. When he quit smoking, the rest of the nation had to as well. He also prohibited circuses, opera, and ballet, as well as the playing of music at public events, on television, and on car radios.

Although Turkmenistan is rich in gas reserves, its people are poor and its infrastructure is failing. Despite having the region's highest infant mortalities and lowest life expectancies, Turkmenbashi spent more money on his pet projects than his people, placing his priorities on building a lake in the desert and an ice palace in the country's capital. After his death in December 2006, Turkomans, having learned their lesson, elected a new president to a five-year term limit.

📺 Behind the TV Shows of Our Time

- An original proposed title for *Friends* was *Insomnia Café.* Other titles considered included *Friends Like Us, Six of One,* and *Across the Hall.*

- The empty frame on Monica's door in *Friends* was supposed to have a mirror on it. After a crewmember accidentally broke it, however, producers decided they liked the way it looked and left it.

- The role of *Friends* coffee shop owner Gunther was originally written without any lines.

- James Michael Tyler, who played Gunther on *Friends,* actually worked at a coffee shop when he got the part. He continued to do so throughout the first four seasons.

- The soundstage that housed *Full House* in its last two seasons went on to become the set of *Friends.* The pilot of *Friends,* however, was filmed on the soundstage used for *Living Single,* while the first season was filmed at what became the permanent home of *Everybody Loves Raymond.*

- The original concept of *Friends* involved Monica and Joey as the main love interests. It wasn't until after casting that writers made the switch to Ross and Rachel.

- *Friends* producers considered making the character of Chandler a homosexual.

- *Frasier* radio producer Roz Doyle is named after a real producer, albeit a TV one. The real Roz Doyle produced *Wings,* which was created by the same people who made *Frasier.*

- Paul Reiser actually plays the piano in the opening theme to *Mad About You.*

- Helen Hunt's role of Jamie Buchman on *Mad About You* almost went to Teri Hatcher. Hunt won out at the final round of auditions.

- Paul Reiser was almost cast as Danny Tanner in *Full House.* The final auditions came down to him and Bob Saget.

The Face of Technology

❖ ❖ ❖ ❖

Hedy Lamarr's beauty camouflaged the
genius that dwelled within.

Beauty and Brains

Cell phones are one of many marvels of today's high technology. But many people would be surprised to learn that one of the progenitors of modern telecommunications is actually a famous Hollywood figure of the past.

Hedy Lamarr had a classically beautiful face that instantly stole men's hearts. Throughout the 1930s and '40s she was MGM's "It" girl, starring in such movies as *Samson and Delilah* and *Algiers*. But to tell of Lamarr's film exploits is only to reveal half the picture—this beauty was as smart as she was seductive.

Ahead of Her Time

Born in 1913 as Hedwig Eva Maria Kiesler, the Austrian-born beauty swapped monikers when she hit Hollywood in 1937. Not only was she gorgeous, Lamarr was also mathematically gifted and had a head for scientific thinking. It was through her first husband, a munitions manufacturer, that she first became interested in weapons and how they work.

When America entered World War II, Lamarr learned that radio-controlled missiles were being blocked when the enemy discovered their operational frequencies. She reasoned that if frequencies could be switched simultaneously at the transmitting *and* receiving ends, then the enemy couldn't block the signal. Her hunch was ultimately correct but ahead of its time. Nevertheless, with the aid of composer and inventor George Antheil, Lamarr would patent their "Secret Communication System" in 1942.

After the transistor broke onto the scene in 1947, Lamarr's idea was updated and adopted by the U.S. Navy for use in its telecommunications sector in 1962. Years later, it would be applied to cellular technology. When asked her preference, acting or inventing, Lamarr replied, "Films have a certain place in a certain time period. Technology is forever."

Odd Ordinances

- In Chicago, serving whiskey to a dog is against the law.

- Fishing tackle isn't allowed in cemeteries in Muncie, Indiana.

- Shooting rabbits from motorboats is illegal in Kansas.

- You can't take your French poodles to the opera in Chicago.

- Hartford, Connecticut, has made it illegal for dogs to go to school.

- Cats and dogs can't fight in the town of Barber, North Carolina.

- A dentist who pulls the wrong tooth from a patient in South Foster, Rhode Island, can be required to have the same tooth removed from his own mouth by a blacksmith.

- Mannequins can only be dressed behind closed shades in Atlanta.

- Any woman weighing 200 pounds is forbidden from riding a horse while wearing shorts in the town of Gurnee, Illinois.

- Putting a skunk in a boss's desk is a crime in Michigan.

- It's illegal to fall asleep during a haircut in Erie, Pennsylvania.

- In Florida, snoozing under the hair dryer is prohibited.

- Sleeping in the fridge is illegal in Pittsburgh.

- Any man shaving his chest is breaking the law in Omaha, Nebraska.

- Mispronouncing the city name is illegal in Joliet, Illinois.

- Snoring so loudly that your neighbors can hear you is illegal in Dunn, North Carolina.

- Throwing a knife at anyone wearing a striped suit is illegal in Natoma, Kansas.

- Oxford and Cleveland, Ohio, made it illegal for women to wear leather shoes at voting polls.

Freedom Ain't Free: Living The Freegan Lifestyle

*Move over vegetarians and vegans—there's a
new eco-conscious lifestyle in town.*

The Freegan Basics

Whether you like it or not, first-world countries in the West are
monsters of consumption. We eat a lot, take up a lot of space, build a
lot of stuff, and generally spend an incalculable amount of money on
things we don't *really* need.

All that consumption can be exhausting for anyone, but a new
subculture of people who call themselves "freegans" are beyond fed
up, and they're determined to opt out of the game altogether.

Using a combination of the word "free" and "vegan," the freegan
lifestyle was first applied to food. Freegans feel that the amount of
perfectly good food thrown away by restaurants, grocery stores, and
everyday folks is despicable when so many people in the world are
starving. Also known as "dumpster diving," "trash tours," or "skips,"
freegans grocery shop in alley garbage cans. Freegans swear that
they eat like kings simply by salvaging food from the garbage. They
never spend a penny, and they cut down on the waste produced by,
well, everyone.

Granted, there aren't too many people interested in searching
through trash bags for dinner; nevertheless, the freegan lifestyle
spread across the United States and into European cities as well.
Soon, "urban foragers" were connecting across time zones to discuss
their philosophy online.

Look, Ma: No Money!

Most freegans aren't content with reducing the world's waste just
by noshing on semi-wilted veggies. Many of these anti-consumerists
find numerous other ways to live for free off the fat of the land.

Clothes and appliances are easily scavenged. Dumpster divers
boast of cast-off sporting equipment, artwork, furniture, musical

instruments, and computers—much of it in near-perfect or perfect condition. Those handy with a needle and thread transform some of the apparel they find into designerlike duds. And many freegans participate in "freemeets," flea markets where anti-capitalists meet to trade goods they've found; no money is exchanged and little trading takes place—it is, quite literally, a free-for-all.

All of this swapping and foraging means these folks have little use for money, which means that the majority of freegans don't have jobs. One of the tenants of the freegan philosophy is that working as a slave to a corporation or unscrupulous business is both demoralizing to the worker and to blame for disastrous results of mass consumerism—i.e., if you work for these people, you're implicated, too. Freegans don't let anyone off the hook.

Hardcore freegans are often squatters, living in abandoned, condemned, or otherwise vacant houses or buildings. Others are content to live in homes that are communal structures. Many freegans don't take their lifestyle quite this far, however; quite a few freegans live in apartments or houses they've furnished with items they've rescued from the curb.

The Freegan Flack

Not everyone thinks the city scavenger way of life is a good thing. Some critics can get past the whole "I-found-this-tasty-sandwich-in-the-dump" part but take issue with the heart of the freegan philosophy.

Some people feel that living off the waste of others isn't what the freegans like to call "symbiosis," but more like "free-loading." Others point out the inherent hypocrisy in the freegan lifestyle: Freegans may effectively reduce a small amount of waste, but if there wasn't any waste, there wouldn't be any freegans. Still others claim that if freegans would buy goods from the store in the first place, there wouldn't be as much to throw away.

Although the world continues to get "greener" as the public's eco-consciousness grows, we're still a long way from a waste-free society. As long as there are trash bins, there will be people to dig through them—whether you call them Freegans, saints, thieves, or nuts is really a matter of opinion.

The Times They Are A-Changin'

1953

- The first 3-D movie, *The House of Wax,* is released.

- On May 29, Sir Edmund Hillary and Tenzing Norgay complete the first successful ascent of Mount Everest.

- Julius and Ethel Rosenberg are executed for passing information regarding atomic weapons to the Soviet Union. The Rosenbergs are the only American citizens executed for espionage during the Cold War.

- Americans tune in to watch Lucy give birth on the hit television show, *I Love Lucy.*

- On April 8, Jomo Kenyatta and five other Kikuyu nationalists are convicted of orchestrating the Mau Mau uprising in Kenya, beginning a ten-year campaign for Kenya's independence from Great Britain.

- After two years of military deadlock and stalled peace negotiations, the United Nations Command and military commanders from China and North Korea sign an armistice that effectively ends the Korean War, though no peace treaty is ever signed. Interestingly, the agreed-upon border between North and South Korea in the armistice is almost identical to the border when the war began in 1950.

- *Playboy* magazine debuts, featuring Marilyn Monroe on its cover.

- Biologist Alfred C. Kinsey publishes *Sexual Behavior in the Human Female,* popularly known as the *Kinsey Report.*

- Russian leader Joseph Stalin suffers a massive stroke on March 1. He dies four days later, having led the Soviet Union for 31 years. Nikita Khrushchev is appointed First Secretary of the Central Comintern of the Communist Party following the death of Stalin.

- James Watson and Francis Crick discover the double helix structure of DNA.

- Jonas Salk develops the first vaccine for polio.

The Medical Uses of Bee Venom

Believe it or not, that pesky bee buzzing around
your fruit salad could one day save your life.

All-Natural Apitherapy

Do you suffer from apiphobia? In other words: Do you freak out when you see a bee? You might want to get over that—it turns out bees can make you better. For more than 4,000 years, the common honeybee has been used to treat everything from multiple sclerosis to rheuma-toid arthritis, gout, asthma, impotence, epilepsy, depression, bursitis, shingles, tendonitis, and even some types of cancer. As part of a unique alternative-medical approach called apitherapy, practitioners use natu-ral bee by-products such as raw honey, beeswax, pollen, royal jelly, and even bee venom to treat medical conditions that may be unresponsive to traditional medicine.

Facing the Stinger

Bee venom is currently being used to reduce inflammation and pain and to treat resistant skin diseases such as psoriasis. Although research-ers have already identified more than 40 pharmacologically active substances in bee venom, very little is known about them or what they can do. One protein that is understood is *melittin,* which has been shown to stimulate the adrenal glands, which produce *cortisol.* Cortisol is a naturally occurring anti-inflammatory that promotes healing in the body. In multiple sclerosis patients, bee venom is thought to dissolve scar tissue on myelin sheaths, improving nerve transmissions.

Bee venom can be administered directly from the bee's stinger or via injection by a trained healthcare professional. After identifying the affected area, the venom is injected, often at key acupuncture points, hence the term, "bee acupuncture."

While few published studies exist supporting the use of bee venom, there are hundreds of stories that attest to its effectiveness. A man in India accidentally disturbed a hive and was stung more than 20 times. While no doubt the punctures were painful, the psoriasis on his scalp and the arthritis in his knees disappeared in less than three months.

Fast Facts

- Some fans swear that Shirley Temple had exactly 56 curls in her hair in every one of her movies.

- Women tend to shave about 412 square inches of their bodies, while men shave only 48.

- Grab your shades: Earth is closest to the sun at the beginning of the year, on January 3.

- Tap water in New York City is considered non-kosher, as it has been found to contain microorganisms that qualify as shellfish.

- The player silhouette in the NBA logo was created from the image of former Los Angeles Laker Jerry West.

- Using proper form, the word "stewardess" is typed using only the left hand.

- December is the most common month for children to be conceived.

- Scrabble was originally called Criss-Cross when an unemployed architect came up with the idea in 1931.

- A typical American family goes through 6,000 pounds of food in any given year.

- You can see parts of Las Vegas from space.

- The soda 7-Up originally contained lithium.

- Crooks in Canada must pay income tax on their ill-gotten gains, but they are allowed to write off expenses against the gross take. On the other hand, lottery and gambling winnings are tax-free unless the taxpayer registers as a professional gambler.

All Creatures Great and Obscure

The animal kingdom is vast and varied, full of exotic specimens such as giraffes, penguins, and monkeys. Yet, there are quite a few other inhabitants of the animal kingdom that you've probably never heard of. Here are a few that might fascinate and amaze you... or just give you the creeps.

- **Raccoon Dog:** Named for the similarity in appearance to that of a raccoon, this solitary creature is actually an omnivorous member of the canine family. Found in China, Korea, and Japan, the raccoon dog has the least-sharp teeth of the canine family. It also plays dead to avoid predators and other natural enemies.

- **Cookiecutter Shark:** This small shark, infrequently seen by human eyes, has big lips and a belly that glows a pale blue-green color to help camouflage it from prey. Its name comes from the small, cookie-shape bite marks it leaves.

- **Vampire Squid:** This fast-moving gelatinous little squid has the largest eyes relative to its body of any animal in the world. Though it has no ink sack, with the aid of photophores it is able to light up its entire body. It is also able to invert itself, making it appear as if it's covered in suckers and sharp spikes.

- **Blobfish:** Found lurking in the depths off the coasts of Australia and Tasmania, this strange-looking creature has been called the "most disgusting fish in the world." The blobfish does not have (nor need) muscles because its jellylike flesh is lighter than water, allowing it to simply float in the high-pressure areas of the ocean.

- **Emperor Tamarin:** This rainforest-dwelling, squirrel-size monkey is named for its mustachioed resemblance to German Emperor Wilhelm II.

- **Pistol Shrimp:** These striped crustaceans differ from other shrimp in that they have claws of differing sizes, one larger than the other. The pistol shrimp pulls back the larger claw and snaps it shut, producing a loud sound that stuns its prey. It has been said that the noise produced by a colony of these shrimp snapping their claws in unison is so loud it can block the sonar tracking of nearby submarines.

- **Shoebill:** Discovered in the 19th century, this large bird is named for its beak, which is indeed shaped like a shoe. A long-legged, broad-winged relative of the stork, the shoebill stands four feet tall and has a seven-foot-wide wingspan. It also has a sharp hook on the end of its hefty beak, which is used for catching prey such as catfish.

- **Suckerfooted Bat:** A rare, diminutive bat, the suckerfoot is found in the western forests of Madagascar. It has small suction cups on its hands allowing them to cling to smooth surfaces as they glide through the forests in search of their next meal.

- **The Yeti Crab:** The pincers of this recently discovered crustacean from the depths of the South Pacific Ocean are covered in yellowish, bacteria-filled hair. Scientists hypothesize that the crabs possibly eat the bacteria, or perhaps use it to detoxify poisonous minerals.

- **Chinese Giant Salamander:** This particular salamander, found in the lakes and streams of China, is the world's largest living amphibian. Though its wrinkled appearance is similar to that of other salamanders, this variety can grow to over five feet in length, making it the undisputed king of salamanders.

- **Shrike:** At first glance, this little bird seems gentle and charming; however, the shrike is infamous for catching and impaling its prey (usually insects, lizards, or small mammals) on thorns. This ultimately helps the bird tear its victims apart, for smaller, more manageable meals. The torn carcasses are then left on the thorns, so the shrike can return for later snacks.

- **Star-Nosed Mole:** This lowland-living critter resembles a common mole, but with a nose that resembles a pink, many-armed starfish. Still, those weird nasal tentacles have nearly 100,000 minute touch receptors. Scientists have recently found that the star-nosed mole is also able to sniff underwater, by quickly inhaling the air bubbles that are blown out through its nostrils.

WHO KNEW?

Debuting the Drive-Through

While waiting for your burger and fries, have you ever wondered about the details of the first drive-through window? Well, the first drive-through window on record was in a McDonald's restaurant in Sierra Vista, Arizona, on January 24, 1975. The command-ers of nearby Fort Huachuca asked the restaurant to install the window because the military base prohibited uniformed soldiers from entering civilian places of business. To make it easier for the soldiers, McDonald's installed a drive-through window so they could enjoy their meals without entering the building. The original window endured until May 1999, when it was torn down and replaced with a newer, more efficient model.

Last Laugh

In 1975, Alex Mitchell and his wife settled down to watch their favorite British television show, *The Goodies*. During the show, one of the skits consisted of an exercise in self-defense called the "Ecky Thump." Halfway into the skit, Mitchell was seized with a bout of uncontrollable laughter that went on for over a half an hour until he eventually succumbed to a fatal heart attack. After the funeral, Mrs. Mitchell penned a note to the produc-ers of *The Goodies* thanking them for making her husband's last minutes alive so enjoyable. Interestingly, "Ecky thump," or "icky thump," is also an exclamation of surprise used in Northern England.

First Kisses

On the subject of romance, the first kiss recorded in a movie was cap-tured between John Rice and May Irwin in the 1896 movie *The Kiss*. The first interracial kiss was filmed on November 22, 1968, with Captain James T. Kirk (played by William Shatner) and Lieutenant Uhura (Nichelle Nichols) in an early episode of *Star Trek*.

And the Winner Is...Me!

With sales of more than 100 million copies since it was first published in 1955 as a beer sales gimmick by Guinness Brewery, in 2003 the *Guin-ness Book of Records* announced that it was the best-selling copyrighted book series in history—itself a Guinness Record.

High Art in Low Places: The Work of Banksy

Armed with spray paint and stencils, a mysterious graffiti artist named Banksy is hard at work right now, offering incendiary street art to the people of the urban world. Is his work vandalism or high art? To his fans, it's a little of both.

Graffiti Art and the Rise of Banksy

The early 1990s saw a boom in both hip-hop music and graffiti. In L.A., New York, and England especially, young men (and a few women) were expressing themselves through dance moves, record scratching, and spray-painting "tags," or embellished graffiti signatures. The first two modes of self-expression weren't illegal—but graffiti was.

City officials didn't see graffiti as a new art form: They felt it undermined authority and lowered property values. Others saw the artistry inherent in the work of taggers and graffiti artists, and felt the art represented people living in "the real world."

In Bristol, England (which has been referred to as the graffiti capital of the world), a rising star in the tagging scene emerged. His tag  name was Banksy, and in 1998, he decided to organize some of the best taggers from the UK and America at an event called "Walls on Fire." Ideally, it was a meeting of the minds, a collaborative project, and a way to legitimize the art form to outsiders. The event was a huge success. Across the world, people increasingly saw graffiti artists as serious artists. As for Banksy, he gained a reputation for not only being a tremendously talented tagger but a voice for the community at large.

Found Art

The projects Banksy organized were really only side projects—his main work has always been the art. And the art definitely gives one pause, whether it ought to be on the wall of a government building or not.

Utilizing stencils and often incorporating slogans or pithy phrases, Banksy mostly paints children, adults, or animals engaged in activity—and always with a clever, unexpected twist. Some of the work is political, and some is just fun: A child might be fishing out of a bucket, but there's a syringe on the end of his line. A young girl hugs a bomb like she would hug a puppy. A pair of English policemen hold each other in a passionate embrace. A cat launches a caped rat into the air via a spoon catapult.

These scenes are depicted on concrete walls, under highway overpasses, high on city buildings, next to sewer grates, and everywhere in between. Fans of Bansky (of which there are legions) go on "treasure hunts" to find works by the artist. One gallery in Bristol does offer some Banksy works for sale, but since the artist paints murals on immovable surfaces and has chosen to remain totally off the media grid, the buying and selling of his art doesn't come easily—and that's just the way he likes it.

The Hunt for Banksy

The fact that no one truly knows Banksy's real identity drives theorists batty. Reporters who have spoken with Banksy usually do so via e-mail. Some speculators believe Banksy to be a male of about 30 years of age. One reporter claimed he met the artist and that he was scruffy and grimy and sported a silver tooth. Others believe that he's not really a single person but is a collaboration of artists. Still others think he could be the man who runs the gallery where some of Banksy's work is sold.

In mid-July 2008, the British tabloid *Mail on Sunday* reported that they had unmasked the elusive Banksy. According to the paper, they identified a man in a photograph taken four years prior as Robin Gunningham. A spokeswoman for Banksy commented to the BBC: "We get these calls all the time. I'll say what I always say: I never confirm or deny these stories."

Bad Ad Grab Bag

"If it's in stock, we have it!"

"Nice parachute never opened, used once slightly stained."

"Joining nudist colony, must sell washer & dryer—$300."

"Stops that irritating whine." *Found in an ad for wedding rings.*

"Lambskin Leather Gloves Offer Unsurpassed Warmth and Softness... Be assured, no lambs are killed in order to make these gloves."

"Light Up Ghost...Not A Real Ghost, $12.99."

"Valentine's Day Sweetheart Special—Free Handgun, Today Thru Valentine's Day!"

"Fresh, Locally Grown ICE."

"Your Trade Is Worth $4,000."* (*If your trade-in is worth $4,000)

Sportcraft Roller Dice: "Teach your kids the elements of dice before sending them to the casino."

"Check Out Our Huge Selection of Newly & Gently Used Goods! Toilet Tissue just 25¢/roll."

"1 bag of boys 18–24 months, $25, takes it all!"

"Polly Miller works in the kitchen of St. Stephen School preparing for the school's annual soup festival....Those attending are asked to bring their own soup and bowl."

"City Market Food & Pharmacy, Career Opportunity—$9.70/hr., with wages possible after just 12 weeks."

"Cows, calves never bred...also 1 gay bull for sale."

"'83 Toyota hunchback—$2,000."

"Management Positions Available—Contact Tony—Vacation, uniforms, meals and possible salary."

Red-Hot Redheads

❖ ❖ ❖ ❖

*Fiery-tempered. Mischievous. Sensual. Stereotypes aside,
redheads demand attention. The following carrot-tops
parlayed their locks of flame into positions of fame.*

Today, less than 4 percent of the world's population possesses naturally red tresses. Some scientists even predict real redheads will near extinction by 2100. This fair-skinned species needs our protection; after all, the world would be a far less colorful place without redheads.

Ruling Reds

- **Pharaoh Ramses II, a.k.a. Ramses the Great:** During his prolific 67-year reign, this son of Seti I constructed countless temples, monuments, and statues—and sired up to 100 offspring.

- **King David:** Goliath should have known better than to mess with a redhead! This feisty fireball eventually became king of Judah and established Jerusalem as its capital city.

- **Elizabeth I:** The red-crowned daughter of Henry VIII and Anne Boleyn reigned as queen for 45 years and is considered by many to be England's greatest monarch.

- **U.S. presidents:** George Washington, Thomas Jefferson, and Martin Van Buren were all undisputed redheads.

Creative Carrot-tops

- **William Shakespeare:** Proud redheads the world over claim Shakespeare as one of their own. Unfortunately, since no descriptions or portraits of the Bard's appearance were recorded during his lifetime, it's a little hard to prove.

- **Samuel Clemens:** Generally known as Mark Twain, this celebrated writer also wrote under the pen name Thomas Jefferson Snodgrass. Defiantly proud of his red hair, Clemens alleged that Adam and Eve were redheads and admonished that "deteriorated black headed descendants" who disdained red hair showed a taste-less "departure from original beauty."

- **Vincent van Gogh:** Ridiculed by the townspeople of Arles, who wanted the mayor to lock up the artist, van Gogh was called *"fou-rou"* (crazy redhead).

Redheaded Rebels

- **Judas Iscariot:** Whether Jesus's betrayer was truly a redhead is unknown, but early artists are thought to have painted Judas's hair red to exploit traditional prejudices against redheads.

- **Jesse James:** Rumor has it this preacher's-kid-turned-bank-robber outsmarted the law by faking his own death. Could be, since the corpse laid to rest in James's grave is reported to have had dark hair, while the outlaw's hair was fiery red.

- **Robert MacGregor:** This early 18th-century Scottish clansman (a.k.a. Rob Roy or Red Rob) was immortalized by novelist Sir Walter Scott and poet William Wordsworth as a Scottish Robin Hood.

Rumors of Redness

- **Lucille Ball:** Arguably the world's most beloved redhead, Lucy's trademark locks were contrived to capitalize on television's Technicolor revolution. Lucy joked that she kept Egypt's economy afloat with the henna used to maintain her carrot-top mop.

- **Lizzie Borden:** Despite the fact that this infa-mous alleged murderess sported a mousy, light-brown mane, a more sensational image persists of Borden as a hot-tempered, axe-wielding redhead.

- **Jesus Christ:** Some assert that Jesus inherited red hair from his ancestor King David. Original paintings uncovered in circa A.D. 586 Rabula Gospels depict Jesus with curly red hair.

- *Blondes are noticed but redheads are never forgotten.*
  —Unknown

The Shocking Death of William Kemmler

William Kemmler was certainly no angel—after all, the guy admitted to bludgeoning his wife to death. Yet his shocking demise sparked death penalty protests and electrified a rivalry between powerhouse energy pioneers Thomas Edison and George Westinghouse.

William Kemmler was an illiterate street peddler in Buffalo, New York, who possessed a jealous streak and a penchant for drinking—a dangerous combination. His common-law wife, Tillie Ziegler, suffered the consequences of these demons in March 1889, when a drunk Kemmler brutally killed her with a hatchet. He confessed to a neighbor, saying that he would willingly "take the rope" for his intentional actions. But instead of swinging for his sins, Kemmler went down in history as the first person ever to be executed by electrocution.

An Undercurrent of Rivalry

Given his guilty admission, Kemmler's trial was swift. By May 13, he was sentenced to death by electrocution—a manner of capital punishment the New York legislature had recently deemed to be "less barbarous" than the noose.

Then a high-price lawyer mysteriously materialized in time to appeal Kemmler's death sentence on the grounds that electrocution was cruel and unusual punishment. When the appellate court upheld the electric chair as humane, another high-profile attorney argued Kemmler's case to the U.S. Supreme Court—again, unsuccessfully.

Although Kemmler's attorneys professed to be acting out of purely humanitarian interests, they were thought to be bankrolled by George Westinghouse, a pioneer in the burgeoning electric industry. Westinghouse, an alternating-current proponent, was desperately trying to defend the merits of AC so that it would gain public favor as the preferred mode of electrical transmission. Thomas Edison, his direct-current rival, hoped to solidify DC's market share by vigorously publicizing the dangers of AC's high-voltage currents.

Sparks Fly

To secure the subliminal link between AC-generated electricity and death, Edison's allies made certain the electric chair would be powered with Westinghouse generators. This was no easy feat, since Westinghouse vigilantly attempted to block all generator sales suspected of connection with Edison or the electric chair.

Electrician Harold Brown was commissioned to create the first deadly device. Rumored to be an Edison agent, Brown favored AC as a power source. He also cunningly sidestepped Westinghouse: By orchestrating the shipment of Westinghouse "dynamos" to Brazil, Brown rerouted the generators back to the United States for use in developing the electric chair.

Onlookers Shocked

Sober and reborn as a Christian, Kemmler calmly approached the electric chair on August 6, 1890. As the warden shakily attached electrodes to Kemmler's body, the prisoner advised him to take his time and keep calm. In fact, according to an eyewitness, Kemmler was the coolest person in the room.

Accounts of the day vary, but all agree Kemmler's electrocution was badly bungled. The executioners seemed unclear on the amount of time the electricity was to be administered, volleying suggestions ranging from a few seconds to fifteen. Finally, ten seconds was agreed upon, and the switch was flipped. Kemmler's body convulsed and turned bright red, but to the horror of onlookers, he appeared to remain alive, groaning and gasping. Additional shocks were applied until at last he succumbed.

By some accounts, Kemmler died instantly—his latent reactions were compared to the phenomenon of a chicken running around after its head has been cut off. By other accounts, Kemmler suffered a slow, painful, and torturous death. Whatever the story, the Westinghouse and Edison camps placed their spin on the event, using Kemmler's death to further their own ambitions.

In the long run, neither side prevailed. Although alternating current became the standard, financial woes eventually caused Westinghouse to lose control of his company. Bankers later took over Edison's companies, which ultimately became General Electric.

Word Histories

Video: Though one might normally associate this term with modern technology, it is borrowed directly from the Latin verb *video* meaning, "to see."

Sputnik: Meaning "fellow traveler," this word is used in Russia to refer to any space vehicle; however, Westerners use it only to refer to the first such vehicle of its kind.

Taxi: Manhattan resident Harry N. Allen coined this term from the French *cabriolet*. He combined it with the "taximeter" device installed in the 16-horsepower cabs he funded to counteract the increasingly high fares being charged by the city's horse-drawn variety.

Tabloid: This word used to refer to a type of pill comprising several medicines compressed into one tablet and manufactured exclusively by the Burroughs, Wellcome and Company of Great Britain. However, in 1902, *The Westminster Gazette* won a court case to use the word, which the pharmaceutical company believed it owned, to refer to their new publication.

Threshold: Long before it was used to refer to the entryway of a house, this word was used by farmers to refer to the process of separating the grain from the chaff by stepping upon it.

Slang: Nobody can say for certain where this word came from, but many believe it is derived from the Norwegian word *slengjakeften*, literally, "to sling the jaw" or "to abuse."

Tarmac: An abbreviation for the tar used in constructing this substance and the macadam roadways that preceded its invention.

Fore: Every golfer knows to yell this word when a shot goes awry, but they probably don't realize that its use did not begin until the late 19th century when golf balls began to be constructed of harder materials. The word itself is a shortened form of "before."

Flamingo: What could these colorful, lively, tropical birds have to do with the Flemish people? The pink birds reminded the Spanish explorers, who were the first Europeans to encounter them, of the equally colorful and lively residents of Flanders, or *Flamingos* in Spanish.

Strangest Baseball Injuries

❖ ❖ ❖ ❖

Athletes are famous for sustaining injuries, but baseball players seem to have a knack for scoring some of the strangest afflictions of all.

Lingerie Laceration

Former Giants manager Roger Craig actually cut his hand while trying to undo a bra strap. No word on what kind of emotional damage was done to the lady.

Eating Exertion

First baseman Ryan Klesko pulled a muscle while with the Braves— by lifting his lunch tray.

Chili Power

Former second baseman Bret Barberie had to sit out during a Marlins game after accidentally rubbing some chili juice in his eye.

Butter Slip

Another dinner winner, former Rangers outfielder Oddibe McDowell ended up slicing his hand open while trying to butter a roll at a celebration luncheon.

Belly Achin'

A knife nearly caused then-Padres player Adam Eaton to pass out. Eaton was using a blade in an attempt to get a DVD out of its wrapper when he slipped and stabbed himself in the abdomen.

Food Force

Former Mets and Giants outfielder Kevin Mitchell may take the cake when it comes to food flaps. He once made the disabled list by straining his rib muscles while vomiting. Mitchell also missed the first four days of spring training after hurting himself while scarfing down a microwaved donut. He is also rumored to have injured himself eating a cupcake at some point.

Given the Boot

Hall of Fame third baseman Wade Boggs got a little too excited putting on cowboy boots and was injured as a result. Boggs ended up missing seven games because of the back strain he incurred.

Toe Trouble

Not to be outdone, former Tigers catcher Mickey Tettleton tied his shoes so tightly that he gave himself a severe case of athlete's foot.

Protection Problems

Outfielder Ken Griffey Jr. found his protection to be his problem: Griffey had to miss a Mariners game after his protective cup apparently slipped and pinched the goods in a not-so-good way.

Virtual Spiders

One-time Blue Jay outfielder Glenallen Hill smashed a glass table while asleep. He dreamt that spiders were attacking him.

Not-So-Cool Moves

Former Oriole pitcher Mark Smith hurt his hand when he reached into an air conditioning unit. He said he wanted to find out why it wasn't working.

Iron Man

Braves pitcher John Smoltz smoldered when he tried to iron a shirt—while he was wearing it. Smoltz ended up burning his chest.

Operator Error

Former pitcher Steve Sparks wanted to show off his Brewers strength by tearing a phone book in half. Instead, he had to show off a dislocated shoulder.

Stressful Sneezes

Former outfielder Sammy Sosa suffered more than a stuffy nose when two sneezes struck him right before a Cubs game. The powerful projections caused Sosa to have back spasms, and he spent the rest of the afternoon getting treatment.

Misheard Lyrics

Elton John, "Tiny Dancer"
Correct: "Hold me closer tiny dancer"
Wrong: "Hold me closer Tony Danza"

Britney Spears, "Oops!...I Did It Again"
Correct: "Oops, I did it again"
Wrong: "Oops, I dated a pen"

Outkast, "Hey Ya"
Correct: "Shake it like a Polaroid picture"
Wrong: "Shake it like a polar bear ninja"

Justin Timberlake, "Sexy Back"
Correct: "Get your sexy on"
Wrong: "Who's a sexy goat?"

Eurythmics, "Sweet Dreams (Are Made of This)"
Correct: "Sweet dreams are made of these. Who am I to disagree?
Traveled the world and the seven seas"
Wrong: "Sweet cream is made of cheese. Who am I to disagree?
Traveled the world in generic jeans"

Johnny Rivers, "Secret Agent Man"
Correct: "Secret Agent Man"
Wrong: "Seasick Asian man"

Pat Benatar, "Hit Me With Your Best Shot"
Correct: "Hit me with your best shot"
Wrong: "Hit me with your pet shark"

Eddie Money, "Two Tickets to Paradise"
Correct: "I've got two tickets to paradise"
Wrong: I've got flu, rickets, and parasites"

Ramones, "I Want to Be Sedated"
Correct: "I want to be sedated"
Wrong: "I want a piece of bacon

Love Bytes: The Origins of Computer Dating

What do four randy college students, a quiz show, and a Supreme Court nominee have in common? Computer dating!

Turning Data Entry Into Dating

In 1965, frustrated with the only two seemingly available means of meeting women—blind dates and mixers—Harvard undergrads Jeff Tarr, Vaughan Morrill, David Crump, and Cornell student Douglas Ginsburg came up with an idea to use computers to arrange compatible dates between Ivy League students. This was decades before the Internet came of age, so Tarr and Vaughan hatched a plan to complete compatibility questionnaires and feed them into a computer, which would then provide the names and telephone numbers of students who would make well-matched couples. According to Tarr, "The goal was never to make money—just meet some attractive ladies."

Fill in the Blanks

After conferring with a number of business executives, lawyers, and computer scientists, Tarr was assured that his harebrained plan could actually work. The four budding matchmakers began writing a questionnaire that would be available for $3 each. Here's a sample question:

1. Your roommate gets you a blind date for the big dance. Good-looking, your roommate says. When you meet your date, you are sure it's your roommate who is blind—your date is friendly, but embarrassingly unattractive. You:
(a) Suggest going to a movie instead.
(b) Monopolize your roommate's date, leaving your roommate with only one noble alternative.
(c) Dance with your date, smiling weakly, but end the evening as early as possible.
(d) Act very friendly the whole time and run the risk of getting trapped into a second date.

National Attention

Several months later, the group realized that they had under-estimated the number of questionnaires it would take to keep the venture afloat and began looking for outside financing. Luckily, the popular TV quiz show *To Tell the Truth* and a 19-year-old coed from UCLA happened to save the day.

Producers from the quiz show contacted Morrill and asked him to appear on the air as one of their "mystery personalities." The spot netted the matchmakers free nationwide publicity for their new venture. At the same time, the guys invited Vicki Albright, Harvard law school's "Woman of the Year" and recent cover subject in *News-week,* to participate in their computerized dating service and osten-sibly to find her the ideal date. The results named a lucky bachelor. The Associated Press picked up news of the computer match; the story was printed in newspapers from coast to coast—more free advertising.

Speed Bumps

Even with the early success of the new dating service, financing con-tinued to plague the group. Finally, Tarr talked a New York-based data processing firm into keeping the business going by forming a new company called Compatibility Research. But spending time on the computer was expensive in the 1960s—even with outside resources helping financially, it just wasn't enough. Tarr paid a fellow classmate $100 to write a computer program that would read the completed questionnaires, transfer the answers to punch cards, and set up the compatible matches. Since the only affordable computer time was between 2 A.M. and 4 P.M. on Sundays, it took nearly six weeks to produce a single list of compatible partners.

Despite these problems, computer dating continued to grow. By 1968, Operation Match had become a cultural phenomenon with over a million respondents, some of whom even went on to marry their computer-made match. Today, computer dating has become a multimillion-dollar industry, fueled largely by the popularity of the Internet. Services like Match.com, eHarmony.com, and dozens of others compete for the attention of singles.

Riddles in Rhymes

A 2004 English study found ten times more violence in nursery rhymes than on prime-time television. Just look at what happened to Jack and Jill or Humpty Dumpty: contusions and possible murder. Learn more about the origins of some famous nursery rhymes.

Who Said That?

The origins of many nursery rhymes can be found in historic references, which often had to be subtle because overt ridicule or criticism could have cost the composer his or her life. Some of these include:

- "Baa Baa Black Sheep"—A medieval peasant's protest against crippling taxation.

- "A Frog He Would Awooing Go"—A derisive objection to the relationship between Queen Elizabeth I and France's Duc d'Alencon.

- "Jack Horner"—A description of a land swindle perpetrated during the time of King Henry VIII.

- "Wee Willie Winkie"—In its earliest form, this was a tongue-in-cheek dissing of King William III.

Rating the Rhymes

Some nursery rhymes would likely deserve a PG rating today. "Ride a Cock Horse to Banbury Cross" (or Coventry) is said to refer to Lady Godiva's famous ride in the buff. Meanwhile, "Little Jumping Joan" was a brief paean about a celebrated bawd. Other rhymes such as "Goosey Goosey Gander" and "Mary, Mary Quite Contrary" display religious intolerance, while "Tom Tom of Islington" and "Punch and Judy" spotlight spousal abuse.

The most gruesome nursery rhymes may be "Ring Around the Rosy" and "London Bridge." The former makes light of the horrors surrounding the Black Death, as a (rosy) red rash was one of the symptoms of the plague. "London Bridge" alludes to the legend of live children interred in the bridge's foundation to ensure the bridge didn't fall down.

It's Not What You Think:
Famous Faked Photos

*Some photographs are so iconic that it's nearly impossible to
separate the image from the event: President John F. Kennedy's
funeral, the Eagle spacecraft landing on the moon, the raising
of the flag at Iwo Jima. But seeing is not always believing.*

A New Era
In the brave new world of digital photography, photographers can
manipulate images with ease while media mavens worry over the
ethics of photographic alterations. But photographers were edit-
ing reality long before the computer: As early as the Civil War,
photographers posed battlefield shots to get the best effect. Nine-
teenth-century photographers used double exposures and other
darkroom sleight-of-hand to create photographs of spirits and the
supernatural. In Stalinist Russia, discredited leaders were removed
from the picture—in more ways than one. Check out these famous
"faked" photographs from the days before Photoshop.

The Loch Ness Monster
In 1934, London surgeon Robert Kenneth Wilson sold a photograph he had taken while on a birding expedition to the *London
Daily Mail.* In the photo, the long slender neck of an unknown
animal rises from the water of Scotland's Loch Ness.

Wilson's story held for 60 years until 1994, when a Loch Ness
Monster believer named Alastair Boyd uncovered evidence that
the photograph was a hoax. It turned out that in 1933, the *Daily
Mail* had hired big-game hunter Marmaduke Wetherell to investigate reported sightings at Loch Ness and find the monster. Instead
of Nessie, however, Wetherell found tracks that had been faked
with a dried hippo foot. Working with his son and stepson,
Wetherell staged the Loch Ness photograph in revenge, attaching
a head and neck crafted from plasticine to the conning tower of a
toy submarine. A friend convinced Wilson to be the front man.

It was Wetherell's stepson who broke the story, admitting his part in the hoax to Boyd in 1994. However, Wetherell's son Ian had published his own version of the hoax in an obscure article in 1975.

Raising the Flag at Iwo Jima

Associated Press photographer Joe Rosenthal won a Pulitzer Prize for his photograph of American servicemen raising the flag at the Battle of Iwo Jima during WWII. He spent the rest of his life fighting charges that the picture had been posed.

The charges were based on a misunderstanding. Rosenthal was halfway up Mount Suribachi when he learned he had missed the flag-raising. Told the view was worth the climb, he continued up the mountain where he found the Marine commanders had decided to replace the original flag with a larger one.

Trying to get a shot of the second flag going up, he stood on a pile of stones to get a better angle and almost missed the second flag-raising as well. When he saw the flag go up out of the corner of his eye, he swung his camera and shot. Knowing a single exposure taken on the fly was a gamble, and wanting to be sure he had something worth printing, Rosenthal took a picture of jubilant Marines gathered under the flag, a photo he called the "gung-ho" shot. He then sent his film to the military press center and left for his next assignment.

Rosenthal had no way of knowing his first, off-the-cuff shot had succeeded, and the congratulatory wire he received from the Associated Press didn't tell him which picture they were congratulating him for. When someone asked him a few days later if he had posed the picture, Rosenthal assumed they were talking about the "gung-ho" shot and said "Sure." A few days later, *TIME* magazine's radio program reported the picture had been posed. *TIME* retracted the story a few days later, but the misunderstanding haunted Rosenthal for the rest of his life.

Makeshift Propaganda

When Soviet war photographer Yevgeny Khaldei entered Nazi Berlin with the Red Army in 1945, he was looking for one thing: his own "Iwo Jima shot." When he didn't find one, he created it.

Khaldei chose the Reichstag building as the site for his photograph, and then discovered he didn't have a Soviet flag to raise. He flew back to Moscow, took three red tablecloths his news agency used for official events, and spent the night sewing a Soviet flag to take back to Berlin.

But the Reichstag was heavily defended—it took two days of fighting before Russians gained control of the roof. On the morning of May 2, while the Germans surrendered the building, a team of soldiers chosen for their political significance stood on the roof and Khaldei posed his masterpiece of Soviet propaganda.

Manipulation of the image didn't end with the pose. Official censors noticed one of the soldiers was wearing two watches, presumably acquired while looting. Khaldei was ordered to edit out the evidence. He also added smoke to the background to heighten the drama.

Khaldei later justified posing his wartime photos by claiming that pictures should match the importance of the event.

Kisses Both Real and Fake

Alfred Eisenstaedt's photograph of a sailor kissing a nurse in a white uniform in Times Square on V-J Day, August 14, 1945, was real enough, snapped on the fly as the seaman exuberantly kissed his way through the crowd.

French photographer Robert Doisneau, however, posed his seemingly spontaneous "Kiss by the Hotel De Ville" for a 1950 *LIFE* magazine photo spread on Parisian lovers, using theater student Françoise Bornet and her then-boyfriend Jacques Carteaud as models. The photo found new life as an icon of romantic love when a poster company rediscovered it in the '80s.

Fast Facts

- *The top-selling tie color is blue.*

- *Honey was used to pay tax in ancient Rome.*

- *Domino's has marketed a reindeer sausage pizza in Iceland.*

- *Apples are considered the most popular fruit in America.*

- *Blondes typically have more individual hairs on their heads than brunettes. Redheads have the fewest of the three.*

- *An average human eyebrow has 550 hairs.*

- *An average human beard has more than 15,000 hairs.*

- *The longest recorded underwater kiss is 2 minutes and 18 seconds.*

- *An average office chair moves around a total of eight miles over the course of a year.*

- *The chili and the frijole are the official vegetables of New Mexico.*

- *The square dance is the official folk dance of Utah.*

- *Princess Diana appeared on the cover of* People *magazine more than 50 times.*

- *John Lennon was the first person to be featured on the cover of* Rolling Stone *magazine.*

- *Manhattan is about half the size of Disney World.*

- *A caterpillar has nearly five to six times as many muscles in its body as a human.*

The Double Life of Billy Tipton

❖ ❖ ❖ ❖

*It's cool for girls to be über-successful music artists
these days, as evidenced by stars such as Madonna, Gwen Stefani,
and Alanis Morrissette. But not long ago, if a lady wanted to
make a life for herself in the music business, she had to face quite
a few obstacles. Read on for the incredible story of one person
who didn't let gender stand in the way of a lifelong dream.*

It's a Girl!

Dorothy Lucille Tipton was born in 1914 in Oklahoma City to
parents already on the brink of divorce. After the Tiptons split,
Dorothy, or "Tippy," as her friends called her, was sent to live with
an aunt in Kansas City, Missouri. It was there that she first fell in
love with music. Tippy tried to join the high school band, but was
told that girls weren't allowed.

Tippy moved back to Oklahoma, and for the majority of her
young adulthood, she studied piano and saxaphone on her own
while working odd jobs to pay the bills. Her career was going
nowhere on account of her gender, however, so Tippy decided to
take a risky step that would change the course of her life.

That's "Mr. Tipton" to You

In 1933, at age 19, "Tippy" started dressing as a man and adopted
the name "Billy" so as to be taken seriously at jazz band auditions.
The ruse was successful; soon Tipton was cross-dressing for her
professional career. By binding her breasts and, er, getting creative
with an athletic supporter and a sock, Tipton was now fully identifying (and identifiable) as a "he."

Although the work involved in passing as a man was tough, it
was beginning to pay off. Tipton was quickly gaining popularity as
a talented, amiable musician, and the jobs started rolling in. Tipton
scored radio performances, posh hotel gigs, national tours, and
album deals. He also shared the stage with prestigious names such
as The Ink Spots, the Delta Rhythm Boys, and big-band leaders

such as Billy Eckstine. Tipton was officially a successful musician—with a big secret.

Love at First Sight

Initially, Tipton was a woman in her private life, but eventually she cross-dressed fulltime. Incredibly, no one could tell that underneath the suit and tie was a female body—including more than a few women. After Tipton became "Billy," he had long-term relationships with women—including five wives—who never knew his true identity.

For seven years, Billy and a woman named Betty Cox lived together in what Cox has described as a rewarding, heterosexual relationship. Tipton told Cox his genitals had been damaged in a car accident and that he would forever have to bind his chest as a result of upper-body injuries. This was enough for Cox, who says Tipton was "the most fantastic love of my life."

In 1962, Tipton married an exotic dancer named Kitty Oakes. Oakes said they never had sex on account of her ill health and Tipton's "injuries." The couple eventually adopted three children. Tipton was a fully engaged parent, involving himself in the PTA, the Boy Scouts, and every charity event in town. Eventually, the couple divorced in 1980.

A Secret Revealed

When Tipton passed away in 1989 at age 74 from hemorrhaging ulcers, the coroners discovered his long-held secret. Oakes swore she had no idea of Tipton's true gender, but her shocked sons believed differently. Oakes ran immediately to the Spokane papers, pleading with them to keep the story under wraps, but she was too late—one of the Tipton boys had already agreed to speak to the press. The sensational story made it all the way to *The New York Times*. But Tipton's double life has served as an inspirational story to some: He's now regarded as a poster boy/girl for transgendered people around the world.

INSPIRATION STATION

Finnegan Would Be Proud

Thorton Wilder reportedly was inspired to write the Pulitzer Prize–winning play, *The Skin of Our Teeth,* after a prop rubber chicken fell from the stage into his lap during a performance of the hit Broadway revue *Hellzapoppin.* But that's just one theory as to how Wilder's bizarre modern allegory (which blended Bible stories, dinosaurs, and the Miss America Pageant, among other things) came to be. Most scholars understand that Wilder was directly inspired by James Joyce's experimental novel, *Finnegan's Wake,* and wrote the play as a response. Some people believe the similarities between the two expressionist works are a little too close for comfort, claiming that of the two epic cyclical histories, Joyce's is the true avant-garde example.

Prince, *The Godfather,* and Apollonia

The brilliant and ever-eclectic (and eccentric) musician Prince seems to find inspiration everywhere he goes, including the movies. In the early 1980s, Prince held auditions to find a singer for an all-female pop group; Spanish-Italian model and vocalist Patricia Kotero got the job. In order to add more sass to her image, however, a name change was in order. Prince had recently seen Francis Ford Coppola's *The Godfather* and was inspired by the character of Apollonia, the beautiful, doomed Italian woman Michael Corleone marries while he's hiding in Italy. Kotero was renamed Apollonia and went on to star opposite Prince in the hit movie *Purple Rain.*

The Two Towers: King and Browning

To the frustration of fans worldwide, horror maven Stephen King's seven-part series *The Dark Tower* has been written and published separately over a period of 22 years, starting in 1970. At age 19, King came across a poem by Robert Browning titled, "Childe Rowland to the Dark Tower Came," and found in it inspiration for his own epic journey. Inspired by Tolkien's *Lord of the Rings* saga, the series follows the hero, Roland, on his quest to the literal and figurative Dark Tower. The *Dark Tower* story has been made into films and graphic novels, and the characters in the story have gone on to inspire musicians and writers to create related works.

A Wealth of Chocolate

In the 16th century, one of the treasures that Spanish conquistadors found was far more delicious than gold.

Chocolate Money

It's hard to believe now, with candy bars sold at nearly every store, but at one time, the cacao plant (used to make chocolate) was so valuable that the beans were used as currency. In the Americas, 100 cacao beans could buy a slave or a turkey hen; one bean could buy a tamale. The Spanish wrote that after the Aztecs conquered the tropical lowland areas of Central America in the 1400s, tribute was often paid in precious cacao beans. In fact, the Aztecs invaded the region of Xoconochco in part because of its production of high-quality cacao. Thereafter, local leaders had to pay tribute to the Aztec empire in precious items such as jaguar skins, the brilliant blue feathers of a cotinga bird, and hundreds of loads of cacao beans.

Not for Everyone

Aztec society was extremely stratified. Only the elite were allowed to drink *xocoatl* or "bitter water," a hot beverage made from cacao beans that had been ground into a paste and flavored with chilies, herbs, or honey. Franciscan missionary Fray Bernardino de Sahagún listed the different chocolate drinks served to the emperor: "green cacao-pods, honeyed chocolate, flowered chocolate, flavored with green vanilla, bright red chocolate, huitztecolli-flower chocolate, black chocolate, [and] white chocolate."

This hot chocolate was hardly the stuff of Swiss Miss. Once mixed, the chocolate was poured from container to container to produce the stiff head of foam that was an important element of the drink.

Modern Mexicans still enjoy chocolate in all its forms. In fact, a descendent of the ancient Aztec royal beverage remains popular in the form of Mexican hot chocolate, a frothy drink flavored with cinnamon, almonds, vanilla extract, and even chili powder.

Down for the Count:
The Sad Life of Bela Lugosi

*The man who once thrilled millions of moviegoers with his
sexual magnetism, catlike movements, and creepy portrayals
died a wizened, nearly penniless, recovering drug addict.*

Hungarian Heartthrob

Bela Lugosi was born Bela Ferenc Dezso Blasko on October 20, 1882,
near the western border of Transylvania, then a part of Hungary. The
youngest of four children, he was raised in the town of Lugos, the name
he would eventually adopt. Never fond of school, Lugosi left home in
1894 to pursue his dream of acting. By 1907, he was a leading figure
on the Hungarian stage, going on to become a featured performer with
the National Theatre in 1913. Although National Theater actors were
exempt from military service, Lugosi enlisted in the army at the start
of World War I. He returned to find his country politically unstable.
Targeted for his activism, he fled Budapest in 1919, barely escaping with
his life.

In 1921, Lugosi came to the United States. Six years later, he was
awarded the lead role in the New York stage version of *Dracula*. The play
was a smash, running for 500 performances. Yet Lugosi only received the
role in Universal Studios' 1931 film version of *Dracula* because of the
untimely death of silent-movie superstar Lon Chaney. Lugosi signed on
for a meager $500 a week; in fact, he only made $3,500 from *Dracula*,
one of the most successful pictures in movie history. Lugosi infused the
otherwise turgid movie with energy, and in the process he created one
of history's most iconic screen characters. Yet the moment of his greatest
artistic triumph was also the beginning of his downward spiral.

Always the Monster, Never the Evil Genius

Universal planned for Lugosi to succeed Chaney as their next "Man of
a Thousand Faces." However, creative differences scuttled his participation as the monster in the follow-up film *Frankenstein*. Lugosi's lost
opportunity opened the door for the man who would eclipse him as a
horror star: Boris Karloff.

Although Lugosi hoped to capitalize on his *Dracula* fame with good roles, he discovered that he was now irrevocably typecast as a horror actor. He spent much of the remainder of the 1930s starring in forgettable potboilers such as *Island of Lost Souls.*

Occasionally he was given decent material; he worked to rise above the travails of typecasting, such as in *Son of Frankenstein,* in which he played the grizzled Ygor. However, as the '40s progressed, Lugosi's films were increasingly low budget. Even when he got a decent part, something bad always seemed to happen. In 1943, Lugosi finally had the opportunity to play the monster in *Frankenstein Meets the Wolf Man.* But Universal executives panicked at the idea of the monster with a Hungarian accent. They cut all of Lugosi's dialogue, as well as the much-needed explanation that the character was blind. On-screen, Lugosi's shuffling, lurching performance made no sense, and the film was resolutely panned.

Ed Wood and Addiction

In 1948, his film career virtually over, Lugosi played Dracula for only the second time on-screen in the daffy *Abbott and Costello Meet Frankenstein.* By then he had become increasingly dependent on morphine—an addiction that had begun when he first received the drug to relieve back pain. As work grew scarce and finances tight, his drug use increased.

In the early '50s Lugosi's desperate need for paying work led him to work with eccentric film producer Ed Wood, who had a reputation for creating extremely low-budget schlock (see: rubber octopuses and bouncing tombstones). Finally, in 1955, a gaunt, shrunken Lugosi voluntarily committed himself to a hospital because of his drug use. Three months later he emerged and returned to Wood for work.

Lugosi died on August 16, 1956, while working on Wood's *Plan 9 From Outer Space*—popularly considered the worst movie ever. The man who played the most iconic vampire was buried in one of his Dracula capes.

FROM THE VAULTS OF HISTORY

A Family That Stays Together...

In the long list of infamous criminals, few surpass the grisly accomplishments of Alexander "Sawney" Bean. Bean was the renowned head of a 48-member clan in 16th-century Scotland who has been accused of murdering and cannibalizing more than 40 people. While many historians claim that Bean never existed, his reputation for ambushing and eating innocent victims after hauling them back to his cave has fueled the Edinburgh tourism industry for hundreds of years.

According to legend, Bean and his family would ambush small groups of travelers. They would then rob and murder the victims, afterward dismembering and cannibalizing them. The leftovers were then carelessly tossed into the sea from the door of their secret cave. Eventually, the bodies would wash up on shore. The Beans' crime spree continued until they were captured alive and convicted of high crimes against humanity. The men were drawn and quartered and the women were burned at the stake. The story of the Beans has been made into a number of movies including Wes Craven's *The Hills Have Eyes*, Gary Sherman's *Death Line*, and Christian Viel's *Evil Breed*.

A Magnificent Mind

As a painter, Leonardo da Vinci is world renowned for his ability to inject life and emotion into his subjects, but surprisingly, he was not a proliferate painter—he painted only 31 pieces in his lifetime. Not to mention that one painting, *Virgin of the Rock* took more than 25 years to complete.

What undoubtedly consumed Leonardo's time were his interests as an Italian polymath, writer, architect, inventor, engineer, musician, painter, botanist, anatomist, and sculptor. He is credited with designing the first armored car in 1485, as well as the machine gun, the bicycle, glider, turnspit (for roasting meat), concave mirrors, water pump, movable bridge, parachute, the revolving stage, and even the first inflatable tube. Leonardo is also noted for his thorough study into the flight of birds as well as for his accurate drawings of human anatomy. One of the reasons historians have had a difficult time interpreting Leonardo's work is that he wrote all of his notes backward as mirror images.

Science vs. Séance

In which we examine the curious nature of ectoplasm and the story of famed medium and ectoplasm producer Margery Crandon's examination by a scientific committee.

The Essence of Ectoplasm

Today most people associate the term "ectoplasm" with the film *Ghostbusters* in which Bill Murray's character gets slimed by a slovenly ghost. To spiritualists of the late 18th and early 19th centuries, however, ectoplasm was an essential substance produced by mediums during a séance.

The ectoplasm was typically white and often luminescent, and it appeared to have the consistency of cheesecloth (which, skeptics wryly observed, was due to it actually being cheesecloth). While many believers regarded ectoplasm as a physical manifestation of the spiritual realm, to others it was part of the 19th-century spiritualism craze.

The first use of the word *ectoplasm* is credited to French scientist and 1913 Nobel Prize winner Charles Richet, who used it to describe the substance produced by a European medium during a séance in 1894. That a highly regarded scientist such as Richet should have a deep and abiding interest in spiritualism did not strike his contemporaries as a contradiction of interests. In fact, the idea that the spiritual world could transfer messages and substances into the world of the living was an appealing notion to Victorians. It was, after all, an era that bridged widespread Victorian beliefs in the metaphysical with the emerging fields of quantum theory and technological experimentation.

Enter Margery, Mistress of Ectoplasm

In 1924, Mina "Margery" Crandon, the wife of a Boston society surgeon, was on her way to becoming the world's most celebrated medium. With the alleged cooperation of Walter, her long-dead brother and spirit-world contact, Crandon had been able to levitate objects, manifest writing, and produce auditory emanations. She had traveled to Europe and submitted to scientific tests in Paris and London to prove her supernatural talents. Upon Crandon's return to the United States, she perfected the art of producing copious amounts of ectoplasm in the form of glowing strands, hands, rods and, in one instance, the fully formed figure of a tiny girl. At different times the ectoplasm streamed from all of her orifices, including mouth, nose, ears, and vagina.

Put to the Test

In 1923, *Scientific American* magazine offered $2,500 to any medium that could conduct a successful séance while under professional scientific scrutiny. Several amateur mediums tried and were proven frauds. Finally, the magazine's associate editor, J. Malcolm Bird, convinced Crandon to sit for the committee.

The individuals who observed Crandon in Boston in the spring and summer of 1924 included Dr. William McDougall, professor of psychology at Harvard; Dr. Daniel Comstock, former Massachusetts Institute of Technology professor; professional magician and spiritualist skeptic Harry Houdini; Dr. Walter Prince, researcher at the American Society of Psychical Research; and amateur magician and author Hereward Carrington.

Although Crandon was able to provide many examples of her intimacy with the spirit world, including the production of ectoplasm, Houdini became convinced that Crandon was a fraud. He delivered a series of lectures denouncing her and accusing Bird of incompetence and collaboration.

Mired in mistrust, the committee members published their disparate findings separately in November 1924. The committee's inability to disprove Crandon's abilities, however, catapulted Margery Crandon into national prominence. Her career peaked several years later when she manifested her deceased brother's fingerprint in dental wax. Subsequent examination, however, showed that the fingerprint was that of her very much living dentist. This episode, coupled with Bird's admission that Crandon's husband had asked him to collaborate in fooling the *Scientific American* committee, thoroughly debunked her abilities.

Odd Ordinances

- It's illegal to smoke a pipe after sunset in Newport, Rhode Island.

- Arresting a dead man for debt is a crime in the state of New York.

- Swearing around dead people is illegal at funeral homes in Nevada.

- Hitting a baseball out of the park is a crime in Muskogee, Oklahoma.

- Playing baseball in any public place is against the law in Wentachee, Washington.

- In Alabama, you can't play dominos on a Sunday.

- In Kansas, you can't sell cherry pie with ice cream on a Sunday.

- Providence, Rhode Island, doesn't allow stores to sell toothpaste on a Sunday.

- Columbus, Ohio, made it illegal to sell corn flakes on a Sunday.

- You can't even cross the street on a Sunday in Marblehead, Massachusetts.

- Selling suntan oil after noon on a Sunday is a crime in Provincetown, Massachusetts.

- Humming on the street on a Sunday is illegal in Cicero, Illinois.

- Hunting is illegal in Virginia on Sundays. That is, except for raccoons—you can hunt them until 2 A.M.

- Kissing your wife is a Sunday no-no in Hartford, Connecticut.

- In Houston, it's illegal to sell Limburger cheese on Sundays.

- Playing hopscotch on a sidewalk is forbidden on Sundays in Missouri.

- In 1845, there was a British law that made attempting suicide punishable by hanging. One can only wonder what the penalty would have been for succeeding.

- It is illegal to fish for whales on land in Oklahoma but legal to hunt them off the "coast."

Have You Lost Weight?
Canada's Gravity Dips

*Ah, gravity. It keeps our feet—and everything
else—firmly on the ground. But due to some
(literally) heavy geological history, in some parts
of Canada, gravity is a matter of opinion.*

Ice, Ice Baby

If you had been hanging out in North America 20,000 years ago,
you would have needed to bundle up. At the time, the world was
enduring the last major Ice Age, and glaciers covered a sizable
chunk of the continent. In some places, the ice sheet was about
two miles thick.

As you can imagine, that ice was also pretty heavy. In fact,
the ice sheet was so dense that the Earth's crust sagged under its
weight until it finally melted away approximately 14,000 years ago.
After the big melt, most of the ground popped up to its original
shape, but parts of Canada have yet to bounce back.

Up, Up, and Away!

The result of these still-sagging areas of the Earth is what scientists
call a "gravity dip." The anomaly seems to be centered around the
Hudson River region. These dips occur when parts of the ice-
squashed earth get stuck in their Ice Age positions. Some people
would regard the result as unfair: Most people who step on a scale
in that area will weigh less than you, even if pound for pound, the
two of you weighed the same. Scientists believe that in addition
to the crust-sagging activity that occurred, a layer of lava in the
Earth's mantle also plays a role in creating the gravity dips.

Whatever the reason, don't get too excited: A gravity dip doesn't
mean that your sandwich is going to float off into space. Most of
the benefits are purely scientific. As one researcher said, "We are
able to show that the ghost of the ice age still hangs over North
America."

Fast Facts

- *The first chalkboard for classroom use was recorded in 1714.*

- *The first recorded e-mail was sent in 1972.*

- *About a quarter of a cup of sweat comes out of your feet in any given day.*

- *When the first location opened in 1955, a McDonald's hamburger sold for 15 cents.*

- *An average McDonald's Big Mac bun has 178 sesame seeds.*

- *The word "spa" dates back almost 2,000 years to when Roman soldiers, marching home from battle, stopped overnight in a Belgian village that had hot mineral springs. The town, named "Spa," became a popular resting spot for Roman soldiers returning from battle.*

- *If you add up all the time you blink during a day, you'd have about half an hour of shut-eye.*

- *Coffee is technically a fruit, as its beans are made from fruit pits.*

- *If Pablo Picasso had signed his full name on his paintings, he'd have had little room left for the painting itself. Picasso's full name was Pablo Diego José Francisco de Paula Juan Nepomuceno María de los Remedios Cipriano de la Santícima Trinidad Clito Ruiz y Picasso.*

- *Many doctors think babies dream in the womb.*

- *American presidents who were bald include John Quincy Adams, Martin Van Buren, and Dwight D. Eisenhower.*

Writing What You Know

In 1994, fans of novelist Anne Perry's Victorian murder mysteries were shocked to learn that the best-selling writer knew her topic a little too well.

Best Friends

It started out innocently enough: Juliet Hulme arrived in New Zealand in 1948, where she met Pauline Parker. Sixteen-year-old Parker and fifteen-year-old Hulme quickly became best friends, particularly over their shared experience of serious illness and its related isolation. As a young girl, Parker had suffered from osteomyelitis, an infection of the bone marrow that required several painful surgeries. Hulme, meanwhile, had recurring bouts of respiratory ailments, culminating with tuberculosis.

Intelligent and imaginative, the two girls created an increasingly violent fantasy life they called the "Fourth World," which was peopled with fairy-tale princes and Hollywood stars they dubbed the "saints." They wrote constantly, sure their stories were their ticket to the Hollywood of their imagination. At night, the girls would sneak outside to act out stories about the characters they had created.

No Matter What

In 1954, Hulme's parents separated. As her father prepared to return to England, Hulme's parents decided to send Juliet to live with relatives in South Africa. Not only would the climate be better for her health, they reasoned, but also the move would bring an end to a relationship that both girls' parents felt had grown too intense. Ever fantasizing, Hulme and Parker convinced themselves that Parker was also moving to South Africa with Hulme. Not surprisingly, Mrs. Parker refused to allow it. Determined to stay together, the girls decided to kill Parker's mother and flee to America, where they planned to sell their writing and work in the movies that played such an important role in their fantasy life.

On June 22, the girls went on what they described as a farewell outing to Victoria Park with Mrs. Parker. There, they bludgeoned Mrs.

Parker to death with half a brick tied in a stocking. The girls expected the woman to die after a single blow so they could blame the death on a fall, but they were horrifyingly wrong—it took 45 blows to kill her. The hysterical girls then ran back to a park kiosk, screaming and covered in blood. The girls' story that Mrs. Parker had slipped and fallen rapidly disintegrated after the police arrived and found the murder weapon in the surrounding woods.

"Incurably Bad"

The trial, with its titillating accusations of lesbianism and insanity, grabbed international headlines, not only because of the brutality of the murder, but also because of the excerpts from Parker's diary that were used as evidence. The diary revealed the intensity of the relationship between the two girls and the fantasy world they inhabited. The diary also made it clear that the murder, flippantly described in its pages as "moider," was premeditated. The entry for June 22 was titled "The Day of the Happy Event."

Parker and Hulme were found guilty following a six-day trial during which the Crown Prosecutor described them as "not incurably insane, but incurably bad." Because they were under 18 and considered juveniles, they could not be given a capital sentence. Instead, they were sentenced to separate prisons for an unspecified term. After five years, they were released on the condition that they never contact each other again. Hulme returned to England and later took her stepfather's name, Perry. She also changed her first name; as Anne Perry, she went on to write dozens of popular mysteries, many of them falling into the detective fiction and historical murder-mystery genres. Parker, meanwhile, lives in obscurity in an English village.

The murders were fairly forgotten, at least for a time. Years later, Perry's true identity was uncovered as a result of the publicity surrounding the 1994 release of the movie *Heavenly Creatures,* directed by Peter Jackson. The film, starring Kate Winslet as Hulme, focused on the events leading to the murder. Perry was upset about the film. "It's like having some disfigurement and being stripped naked and set up in the High Street for everybody to walk by and pay their penny and have a look," she told *The New York Times.* "I would like to put my clothes on and go home, please, be like anybody else."

Really Wrong Science Predictions

Getting it right isn't always easy, even if you're Albert Einstein. Of course, when Einstein gets it wrong, it goes down in history. But he's not the only one to make a major slip-up when it comes to science and technology predictions.

"I think there is a world market for maybe five computers."
—*IBM Chairman Thomas Watson Sr., 1943*

"I have traveled the length and breadth of this country and talked with the best people, and I can assure you that data processing is a fad that won't last out the year."
—*Prentice Hall business books editor, 1957*

"But what is it good for?"
—*Engineer at the Advanced Computing Systems Division of IBM, commenting on the microchip, 1968*

"There is no reason anyone would want a computer in their home."
—*Digital Equipment Corp. President Ken Olson, 1977*

"This 'telephone' has too many shortcomings to be seriously considered as a means of communication. The device is inherently of no value to us."
—*Western Union internal memo, 1876*

"The wireless music box has no imaginable commercial value. Who would pay for a message sent to nobody in particular?"
—*David Sarnoff's colleagues in response to his urging for radio investment, 1920s*

"The concept is interesting and well-formed, but in order to earn better than a 'C,' the idea must be feasible."
—*A Yale University professor, responding to future Federal Express founder Fred Smith's paper proposing reliable overnight delivery service*

"Airplanes are interesting toys but of no military value."
—*French military strategist Marechal Ferdinand Foch, 1911*

"Everything that can be invented has been invented."
— *U.S. Office of Patents Commissioner Charles H. Duell, 1899*

"640K ought to be enough for anybody."
— *Attributed to former Microsoft chairman Bill Gates, 1981*

"Well-informed people know it is impossible to transmit their voices over wires, and even if it were possible, the thing would not have practical value."
— *Editorial in* The Boston Post, *1865*

"There's a lunatic in the lobby who says he's invented a device for transmitting pictures over the air. Be careful, he may have a razor on him."
— *Editor of the* London Daily Express, *commenting on a visitor*

"Where a calculator on the ENIAC is equipped with 18,000 vacuum tubes and weighs 30 tons, computers in the future may have only 1,000 vacuum tubes and weigh only 1.5 tons."
— Popular Mechanics, *1949*

"The Americans have need of the telephone, but we do not. We have plenty of messenger boys."
— *British Post Officer Chief Engineer Sir William Preece, 1878*

"Radio has no future"; "Heavier-than-air flying machines are impossible"; "X-rays will prove to be a hoax."
— *Royal Society President William Thomson (Lord Kelvin), 1895, 1897*

"While theoretically and technically television may be feasible, commercially and financially it is an impossibility."
— *Radio pioneer Lee DeForest, 1926*

"Who the hell wants to hear actors talk?"
— *Warner Brothers' H. M. Warner, 1927*

The Segway will be "as big a deal as the PC."
— *Apple founder Steve Jobs*

"With over 50 foreign cars already on sale here, the Japanese auto industry isn't likely to carve out a big slice of the U.S. market."
— Business Week, *1958*

He Said, She Said

"Buy land. They ain't making any more of the stuff."

—*Will Rogers*

"Get your facts first, then you can distort them as you please."

—*Mark Twain*

"Ah, yes, divorce...from the Latin word meaning to rip out a man's genitals through his wallet."

—*Robin Williams*

"Whoever named it necking was a poor judge of anatomy."

—*Groucho Marx*

"Things are never so bad they can't be made worse."

—*Humphrey Bogart*

"Always be nice to your children because they are the ones who will choose your rest home."

—*Phyllis Diller*

"What is comedy? Comedy is the art of making people laugh without making them puke."

—*Steve Martin*

"If God had wanted us to vote, he would have given us candidates."

—*Jay Leno*

"I'm at the age where food has taken the place of sex in my life. In fact, I've just had a mirror put over my kitchen table."

—*Rodney Dangerfield*

"I don't exercise. If God had wanted me to bend over, he would have put diamonds on the floor."

—*Joan Rivers*

"Hell, if I'd jumped on all the dames I'm supposed to have jumped on, I'd have had no time to go fishing."

—*Clark Gable*

"Football combines two of the worst things in American life. It is violence punctuated by committee meetings."

—*George Will*

There She Is...

The Miss America beauty pageant is well known for its sleek, tightly choreographed lines of beautiful women. But the early days of the Miss America pageant were anything but tasteful.

The Fall Frolic

In 1920, Atlantic City hotel owner H. Conrad Eckholm had an idea for a way to attract folks to town after Labor Day—typically the slowest time for tourism. The "fall frolic" was moderately successful, and it was decided to repeat the event the following year. One important addition was made to the frolic: a beauty contest.

But this was Atlantic City, a city that reveled in spectacle. Its celebrated boardwalk contained, among other curiosities, a grandiose Moorish estate where the owner fished from his bedroom window. No mere bevy of bathing-suit beauties would compete at this contest! To flesh out the theme and heighten the theatrics, the event coordinators hired 80-year-old Hudson Maxim to preside over the Fall Frolic as Father Neptune. Trident in hand and white beard flowing, on September 8, 1921, Father Neptune floated onto the beach in a seashell barge along with his retinue of beauty queens. The city mayor made a speech, the key to the city was presented, and scores of "sea nymphs" smiled and waved for the cameras. The Fall Frolic beauty pageant was officially underway; its winner would be crowned "Miss America."

Neptune Reigns Supreme

Clearly the star of the show, Father Neptune was dubbed "His Bosship of the Briny" and "Blue Blood of the Breakers" by the local press. Maxim was the inventor of smokeless gunpowder, which made him highly sensitive to odors. "If I were placed next to someone smelling to high heaven with perfume, I'd collapse and fall in a heap," he told reporters. Yet he didn't seem to mind being surrounded by perfume-drenched beauty queens.

The inaugural Fall Frolic was a wild success. It featured lifeguard boat races, fireworks, and vaudeville shows. It seemed as if everyone was in bathing suits, including the police. A bawdy, Mardi Gras-type affair known as "Neptune's Frolique" was held, in which women showed off their "nude limbs." Judging the crowd's applause for which girl they liked best, as well as a panel of "experts," the first Miss America pageant winner was announced: Sixteen-year-old Margaret Gorman of Washington, D.C.

Substance Over Form

The 1923 pageant featured 57 contestants, including Miss Alaska. Although her arduous trek from the snowy hinterlands to the sandy beaches was described as having forced her to use "dog-sled, aeroplane, train, and boat," in reality she was married and lived in dog-sled-free New York City. Exposed as a fraud, she was barred from the competition by red-faced pageant officials. She, in turn, filed a $150,000 lawsuit.

Other problems arose that year when several contestants appeared in the Bather's Revue, (now known as the "swimsuit competition") in revealing (for the time) one-piece bathing suits. The other women, who had worn more traditional and modest bathing attire, immediately staged a "beauty strike." They didn't know, they protested, that "form was to be considered in selecting America's most beautiful bathing girl." Problems continued as Miss Philadelphia was knocked unconscious when the chairs the contestants were standing on collapsed in a heap.

Shedding Its Image

More disasters followed over the next few years. Against regulations that kept the contest to single women, there were several instances when married women competed (including one with a baby). Rumors that the final results were fixed didn't help matters. Eventually—and somewhat incredibly—the pageant was seen as hurting rather than helping Atlantic City's image. It finally was canceled in March 1928.

Resurrected briefly in 1933, the pageant featured Miss New York's collapse on stage due to an abscessed tooth, Miss Oklahoma's emergency appendectomy, another married contestant, and three others disqualified for residing in states other than those claimed.

When the Miss America pageant returned once more in 1935, it had been restructured and regulated to more resemble today's glossy version. No one, it seemed, wanted to recall the "good old days."

Fumbling Felons

Her Number Was Up

Forgery is one of those criminal techniques that takes considerable skill. It also helps to have an iota of common sense.

For one Oregon woman, the time to try her hand at forgery had come. Standing in a convenience store with a state lottery ticket in her hand, she knew her ticket was a loser—just one number away from winning $20—but she didn't care. She wanted that money. The woman slipped to the back of the store, where she furtively altered the wrong number on the ticket into the winning one with a ballpoint pen.

The alert store clerk immediately spotted the forgery and called the police. The woman was arrested and charged with fraud. But then the arresting officer looked closer at the forged ticket. Squinting, he could just make out the original number underneath the pen mark. When he looked up at the chart of winning lottery numbers, he discovered that the original ticket had, in fact, been a winner—of $5,000.

(Try to) Drive My Car

At least the crook in this story had the right idea—getaway cars are for getaways. Of course, it's ideal if the car can actually be entered before the getaway takes place. Call us crazy, but it seems to work better that way.

At a Honolulu mall, a shoplifter grabbed several expensive ladies' handbags. He sprinted out of the store and headed for his car in the parking lot. Alerted by the store clerk, security guards gave chase.

For a moment, it seemed like the story had all the classic cliffhanger elements: a crime, a chase, and a getaway car ready for action. But when the thief dashed to his car, he stopped short. Seconds later, the guards caught up to him. Baffled, they asked why he had stopped when it seemed as if he was going to beat them to his car. The crook pointed inside the car: Dangling in the ignition were the thief's car keys. He had locked himself out.

Pucker Up:
History's Notable Kisses

*From pecks on the cheek to full-on Frenchin', this
pastime garners a lot of cultural attention. Check
out some of history's most notable kisses.*

The Very, Very, Very First Kiss

Whether it was good or bad, everyone remembers their first kiss.
But did you ever wonder where it all started? Some researchers
believe kissing possibly derived from the practice of mothers passing
chewed food to their babies (think of it as an early form of puree).
Anthropologists aren't all in agreement about humanity's very first
kiss, but there are clues as to how ancient this practice really is.
Kissing is often depicted in Egyptian art, leading many scholars to
believe that the kiss has long signified a "giving of life" or "blending
of souls" for people all around the world.

According to anthropologist Vaughn Bryant Jr., evidence has
been found that dates the first romantic kiss to circa 1500 B.C. in
India. Prior to this date, no one has found other examples that
records the kiss.

Et Tu, Judas?

In the Christian New Testament, the Gospels Matthew, Mark, and
Luke tell of a highly controversial kiss involving Jesus Christ and one
of his apostles, Judas Iscariot, whom Jesus had prophesied as the one
who would betray him. One version of the story says Judas led Jesus
to the Romans, and then identified Jesus to his captors by giving him
a kiss on the cheek. Thus Judas is cast as the ultimate betrayer—
calling someone a "Judas" is not a compliment.

However, some scholars argue that according to the Book of
Luke, Jesus and Judas were in on the whole thing together, and that
Judas was simply helping Jesus fulfill the prophecy. Either way, that
kiss, known as "The Betrayal of Christ," is one of the most reproduced kisses in the history of art.

Kiss Me, I'm Sleeping!

When one thinks of the Sleeping Beauty fairy tale, usually the 1959 Disney movie version comes to mind. But the story is far older, going back to the 1697 edition of Charles Perrault's *Tales of Mother Goose*. In the story, a wicked fairy curses a beautiful princess and puts her to sleep for 100 years. A smooch from a handsome prince is the only way out of hibernation. See? Kissing is good for you!

More Than Meets the Lips

Auguste Rodin's famous marble sculpture, *The Kiss*, suggests sex, romance, and...eternal damnation? Unfortunately, the backstory of one of art's most amorous pieces is a lot less romantic than most people believe. Upon first glance, the piece seems to depict two innocent, carefree lovers locked in a passionate embrace. Instead, the kissing couple actually represent two damned characters from Dante's *Inferno*. The sculpture, created in 1889, was initially part of a colossal work by Rodin called *The Gates of Hell*, but the two lovers were eventually removed from the larger work to stand on their own.

I'm Ready for My (Really) Close-up

The first kiss to be recorded in a film occurred in Thomas Edison's 47-second-long film *The Kiss*. Recorded in the spring of 1896 for nickelodeon audiences, the smooch was between actors John C. Rice and May Irwin. Although the kiss lasts only about 20 seconds, it managed to outrage plenty of people. The long, hard battle between filmmakers and censors had begun.

The Timed Kiss

During the golden age of film censorship, on-screen kisses couldn't last too long or look too passionate. In the 1941 comedy *You're in the Army Now*, the characters played by Jane Wyman and Regis Toomey enjoy a full, three-minute kiss. Scandalous!

Girls Kissing Girls = Great Ratings

Many people remember the hullabaloo surrounding the 1997 episode of *Ellen*, when comedienne Ellen DeGeneres announced she was gay and shared an onscreen kiss with actress Laura Dern.

But there were other girl-girl kisses on television before that. In 1991, two women puckered up on *L.A. Law,* and a 1994 episode of *Roseanne* featured a kiss between Roseanne Arnold and Mariel Hemingway. Huge controversy occurred among conservative *and* liberal audiences in all the above incidences—conservative viewers thought networks had gone too far, while liberal groups thought the kisses weren't properly handled. Judging by the sky-high ratings garnered for these episodes, we're guessing that there will be more opportunities for the major networks to get it right.

Les Kisses Dangereuse
Of all the scandalous kissing that happened on the 1980s TV drama *Dynasty,* one topped them all in terms of controversy—more than a year after it happened. In 1984, Daniel Reece, played by Rock Hudson, planted a big kiss on Krystle Carrington, played by Linda Evans. Then in 1985, Hudson issued a press release stating that he was dying of AIDS. He had known he was infected with the HIV virus when he kissed Evans; since very little was known about the virus at that time, the public panicked. Unfortunately, the illness combined with the stress of the media frenzy proved to be too much for Hudson to handle, and he died later that year. However, the panic led to more research and eventually a better understanding of the virus.

Black and White and Kissed All Over
In 1945, when it was announced that Japan surrendered during the Second World War, Times Square in New York City erupted into joyous chaos. *LIFE* magazine photojournalist Alfred Eisenstaedt was there at the time, and he snapped a picture of a sailor throwing a nurse back in a celebratory kiss. The picture became an icon of America's return to prosperity (although there are stories that the woman smacked the soldier after she was back on her feet). The people in the photo have never been positively identified, but that hasn't kept it from being one of the most reproduced pictures in the world.

🎼 Behind the Music of Our Time

- Bruce Springsteen's 1984 album *Born in the U.S.A.* was, rather fittingly, the first compact disc ever made in the United States.

- The name Mony in the song "Mony Mony"—first recorded by Tommy James and the Shondells in 1968 and made famous again by Billy Idol in 1987—actually comes from the name of a New York bank. James was staying in a hotel across from the Mutual of New York (MONY) bank and says he saw the acronym flashing on and off from his window.

- Janet Jackson apparently has a tattoo said to show Mickey and Minnie Mouse having sex—though you'd have to view Ms. Jackson in the buff to be able to see it.

- Buddy Holly's real name was Charles "Buddy" Holley. Decca Records misspelled his last name on his original recording contract, and he decided just to stick with the e-free version.

- A printing mistake also led to Dionne Warwick's last name: The diva was Dionne Warrick until her first single, "Don't Make Me Over," came out with a typo. She also opted to stick with the altered alias.

- Singer and pianist Tori Amos was expelled from the prestigious Peabody Conservatory music school in Baltimore when she was 11 years old. Apparently she hated to read sheet music.

- The beach hit "Wipe Out" was written on a lark. The Surfaris needed a quick ditty to fill the b-side of their "Surfer Joe" single. "Joe" didn't make much of a dent, but "Wipe Out" became a surfer standard.

- Depeche Mode was originally named Composition of Sound.

- The band Chicago was first called Big Thing.

- The Beach Boys' original band name was Carl and the Passions.

- Simon and Garfunkel first formed under the name Tom and Jerry, after the cartoon characters.

- Lynyrd Skynyrd initially called themselves My Backyard before settling on their now-famous moniker.

Toad-ally High

❖ ❖ ❖ ❖

Bored with all of the traditional ways of getting high: marijuana, cocaine, and Ecstasy? Looking for a new disgusting and unhygienic way to tune out for a while? Look no further than the banks of the Colorado River, dude.

Hopping along the river's shores in southern Arizona, California, and northern New Mexico, the *Bufo alvarius* (also called the "Cane Toad" and "Colorado River Toad") would normally be in danger of being the main course for a wolf or Gila monster. That is, it would if it weren't for a highly toxic venom that this carnivorous toad produces whenever it gets agitated: the same venom that can get you high as a kite if properly ingested.

The toad's venom is a concentrated chemical called bufotenine that also happens to contain the powerful hallucinogen 5-MeO-DMT (or 5-methoxy-dimethyltryptamine). Ingested directly from the toad's skin in toxic doses (such as licking its skin), bufotenine is powerful enough to kill dogs and other small animals. However, when ingested in other ways—such as smoking the toad's venom—the toxic bufotenine burns off, leaving only the 5-MeO-DMT chemicals. Those can produce an intense, albeit, short-lived rush that has been described as 100 times more powerful than LSD or magic mushrooms, even if it takes a lot more work to get it.

As one of the few animals that excrete 5-MeO-DMT, *Bufo alvarius* are leathery, greenish-gray or brown critters that can grow up to seven inches long. They have four large glands that are located above the ear membranes and where their hind legs meet their bodies. Toad-smokers first milk the venom from the amphibian by rubbing its glands, which causes it to excrete the bufotenine. Then they catch the milky white liquid in a glass dish or other container. After the bufotenine has evaporated into a crystalline substance, it is collected using a razor blade or other sharp instrument and put in a glass-smoking pipe, and then lit and inhaled. Sounds, uh, fun!

The Riots of Spring

Combine three headstrong Russians, a ballet company, and an angry audience, and what do you get? The infamous premiere of Le Sacre du Printemps, *a.k.a.* The Rite of Spring.

On a hot night on May 29, 1913, the influential Ballets Russes premiered a work at the newly built Théâtre des Champs-Élysées in Paris. But the opening was hardly the heady event that one would expect—from the first bassoon note, the audience began to whistle and catcall. Tempers flared between those who wanted to hear the work and those who wished to shout it down. Society ladies reportedly threw vegetables, and several fistfights erupted in the aisles. The reason behind the uproar originated with three Russian artists whose vision for a new understanding of ballet and theater directly challenged the old traditions. Audiences, however, didn't necessarily approve of the revision. Here are the main players:

Diaghilev

In 1913, dance in Europe was seen as a transcendent art form. After centuries of marginalization to either peasant folk festivals or formalized society ballrooms, dance had reemerged as a powerful form of intellectual and aesthetic expression. Leading the revival was the Ballets Russes ballet company under the direction of impresario Sergei Pavlovich Diaghilev. While he was enormously successful in his home country, a 1908 trip to Paris made him realize that the daring style of Russian dance was fairly unknown to anyone but Russians. Diaghilev had long believed that true art was first and foremost a tool with the power to regenerate society: It did not teach but inspire. It did not satisfy, but excite. Paris, he realized, was a city ripe for the taking.

Nijinsky

Dismissed from the Russian Imperial Ballet in 1911 for wearing revealing tights, young Vaslav Nijinksy became an international star as a principal dancer of the Ballets Russes. Audiences thrilled at his athletic ability—he seemed to literally hang in the air during leaps—and were smitten by the brutal beauty of his performances.

But Nijinsky was not without plenty of melodrama. His choreographed Debussy's *L'Après-midi d'un faune* in 1912 shocked and disappointed audiences. They watched as the most talented dancer in the world made stiff steps that culminated in a highly eroticized series of movements with a scarf—no leaps, no athleticism. Many were convinced that Nijinsky had overstepped his role. But, in fact, Nijinsky had only just begun.

Stravinsky

By 1912, the Ballets Russes had already achieved great success in their collaborations with the Russian composer Igor Stravinsky. Shortly after the debut of his successful *Firebird Suite,* Stravinsky dreamed of a pagan ceremony on the Slavic steppes culminating in the sacrifice of a virgin who dances herself to death. The compelling, rhythmic music that accompanied this dream was unlike anything heard in the Western world. Once he heard it, Diaghilev was convinced that this strange, primitive music needed to be let loose into the world.

Setting the Stage

On the morning of May 28, 1913, an advertisement was posted proclaiming the performance of a new work that would offer "the most surprising realization that the admirable troupe of M. Serge de Diaghilev has ever attempted . . . which will surely raise passionate discussions." No kidding. In fact, knowing that *The Rite of Spring* would be controversial, Diaghilev wanted to raise the audience's expectations to a fever pitch. Rumors had already circulated that Stravinsky and Nijinsky had fought over the work, and that many of the musicians and performers considered the piece punishing and contrary to form.

Well, they weren't so much rumors as fact. Diaghilev, ever the plotter, knew that Stravinsky and Nijinsky would be an incendiary pairing, and he chose the distinctly modern Théâtre des Champs-Élysées, itself a work of significant artistic controversy, as the place to set his fire. The theater also featured seating that allowed the straggly bohemians to sit alarmingly close to the aristocrats. Again, it was all a part of Diaghilev's master plan: To defend the work against the convention-bound dowagers and society gentlemen, he invited plenty of the wild boho set, eager to embrace anything that shocked the bourgeoisie.

The Assault

Well, it worked. At the premiere on May 29, Stravinsky's new composition was a cacophony of rhythm and dissonance, lacking standard forms or coherent thematic development. Requiring a huge orchestra dominated by percussion, it was a direct assault upon the senses. Nijinsky's choreography was equally daring, performed with toes pointed inward and elbows jutting from bodies. Wearing costumes of heavy sacks painted with squares and circles, the troupe defied every convention of ballet.

It didn't go over well. Melee ensued as the noise of public protest challenged that of the orchestra. Stravinsky, openly enraged at the audience, tried to keep Nijinsky from rushing onstage as he shouted the count to his dancers who were having trouble hearing the music. Pandemonium ruled, and a musicologist later remarked that the pagans onstage had made pagans of the audience. After a brief intermission, the performance resumed—as did the protests. Diaghilev attempted to quiet the audience but to no avail. Finally, the music was finished—all 33 minutes of it—and history had been made.

Victory of the Moderns

Curiously, later performances of the work met with no resistance. It was performed to receptive (if not sparse) audiences in London. Only a year later, Stravinsky was carried triumphantly from the concert hall following a performance of the work. In the weeks, months, and years that followed that tumultuous first night, many who had not attended claimed to have been there, and those who were bragged about the sheer magnitude and excitement of *The Rite of Spring* opening.

- *The music from* The Rite of Spring *has been used in scores of films, most notably in Disney's groundbreaking film* Fantasia.

- *Nijinsky, who had been Diaghilev's lover since joining the Ballets Russes, was dismissed from the troop when he left Diaghilev for the dancer Romola de Pulszky.*

Talk to the Expert

PET PSYCHIC

Q: Why do people call for your services?
A: About 90 percent of the cases I work with are "lost pet" cases. The other work I do is with pets that have behavioral problems, like cats who are eliminating outside their litter boxes.

Q: You say humans need to create images to communicate with animals. Can you describe that process?
A: What you want to do is send a picture to the animal. The easiest way to do that is to either describe it out loud or write it down. If you're trying to send a cat a message that you're going to be leaving for several days, but there's going to be a pet sitter coming in, you'd want to say something like, "I'll be leaving through the door, which is brown, and I'll be driving in my car, which is blue, but then somebody will come in." So basically you're using as much description as possible.

Q: Are images also how you perceive what's going on with animals?
A: Right, it's mostly pictures. Sometimes it's the sense of fear, or it's raw emotions. Sometimes it's feelings—if an animal is having pain in the chest, I'll get an empathetic chest pain.

Q: Which animals have the most to say, and which ones are the toughest to "crack"?
A: In my work with lost animals, I won't work with ferrets, snakes, turtles, hamsters, or spiders. Those are animals that often go into holes, and they don't pay attention to what's around the holes. So for me to figure out what they're seeing is impossible. Other than that, each individual species has certain things that are more important to them. Horses talk a lot about the emotions that they have or the feelings that they're getting from their human companions. Dogs will communicate about how they see their role in the house or what they can do to get our attention.

Fast Facts

- Root beer used to be the most popular soda in the United States, but now it's only about 5 percent of the market.

- Americans drink 50 times more soda now than they did a century ago.

- It takes about 2,893 licks to get to the center of a typical Tootsie Pop.

- Parsley is the most popular herb worldwide.

- A pelican doesn't have nostrils.

- A Twinkie contains 68 percent air.

- In 1995, blue M&Ms replaced tan M&Ms.

- If you use lipstick, the odds are high that you've spread fish scales on your lips. A common makeup ingredient called "pearl essence" or "pearlescence" uses fish compounds to create a shimmer effect.

- Muhammad is the most common name in the world.

- Max is the most common dog name in the United States.

- The first Hummer made for nonmilitary use was sold to Arnold Schwarzenegger. The "Governator" bought the vehicle in 1992.

- Each year, Parker Brothers prints up about $50 million in Monopoly money—far more than the U.S. Treasury prints in real currency.

- Monrovia, the capital of Liberia, Africa, is the only foreign capital city named after a U.S. president. James Monroe was president when the city was founded in 1822 as a refuge for freed slaves.

Fore! The Story of Jeanne Carmen

❖ ❖ ❖ ❖

Bottle-blonde Jeanne Carmen enjoyed a wild life. She was a '50s-era pinup model who could rival Bettie Page, earned the crown "Queen of the B-Movies" for her work on the big screen, and boasted friendships with Marilyn Monroe and Elvis Presley. What many people don't know, however, is that Carmen was also the first professional female trick-shot golfer.

From Farm Girl to Model

Disillusioned with life on an Arkansas cotton farm, 13-year-old Jeanne Carmen ran away from home with dreams of becoming a movie star. She landed a job as a burlesque dancer in New York before becoming a model. In 1949, she took an assignment to model golf clothes for a Manhattan store. During the shoot, she discovered she had a natural ability for the game of golf. She began honing her various golf tricks—eventually using them to gain wealth and notoriety.

Carmen's tricks included stacking three golf balls on top of each other, then driving the middle ball over 200 yards without disturbing the bottom ball. She could also hit the flagstick from 150 yards away one out of every three attempts. Her most popular trick, though, was to drive a golf ball off a tee that was clenched between the teeth of a prone (invariably male) volunteer without so much as grazing his whiskers. Carmen became so adept at these tricks that she demonstrated them for former President Dwight D. Eisenhower and gave golfing lessons to Hollywood celebrities such as Jayne Mansfield.

Hustling for the Mob

Carmen put her modeling career on hold and spent the early '50s traveling the East Coast, earning up to $1,000 a day performing trick shots. It was during this time that she met Chicago mobster Johnny Roselli, one of Sam Giancana's mobsters. He took her to Las Vegas and set her up hustling naive tourists on the links.

The hustle was a simple one: Roselli would find wealthy hotel guests and point to the curvy, glamorous Carmen and bet them that they couldn't beat her. For the first few holes she'd play like the ditzy blonde people expected her to be and let them get ahead. Suddenly, she'd make an amazing improvement. Roselli never lost a bet.

Carmen eventually tired of the lifestyle. When one of her beaten opponents refused to pay, Roselli dangled him from the top of a Vegas hotel and threatened to drop him. It was time to move on.

Marilyn's Buddy

By 1952, Carmen was on the cover of the *Esquire Girl* calendar, living in Hollywood, and was neighbors with Marilyn Monroe—with whom Carmen claimed to have shared some wild nights in the company of such luminaries as Elvis Presley, Frank Sinatra, Clark Gable, Errol Flynn, and John and Bobby Kennedy. Carmen also landed roles in a host of forgettable B-movies such as *Guns Don't Argue* and *The Three Outlaws,* a western that was later remade as *Butch Cassidy and the Sundance Kid.*

Carmen's hopes of graduating to A-list movies perished on August 5, 1962—the night Monroe died. Carmen had spoken to Monroe earlier that evening, and she always refuted the idea that the pop icon had committed suicide. She believed Marilyn was murdered by the mob. Carmen's old friend Roselli called her up soon after and advised her to dye her hair brown and leave Los Angeles. Carmen followed his advice and began a new life in Scottsdale, Arizona, where she married and started a family. She kept her colorful past a secret, but she continued to play golf—although never for money, and she kept the trick shots to a minimum lest she be recognized.

In 1976, Carmen returned to California with her family after Roselli informed her that mob boss Sam Giancana was dead and she was finally safe. Carmen died in 2007, only chipping distance from a golf club where the older members still talk about the blonde beauty who could hit a trick shot better than anyone.

The Times They Are A-Changin'

1963

- On August 28, Dr. Martin Luther King Jr. makes his "I have a dream speech" at the Lincoln Memorial, commemorating the centennial of the Emancipation Proclamation. King leads 200,000 Freedom Marchers through Washington, D.C., to demonstrate support for the civil rights movement.

- The Beatles release their first album, *Please, Please Me*, on March 22. Beatlemania is born.

- Russian astronaut Valentina Tereshkova makes a three-day space flight, becoming the first woman in space.

- The U.S. Supreme Court rules that Bible readings and prayer in public schools are unconstitutional.

- Tony Bennett wins the Grammy for Record of the Year with his album, *I Left My Heart in San Francisco.*

- The United States, the USSR, and Great Britain sign the Nuclear Test Ban Treaty, prohibiting all aboveground nuclear testing.

- Super-spy James Bond is introduced to the world with the April publication of *Casino Royale.*

- A 24-hour "hot line" is activated between the White House and the Kremlin, in the hope that rapid, secure communication between the two superpowers will avoid a repetition of the Cuban missile crisis.

- As a result of violent repression of the Buddhist majority, South Vietnamese president Ngo Dinh Diem is assassinated in a military coup on November 2.

- President John F. Kennedy is assassinated in Dallas on November 22. Two days later, Jack Ruby murders the alleged assassin, Lee Harvey Oswald, in the city jail as he is being moved to a more secure facility.

- Coca-Cola introduces its first diet soda, Tab.

Bad MOVE in Philly

*Looking more like a war zone than the
City of Brotherly Love, Philadelphia was ignited
under a police-induced firestorm in 1985.*

Tensions Begin

They called themselves MOVE, short for the word "movement."
Formed around 1972 by Donald and John "Africa" Glassey, the radical organization was comprised predominantly of African Americans
who believed that a back-to-nature approach was central to living a
full life. MOVE preached vigorously against the ills of technology
and strongly embraced the idea of a society without government
or police. Not surprisingly, their actions drew the suspicion and ire
of the Philadelphia police. Eventually, tensions between the two
groups would climax in the police bombing of MOVE's headquarters
in 1985. To this day the incident is still vigorously criticized.

Hostilities started in 1978, when MOVE members were living
communally in a house owned by Donald Glassey. Philadelphia
police were wary of the group's actions there, and they released a
court order demanding that MOVE, well, move. The radical group
refused to relocate, however, and the ensuing confrontation claimed
the life of Officer James Ramp and also injured several people. Nine
MOVE members were subsequently tried, convicted of third-degree
murder, and sentenced to 30 years in prison for their part in the
shooting.

The Situation Escalates

By 1985, the remaining MOVE members were living in a row house
at 6221 Osage Avenue. But they weren't quiet about their new
residence—group members were heard shouting obscenities over
bullhorns during the early hours of the morning. MOVE was suspected of hoarding weapons, and from what the police could see,
they had even built a wooden bunker on their roof. Additionally,
every window and door of their house was barricaded with plywood.

Their actions not only made the police nervous, but it also frightened the group's neighbors, who turned to city officials for help.

Devastating Destruction

Many Philadelphians will never forget May 13, 1985. On that morning, an organized force of police, firefighters, and city officials converged on the residence in an attempt to force MOVE members from their antisocial haven. In short order, a standoff ensued; MOVE exchanged gunfire with the police. Possibly fearing a repeat of the 1978 incident, Philadelphia police planned a proactive, though ultimately fateful, strategy. At 5:30 that evening, they maneuvered a police helicopter over the house and released a bomb containing C-4 explosive. Although police claimed the bomb was only intended to destroy the bunker, it did far more than that.

Within minutes, the house was engulfed in a firestorm so powerful it would leapfrog streets and spread to adjacent homes. The only survivors to come out of the MOVE house were Ramona Africa (most MOVE members had taken the surname Africa) and a 13-year-old boy. In all, within four hours 11 people were dead (including five children) and 61 residences were decimated.

The Aftermath

Almost immediately, public opinion turned against the police. Questions soon arose: Why had the police dropped a bomb when they knew innocent women and children were inside the residence? Why had the fire department neglected to put out the fire? And other than noisemaking and unruliness, what had the MOVE group done at the Osage residence to merit such an attack? To this day, these questions remain largely unanswered.

Ramona Africa was charged with conspiracy, riot, and multiple counts of assault and served seven years in prison. In 1996, she was awarded $500,000 in a civil suit against the city. When asked her opinion of the bombing during a 2003 interview, Africa was blunt: "If the government is saying that their solution to a neighborhood dispute is to bomb the neighborhood and burn it down, then there wouldn't be a single neighborhood standing."

ESCAPE!

SHARK ATTACK

Sure, the odds of a face-to-face encounter with Jaws are low, but being prepared could save your life.

Don't Play Dead

Calmly floating is a sure way to let a shark get the best of you. Instead, oceanologists say it's best to fight back. If a shark is coming toward you, hit it in the eyes or gills—those are the animal's most sensitive areas. Use anything you have to make your strike: a surfboard, scuba gear, or, as a last resort, your fist. If you're feeling wily, you can even try getting your hands into the gill openings to really cause the shark some pain.

Keep On Fighting

Remember that a shark is a predator and its instinct is to attack vulnerable prey, so keep fighting. If you can show it that you are not defenseless, it's more likely to move on to an easier target.

Get Away Fast

It seems obvious, but get yourself out of the water as soon as you can. If you're diving underwater, the safest place to be is close to the sea floor.

Steer Away From Danger

You can decrease the odds of an attack by following some simple precautionary steps:

- Stay out of the water if you have any open wounds or if you're bleeding (including menstruating).

- Don't wear shiny jewelry in the ocean.

- Stay in groups.

- Don't swim at night.

- Avoid areas inshore of sandbars or between sandbars. This is where sharks most often gather to find their prey.

HOW IT ALL BEGAN

Bye-Bye Birdie Droppings

Both spandex and Velcro are remarkably versatile materials. That may be why they were selected as the major components in bird diapers. In 1999, Lorraine and Mark Moore of Watkins Glen, New York, applied for a patent for their bird diaper design. These diapers are advertised as ideal for pet birds that are allowed to flutter about and do their business outside their cage.

Tomcatting Made Easy

Keeping an indoor/outdoor cat can be a hassle. That's why many owners install kitty doors. Resident cats quickly learn to use them. Unfortunately, so does every stray in the neighborhood. To solve the problem, David Chamberlain invented a microchip for the door that scans a recognition microchip implanted in the resident cat.

But, what happens when the resident feline brings home a trophy mouse, mole, or bird? For these intrepid hunters, one owner came up with image recognition software hooked up to a minicam. How long, one wonders, before a pet owner-cum-inventor dreams up a meow-recognition kitty door?

The Nose Knows

In 2008, 38.4 million American households owned cats; 56 percent of them owned two or more cats. That's a lot of kitty litter—and a whole lot of smelly litter boxes.

Brad Baxter of Pontiac, Michigan, came to the rescue, possibly making himself a cat owner's best friend. About ten years ago, he developed an automated self-cleaning litter box. Built-in pressure plates alert the box when the cat climbs in, then again when it has done its business. A small electric motor rotates the box, dropping the clump of whatever into a plastic bag, and that's about it. Once a week the owner changes bags and tops off the litter. No yuck whatsoever. Unfortunately, it only comes in two colors but custom designer colors for finicky cats probably aren't far in the future.

The Forbidden Allure of Absinthe

❖ ❖ ❖ ❖

After a 95-year ban, absinthe is again legal in the United States.

The Green-Eyed Muse

Absinthe: The peridot-green liqueur is synonymous with the bohemian excesses of the turn of the 19th century. Poets and artists often sought inspiration from the "green-eyed muse." Toulouse-Lautrec carried it in a hollow cane. Van Gogh, Manet, Degas, and Picasso not only drank "the green fairy," they painted haunting portraits of absinthe drinkers. Many claimed they found a heightened sense of clarity and invention from drinking it, different from the effects of any other alcohol. As the writer Oscar Wilde described the effects, "After the first glass, you see things as you wish they were. After the second, you see them as they are not. Finally you see things as they really are, and that is the most horrible thing in the world."

The Making of a Legend

Originally produced in Switzerland around 1790 as an herbal cure-all, absinthe became popular as an aperitif following the French invasion of Algeria in 1832. The bitter drink was also issued as an anti-malarial to French soldiers, who mixed it in wine to make it more palatable. Returning soldiers brought back a taste for the bitter drink along with their other souvenirs of the North African campaign. With the rise of café culture in the 1870s, absinthe became an essential element in the Parisian boulevard stroll known as *l'heure vert* (the green hour).

At the height of its popularity, drinking absinthe involved as much ritual as a Japanese tea ceremony. The liqueur was poured into a special glass marked to measure the "dose." A sugar cube was placed on a flat slotted spoon over the glass, and then ice water was dripped onto the cube until it dissolved into the alcohol. As the alcohol was diluted, the essential oils came out, transforming the green liqueur into an opalescent white in a process called *louching*. Watching the drink change color was an important part of the ritual.

Serious absinthe drinkers let the ice water fall drop by drop so they could watch trails of opal swirl through the green liquid.

The major ingredients in absinthe were wormwood essence and alcohol. The classical formulation of the liqueur was made from grand wormwood *(Artemisia absinthium)*, green anise, and fennel, which were steeped in an alcohol base and then distilled. The process was completed with an additional infusion of Roman wormwood *(Artemisia pontica)*, hyssop, and lemon balm. Once it was filtered, the result was a clear green liqueur with undertones of licorice.

The Ill Effects

From the late 1850s on, doctors were concerned with the effects of excessive drinking of absinthe. A condition known as "absinthism" was identified with symptoms that one French doctor described as "sudden delirium, epileptic attacks, vertigo, [and] hallucinatory delirium." Others speculated that there was an increased risk of madness and suicide among serious absinthe drinkers. Scientists pinned the blame on *thujone,* a chemical derived from wormwood that possibly produced psychedelic effects. Despite medical warnings, consumers convinced themselves that the benefits of what the poet Verlaine described as "the green and terrible drink" were worth the risk.

Absinthe's Return

Between 1905 and 1913, absinthe was banned in Belgium, Switzerland, the United States, and Italy. France, the center of absinthe culture, held out until 1915, only banning the liqueur when it was perceived as a threat to national defense at the beginning of World War I. By 1920, absinthe had been effectively banned worldwide.

Absinthe began to reappear in the European market in 1989, with legal restrictions on the levels of thujone. In 2007, absinthe was legally imported to the United States for the first time since 1912. The green fairy is back, but her wings have been clipped.

Word Histories

Engine: This word was once used in reference to wit or inborn talent. In the 13th century, however, "engine" (from the Latin *ingenium,* or "the powers inborn") became used for military mechanical devices. William Shakespeare used the word to reference both meanings. It was not until the mid-18th century that "engineer" appeared in reference to those who built and operated machinery and public works.

Ermine: Although the term now refers to a particularly smooth and beautiful fur often used for luxury coats and coverings, it's derived from the Latin word for weasel, *Armenius mus,* which was originally believed to be a rat from Armenia.

Eskimo: This is the Algonquin word for "eaters of raw flesh," which is why the people to whom it refers call themselves *Inuit* or "the People."

"Expletive Deleted": This phrase came into popular usage following the Nixon-era Watergate imbroglio, in which court transcripts used the phrase in place of profane utterances.

Extraterrestrial: H. G. Wells may have been the first to use this word as an adjective, but credit for using it to refer to beings from another planet goes to L. Sprague de Camp. De Camp used both "extraterrestrial" and its abbreviation, "E.T.," as a noun in the same 1939 *Astounding Science Fiction* article.

Fee: Next time you have to pay a fee, remember that the term originally referred to Anglo-Saxon cattle, called *feoh,* which were used to pay taxes in the Middle Ages. Now consider whether it's easier to carry a credit card or a cow to the store.

Sandwich: Although John Montagu, consummate gambler, hasty eater, and the fourth Earl of Sandwich (1718–1792), is responsible for the name for this meal, people had eaten sandwiches long before the Earl made them trendy.

War: The Romans called it *bellum,* but 12th-century Germans, perhaps uncomfortable with its similarity to *belle,* or "beauty," began using the word "war" instead. War is derived from Old High Germanic; both the word and the act have persisted through the ages.

Wanted: The Few, the Proud, the Foolhardy

❖ ❖ ❖ ❖

Looking for a career change? Here are some job descriptions to (re)consider before your next interview.

Floating Cities

Just offshore from any wartime conflict are floating cities populated with more than 5,000 men and women: aircraft carriers. Twenty-four hours a day, seven days a week, the crews on aircraft carriers risk their lives by being blown overboard by jet blasts as they launch multimillion-dollar fighter planes from runways that are less than 1,000 feet long. Add to that four steam-powered catapults that can send a 49,201-pound F/A-18 into the air at 165 miles per hour in less than 2 seconds, and you have all the makings of one of the most dangerous workplaces on Earth.

The Big Snow Job

The next time you're enjoying a ski vacation, take a moment to remember the avalanche crew. While you're still slumbering under your down comforter, members of the resort's ski patrol avalanche crew have already made their way up to the top of the mountain to inspect the runs you'll be skiing and to set off avalanches before the snow has a chance to slide.

The primary purpose of setting off avalanches at popular ski resorts is to prevent heavy accumulations of snow from endangering the lives of guests. This often means hiking up slippery mountain ridges long before dawn, rappelling off precarious cornices, and tossing dynamite charges into unstable areas. In places where the snow is ready to slide, avalanche crewmembers will "ski cut" a run and try to set off the snow before the first guests have finished their lattes.

Down You Go

If you're looking for hard, dirty, and dangerous work, then you've come to the right place. The business of coal mining has a long history of wall failures, vehicle collisions, collapsed roofs, and gas explosions. Even under the best circumstances, coal mining is highly unpredictable work—especially in under-developed countries where miners are forced to endure unsafe working conditions, shoddy material, and outdated machinery.

However, even with sophisticated monitoring devices, gas drainage, and improved ventilation techniques, miners are constantly threatened with suffocation due to carbon monoxide, methane, and sulfur accumulations. It's a dangerous job, but someone has to do it.

Hide and Seek

It's the middle of the night, and the Sheriff's Department needs your help—a 14-year-old boy is missing from his Scout camp and it's beginning to snow.

Search and Rescue crews are volunteers who save the lives of those who have lost their way in rugged terrain, fallen from steep ledges, need emergency medical treatment, or all of the above. Although most volunteers are trained mountaineers and emergency medical technicians, it's rarely enough training when it's just you against the elements. During the summer months, crews contend with bears, mountain lions, and poisonous snakes. In the winter, the worry is the threat of getting lost in a snowstorm or being buried by an avalanche while battling frostbite.

Take a Left on 45th Street

Perhaps one of the most dangerous places to be on a Friday night is the front seat of a taxicab—especially in large metropolitan cities. Driving a taxi gives new meaning to the phrase "anything goes." Working long hours for relatively low pay, many taxi drivers voluntarily put themselves at risk for any form of violence that slides into their back seat. Although many cabs are fitted with cages that separate drivers from their customers, it's almost impossible to prevent an attack from a gun, knife, or other object—all while trying to keep their eyes on the road.

How to Beat a Lie Detector Test

If you've been told that you'll need to take a polygraph test before accepting a job or to be cleared of a crime, watch out—you're about to be duped. The polygraph or "lie detector" test is one of the most misunderstood tests used in law enforcement and industry.

Many experts will tell you that lie detector tests are based on fallible data—regardless of how scientific the equipment appears, there's no sure way a person can tell whether or not someone is lying. Since the test is so imperfect, be suspicious of anyone who makes your fate contingent upon the results of a polygraph test. Still, here are a few suggestions on how to beat one:

1. Unless you're applying for a job, refuse to take the poly graph test. There are no laws that can compel anyone to take it.

2. Keep your answers short and to the point. Most questions asked of you can be answered with a "yes" or "no." Keep it simple.

3. During the polygraph test, you'll be asked three types of questions: irrelevant, relevant, and control questions. Irrelevant questions generally take the form of, "Is the color of this room white?" Relevant questions are the areas that get you into trouble. Control questions are designed to "calibrate" your responses during the test. See the next point.

4. Control questions are asked so that the technician can compare the responses to questions against a known entity. The easiest way to beat a lie detector test is to invalidate the control questions. Try these simple techniques when asked a control question:

   • Change your breathing rate and depth from the normal 15 to 30 breaths per minute to anything faster or slower.

   • Solve a math problem in your head, or count backward from 100 by 7.

   • Bite the sides of your tongue until it begins to hurt.

Fumbling Felons

Bear Facts

For someone to shift the blame for their criminal behavior is one thing, but it always works best if the other person or thing happens to be alive. Police are sort of quick to catch on otherwise.

A police officer in Florida saw this firsthand when he stopped a van that was driving erratically. As he approached the van, he saw the driver was now sitting in the passenger seat. When the cop asked for the man's license and registration, the man indignantly informed him, "I wasn't driving. The guy in the back was." When the officer looked in the back of the van, all he saw was a huge stuffed teddy bear. However, since the teddy refused to bear all, the man was taken into custody.

The Eyes Have It

Two teenage thieves in Liverpool, England, had been quite successful at their previous scheme: driving around, then suddenly stopping at a random parked car. One would break into the auto while the other drove around the block. By the time he came back, his buddy would be waiting for him with the car radio, CD player, and whatever else they wanted. After successfully fencing the goods, the two hoods would be back on the street, looking for another victim.

The case was a difficult one for police to solve, particularly because of the random nature of the crimes. All the cops could do was increase their patrols of the area.

One night two cops were slowly cruising down the street when their squad car's back door opened. In hopped a youth holding a car radio. "Hit it!" he yelled.

Obediently, the cops did; they raced the squad car around the block, and they handcuffed the unwitting thief. Quickly returning to the scene of the crime, the officers caught the hoodlum's accomplice as well. When they inquired why the boy with the radio had jumped into their vehicle, they discovered that he was nearsighted and had forgotten his glasses that evening. He had simply picked out a car that he thought was his friend's and hopped in.

Mothers of Atrocity:
The Women of the SS

*Hitler's infamous Nazi Schutzstaffel force, better known as the
SS, was responsible for countless war atrocities, including the
annihilation of six million Jews during the Holocaust. They wore
black uniforms with a skull on their hats and committed crimes
against humanity with merciless ease. But Hitler's racist ideology
attracted not just men of brutality and violence, but women as well.*

Germany's Women Enlist

As World War II dwindled, many German men were diverted to
the front lines. To replace their positions, many German women
were forced to join the SS-Gefolge, the female auxiliary of the SS.
There they served as guards at the concentration camps. However,
plenty of other women readily volunteered, eager to show their
love for the Reich. Most female guards were trained at the infamous Ravensbrück women's concentration camp in Northern Germany where it's estimated that more than 130,000 female prisoners
lost their lives. Female guards were called *Aufseherin;* as the war
crimes trials later revealed, they were every bit as cruel and callous
as their male counterparts. Here are the grisly stories of just four
of the approximately 4,000 female SS concentration camp guards.

Irma Grese: The Most Notorious
Female War Criminal Ever

Twenty-year-old Irma Grese worked at Ravensbrück before transfer-
ring to Auschwitz in 1943. There she rose to the rank of Senior SS-
Supervisor, the second highest rank attainable in the SS-Gefolge, and
oversaw about 30,000 Jewish and Polish female prisoners. As well as
selecting women for the gas chamber, Grese carried a whip and pistol
with which she would frequently either beat prisoners to death or randomly shoot them. She also enjoyed watching prisoners being savaged
by her pack of well-trained (and half-starved) dogs.

When Allied forces liberated the concentration camp at the end
of the war, they made a ghastly discovery in her living hut: Grese had

the skins of three prisoners fashioned into lampshades. She was tried by a British war crimes court at Lüneburg and to the end, Grese was remorseless for her actions. She was sentenced to death by hanging. Famously, Grese refused a hood, and her last words commanded, "*Snell*," German for "quick." Grese was executed on December 13, 1945.

Ilse Koch: The Bitch of Buchenwald

The wife of Karl Koch, the Commandant of the Buchenwald camp, Ilse Koch's sadistic behavior earned her the moniker, the "Bitch of Buchenwald." She enjoyed riding around the camp on her horse, whipping any prisoners that caught her eye. She also shared Grese's similar depraved taste in home furnishings. As she rode around Buchenwald, Koch would select any prisoners with distinctive tattoos. SS guards would then kill and skin the selected prisoners and Koch would fashion the tattooed skins into such ornamental items as lampshades, book covers, handbags, or gloves.

Koch was sentenced to life imprisonment by an American military tribunal in 1947. She was pardoned two years later, but was then arrested and tried before a West German court. More than 20 years later, she committed suicide in a German prison.

Herta Oberheuser: A Doctor of Death

Dr. Herta Oberheuser was the only female defendant at the 1946 Nuremburg Medical Trails. Like the infamous "Angel of Death" Dr. Josef Mengele, Oberheuser conducted horrific human experiments on prisoners.

In some experiments, Oberheuser—not using anesthetic—would brutally wound prisoners to replicate the injuries suffered by soldiers in battle. She would then contaminate the open wounds by scouring them with glass, sawdust, or rusty nails to study the body's reaction.

Having conducted some of the most gruesome human experiments on record, Oberheuser received a 20-year prison sentence. However, she was released in 1952 for good conduct and went on to serve as a family doctor in Stocksee, Germany. Her license was revoked in 1958 after protests from the Association of Former Ravensbrück Concentration Camp Prisoners. Oberheuser died in 1978.

A Nazi Among Us

In 2006, 84-year-old Elfriede Rinkel was deported from her home in San Francisco back to Germany. For more than 60 years she had managed to hide her horrific secret, not only from U.S. immigration officials but also from her Jewish husband. In truth, Rinkel had worked as one of Hitler's women of the SS, a guard at a Nazi concentration camp during World War II.

Born Elfriede Huth, Rinkel worked for ten months at the infamous Ravensbrück concentration camp after responding to a want ad for guards. She volunteered to work with an SS-trained attack dog, brutalized female inmates, forced them to march to slave labor sites, and subjected them to inhumane conditions. During Rinkel's time at the camp, nearly 10,000 women died, either in the gas chambers, during medical experiments, or from malnutrition and disease.

When Rinkel moved to the United States in 1959, she managed to conceal her concentration camp service from immigration authorities. She met her late husband at a German-American club in San Francisco. A German Jew, he fled to the United States to escape the Holocaust. He was an active member of the Jewish organization B'nai B'rith until his death in 2004. Friends say that he never suspected his wife was hiding such a dark secret; after all, they pointed out, she used to attend the synagogue with him and even contributed to Jewish charities. In a 2006 interview with the *San Francisco Chronicle,* Rinkel offered little explanation for why she kept her past hidden from her husband for 42 years. "That was my business," she said.

The Justice Department's Office of Special Investigations, formed in 1979 to track down Nazis living in the United States, finally uncovered Rinkel's history by comparing guard rosters and other Nazi documents with immigration records. Rinkel was the first woman prosecuted by the office. She now lives in the German city of Willich. Due to Germany's statute of limitations, she is unlikely to ever be prosecuted for her crimes.

Fast Facts

- The term "soap opera" comes from the fact that the shows used to work advertisements for soap powder into the plotlines.

- The last letter added to the English alphabet was "J."

- The first bubble gum was invented in 1906, but it failed miserably. It wasn't until 1928, when Dubble Bubble came out with its famous pink gum, that the stuff started to catch on.

- Three Musketeers candy bars got their name because they used to have three layers: vanilla, chocolate, and strawberry. Now, the bars only have chocolate.

- A cat sweats through its paws.

- A cell phone in 1984 would have cost you just under $4,000.

- The screwdriver was somehow invented before the screw.

- Belgium once experimented with using cats to deliver mail.

- The human ear has nine muscles, though they are mostly nonfunctional.

- Nintendo's Mario character was originally named "Jumpman" when he appeared in the 1981 arcade version of Donkey Kong. The name was eventually changed to Mario as homage to the landlord of Nintendo's old office, Mario Segali, who was said to resemble the animated little fellow.

- Reading about yawning is enough to make many people yawn.

- An average male beard would grow 13 feet long over a lifetime if never shaved.

FROM THE VAULTS OF HISTORY

Amiable and Unarmed

Indira Gandhi once said, "You can't shake hands with a closed fist." While that may be true, it's interesting that this gesture of friendliness has origins in armature. Most historians agree that the custom of the handshake began several hundred years ago in England as not only a way to greet someone but also to communicate to the other that you were unarmed and empty handed. Years ago, gentlemen often concealed weapons up their left sleeve, so shaking hands was done with the left hand as a gesture of trust. As the handshake grew in popularity, it naturally shifted to the right hand as a matter of convenience.

Put 'Er There

The gesture of shaking hands is found all over the world, but in many different variations. If you're a world traveler, it's a good idea to study up on a country's handshaking customs. For instance, in Japan, the handshake is often substituted with a bow. Russians frequently shake hands but always without wearing gloves. In fact, many Eastern European nations consider shaking hands while wearing gloves to be completely rude. The Chinese enjoy a brisk "pumping" handshake, but many Middle Eastern cultures encourage men to offer a limp wet noodle of a handshake. The French always shake each others' hands in business meetings but when outside the conference room it's customary to briskly buss each others' cheeks. In Kuwait, shaking hands is reserved for men—shaking hands with an unfamiliar woman is considered taboo. That also goes for folks of the Orthodox Jewish faith.

Finally, if for any reason, you can't shake hands (due to arthritis, an injury, or you just sneezed in your hand), be prepared to immediately offer a polite apology. In many countries, not shaking hands is one of the easiest ways to insult a stranger.

"The biggest danger for a politician is to shake hands with a man who is physically stronger, has been drinking, and is voting for the other guy."
—Senator William Proxmire

Beach Squeaks and Dune Booms

❖ ❖ ❖ ❖

There are two types of sonorous sand in the world, which create sounds when stepped on or moved. Marco Polo attributed their strange songs to musical evil spirits, but scientists now know better.

Sand Symphonies

"Singing sand" is generally classified as either "squeaking" or "booming." Squeaking sands are found near shorelines and, when compressed with a wave or footstep, emit a high-pitched chirp or croak that lasts only a fraction of a second. The real songsters of the silica world are the booming dunes, of which only 35 exist worldwide. Their sound is described as whistling or roaring, and has been compared to a kettledrum, foghorn, or pipe organ. Their pitch is low, between D and G sharp, two octaves below middle C. The sound is surprisingly loud, carrying up to six miles away and measuring a raucous 115 decibels—comparable to a rock concert or a revving motorcycle.

We Have Ways of Making You Talk

Booming is more complicated than squeaking. Booming dunes are made of highly polished, perfectly spherical sand that is extremely dry (as little as 0.1 percent moisture can impede the sand's ability to sing).

The dunes are quite tall—at least 150 feet—and when the slopes reach approximately 35 degrees, the sand is prone to avalanche. The grains collide approximately 100 times per second, slipping off one another and creating sound. The waves caused by these collisions synchronize them, so the grains collide in tempo, creating a unified pitch. This vibrating exterior layer of sand, looser and less dense than the inner layer, causes the air around the dune to vibrate, amplifying the sound like a loudspeaker.

Although scientists have long been interested in singing sands, recording artists are now incorporating this strange music into their work. But not all sands are equally talented. The most beautiful music comes from dunes in the Arabian country of Oman, whereas some Chinese sands can only occasionally be coaxed to sing.

ANAGRAMS

An anagram is a word or phrase that exactly reproduces the letters in another word or phrase. The most interesting of them reflect or comment on the subject of the first.

Action man—Cannot aim

Shower Time—Where moist

Santa Monica—Satanic moan

Goodbye—Obey God

iPod lover—Poor devil

Narcissism—Man's crisis

Hot water—Worth tea

Television programming—Permeating living rooms

Margaret Thatcher—That great charmer

Clint Eastwood—Old West action

Sheryl Crow—Her slow cry

Ladybug—Bald guy

Astronomers—No more stars

David Letterman—Nerd amid late T.V.

Princess Diana—End is a car spin

Statue of Liberty—Built to stay free

Laxative—Exit lava

Evangelist—Evil's agent

Desperation—A rope ends it

Sherlock Holmes—He'll mesh crooks

George W. Bush—He grew bogus

Madonna Louise Ciccone—One cool dance musician

The Art of the Insult

❖ ❖ ❖ ❖

Over time, English invective, having been limited to a half-dozen simple-minded obscenities, has lost its sting. But in the Elizabethan era, insults were inventive, rich, and varied. Want to add force to your anger and clean up your language at the same time? Borrow a few blasts from the Bard himself, William Shakespeare.

"More validity, more honorable state, more courtship lives in carrion flies."

—*Romeo and Juliet*

Translation: You're lower than a maggot.

"I knew him to be a dangerous and lascivious boy, who is a whale to virginity, and devours up all the fry it finds."

—*All's Well That Ends Well*

Translation: He's a cheatin' bastard.

"Where wilt thou find a cavern dark enough to mask thy monstrous visage?"

—*Julius Caesar*

Translation: You're so ugly you should wear a bag over your head.

"Get gone, you dwarf, you minimus, of hindering knot-grass made, you bead, you acorn."

—*A Midsummer Night's Dream*

Translation: Scram, shorty.

"You blocks, you stones, you worse than senseless things!"

—*Julius Caesar*

Translation: Not a brain in the bunch of you.

"Eat my leek."

—*Henry V*

Translation: Bite me.

Open Up and Say "Ugh"!

❖ ❖ ❖ ❖

One of the last things a patient wants to see as they look across a sterile operating room are leeches, maggots, and scum-sucking fish. But all three have earned a solid place in the medical community—simply by doing what comes naturally.

The Flies Have It

Maggots are nothing more than fly larvae—one of the most basic forms of life. But to many patients with wounds that refuse to respond to conventional treatment, they are a godsend. For the majority of people recovering from life-threatening wounds, contusions, and limb reattachments, antibiotics provide much of the follow-up care they need. But for a small percentage of patients who do not respond to modern medicines, maggots slither in to fill the gap.

Applied to a dressing that is made in the form of a small "cage," maggots are applied to almost any area that does not respond well to conventional treatment. The maggot thrives on consuming dead tissue (a process called "debridement"), while ignoring the healthy areas. After several days, the maggots are removed—but only after they have consumed up to ten times their own weight in dead tissue, cleaned the wound, and left an ammonialike antimicrobial enzyme behind.

While maggot therapy may not be everyone's cup of tea, it is effective in treating diseases like diabetes where restricting circulation for any reason can often result in nerve damage and even loss of limb.

Golden Age of Leeches

Similar to the maggot, leeches are small animal organisms that have been used by physicians and barbers (who, in the olden days, were also considered surgeons) for over 2,500 years for treating everything from headaches and mental illnesses to—gulp—hemorrhoids. And while they might appear to be on the low end of the evolution scale, leeches actually have 32 brains!

Leeches are raised commercially around the world with the majority coming from France, Hungary, Ukraine, Romania, Egypt, Algeria, Turkey, and the United States. Used extensively until the 19th century, the "Golden Age of Leeches" was usurped by the adoption of modern concepts of pathology and microbiology. *Hirudotherapy,* or the medicinal use of leeches, has enjoyed a recent resurgence after their demonstrated ability to heal patients when other means have failed.

Leeches feed on the blood of humans and other animals by piercing the skin with a long proboscis. Oftentimes this is the most effective way to drain a postsurgical area of blood, and it can actually facilitate the healing process. At the same time leeches attach to their host, they inject a blood-thinning anticoagulant; they continue until they have consumed up to five times their body weight in blood. The host rarely feels the bite because the leech also injects a local anesthetic before it pierces the skin.

The Doctor (Fish) Is In

Another unlikely ally to the medical community is the doctor fish, found in bathing pools in the small Turkish town of Kangal. The therapeutic pools in Kangal are a popular destination for people suffering from fractures, joint traumas, gynecological maladies, and skin diseases. While the pools themselves have a number of beneficial qualities such as the presence of selenium (a mineral that protects against free radicals and helps with wound healing), they are most famous for the doctor fish that live there.

At only 15 to 20 centimeters in length, doctor fish are relatively small and do not physically attach themselves to their host like leeches or maggots. Instead, they surround a person's skin, striking and licking it. They are particularly fond of eating psoriatic plaque and other skin diseases that have been softened by the water, eating only the dead and hyper-keratinized tissue while leaving the healthy tissue behind.

While many people might be uncomfortable at the thought of being surrounded by a school of fish feasting on their skin, many actually enjoy the pleasant and relaxing sensation of getting a "micro-massage."

🎥 Behind the Films of Our Time

- The name James Bond is believed to have come from a real-life ornithologist, or bird enthusiast, with the same name.

- The makers of *The Wizard of Oz* paid the dog portraying Toto $125 per week for appearing in the film.

- Tom Hanks's 1988 hit *Big* was originally written with a drastically different ending. In the film, Hanks plays a 12-year-old named Josh who inadvertently transforms himself into an adult by wishing on a carnival fortune-teller machine. The adult Josh develops a relationship with an adult woman named Susan, but in the end, of course, he becomes a kid again and leaves her behind. The original version, however, ended with a girl named Susan showing up at his school soon thereafter— in other words, the adult Susan visited the same carnival machine to wish herself a child so she could rejoin him. Apparently, test audiences didn't like it; the movie's makers cut it at the last minute.

- James Earl Jones, the man who gave *Star Wars*'s Darth Vader his signature deep, booming voice, never met the man who played the villain's body, David Prowse. In addition to Jones and Prowse, two people helped make the Vader character come to life: Sebastian Shaw played the unmasked face, and Ben Burtt, the film's sound designer, did the infamous breathing effects.

- The sound of E.T. walking, in the movie *E.T.: The Extra-Terrestrial*, was created by a crewmember playing with jelly in her hands.

- Some of the guts that spring out when the shark explodes in 1983's *Jaws 3-D* were actually made out of unsold E.T. dolls.

- Actress Debra Winger provided the voice of E.T.

- Actor Jean-Claude Van Damme plays the costumed alien in parts of the Arnold Schwarzenegger hit *Predator*. Van Damme left filming early but is said to be in most of the climbing scenes.

- For the 2005 remake of *Charlie and the Chocolate Factory*, legend has it director Tim Burton spent lots of time and money training actual squirrels to crack nuts.

Nobody Puts Josie in the Corner: Josephine Baker at the Stork Club

It's hard to imagine Beyoncé being denied a table in a fancy club or restaurant. Nowadays, a major recording artist—regardless of color—can go into pretty much any place he or she wants and receive serious VIP treatment. But it wasn't always this way.

That's Ms. Baker to You

By the time St. Louis native Josephine Baker was 19 years old, her legendary career was well under way. The exceedingly talented, exceptionally pretty African American singer had a way with song, dance, and stage banter—and as a stripper, her sex appeal couldn't be denied, either. The total package catapulted her into fame first across Europe and then the United States, where she performed her act to sold-out crowds.

During World War II, Baker spent much of her time performing for troops in Africa, the Middle East, and across her home country while still finding time to gather intelligence for the French resistance. She was a tireless volunteer for the Red Cross, and after the war, she and her husband adopted 12 children from around the world—not quite a Baker's dozen. Baker's wish was to make her family "a World Village." The group returned to America in 1950 with the hopes of creating a kind of multicultural utopia.

Sorry, Ma'am, We're Full

You'd think that with her significant fame and tireless war efforts people would be falling all over themselves to offer the great Josephine Baker pretty much anything she wanted. Unfortunately, this was America in the 1950s, which meant that if you were black you were considered a second-class citizen.

In 1951, Baker wanted to dine at the famous Stork Club in New York City. The Stork Club was a "see-and-be-seen" establishment, full of the city's elite in entertainment, politics, and culture. But, classy joint or not, the Stork Club refused to serve Baker simply on the basis of her skin color.

Baker didn't take the news well. She caused quite a row and was asked to leave, but not before being accused of being a Communist sympathizer (remember, this was America in the 1950s). Grace Kelly was at the club at the time, and she came to the aid of the embarrassed and furious entertainer. Kelly vowed never to return to the club, and she kept her promise. After Baker left, with Kelly by her side, she vowed to get her revenge on the Stork Club by dedicating her life to the fight for equality among all people of color.

Igniting the Fight

Baker started by suing the club, forcing its discrimination policy into the open after the public confrontation. She also immediately began refusing gigs that didn't take place in integrated venues. This had a major effect on many establishments that couldn't afford to *not* change the policy. In particular, Las Vegas nightclubs were forced to look at their admittance policies, which set the ball rolling for much of the rest of the entertainment industry.

In 1963, Martin Luther King Jr. asked Baker to speak at his legendary March on Washington. Baker was the only woman speaker featured that day. As she surveyed the audience, she was pleased. "Salt and pepper. Just what it should be," she said. However, when King's widow, Coretta Scott King, asked her to step into her husband's shoes as leader of the American Civil Rights Movement, Baker declined. She wanted to raise her family and lead a quieter life. Indeed, Baker and her "Rainbow Tribe" of children lived in a castle in France in relative peace.

By the time of her death in 1975, Baker had made a career comeback. More than 20,000 people came to pay their respects at her funeral. To this day, Baker's name is invoked among musicians, performers, and civil rights activists.

"Surely the day will come when color means nothing more than the skin tone, when religion is seen uniquely as a way to speak one's soul; when birth places have the weight of a throw of the dice and all men are born free, when understanding breeds love and brotherhood."
—*Josephine Baker*

chiropractors listened for a high-pitched "squeak" that meant that the device had detected areas of neurological stress, characterized by high levels of radiation. The device was widely used until 1984 when it was deemed worthless by the Food and Drug Administration.

- **The Foot Operated Breast Enlarger Pump:** In the mid-1970s, silicone breast implant technology was still in its infancy. Instead, many women pining for larger breasts spent $9.95 for a foot-operated vacuum pump and a series of cups that promised "larger, firmer and more shapely breasts in only 8 weeks." As it turned out, more than four million women were duped into buying a device that produced nothing more than bruising.

- **The Crystaldyne Pain Reliever:** In 1996, one of the most popular pain relievers on the market was nothing more than a gas grill igniter. When the sufferer pushed on the plunger, the device sent a short burst of sparks and electrical shocks through the skin to cure headaches, stress, arthritis, menstrual cramps, earaches, flu, and nosebleeds. After being subjected to FDA regulations, however, the company disappeared with thousands of dollars, falsely telling their consumers that "their devices were in the mail."

- **The Prostate Gland Warmer** and **The Recto Rotor:** Even someone without the slightest bit of imagination would cringe at the idea of inserting a 4½-inch probe connected to a 9-foot electrical cord into their rectum. However, for thousands of adventurous consumers in the 1910s, the Prostate Gland Warmer (featuring a blue lightbulb that would light up when plugged in) and the Recto Rotor promised the latest in quick relief from prostate problems, constipation, and piles.

- **The Radium Ore Revigator:** In 1925, thousands of unknowing consumers plunked down their hard-earned cash for a clay jar with walls that were impregnated with low-grade radioactive ore. The radioactive material was nothing more than that found in the dial of an inexpensive wristwatch, but the Revigator still promised to invigorate "tired" or "wilted" water that was put into it—"the cause of illness in one hundred and nine million out of the hundred and ten million people of the United States."

- **Hall's Hair Renewer:** For as long as there's been hair loss, there has probably been hair-loss cures. One of the better-known snake oils in the 19th century was Hall's Vegetable Sicilian Hair Renewer, which Reuben P. Hall began selling in 1894. According to the inventor, an Italian sailor passed the recipe onto him; the results promised hair growth and decreased grayness. The first version was composed of water, glycerine, lead sugar, and traces of sulfer, sage, raspberry leaves, tea, and oil of citronella. Eventually, the formula was adjusted to include two kinds of rum and trace amounts of lead and salt. Of course, lead is poisonous, and the ingredients had to be changed once again. Still, the product sold into the 1930s. Perhaps it was its promise that "As a dressing it keeps the hair lustrous, soft and silken, and easy to arrange. Merit wins."

- **The Relaxacisor:** For anyone who hated to exercise but still wanted a lithe, athletic body, the Relaxacisor was the answer. Produced in the early 1970s, the Relaxacisor came with four adhesive pads that were applied to the skin and connected by electrodes to a control panel. The device would deliver a series of electrical jolts to the body, "taking the place of regular exercise" while the user reclined on a sofa. All 400,000 devices were recalled for putting consumers at risk for miscarriages, hernias, ulcers, varicose veins, epilepsy, and exacerbating preexisting medical conditions.

- **The Timely Warning:** In 1888, one of the most embarrassing and debilitating experiences a man could endure was an "amorous dream" or "night emission." Fortunately, Dr. E. B. Foote came up with the "Timely Warning," a circular, aluminum ring that was worn to prevent "the loss of the most vital fluids of the system—those secreted by the testicular glands." For better or for worse, no diagrams have been found to illustrate exactly just *how* the device was worn.

Odd Ordinances

- It's illegal to hunt or kill a deer if you're in the midst of swimming in Florida.

- You can't kill a moth under a streetlight in Los Angeles.

- Catching a mouse without a hunting license isn't allowed in Cleveland, Ohio.

- Louisiana has a law prohibiting public gargling in the city.

- Better not blow your nose in public if you're in Waterville, Maine; it's illegal.

- Public sneezing is never allowed in the state of Nebraska.

- Driving a motorboat down a street is illegal in Brewton, Alabama.

- Whistling underwater is a crime anywhere in the state of Vermont.

- Leaving puddles of rain on your lawn for more than 12 hours is against the law in Lake Charles, Louisiana.

- Swimming is allowed only at night in Durango, Colorado.

- Swimming nude is allowed only between 8:30 P.M. and 5 A.M. in Spring Valley, New York.

- Crying on the witness stand is against the law in Los Angeles.

- *Merriam-Webster's Dictionary* was once banned in Carlsbad, New Mexico, because it was believed to contain obscene words.

- Politicians are never allowed to hand out cigars on an election day in Kansas (any other day is fine).

- Making a dead person serve on a jury is a crime in Oregon.

- In Fountain Inn, South Carolina, horses were once required to wear pants when in public.

- Driving livestock on a school bus is illegal in Florida.

There's Something About Mary

The Virgin Mary seems to pop up in the darndest places: on the sides of buildings, on underpasses, and even in muffins. Below, we've listed some of her more interesting sightings.

One famous 1996 Mary appearance was a 60-foot-tall image on the side of a windowed **office building** in Clearwater, Florida. Tragedy struck on March 1, 2004, when a teenage hooligan decided to knock the windows out with a slingshot. According to the Roadside America website, part of the image is still visible.

In August 2006, the Virgin Mary appeared on a Chicago woman's **pet turtle** that just happened to be named "Mary." Owner Shirley McVane said her friends doubted her claims that the shape on her terrapin's tummy was indeed that of the mother of Jesus Christ, saying, "They said, 'Oh, Shirley, you're getting nuts; you're 81 years old.'"

Dorchester, Massachusetts, resident Susan McGuinness claimed that the **burnt label** on her roasting pan on March 17, 2005, looked like Mary holding the baby Jesus. McGuinness promised not to wash or cook on the pan again, but said she probably would sell it on eBay.com.

Speaking of which, in 2004, a woman named Diana Duyser put half of her ten-year-old **grilled cheese sandwich** bearing the Virgin Mary's likeness up for auction on eBay. The sandwich actually drew bids of up to $22,000 before eBay pulled it. But then, the sandwich reappeared on the bidding block after eBay allowed its sale. A miracle!

In September 2007, Marty Nance of Watauga, Texas, saw the Virgin Mary's face in a **lemon** that he was cutting at his father's bar. Nance said, "Some people say it looked like Mother Teresa or the Virgin Mary…and some people say it looked like Nicole Kidman."

In 2006, candy makers at Bodega Chocolates in Fountain Valley, California, reported a two-inch-tall lump of **chocolate drippings** that bore a resemblance to the Virgin Mary. Apparently, employees spent much of their time hovering over the small figure, placing candles around it, and praying. Talk about heavenly chocolate!

INSPIRATION STATION

Painting a Play

August Wilson's ten-play epic, *Pittsburgh Cycle,* depicts the experiences of Black America in each decade of the 20th century. The installment set in the 1930s, *The Piano Lesson,* won Wilson his second Pulitzer Prize and is regarded as one of his finest works. What some people don't know is that the play was inspired by a painting of the same name by artist Romare Bearden. The story goes that Wilson was viewing the painting when he suddenly turned to a friend and announced, "This is my next play." Wilson, who wrote *The Piano Lesson* in 1989 and passed away in 2005, said, "In Bearden I found my artistic mentor and sought, and still aspire, to make my plays the equal of his canvasses."

The Weirder, the Better

Pretty pictures of idyllic landscapes, tidy portraits of good-looking people—this was not the stuff that moved legendary photographer Diane Arbus to take pictures. Instead, Arbus was inspired by what society deemed ugly and captured the image with a camera that inspired her, as well. Fascinated by the "freaks" exhibited at circus sideshows and the down-and-out characters that lurked in New York's seedy Bowery district, Arbus treated all of her ragged subjects with awed respect and referred to them as "aristocrats." "I really believe there are things nobody would see if I didn't photograph them," she said.

In 1962, Arbus found inspiration in the tool she used to make the art itself: She swapped her old Nikon for a larger-format camera that produced large, square negatives and finished prints that made everyone (even conventionally attractive celebrities like Mae West) look grotesque and stark. The result was arresting. The images inspire in the viewer a range of feelings, everything from fear to pity, from reverence to love.

"I work from awkwardness. By that I mean I don't like to arrange things. If I stand in front of something, instead of arranging it, I arrange myself.
—*Diane Arbus*

Sail by the Stars, Plant by the Moon

❖ ❖ ❖ ❖

Before the advent of meteorology, people forecast the weather by other means. Natural forecasting may seem like folkloric fancy to some, but often there is a kernel of truth behind the sayings.

Red Sky at Morning

While many means of natural weather forecasting are relatively arbitrary, some actually have a basis in science. The oft-quoted proverb, "Red sky at morning, sailor take warning; red sky at night, sailor's delight" is actually a reasonable indicator of short-term weather trends, particularly in the middle latitudes of the Northern Hemisphere. The sinking air mass in a high-air pressure area holds air filled with particulates closer to the earth. This air tends to dispel shorter wavelengths of light and allow the longer (and redder) wavelengths, which cause a red sky at sunset. Since high-pressure systems typically herald fair weather, any sailors observing the sunset could rest easy knowing that clear weather and good sailing is on its way.

However, a red sky at sunrise indicates that the high-pressure front has already passed, as weather systems most often move from west to east in the mid-northern latitudes. A low-pressure system is likely to follow, with the likelihood of clouds and precipitation.

Other weather proverbs have some meteorological basis as well. "Mare's tails and mackerel scales make tall ships take in their sails" is a reference to two types of cloud: the cirrus (the mare's tails) and cirrocumulus (the mackerel scales). Both are harbingers of a warm front, bringing a change in wind pattern and possible precipitation.

The Farmer's Friend

Farmers also need some indication of coming weather to plan their crops. The heavenly bodies seem to be a good indicator, as both "Clear moon, frost soon," and "When the stars begin to huddle, the earth will soon become a puddle" have some basis in science. The "huddle" is in reference to groups of stars only visible through gaps in cloud cover.

Some weather lore, like "A year of snow, a year of plenty" is fairly reliable, as late snow cover prevents fruit from blossoming until the time of the killing frosts has gone. However, plenty of weather proverbs are simply without basis.

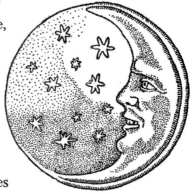

Fauna and Flora Forecasters

Sailors and farmers aren't the only ones keeping their eyes on the skies—many animals are extremely sensitive to changes in weather. So while it may seem as if an animal is "predicting" future weather, in fact, it is just responding to a preexisting condition. For instance, companion animals such as dogs and cats are well known for becoming restless before large-scale weather events such as tornadoes, hurricanes, or extreme electrical storms.

Low-flying swallows or low-nesting crows are both indicators of poor weather to come—a phenomenon supported by the fact that falling air pressure causes discomfort in birds' ears, so they fly low to mitigate it. These same pressure systems can cause deer and elk to seek the shelter of lower ground in anticipation of inclement weather.

As is the case with most natural forecasting, one just needs to take note of what's happening around them. For instance, farmers have noticed that cows tend to group together and lie down if a storm is approaching. Also, ants tend to increase the slope of their hills and cats tend to wash behind their ears with greater frequency just before a rain.

While observations of animal behavior are dependent upon the interpretations of the observer, watching flora is more reliable. The scales of pinecones open and stiffen in dry weather, but they return to their relaxed state in times of moisture.

Even humans are not immune to these changes in barometric pressure. Many people report suffering from headaches, and aching or pressure in their arthritic joints, recently healed fractures, or corns and bunions when the weather changes.

11 Stupid Legal Warnings

Our lawsuit-obsessed society has forced product manufacturers to cover their "you-know-whats" by writing warning labels to protect us from ourselves. Some are funny, some are absolutely ridiculous, but all are guaranteed to stand up in court.

1. Child-size Superman and Batman costumes come with this warning label: "Wearing of this garment does not enable you to fly."

2. A clothes iron comes with this caution: "Warning: Never iron clothes on the body." Ouch!

3. The instructions for a medical thermometer advise: "Do not use orally after using rectally."

4. The side of a Slush Puppy cup warns: "This ice may be cold." The only thing dumber than this would be a disclaimer stating: "No puppies were harmed in the making of this product."

5. The box of a 500-piece puzzle reads: "Some assembly required."

6. A Power Puff Girls costume discourages: "You cannot save the world!"

7. A box of PMS relief tablets has this advice: "Warning: Do not use if you have prostate problems."

8. Cans of Easy Cheese contain this instruction: "For best results, remove cap."

9. A warning label on a nighttime sleep-aid reads: "Warning: May cause drowsiness."

10. Cans of self-defense pepper spray caution: "May irritate eyes."

11. Both boys and girls should read the label on the Harry Potter toy broom: "This broom does not actually fly."

Tulipmania

❖ ❖ ❖ ❖

Cabbage Patch Kids, Tickle Me Elmo, Nintendo Wii—there have definitely been some big buying fads in the past. But in the winter of 1636–37, the Netherlands went crazy for tulips.

A Growing Commodity

The tulip had first reached Europe from Ottoman Turkey around 1560, brought home by diplomats and merchants who admired the flowers in the gardens of Istanbul. By 1633, about 500 different varieties were being grown in the Dutch Republic alone. Fashionable varieties prized by connoisseurs for their brilliant color and unpredictable "flamed," "feathered," and striped patterns, were sold by the bulb, the price based on rarity and the weight of the bulb. The more common, single-color varieties were sold by the basket.

At first, the sale of bulbs was tied to the growing season. Bulbs were bought between June, when they were "lifted" from the ground after they had bloomed, and October, when they were planted again. But around 1634, growers began to sell tulips in the winter for future delivery, adding new instability to the unregulated tulip market. Sales contracts were written for a particular bulb from a particular location, to be delivered and paid for when the bulbs were lifted the following June. Some tulips changed hands several times before they even bloomed.

The Tulip Boom

Between 1634 and 1635, people began to go bonkers for bulbs. The plague had ravaged the Netherlands between 1633 and 1635, causing a serious labor shortage. Still, wages were high, and people could afford small luxuries. Skilled tradesmen might not be able to afford a fashionable bulb, but they could easily afford a basket of common bulbs or even a single-color breeder bulb. At the same time, tulips became fashionable in France. Women wore clusters of tulips in their bosoms, and wealthy men competed to buy the most dramatic blooms. The supply of bulbs could not keep up with increased demand from both the bottom and the top of the market. Prices began to rise.

When the lifting season arrived in 1636, many varieties had already doubled in price. By December, prices were rising so quickly that the value of some bulbs doubled in little more than a week. An Admiral van der Eyck bulb was offered for 1,000 guilders—the price of a modest house. The price for common bulbs rose even more quickly than those for rare varieties, increasing 20 times over the course of a few weeks.

Bulb Bust
The tulip market reached its height at the auction of a private bulb collection in Alkmaar on February 5, 1637. Buyers came from all over the Netherlands to bid on the bulbs, whose owners also ran an orphanage. By the end of the day, the auctioneers had raised 90,000 guilders for the orphaned children. (A skilled tradesman in Amsterdam earned an average of 250 guilders a year.)

A week later, the market crashed due to doubts as to whether or not prices would increase. Bulb prices dropped by the hour, and sellers began to worry they would not be paid for bulbs that already had been pre-sold. Meanwhile, buyers feared they would be forced to pay inflated prices for now worthless bulbs. The scramble was on, and conflicts over the sale of bulbs were so common that the High Court of Holland allowed tulip-related claims in the courts only if the parties could not work it out for themselves.

A Healthy Bloom
The tulip market recovered its equilibrium quickly. Connoisseurs continued to buy rare bulbs at high prices. As first the tulip and then the hyacinth became fashionable in other European countries, Dutch growers developed a thriving export trade in flower bulbs. Ironically, Dutch tulip growers shipped tens of thousands of tulip bulbs to the Ottoman court, which was rocked by its own version of tulipmania in the 1690s. Today the Netherlands produces 60 percent of the commercially grown flowers in the world; of these flowers, tulips are still the most popular.

He Said, She Said

"I grew up with six brothers. That's how I learned to dance—waiting for the bathroom."

—*Bob Hope*

"Kids. They're not easy. But there has to be some penalty for sex."

—*Bill Maher*

"Life would be infinitely happier if we could only be born at the age of 80 and gradually approach 18."

—*Mark Twain*

"Frisbeetarianism is the belief that when you die, your soul goes up on the roof and gets stuck."

—*George Carlin*

"I don't make jokes. I just watch the government and report the facts."

—*Will Rogers*

"Everybody knows how to raise children, except the people who have them."

—*P. J. O'Rourke*

"The Supreme Court has ruled that they cannot have a nativity scene in Washington, D.C. This wasn't for any religious reasons. They couldn't find three wise men and a virgin."

—*Jay Leno*

"Adults are always asking kids what they want to be when they grow up because they are looking for ideas."

—*Paula Poundstone*

"Women won't let me stay single and I won't let me stay married."

—*Errol Flynn*

"Boxing is a lot of white men watching two black men beat each other up."

—*Muhammad Ali*

"Marriages don't last. When I meet a guy, the first question I ask myself is: Is this the man I want my children to spend their weekends with?"

—*Rita Rudner*

The Trials of a Ball Turret Gunner

❖ ❖ ❖ ❖

Depending on whom you talk to, the job of a ball turret gunner or belly gunner was either the best or the worst job to have on a B-17 Flying Fortress flight crew during World War II. Chosen because of their small stature, ball turret gunners had to withstand extremely cramped quarters, hours of subzero temperatures, extreme heights, and death—all without the benefit of wearing a parachute.

All the Comforts of Home

During the Second World War, the B-17 Flying Fortresses were the mainstays in thousands of combat missions flown over enemy lines. Each bomber depended on ten crewmembers; the smallest and most nimble were assigned to sit in the ball turret.

The ball turret was a small, bubblelike compartment made of glass and plastic that housed two .50-caliber machine guns. Mounted on the underside of the aircraft, the ball turret was so small that the gunner could only be lowered into the turret through an escape door after takeoff while the guns were pointing straight down. Once inside the turret, the gunner sat curled up in a fetal position with his feet secured in overhead stirrups, straddling a 13-inch armored-glass window that was his main vantage point during battle. The gunner looked through his knees and operated a red sight with his left foot that framed the target. The ends of the machine guns projected backward (as did the gunners), just inches from either side of the gunner's head. Two handles on either side of the window allowed him to rotate the turret 90° up and down and 360° in either direction and fire the machine guns.

Bunny Suits to the Rescue

Unlike the other crew members' toasty, wool-lined flight suits, the ball turret gunners were extremely limited by space, so they depended on thin fabric flight suits that were worn over electrically heated "blue bunny suits" to ward off the cold. After sliding into the turret, the gunners would plug into an electrical outlet that would heat their blue bunny suits—

It was fairly common for ball turret gunners to spend 10 to 12 continuous hours suspended inside their turret—definitely in excess of one's average bladder-retention capability. "Having to relieve oneself was a constant," said Harold "Diz"

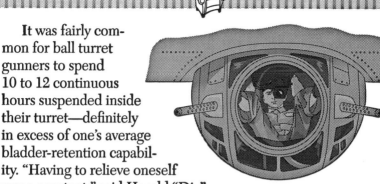

Kronenberg, a World War II ball turret gunner. "Relief tubes in the fuselage benefited the other crewmen but were of little value to a ball turret gunner... at high altitudes, the relief tubes often froze up and were, therefore, of no value to anyone." Just in case, Kronenberg said, gunners always brought along an empty can.

The Good News and the Bad News

While many B-17 crewmembers considered the ball turret the worst crew assignment on the aircraft, they also agreed that it was the safest. Because the turret could rotate up and down as well as in both directions, they also enjoyed one of the best views and were the first to notice incoming attackers. Ironically, postwar analysis of fatality records showed they also experienced the fewest number of battle wounds.

Of course, it wasn't all high flying. On January 3, 1943, Alan Magee was a ball turret gunner who was wounded while flying his seventh mission in a B-17 dubbed *Snap! Crackle! Pop!* During a daytime bombing raid over Saint-Nazaire, France, a German fighter shot off part of the bomber's right wing, sending it into a tailspin toward the ground.

Magee managed to climb out of his ball turret but had to leap from the plane without a parachute and fell more than four miles before crashing through a glass roof of a train station. Although the roof helped break his fall, Magee sustained 28 shrapnel wounds, several broken bones, damage to his nose, an eye, lung, kidney, and he nearly severed an arm. After being interned behind enemy lines, Magee was liberated by U.S. troops in May 1945. He received the Air Medal for meritorious conduct and a Purple Heart for his efforts.

FLUBBED HEADLINES

"Man Minus Ear Waives Hearing"

"Bank Drive-in Window Blocked by Board"

"Hospitals Are Sued by 7 Foot Doctors"

"Marijuana Issue Sent To a Joint Committee"

"Include Your Children When Baking Cookies"

"Something Went Wrong in Jet Crash, Experts Say"

"Police Begin Campaign to Run Down Jaywalkers"

"Drunks Get Nine Months in Violin Case"

"Governor Chiles Offers Rare Opportunity to Goose Hunters"

"Iraqi Head Seeks Arms"

"Panda Mating Fails; Veterinarian Takes Over"

"Miners Refuse to Work After Death"

"Stolen Painting Found by Tree"

"If Strike Isn't Settled Quickly, It May Last a While"

"Farmer Bill Dies in House"

"Gasoline Stations Will Also Offer Mammograms"

"Squad Helps Dog Bite Victim"

"Enraged Cow Injures Farmer with Ax"

"Cold Wave Linked to Temperatures"

"Chef Throws His Heart into Helping Feed Needy"

"Deaf College Opens Doors to Hearing"

"Old School Pillars Are Replaced by Alumni"

"Some Pieces of Rock Hudson Sold at Auction"

"Sex Education Delayed, Teachers Request Training"

"Yellow Snow Studied to Test Nutrition"

Sitting on the Laps of Power

❖ ❖ ❖ ❖

Former Secretary of State Henry Kissinger called power
"the ultimate aphrodisiac." For centuries, influential—and
married—men have been attracting women drawn by power.

Presidential Follies

American presidential dalliances seemed almost
commonplace in the 20th century. Bill Clinton
had Monica Lewinsky. Franklin D. Roosevelt
had a decades-long affair with Lucy Mercer
(later Rutherfurd). In fact, it was she, and not his
wife Eleanor, who was with him when he died
at Warm Springs, Georgia, in 1945. John
Kennedy allegedly had Angie Dickinson,
Marilyn Monroe, Jayne Mansfield, and
Judith Campbell Exner, among others.

Lucy Mercer

Warren G. Harding worked as a genial
former newspaper editor and U.S. senator
from Ohio before he decided to capitalize
on America's war-weariness by running for president. He became the
nation's 29th president in 1920, and he promised America a "return
to normalcy." However, despite being married to a woman he called
"Duchess," Harding had previously carried on a 15-year-long affair
with Carrie Phillips, the wife of a good friend.

When that affair ended, he took up with Nan Britton, a much
younger woman who was rumored to still be a virgin when she began
seeing Harding. The innocence didn't last long—after one particular
night of passion in the Senate Office Building in January 1919, she
conceived a child. After Harding's death in 1927, Britton published
a tell-all book of their trysts, *The President's Daughter.* So much for
"normalcy."

Amorous Also-Rans

Sometimes a man lusting after both the presidency and other
women finds the two desires don't mix well. Such was the case in
July 1791, when U.S. Treasury Secretary Alexander Hamilton began

an affair with Maria Reynolds, a pretty 23-year-old woman who tearfully implored him for help as her husband had left her. A few months later Reynolds's husband James, a professional con man, mysteriously returned, and blackmailed Hamilton. Although he paid $1,750 to keep the affair quiet, Hamilton learned the sad truth that blackmailers are never satisfied. In 1797, the affair came to light, creating one of the first sex scandals in American politics. Although Hamilton apologized, many historians believe the damage to his reputation cost him the presidency he so coveted.

Another man who saw his presidential chances wrecked on the rocks of infidelity was Gary Hart. The odds-on favorite to win the 1988 Democratic presidential nomination, the married senator from Colorado was caught by the press in April 1987, in the company of Donna Rice, a blonde 29-year-old actress and model. One of the places they had allegedly been together was on a yacht called, appropriately enough, *Monkey Business.* After several days of feverish headlines, Hart withdrew from the presidential race. Although he reentered the race later that year, Hart's monkey business had finished him as a force in national politics.

Political cost was likely not on the mind of Thomas Jefferson if, and when, he began an affair with Sally Hemings, a slave at Monticello. Although he was a powerful political figure, Jefferson was also a lonely widower who had promised his dying wife in 1782 that he would never remarry. At the time, scholars hypothesize, that he began the affair with Hemings, the presidency must have seemed a distant dream. However, in 1800, Jefferson became president. Two years later, a newspaper editor named James Callendar first published the charge that Jefferson and Hemings were an item, thus igniting a historical controversy that still rages today. Even modern methods like DNA testing have failed to positively identify Thomas Jefferson as the father of Hemings's children. The only thing certain is that this story is far from over.

Foreign Affairs

Of course, it is not only American political figures that have had a roving eye. Charles Stewart Parnell was a leader of the Ireland's Independence Movement in the 1880s. It seemed as if British Prime Minister William Gladstone was about to support Parnell and

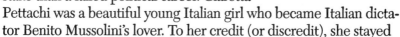

finally give Ireland its freedom, but in November 1890, it was revealed that Parnell had long been involved with Kitty O'Shea, the wife of William Henry O'Shea. The disclosure rocked prim-and-proper England, causing Gladstone to distance himself from Parnell and pull back from endorsing Irish independence. Thus not just a political career, but also the fate of an entire nation was affected by one man's indiscretion.

Kitty O' Shea

Of course, there's much more at stake than a failed political career. Claretta Pettachi was a beautiful young Italian girl who became Italian dictator Benito Mussolini's lover. To her credit (or discredit), she stayed loyal to him to the end. In April 1945, she and Mussolini were captured as they tried to flee Italy. According to legend, Pettachi was offered her freedom but refused, and she threw her body in front of Mussolini's in a vain attempt to shield him from a firing squad's bullets. Photos show their bodies, which were subsequently hung upside down in a public square.

Claretta Pettachi

Pettachi's devotion to her fascist lover is perhaps only topped by that of Prince Pedro of Portugal. Pedro began an affair with one of his wife's maids, Inês de Castro, who bore him two children. His wife died in 1349, and de Castro was put to death in 1355. When Pedro became king in 1357, he had his mistress' body exhumed, married the corpse, and forced his entire court to honor her remains.

History is filled with many more examples of famous men and the women they attracted. However, the attraction doesn't seem to work in the opposite direction—stories of powerful women and the men they attracted are much less common. Perhaps it is as Eleanor Roosevelt once observed: "[How] men despise women who have real power."

27 Silly Presidential Nicknames

❖ ❖ ❖ ❖

President	Nickname
1. James Monroe	Last Cocked Hat
2. John Quincy Adams	Old Man Eloquent
3. Martin Van Buren	The Little Magician; Martin Van Ruin
4. John Tyler	His Accidency
5. Zachary Taylor	Old Rough and Ready
6. Millard Fillmore	His Accidency
7. James Buchanan	The Bachelor President; Old Buck
8. Andrew Johnson	King Andy; Sir Veto
9. Ulysses S. Grant	Useless; Unconditional Surrender
10. Rutherford B. Hayes	Rutherfraud Hayes; His Fraudulency
11. James Garfield	The Preacher; The Teacher President
12. Grover Cleveland	Uncle Jumbo; His Obstinacy
13. Benjamin Harrison	Little Ben; White House Iceberg
14. William McKinley	Wobbly Willie; Idol of Ohio
15. Woodrow Wilson	The Schoolmaster
16. Warren Harding	Wobbly Warren
17. Herbert Hoover	The Great Engineer
18. Harry Truman	The Haberdasher
19. John F. Kennedy	King of Camelot
20. Lyndon B. Johnson	Big Daddy
21. Richard M. Nixon	Tricky Dick
22. Gerald Ford	The Accidental President
23. Jimmy Carter	The Peanut Farmer
24. Ronald Reagan	Dutch; The Gipper; The Great Communicator
25. George H. W. Bush	Poppy
26. Bill Clinton	Bubba; Slick Willie; The Comeback Kid
27. George W. Bush	Junior; W; Dubya

Footnotes: The Who, What, and Wear of Shoes

❖ ❖ ❖ ❖

Look down at your feet—do your shoes give away your birthplace, income level, or your social status? Do they tell the world what you do for a living, what your hobbies are, or whether you're married? Well, they certainly did in the past.

When Moses climbed Mount Sinai to chat with God, he was commanded by God to "Put off thy shoes, for the ground whereon thou standest is holy." At that moment, Moses learned one of the first important lessons about footwear; since then, many societies have dictated that discarding one's shoes is a demonstration of humility and piety. For the rest of us, shoes continue to speak volumes about who we are, how much money we make, and what we do for a living. Read on for some shoe-related facts!

Early Functions of Shoes

- Even though shoes had been around for centuries, it wasn't until the Middle Ages that simple sandals had evolved into shoes that were designed for comfort as much as functionality. For the first time, shoes were made with leather uppers, mainly for warmth and protection from the elements. The *sabot* was a primitive shoe that was made in only two sizes: big and bigger. They tended to be very uncomfortable for two reasons: first, men's and women's hosiery were not always available and second, shoes were made on a single last, so there were no "right" or "left" shoes.

- 1818 proved to be a big year for footwear: Shoes were finally made with unique right and left lasts. The sabot was replaced by the English clog, which had a wood sole and a fabric upper.

- By the 1900s, shoes were being made in part by machines, and they came in more than 150 sizes. Even today, the average American woman buys more than five pairs of shoes a year, whereas men buy only two pairs.

- During the Christian Crusades, parishioners who wore shoes whose toes were so long that the footwear prevented them from being able to kneel in church often outraged clergymen. As a result, they decreed that no one wearing shoes with toes longer than two inches could attend services.

- To standardize sizing, English King Edward II determined in 1324 that an "average" size shoe measured 39 barleycorns when laid end to end. This length was rather arbitrarily decided to be a size 13. All other sizes are based on this standard.

- The largest shoe size on record belongs to a Florida man who wears a size 42 shoe (or 68 barleycorns).

Fashion Takes Over the Shoe Industry

- The Egyptians were one of the first people to wear shoes that depicted the owner's social status. Peasants tended to wear "comfortable" sandals made from woven papyrus with a flat sole that were lashed to their ankles with reeds. More affluent citizens could be identified by sandals with pointed toes, particularly red or yellow in color. If you were a slave, however, chances are you went without shoes altogether.

- In the 16th century, shoes often inhibited movement instead of facilitating it. Not to be outdone by their predecessors' pumps, French women began wearing shoes with higher and higher heels. Some Venetian women wore shoes that were more than 13 inches high, requiring that they be carried by servants and hoisted in and out of their gondolas. And for centuries, it was considered a status symbol for Chinese women to have "three-inch golden lotuses" for feet. This was done by a method of repeatedly breaking and binding their feet starting at age seven or so.

- During the Crusades, shoes defined the wearer. While peasants and others involved in manual labor wore sturdy, functional shoes, aristocrats often wore shoes that were clearly for show instead of purpose. Some shoes worn by the wealthy featured toes so long that they needed to be supported by chains fastened to their legs, slightly below their knees.

Santa, Is that You?

America's Santa Claus owes a big thank-you to a German artist.

Thomas Nast is famous in American history as the cartoonist whose drawings brought down Boss Tweed. Less well known is that if it wasn't for Nast, jolly ol' Santa Claus might look very different today.

Ho Ho, Er, *Who* Are You?

Initially Santa's image followed his origins as St. Nicholas, and he was often depicted as a stern, lean, patriarchal figure in flowing religious robes. Around 1300, however, St. Nicholas adopted the flowing white beard of the Northern European god Odin. Years passed, and once across the Atlantic Ocean (and in America), Nicholas began to look more like a gnome. He shrunk in physical size, often smoked a Dutch-style pipe, and dressed in various styles of clothing that made him seem like anything from a secondhand-store fugitive to a character from *1001 Arabian Nights.* One eerie 1837 picture shows him with baleful, beady black eyes and an evil smirk.

Santa Savior

Into this muddled situation stepped Nast. As a cartoonist for the national newspaper *Harper's Weekly,* the Bavarian-born Nast often depicted grim subjects such as war and death. When given the option to draw St. Nicholas, he jumped at the opportunity to do something joyful. His first Santa Claus cartoon appeared in January 1863, and he continued to produce them for more than two decades.

Nast put a twinkle in Santa's eye, increased his stature to full-size and round-bellied, and gave him a jolly temperament. Nast's Santa ran a workshop at the North Pole, wore a red suit trimmed in white, and carried around a list of good and bad children.

Nast surrounded Santa Claus with symbols of Christmas: toys, holly, mistletoe, wishful children, a reindeer-drawn sleigh on a snowy roof, and stockings hung by the fireplace. Nast tied all these previously disparate images together to form a complete picture of Santa and Christmas. Other artists later refined Santa Claus, but it was Thomas Nast who first made Santa into a Christmas story.

Grapple and Grind

❖ ❖ ❖ ❖

*From body slams to all-out glam, female grapplers have long been
a featured part of the pro wrestling game. Meet the Fabulous
Moolah and some of the other gals of women's wrestling.*

Rejecting the Status Quo

In the mid-1950s, women's roles were as clearly defined as they
were limited. For many women in the United States, the burgeoning
"baby-boom" spelled out their fate: They would become housewives.
It was also an era of high femininity and manners, where popular
culture dictated what was deemed "ladylike" or not.

Still, amid this model, fringe elements were flowering. In professional wrestling, a new women's division took these accepted roles
of femininity and stood them flat on their cauliflower ears. Under
this entertaining banner, tough, self-assured women were suddenly
tossed into the white-hot spotlight. Literally. Among the standout
acts was a woman named Moolah.

Meet Moolah

Lillian Ellison hit the wrestling game at the
perfect time. Women were screaming for
excitement, and men were eager for the
next gimmick. But timing wasn't something that Ellison was overly concerned
with. She moved to her own beat and set
her own goals. In the early 1950s, she married and became a very young mother as a
teenager. The union would last only two years,
but it reinforced Ellison's free-spirit outlook on life. Despite having a
baby to raise, Ellison, an ardent wrestling fan, decided to suit up and
give the professional ranks a shot. History was about to be made.

As the "Fabulous Moolah" Ellison gave both genders what they
wanted. With her signature moves, such as the "Big Punch," the
"School Girl Roll Up," and the "Spiral Backbreaker," Moolah was
unlike anything wrestling fans had ever seen. In 1956, she would

The Day the Music Died

❖ ❖ ❖ ❖

Death happens to everybody and, whatever the
circumstances, it is always tragic. Read further for stories
of pop stars whose candles burned a little too brightly.

Michael Hutchence, singer for INXS

One of the great inconveniences of death is that the deceased has no
control over what happens immediately after death—there isn't time
to tidy up the house, fix one's hair, or turn off the stove. Or, in the
case of Michael Hutchence, no opportunity to put on some clothes.
Typically, those who choose to take their own life have the advantage of foreknowledge and can make certain arrangements, often
including a note of explanation. Hutchence, however, was reportedly
found nude with a belt nearby. That, and the absence of any written
confession, has led many to conclude that the 37-year-old died as the
accidental result of autoerotic asphyxiation—that is, choking oneself
to achieve sexual gratification. His death, however, was officially
documented as a suicide. An ignoble end to a man who fronted one
of Australia's most successful bands.

Richard Manuel, member of The Band

Canadian singer and pianist Richard Manuel was just 18 years old
when he joined veteran rock 'n' roller Ronnie Hawkins's band,
The Hawks, in 1961. Together, Manuel and his bandmates slogged
through years of clubs and bars; in the process, they became good
friends and built a reputation as one of the world's best road bands,
working with music legends including Bob Dylan.

Eventually, The Hawks signed with Dylan's manager, changed
their name to The Band, and recorded a series of albums that
spawned years of critical and commercial success. Manuel was often
named as the best singer of the group, and he had plenty of admir-
ers, including Eric Clapton, who regarded him with awe. But by
1976, Manuel had deteriorated from a creative, compelling performer to an addict crippled by drugs and alcohol. After the group

broke up (their farewell concert was well documented in the film *The Last Waltz*, directed by Martin Scorsese), Manuel checked himself into rehab. Most of the members of The Band reunited at various times, with limited success. In January 1986, word of manager and longtime friend Albert Grossman's death sent Manuel back to his addictions. On March 14, 1986, Manuel hanged himself in a hotel room in Florida.

Herman Brood, Dutch rock star

He may not be a household name in America, but in Amsterdam the name Herman Brood carries the same weight as Elvis does in Memphis or Jerry Garcia does in San Francisco. Brood was a brilliant artist: a jack-of-all-trades who worked as a musician, painter, actor, and poet. Though he never achieved true international rock stardom, Brood's talent earned him the appreciation of music and art fans around the world.

With a reputation for excessive and unrestrained drug and alcohol abuse, Brood bounced through Dutch society with a buoyancy that defied reason but rarely seemed unmerited—after all, he had cl ss, he had grace, and even his critics had to admit that he was talented. But by the summer of 2001, Brood was depressed and tortured by an intense addiction to heroin, which he kept at bay through a daily diet of alcohol and speed. On July 11, 2001, he threw himself off the rooftop of the Amsterdam Hilton at age 54—a site that now conjures the memory of Holland's most brilliant pop star.

Hank Williams Sr., country music icon

Sure, his professional career lasted a scant five years and he was only 29 when he died in 1953, but Hank Williams Sr. covered a lot of ground during his short life. His 1949 recording of "Lovesick Blues" catapulted him into national prominence and led to a string of hits that cemented him as a country-music icon. To Williams, he was just doing what came naturally. "A song ain't nothin' in the world but a story just wrote with music to it," he said. But by mid-1952, Williams was in a bad state: His drinking was out of control and he was addicted to painkillers.

On December 30, Hank was driven from Montgomery, Alabama, to participate in a regional series of shows. Exactly what happened after that is still hotly debated. Some stories say that before leaving town, Williams had the driver stop at a doctor's office for injections of vitamin B-12 and morphine. After a night in a hotel, Williams and the driver made it as far as Knoxville, Tennessee, where they checked into a hotel. There, the reportedly inebriated Williams insisted on two additional shots of morphine.

Williams's promoter called to inform the driver that the star was still expected to perform in Canton, Ohio, the next day. The driver had two hotel orderlies carry the now-unconscious singer to the car. As the story goes, another driver eventually took over, with Williams apparently sleeping in the back seat. It wasn't until the next morning that the driver realized that Williams was dead. He was officially pronounced dead on January 1, 1953. Despite the rumors surrounding his death, Williams will always be remembered as having died on the way to a show he couldn't miss.

Nikki Sixx, bassist for Mötley Crüe (not dead, though not for lack of trying)

He was the kind of kid that convenience store owners hate: a thief, drug abuser, and foul-mouthed delinquent. Born Frank Carlton Serafino Ferrana, the man who would become known to heavy metal fans as Nikki Sixx, learned to play rock bass in Idaho. In 1975, at age 17, he moved to Los Angeles and changed his name. Sixx drifted in and out of bands, jobs, and drug habits before scoring big with the heavy metal band Mötley Crüe.

The band enjoyed a string of hits, mostly written by Sixx. Overwhelmed by success, Crüe members indulged in every possible vice; Sixx later said that at the time he considered his body a "human chemistry experiment" and would haphazardly mix narcotics and alcohol in search of a new high. On one occasion, he claimed to have overdosed at a London heroin dealer's house and, after being beaten back to life with a wooden club, was unceremoniously deposited in a Dumpster. In December 1987, he overdosed again, and for two minutes he was technically dead at an L.A. hospital. He revived after two shots of adrenaline were injected directly into his heart. Soon afterward the whole band entered rehab, emerging drug free.

Odd Ordinances

- Insulting a rice plant used to be illegal in Cambodia.

- Cab drivers aren't allowed to carry rabid dogs or corpses anywhere in London.

- It's a crime to die while in London's House of Parliament.

- Placing a postage stamp with the British monarch upside down is against the law.

- Naming a pig "Napoleon" in France is illegal.

- Grabbing a taxicab while sick with the plague is strictly prohibited in London.

- Driving while blindfolded could get you arrested in Alabama.

- Any Royal Navy ship going into the Port of London is legally required to give the Tower of London's constable a barrel of rum.

- Male doctors in the Islamic country of Bahrain are only allowed to look at a woman's genitals through a mirror during an examination.

- A pregnant woman is legally allowed to urinate anywhere she desires in the United Kingdom. The law further specifies that even a policeman's helmet is acceptable.

- Skateboarding in a police station is illegal in Miami, Florida.

- Indonesia has outlawed the act of masturbation. It is punishable by decapitation.

- All English boys and men age 14 and older are technically required to practice longbow skills for two hours every day.

- London law specifies that firemen will not have to pay tolls while carrying sheep or geese.

- It is against the law for unmarried women to parachute on a Sunday anywhere in Florida.

All Hail the Emperor!

Meet Mr. Joshua Abraham Norton: businessman, citizen of San Francisco, and the first Emperor of the United States of America.

Humble Beginnings

Joshua Norton, America's first and only "Emperor," was born in England in 1819. Soon after his birth, Norton and his family relocated to South Africa. When his father died, Norton found he was the recipient of $40,000 from his father's estate.

With inheritence money in pocket, 30-year-old Norton headed to San Francisco in 1849 where he quickly set about amassing a small fortune in real estate. However, a failed attempt to corner the San Francisco rice market left Norton in financial ruin. After declaring bankruptcy in 1858, Norton left the Bay area for a short time.

He returned a year later, but the stress and strain caused by his economic downfall had taken its toll on Norton, who not only lost his money, but also his marbles. No longer having use for the United States and its government, on September 17, 1859, Norton officially proclaimed himself "Emperor of These United States."

The Reign of Emperor Norton I

As the self-proclaimed emperor, Norton quickly (though impotently) moved to dissolve Congress, ordered the U.S. Army to forcibly stop the meeting of said body, and abolished both the Republican and Democratic parties.

Norton also demanded the construction of a bridge spanning the bay to connect San Francisco and Oakland. He was a man of the people, and the Emperor spent his days tirelessly inspecting the streets of his hometown until his death on January 8, 1880.

On the occasion of his funeral, more than 20,000 of his subjects, "from capitalists to the pauper, the clergyman to the pickpocket, well-dressed ladies and those whose garb and bearing hinted of the social outcast," took to the streets to show their appreciation for their fallen faux leader.

Weird Theme Restaurants

When good food and service are just not enough, it's comforting to know that there is a plethora of new experiences for the discriminating (and adventurous) diner. Here's a quick look at some of the more imaginative restaurants vying for your dining dollar, and where to find them.

Moscow

Looking for a thrill? **Gogol** is an underground restaurant located in the heart of downtown Moscow. Designed to look like a wartime bunker, guests are alerted when their order is ready to be picked up by an ear-shattering air raid siren.

If that doesn't suit you, try **The Real McCoy.** In order to find the entrance to the restaurant, diners must find the secret door identified by a small plaque. After knocking, a doorman confirms your identity by peering through a small peephole. Inside, The Real McCoy looks like a 1930s Prohibition-era speakeasy, complete with a brass still. Mug shots of the staff (or "inmates") adorn the walls of the bar.

Taiwan

If you long to relive that night spent in the hospital getting your gallbladder removed, you'll simply love the **D.S. Music Restaurant.** Borrowing from the ever-popular medical theme, guests are seated around a hospital bed. Visitors can also order cocktails (called "medicine") served in IV bags administered by sexily clad "nurses."

Just when you thought you've seen it all, the **Modern Toilet** restaurant stands poised to offer its clients the very best in lavatory cuisine. The Modern Toilet "seats" 100 guests on porcelain commodes instead of chairs, where they feast from a menu of items served on miniature toilet seats. Can't find the napkins? Just reach to your side and grab some toilet paper.

The Jail captures all of the memories of your last incarceration with none of the filth or unpleasant smell. From the moment that you pass through the solid steel doors, you'll thrill at the feel of your wrists being shackled as you're escorted to an intimate table located behind bars. Fortunately, The Jail features reasonably priced Chinese cuisine instead of chipped beef on toast.

Tokyo

The restaurant **Alcatraz** offers something a little bit different in service and ambiance. Also known as the Shibuya Medical Prison, Alcatraz guests are shackled from the moment they enter the bar. After determining your blood type, inmates clad in black-and-white striped jailhouse uniforms lead you to a cell where you can order drinks like the "Influenza" and hover over your meal, which is served in a stainless steel kidney-shaped basin.

Some people never grow up. And why should they when they can dine at the **Alice in Wonderland Café**? From the moment you enter the Wonderland Café, you are made to feel like you belong at the Mad Hatter's tea party by an all-female staff of waitresses dressed in skimpy French maid costumes. While the main courses are on par with other restaurants, guests love the White Rabbit crepes and Tweedle Dee and Dum parfait.

United States

Leave it to the Americans to come up with a restaurant that's built around bowls of cereal. **Cereality** is a franchise with cafés located in Ohio, West Virginia, Minnesota, Florida, Texas, and Arizona. With the assistance of pajama-clad "cereologists," customers can choose from a wide variety of hot or cold cereal, doused with—you guessed it—milk!

When you've had enough of low-calorie, low-fat, heart-healthy cuisine, it's time to take the plunge at the **Heart Attack Grill** in Chandler, Arizona. The restaurant makes no apologies for their high-fat, high-cholesterol menu items. Instead, it touts the great taste of their Quadruple Bypass Burger and Flatliner Fries (fried in lard). Wash down the grease with a can of Jolt Cola or an item from their full line of retrograde beers.

Fast Facts

- *"Texas" evolved from the Caddo Indian greeting* te shas. *Since there is no "sh" sound in Spanish, early explorers and missionaries writing about their travels replaced the unfamiliar syllable with an "x" to make "te xas."*

- *The longest overdue book in the United States is 145 years (in Ohio). The longest in the world is 288 years (in Germany). We can't even imagine the late fee.*

- *Roses are the symbol of the Virgin Mary. Catholic "rosaries" were originally made of 165 dried and rolled rose petals.*

- *Corn has an even number of rows on each ear. The average ear has 800 kernels arranged in 16 rows.*

- *Disney's Space Mountain roller coaster was the first thrill attraction to be operated by a computer.*

- *The difference between a fruit and a vegetable is that fruits contain the seeds of the plant (so cucumbers and tomatoes are actually fruits!), while "vegetable" refers more generally to other edible parts of a plant, like lettuce leaves and carrots.*

- *Pizza Hut is the world's largest consumer of cheese: It uses 300 million pounds each year.*

- *Until the early 1800s, Hawaiian law forbade women from eating bananas—under penalty of death.*

- *The popular building block toy Lego takes its name from the Danish phrase* leg godt, *meaning "play well."*

- *The brown bat needs more sleep than any animal (20 hours a day), while the giraffe needs the least amount (only 2 hours a day).*

The Last Days of Pompeii

❖ ❖ ❖ ❖

*In the early days of the new millennium, Pompeii was
a popular, bustling city. In an instant, it was over.*

Calm and Quiet

In August A.D. 79, Pompeii was a bustling Roman city of about
20,000 people. Located in a fertile agricultural region on the Bay
of Naples, the city was the center of Rome's Mediterranean trade.
Only a few days travel from Rome, Pompeii was a popular resort
for wealthy Romans. It was also
famous for the production and sale
of *garum,* a spicy sauce made from
fish entrails.

Mount Vesuvius had been
quiet for 800 years; in fact, it had
been such a long time that
practically no one remem-
bered that the volcano even
existed. However, minor
earthquakes were common,
and there had been a major
earthquake 17 years earlier. After that catastrophe, Pompeii had
rebuilt and carried on. But in mid-August of 79, the earth began to
rumble once more. Streams and wells dried up, and the sea became
unusually turbulent. The townspeople murmured about portents
and omens, but they were not alarmed enough to evacuate the city.

Buried in Ashes

Our only eyewitness accounts of the disaster come from two letters
written by Pliny the Younger, who was a teenager when he watched
the eruption from the town of Misenum, across the Bay of Naples.
According to Pliny, Vesuvius erupted in the early afternoon of August
24, sending a cloud of smoke that billowed into the sky "like an
umbrella pine." Modern scientists estimate that the eruption shot
12 miles into the air. By the time Pliny and his mother decided to

evacuate, "a dense black cloud was coming up behind us, spreading over the earth like a flood." When the darkness finally thinned, "we were horrified to see everything changed, buried deep in ashes like snow drifts."

It looked bad from afar, but the situation was far worse in Pompeii. The disaster began with a light fall of ash, which accelerated into a hail of lava shards and pumice. At first, people retreated into their homes. Clouds of ash filled the air, making it hard to breathe and cloaking the city in darkness. As the falling stones grew larger and volcanic debris began to accumulate at the rate of five to six inches per hour, many people tried to leave the city. Those who fled inland, carrying a few possessions, had a chance for survival. Those who fled toward the sea found their escape blocked by violent waves made more dangerous by floating pumice.

Continuing Horror

By sunset, the volcano's activity seemed to slow. Some Pompeians who had survived the initial eruption dug their way out of their homes and tried to escape the city, scrambling over an accumulation of pumice and ash that was two feet deep. As the evening progressed, the rain of pumice turned from white to gray, and the size of the stones continued to increase. By midnight, first-floor doors and windows were completely blocked. The accumulated volcanic debris was now five feet deep.

Shortly after, the eruptions entered a second, more dangerous, phase. As the volcano's power waned, portions of the crust collapsed. As a result, avalanches of hot ash, pumice, rock fragments, and volcanic gases rushed toward the cities around the Bay of Naples at a speed scientists estimate was approximately 60 to 180 miles per hour. Surge and flow destroyed everything in their path with a deadly combination of heat and speed, and then covered the ruins with a flood of hot volcanic debris.

The first two surges did not get as far as Pompeii; the third surge reached the city in the early morning. Roofs collapsed under the weight of falling rock. Those who were not buried alive died from extreme heat or suffocated from breathing in the hot ash. Three more surges followed in quick succession. By 8 A.M., the city of Pompeii was obliterated, frozen in time by more than 12 feet of volcanic debris.

Behind the TV Shows of Our Time

- The character of Uncle Jesse on *Full House* was originally named Uncle Adam. Actor John Stamos is credited with changing the name. He also changed his character's last name from Cochran to Katsopolis in the show's second season to reflect his own Greek background.

- As the Olsen twins grew older, producers considered splitting up the role of Michelle on *Full House* since they had started looking less similar than when they were toddlers. The girls' popularity, however, convinced the show's creators to keep both on staff despite appearance issues.

- Mary-Kate and Ashley Olsen were originally credited as "Mary-Kate Ashley Olsen" on *Full House,* because producers didn't want people to know two kids were playing the role.

- *Full House* was initially conceived as an adult-oriented comedy called *House of Comics*. Producers decided to change the name and the focus to target a more family-oriented audience.

- Actor Michael Muhney was considered for the lead role of J. D. on *Scrubs*. Producers decided to go with Zach Braff, though, because he seemed quirkier.

- *Scrubs* is filmed in an old abandoned hospital—the North Hollywood Medical Center in the San Fernando Valley. Extra floors are used for production offices and secondary sets.

- The hospital *a cappella* band fronted by *Scrubs* character Ted is actually a real band led by actor Sam Lloyd. The singers started performing together in college as The Blanks.

- The character Janitor on *Scrubs* was intended to never speak with or interact with any other character other than J. D., a concept that held through to part of the second season. Show creator Bill Lawrence wanted to use that as a final plot twist in case the series was canceled.

- In one *Scrubs* episode, Zach Braff and Sarah Chalke bungee jumped together. The stunt doubles who performed as Braff and Chalke previously hadn't met—but they ended up getting married.

ESCAPE!

KILLER BEES

Killer bees are among the most aggressive insects, and their stings can be fatal. Arm yourself with the knowledge to escape and you may end up saving your own life.

Killer bees are notorious for being easy to provoke and hard to escape. The African honeybee, as the killer bee is officially known, will chase humans many times the distance of its more common honeybee cousin (there have been reports of bees giving chase for over 600 yards). They can also stay angry for up to a full 24 hours. Here's what to do if you find yourself in its path:

- Don't hesitate, just run. The majority of human and animal deaths happen because victims don't get away fast enough.

- Keep your hands over your eyes, nose, and mouth as you dash. Bees primarily go after the face and head, so this will give you some form of protection.

- Don't swat; it will only make the bees angrier.

- Head for anywhere indoors, then duck into a dark corner and cover yourself. Bees usually won't follow you inside; if one does, it's likely to become confused and go toward the light at the window.

- If you can't find a building or a car, opt for bushes or high weeds instead. They're your next best protection.

- Never remain still, and never jump into water. Bees are smart enough to know you have to come up sooner or later, and they'll be waiting for you.

- If you do get stung, use a blunt knife or the edge of a credit card to scrape the stinger from your skin as soon as possible. Don't pinch or pull on it, as this could end up increasing the flow of the toxin into the body. And get to a doctor as soon as possible!

Rebel Yell

❖ ❖ ❖ ❖

*You say you want a revolution? Well, what happens when
no one shows up? Read on for some failed uprisings.*

Keep Your Powder Dry

The Gunpowder Plot of 1605 was certainly one of the times when the
rebel script didn't work out. Planned by Guy Fawkes and a few revolutionary cronies over an ale or two in a London pub called the Duck and
Drake, the plan entailed blowing up England's Houses of Parliament
while the Members and Lords were in session. Fawkes assumed that
before the rubble even settled, the oppressed populace would rise in
arms to take over the country.

The conspirators managed to secrete 36 barrels of gunpowder in
the cellar of the Parliament buildings, but Fawkes was nabbed before
he could put flame to fuse. A few of his co-conspirators escaped to the
countryside where they decided to make a last stand. Unfortunately,
their gunpowder was wet. They put the explosive near an open fire to
dry it out, which worked—but then it blew up in their faces.

As for the uprising, no one informed the populace of it happening.
Even so, the citizenry declared November 5 to be Guy Fawkes Day.
For years, a popular saying stated that Fawkes was "the only man ever
to enter Parliament with honest intentions."

Canceled Flights and Lost Luggage

Fidel Castro made a lot of people angry after he ran General Fulgencio
Batista out of Cuba in January 1959. First in line was Cuba's now-
displaced gentry, whom Castro had also chased off. He'd done the
same to some of the American organized crime families who ran
Havana's hotels and casinos. There was tension with the U.S. government, which had helped finance his revolution. Moreover, he cozied
up to the Soviet Union—not at all politic at the height of the Cold War.

But Cuban exiles weren't willing to simply mellow out and work
on their tans in Miami. They wanted their turf back. They vigorously
lobbied the U.S. government, arguing that an incendiary event—say,
an invasion—would spark a popular uprising by the oppressed Cuban

masses. The exiles were prepared to supply the manpower if the United States would train them and provide equipment and air support on the big day. They thought they had a deal.

The exiles rounded up some likely rebels, including 200 veterans of Batista's defeated army, and training got underway. On April 12, 1961, President John F. Kennedy announced that the country would not militarily intervene in Cuban affairs. The ex-pats thought that was a great piece of disinformation. On April 17, 1961, the rebels landed at the Bay of Pigs. Castro's army was there to greet them—the U.S. air support, however, was not. Thereafter, Cubans learned to keep their mouth shut regarding Castro's regime. In fact, any Cubans who did rise up publicly did so to protest the invasion.

Timing Is Everything

Unlike the Gunpowder Plot, the locals had plenty of notice in an 1837 plot in Upper Canada; after all, a "Declaration of Independence" had already been publicized. Its firebrand leader, William Lyon Mackenzie, figured that thanks to the Declaration and his advertisement posting in a local newspaper, at least 5,000 people would show up on the appointed date and time: December 7 at a local pub in York (present-day Toronto).

But word was slow to get around. Then someone changed the date to December 4. Consequently, only a few hundred farmers showed up. The weather was nasty, sleet and ice were on the roads, and the pub ran out of food. Most of the farmers returned home.

Everyone was back at the pub the next morning. The plan was to march into the town, put the run on any resistance, and hang the British-appointed governor. Rebels with muskets led the march, followed by the rank and file armed mostly with clubs and pitchforks. The local sheriff, manned with a couple dozen soldiers, confronted the rabble on the main street. They exchanged a round of musket fire. When the rebel shooters knelt to reload, the farmers following them thought they'd all been shot. Figuring their big guns gone, the farmers promptly hied it back to their respective homesteads.

The townsfolk paid the affair little attention. Top on the agenda at the next town council meeting wasn't the abortive rebellion; instead, they hotly debated a bylaw to prohibit citizens from letting their pigs roam freely on York's streets. The bylaw passed.

18 Odd Items for Sale in Japanese Vending Machines

Japan seems to have a yen for selling unusual products via vending machines—they sell more than any other country. Aside from the usual candy and gum, here are some of the more obscure items available for purchase in Japanese vending machines.

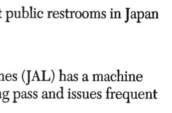

1. Fresh eggs
2. Bags of rice in various sizes
3. Fishing line, fish hooks, and fish bait
4. Toilet paper in small packets—most public restrooms in Japan charge a fee for toilet paper
5. Fresh flowers
6. Frequent flyer miles—Japan Air Lines (JAL) has a machine that reads a credit card and boarding pass and issues frequent flyer miles
7. Beer in cans—or two-liter jugs
8. Film and disposable cameras
9. Pornographic magazines
10. Designer condoms
11. Batteries
12. Live rhinoceros beetles—a popular pet for Japanese children
13. Kerosene for home space heaters
14. Dry ice—sold at supermarkets for keeping frozen food cold until the customer gets home
15. Sake in preheated containers
16. Cups of hot noodles
17. Fortunes—these machines are found at shrines and temples
18. Umbrellas—for both rain and shade

PALINDROMES

A palindrome is a phrase that reads the same in both directions. The word is derived from the Greek palíndromos, *which means running back again (palín = again; drom-, dramein = to run).*

Go hang a salami; I'm a lasagna hog!

Go deliver a dare, vile dog

Dr. Awkward

Oozy rat in a sanitary zoo

A man, a plan, a canal—Panama!

Bird rib

Dee saw a seed

A dog! A panic in a pagoda!

Deer breed

Live not on evil

Devil never even lived

Do offer a ref food

Marge let a moody baby doom a telegram

Doom an evil deed, liven a mood

Draw noses onward

Evil olive

Gary knits a stinky rag

Evade me, Dave

Desserts I desire not, so long no lost one rise distressed

No lemons, no melon

Norah's foes order red rose of Sharon

Harass selfless Sarah

The Multimillion-Dollar Manhattan Mystery

When a family hired an architect to design their new 4,200-square-foot apartment, they had no idea what they'd gotten themselves into.

In 2003, the Klinsky family decided they wanted their recently purchased Manhattan home to be unique. It was an understandable request; after all, they paid $8.5 million for the place. So when the family found architect Eric Clough and heard his impressive vision, they immediately hired him for the job.

Of course, what they didn't know then was that they'd heard only half of Clough's plan for their home—and that the other half wouldn't be discovered until months after they'd moved in.

The Conception
Clough says it all started when Mr. Klinsky handed him a poem he'd written and asked to have it put into a bottle and hidden behind a wall as a sort of time capsule for his family. The concept gave Clough the idea that would eventually make national news: He would set out to create a complex mystery built into the apartment, complete with clues that would take the family on a fictional journey through time. He laboriously researched ciphers and codes, secret compartments, and contraptions and spent years creating the most majestic design he'd ever imagined.

The Discovery
Fast forward to May 2006. The Klinsky family (including mom, dad, four children, and a dog) moved into their apartment. They were pleased with the results; everything looked great and seemed normal. Well, it did for about four months.

The first mystery was discovered when one of the sons and a friend were playing in his bedroom. The boy was looking intently at the room's radiator when he noticed letters carved into the grille. Somehow, the child realized they were in a code (later identified as the Caesar Shift cipher, in which each letter is replaced by a letter three positions lower in the alphabet). Decoded, the words spelled the son's name.

Several more unusual events unfolded, all with Clough refusing to give any explanation. Finally, the family received a cryptic letter with a poem directing them to a hidden panel. That's when the true scavenger hunt began.

The First Clue

Inside the panel, the family found a book that Clough had custom-written and bound. Clue by clue, the story took them through trap doors and hidden compartments within their own home, producing a complex web that took weeks to unravel.

Eighteen difficult clues later, the mystery led them to a set of hallway panels. The Klinskys had to take off two decorative doorknockers and form them together to make a crank. In turn, that crank opened hidden panels in a dining room cabinet that contained another series of keys and keyholes. Once the family figured out what keys matched with what holes, they discovered a set of drawers with a crossword puzzle. The puzzle led to more hidden panels in another room, which led to a hidden magnet, which opened more hidden panels, which contained—at long last—the original poem the father had asked Clough to hide.

The Process

This intense mystery spared no expense. Clough's fee for the renovation was more than $1.2 million—a number he says didn't even begin to cover the project's cost. (Granted, he was only hired for the renovation, and not the mystery.) While the renovation itself took about a year and a half, the creation of the unusual scavenger hunt took a full four years. Clough says he ate most of the overhead, and he had a few dozen friends who volunteered their time. In 2008, it was reported that Paramount Pictures bought the rights to the story of the Klinsky mystery apartment.

Now *that's* what we call a housewarming.

Happy Birthday, Mr. President

❖ ❖ ❖ ❖

*Although two centuries have passed since Abraham
Lincoln was born on February 12, 1809, this farm-boy-cum-
president is still the object of worldwide fascination.*

Lincoln's Looks

Honestly, Abe was no babe. At a gangly
6 feet 4 inches, Lincoln stood nearly a foot
taller than the average man and wore a
size 14 shoe. With a wingspan measuring seven feet, Lincoln's long arms
gave him a decided advantage when
engaged in his favorite sport of
wrestling.

A wart on his cheek and a scar over
his eye marked the right side of Lincoln's
face, a souvenir from an 1828 robbery attack.
Lincoln's thin face was so homely that an 11-year-old girl bribed him
to "let [his] whiskers grow" in exchange for her brothers' votes.

Abe was well aware of his shortcomings in the looks department.
When charged with being "two-faced" by political rival Stephen
Douglas, Lincoln retorted: "If I had another face, do you think I
would wear this one?"

Funny Fellow

With his bawdy wit and knack for storytelling, Honest Abe had the
makings of a grat stand-up comedian. After observing a well-dressed
woman in a plumed hat fall while navigating the muddy streets of
Springfield, Illinois, Lincoln commented, "Reminds me of a duck."
When asked why, Lincoln quipped, "Feathers on her head and down
on her behind." Lincoln had a story for every occasion and often
peppered his legal pleadings and stump speeches with relevant
anecdotes. This gift of gab probably aided Lincoln's political career.
Many voters related to Honest Abe's folksy charm and hardworking
"rail splitter" background.

However, not everyone was amused by Lincoln's offbeat sense of humor. Some cabinet members questioned the president's "buffoonery," especially the time when he delayed the start of a crucial meeting to discuss the Emancipation Proclamation to read aloud a chapter from an amusing book by Artemus Ward.

At the conclusion of the reading, Lincoln laughed heartily while the stone-faced cabinet members refused to crack a smile. So he read them a second chapter. Upon receiving the same cold response, Lincoln threw down the book in exasperation, saying "Gentlemen, why don't you laugh? With the fearful strain that is upon me night and day, if I did not laugh I should die."

Ironies and Oddities

Lincoln was shot on April 14, 1865. It was also a Good Friday, which helped boost the president (who died the next day) into the role of martyr/messiah for many fans. Ironically, Edwin Booth, the brother of Lincoln's assassin John Wilkes Booth, had once saved the life of Lincoln's son Robert. The oldest of Lincoln's four sons, Robert was the only one to survive to adulthood.

Lincoln's wife, Mary Todd, was fascinated with psychic phenomena and publicly frequented spiritualists. After their son Willie's death, she was said to have held a séance at the White House to make contact with his spirit. Lincoln, desolate with grief over the loss of his favorite son, is rumored to have attended.

Lincoln himself reportedly had psychic abilities. Numerous accounts of his visions exist, but perhaps the most chilling of these is the premonition he had prior to his assassination. Lincoln dreamt he heard crying. He went on to dream that upon investigating its source, he discovered a body laid out in the East Room, stationed with guards. When he asked the mourners who had died, they replied, "The president. He was killed by an assassin."

Some people claim that Lincoln must have had a sense of what was to happen. When he left for Ford's Theatre the evening of his assassination, he paused to tell his trusted bodyguard, William Crook, "Goodbye." Crook reports that Lincoln habitually bid him "Good night." It was the first time the president had ever told him otherwise.

FROM THE VAULTS OF HISTORY

A Curious Hobby
In the late 1800s, a convicted forger named A. Schiller was faced with a lot of time on his hands. After spending 25 years in a Sing Sing cell, Schiller was found dead with six silver and one gold regular straight head pins on his person, each with a head that was only $^{47}/_{1000}$ of an inch in diameter. Later, the heads of the pins were examined under high magnification and were found to have carefully carved etchings on them, which turned out to be words to the Lord's Prayer. During the 25 years that Schiller spent in his cell, he used the time to etch on the heads of the pins using a tool that was so small it was almost invisible to the naked eye. Experts estimate that the etchings required more than 1,863 separate strokes to complete the work. Created as a labor of love, the work ultimately cost Schiller his eyesight.

Reagan's Firsts
As president of the United States, Ronald Reagan had many opportunities to create "firsts," but it would take a varied and successful background to be the first president to start his political life as an actor. During Reagan's youth, he worked as a lifeguard and was credited with saving more than 75 lives. After working in a number of jobs, including sports announcer, Reagan became a contract actor who would become the first (and most likely the only) future U.S. president to wear a Nazi uniform, which he wore while filming *Desperate Journey* in 1942. During his show business career, he became the first of future presidents to head a major labor union, as the president of the Screen Actors Guild (serving from 1947 to 1952 and again from 1959 to 1960).

After serving as the governor of California, Reagan tossed his hat into national politics and became the 40th U.S. president. He has also been noted as the nation's oldest president. As he quipped while exiting the hospital after his annual physical, "When I go in for a physical, they no longer ask how old I am. They carbon date me."

The Man Who Tried to Outrun War

❖ ❖ ❖ ❖

*Wilmer McLean knows all too well that "you can
run, but you can't hide." Learn how the Civil War
began and ended on McLean's property.*

Unwelcome Guests

In 1854, Wilmer McLean, a retired grocer, bought a Virginia estate
along the Bull Run Creek near Manassas Junction in Prince William
County. He worked hard and made major improvements to the property, including building a large stone barn.

In April 1861, the Civil War erupted, and Virginia became a focal
point of the conflict. In July, the first major engagement of the war,
Bull Run (or Manassas), was fought by Union and Confederate troops
who trod throughout McLean's land. At one point, an artillery shell
went down a chimney of McLean's farmhouse, fell into the kitchen
fireplace, and exploded in a pot of stew, scattering food all over
the room. During the fight, wounded Confederates were placed in
McLean's large barn, which the federals then shelled and destroyed.

That was enough for McLean. After the armies moved on to other
battles, he bought a farm in an isolated part of southern Virginia, far
away from the Washington–Richmond war corridor. It seemed a good
choice—over the next three years, two more battles occurred around
the Bull Run area.

Parlor Trick

But there's no escaping fate. On Sunday, April 9, 1865, the war found
McLean once again. McLean was walking in the village of Appomat-
tox Court House when a Confederate officer looking for a meeting
place for generals Ulysses S. Grant and Robert E. Lee approached
him. When his first suggested building was rejected, McLean reluctantly offered his handsome home. There, in McLean's front parlor,
the two generals negotiated an end to the Civil War.

The irony was not lost on McLean, who reportedly remarked,
"The [Civil] War began in my front yard and ended in my parlor."

Fumbling Felons

Paper or Plastic?

Disguises can be tricky things—sure, they're great if they work, but every little detail has to be taken into account for that to happen. Especially details like, say, breathing.

An Arkansas thief found this out when he broke into an electronics store. He had forgotten his disguise, so he grabbed the first thing he could find—an opaque plastic bag. But not only did the bag prevent him from seeing where he was going, it also didn't allow in any air. The robber spent several minutes stumbling and tripping through the store, then finally collapsed and crawled away.

However, not willing to throw in the towel just yet, the hardy crook was back a few minutes later with yet another plastic-bag disguise. This time, though, he had cut two eyeholes into the bag, which presumably let in some air as well. Fortified by fresh air, the crook managed to grab thousands of dollars worth of electronic equipment.

When the cops reviewed the surveillance footage, they found that in his haste, the thief had neglected to remove the nametag from his clothing—a security guard's uniform from the mall where the store was located. The cops quickly corralled the crook, and took him to a place where he was issued a number to go with his name.

Criminal Quickies

A police department in Ottawa, Canada, had to expel a cadet from its officer training school when they discovered he'd stolen a car to get to class on time.

In Benecia, California, two armed robbers stuck up a credit union only to discover it was one of many "cashless" credit unions in the state. It would've paid to do some research first.

When Long Beach, California, armed robber James Elliot's revolver misfired, he peered down the barrel to check out the problem. He didn't survive.

The Hidden History of the Jockstrap

On November 28, 2005, the Bike Athletic Company celebrated the production of its 350 millionth jockstrap, which was promptly framed and flown to the company's headquarters. Lets take a closer look at some landmarks in the long history of this piece of men's protective underwear.

The Birth of a Legend

The origin of the jockstrap begins in 1874, thanks to Charles Bennett, who worked for the Chicago-based sporting goods company Sharp & Smith. Originally, Bennett designed his garment to be used by bicyclists in Boston. In 1897, Bennett and his newly formed BIKE Web Company (as Bike Athletic was known then) officially patented his invention.

At the time, a bicycle craze was sweeping the nation. These bikes weren't like today's average cruisers; instead, the bicycles of yore were high-wheeled and quite precarious. Folks raced these bikes around steeply banked velodrome tracks as well as through Boston's bumpy cobblestone streets. The daredevils on the velodromes were known as "bike jockeys," which led to Bennett naming his invention the "BIKE Jockey Strap," later shortened to "jockstrap." Two decades later, the U.S. Army issued jockstraps to World War I soldiers in order to reduce "scrotal fatigue." When the troops came home, the bicycle craze had been replaced by the rough and tumble sport of football; the jockstrap found a new home on the gridiron.

Manly Fact: There is some conjecture that the word "jock" is derived from a slang term for the penis.

Entering Manhood Via the Locker Room

To most men of a certain age, the jockstrap is a right of passage that signals the arrival of puberty and a need to protect the male reproductive organs during vigorous exercise. To the uninitiated (or female), the jockstrap might contain some mystery, but its construction is rather simple. A jockstrap (or athletic supporter) consists of an elastic waistband and leg straps connected to a pouch that holds the testicles and penis close to the body, sometimes with the added plastic cup (ostensibly to avoid injury). The original design, with the addition of the cup, hasn't changed much since the early 1900s.

Manly Fact: Jockstrap size refers to waist size. In this case, bigger isn't necessarily better.

A Milestone Missed

In 1974, the jockstrap turned 100 years old, but the anniversary was a quiet one—alas, no national magazine covers commemorating the garment, no ticker-tape parade. Perhaps it was due to a national feeling of modesty, yet 15 years later, as a journalist writing for the *Orlando Sentinel* remarked, a certain women's undergarment—the bra—received plenty of press for its centennial. In fact, when the bra turned 100, *LIFE* magazine issued six pages to celebrate, along with a pictorial, and a headline shouting "Hurrah for the bra." Ten years later, as the jockstrap turned 125, a *Houston Chronicle* writer wondered why we'd forgotten about the forsaken jockstrap. Perhaps we'd been too distracted by Y2K in 1999, he wrote, or maybe "the jock just isn't in the same league [as the bra].... A bra suggests female mystery; a jock suggests male vulnerability."

Manly Fact: In the early 1900s, the jockstrap influenced the invention of the Heidelberg Alternating Current Electric Belt, which claimed to cure nervous diseases in men and women.

The Decline of the Jock?

In the past few decades, there has been some run on jockstrap territory by the likes of the more free-flowing boxer shorts, jockey shorts, and, for athletic types, "compression shorts." Slowing numbers can be pointed to increased competition, or perhaps men are acting out against years of ridicule by classmates and less-than-tactful gym teachers. Still, after more than 130 years on the market, the jockstrap probably isn't going anywhere just yet.

Fast Facts

- The square most commonly landed on in the game of Monopoly is Illinois Avenue. (The Go space ranks second.)

- The Oklahoma State Penitentiary in McAlester hosts the world's only "behind-the-walls" prison rodeo each year. Convicts compete in events such as bull riding and steer wrestling.

- The original title of the Buddy Holly hit song "Peggy Sue" was "Cindy Lou."

- The city of Nome, Alaska, was mistakenly named when a British mapmaker—with really poor handwriting, apparently—circled the port and wrote "Name?" next to it.

- The first stolen car was reported in St. Louis, Missouri, in 1905.

- In the United Kingdom, the difference between a "village"— a small group of houses and buildings in a rural area—and a "hamlet" is that a village has a church.

- The ice sheet that covers 98 percent of Antarctica is about 6,500 feet thick. That's more than a mile of ice.

- All ferrets are born deaf; they don't begin to hear until they are about 34 days old.

- In 1729, the government of Maine passed a law forbidding the use of tomatoes in any clam chowder made in the state. Since then, all New England clam chowders have been made with cream.

- In Switzerland, it is considered rude to talk with your hands in your pockets.

- Helium was discovered at the University of Kansas in 1905.

Twin Peaks and *Seinfeld:* A Connection About Nothing?

Some TV shows attract fans like flies to honey. The eerie, often-bizarre murder mystery Twin Peaks *is one of those shows; the smart comedy "about nothing,"* Seinfeld, *is another. While the shows couldn't be more different, content- and tone-wise, it turns out they do have a few odd similarities.*

Sure, television actors tend to move around shows—you may see one actor as a bum on a cop drama, and the same actor as a business-man in a comedy. But *Twin Peaks* and *Seinfeld* have shared far more than just a couple actors. Was it insider actor-trading by opportunistic agents? A freaky coincidence? A conspiracy? It's like, what's the *deal* with that? Here are some examples of the oddball connection:

- Warren Frost played the father of George's fiancé on *Seinfeld.* He also showed up on *Twin Peaks* as Doc Hayward, the man who performed the autopsy on the show's dead star, Laura Palmer.

- Grace Zabriskie played the tipsy mother of George's fiancé on *Seinfeld.* She also had a major part on *Twin Peaks* as Laura's mother.

- Brenda Strong played an assassin on *Twin Peaks.* However, she also was "the braless wonder," Sue Ellen Mischke, on *Seinfeld.*

- Most know comedic actress Molly Shannon from *Saturday Night Live* fame. But Shannon also played an adoption agency worker on *Twin Peaks* and Elaine's co-worker on *Seinfeld.*

- The actor who portrayed Elaine's boss, Mr. Pitt, in *Seinfeld* is Ian Abercrombie—who played the insurance adjuster in *Twin Peaks.*

- During an episode of *Seinfeld,* Kramer tries to avoid the cable guy. That cable guy is played by Walter Olkewicz, a.k.a. the evil smuggler on *Twin Peaks.*

- Remember the *Seinfeld* episode when Jerry steals the marble rye from the old lady? That old lady is actress Frances Bay, whom Laura Palmer and her pal Donna Hayward delivered meals to in *Twin Peaks.*

At War on the Air

*During World War II, Axis and Allies alike
unleashed a powerful new weapon: broadcast radio.
Recognizable radio personalities spread disinformation
over the airwaves and attacked enemy morale.*

Lord Haw-Haw

William Joyce—nicknamed Lord Haw-Haw for his nasal drawl—
broadcast propaganda for Germany. A member of the British Union of
Fascists, Joyce fled to Germany in 1939; there, he offered his services
to the Nazis. His weekly broadcasts began with the tagline "Germany
calling" and featured inaccurate reports of British defeats and German
saboteurs in Britain. At the height of the war, Joyce garnered almost as
many listeners as the British BBC station. Even Mel Blanc, the voice of
Bugs Bunny, parodied him in a Looney Tunes cartoon. Joyce's broadcasts to England caused more amusement than dismay.

After his arrest in May 1945, Joyce was tried in England for treason, even though he had been born in the United States and was a
naturalized German citizen. The prosecution argued that Joyce owed
allegiance to Britain as long as he held a British passport, illegal or not.
Joyce was found guilty and hanged.

Tokyo Rose

"Tokyo Rose" was the collective name given by
American servicemen in the Pacific to female
announcers who played popular music and read
disparaging war reports on Radio Tokyo.

After the war, Iva Toguri D'Aquino,
who had broadcast under the name
Orphan Ann, became the face of Tokyo
Rose in America. D'Aquino was an
American citizen of Japanese descent
who had gone to Japan to care for an
ailing aunt. Stranded in Japan after Pearl Harbor, D'Aquino was forced
to broadcast propaganda to American troops. Known for her bouncy

delivery, she opened with, "Greetings, everybody! This is your No. 1 enemy, your favorite playmate, Orphan Ann on Radio Tokyo—the little sunbeam whose throat you'd like to cut." Upon her return to America, D'Aquino was tried for treason as Tokyo Rose. Found guilty in 1949, she served six years of a ten-year sentence. D'Aquino insisted she was innocent and had actually worked with American POWs who helped her write broadcasts that would sabotage the program with on-air flubs, puns, and innuendo. In the 1970s, a public inquiry established D'Aquino's innocence. President Ford pardoned D'Aquino in 1977.

Axis Sally

American actress Mildred Gillars was a familiar voice throughout Europe, the Mediterranean, and North Africa during the war. She identified herself as "Midge on the mike," but to American servicemen she was "Axis Sally." Her program on Radio Berlin, "Home Sweet Home," was a mixture of popular music, anti-Semitic diatribes, and speculation on the infidelity of the girls back home. Gillars made her most famous broadcast just before the Allied invasion of Normandy: a radio drama called "Vision of Invasion," in which an American mother dreams that her son died crossing the English Channel. Gillars was convicted of treason for that broadcast, which was played at her trial. She served 12 years of a 30-year sentence. Afterward, she entered a convent in Columbus, Ohio.

Propaganda by Accident

British writer P. G. Wodehouse, creator of the characters Bertie Wooster and the inimitable Jeeves, was living in Le Tourquet when the Germans invaded France in 1940. Wodehouse was arrested and sent to a German internment camp. He was released shortly before his 60th birthday, but since he was still stranded in Europe, he made five broadcasts on German radio. The broadcasts were classic Wodehouse, poking fun at himself, the Germans, and his fellow internees. The Brits who laughed at Lord Haw-Haw's vitriolic attacks were incensed by Wodehouse's lighthearted description of the trials of internment, and they denounced him as a Nazi sympathizer. A Foreign Office investigation after the war, however, found Wodehouse had made the broadcasts "in all innocence and without any evil intent."

More Really Wrong Science Predictions

"Jupiter's moons are invisible to the naked eye, and therefore can have no influence on the earth, and therefore would be useless, and therefore do not exist."
—Contemporaries of Galileo Galilei, early 1600s

"The proposition that the sun is the centre and does not revolve about the earth is foolish, absurd, false in theology and heretical."
—The Inquisition, on Galileo's theories, early 1600s

"So we went to Atari and said, 'Hey, we've got this amazing thing, even built with some of your parts, and what do you think about funding us? Or we'll give it to you. We just want to do it. Pay our salary, we'll come work for you.' And they said, 'No.' So then we went to Hewlett-Packard, and they said, 'Hey, we don't need you. You haven't got through college yet.'"
—Apple founder Steve Jobs, on trying to pitch his idea of a personal computer

"Drill for oil? You mean drill into the ground to try and find oil? You're crazy."
—Workers after being asked by Edwin L. Drake to help with his oil-drilling project, 1859

"The bomb will never go off. I speak as an expert in explosives."
—Admiral William Leahy, U.S. Atomic Bomb Project, 1943. The first atomic bomb was tested in 1945.

"What can be more palpably absurd than the prospect held out of locomotives traveling twice as fast as stagecoaches?"
—England's Quarterly Review, 1825

"There will never be a bigger plane built."
—A Boeing engineer following the first flight of the 247, a twin-engine plane built to carry ten people, 1933

"Very interesting, Whittle, my boy, but it will never work."
—A Cambridge professor of aeronautical engineering, looking at a plan for the jet engine by future jet-engine inventor Frank Whittle

"Professor Goddard does not know the relation between action and reaction and the need to have something better than a vacuum against which to react. He seems to lack the basic knowledge ladled out daily in high schools."

—The New York Times *editorial, 1921, on future rocket pioneer Robert Goddard*

"Louis Pasteur's theory of germs is ridiculous fiction."

—*Toulouse physiology professor Pierre Pachet, 1872, on future rabies vaccine creator and germ research pioneer Louis Pasteur*

"You want to have consistent and uniform muscle development across all of your muscles? It can't be done. It's just a fact of life. You just have to accept inconsistent muscle development as an unalterable condition of weight training."

—*Early response received by Arthur Jones, future creator of Nautilus fitness machines*

"Brain work will cause women to go bald."

—*Berlin professor, 1914*

"The abdomen, the chest, and the brain will forever be shut from the intrusion of the wise and humane surgeon."

—*Sir John Eric Ericksen, official surgeon of Queen Victoria, 1873*

"The abolishment of pain in surgery is a chimera. It is absurd to go on seeking it. Knife and pain are two words in surgery that must forever be associated in the consciousness of the patient."

—*French surgeon Dr. Alfred Velpeau, 1839*

"There is not the slightest indication that nuclear energy will ever be obtainable. It would mean that the atom would have to be shattered at will."

—*Albert Einstein, 1932. He changed his tune around 1939.*

"I see no good reasons why the views given in this volume should shock the religious sensibilities of anyone."

—*Charles Darwin,* The Origin of Species, *1869*

"That virus is a pussycat."

—*Dr. Peter Duesberg, molecular-biology professor at U.C. Berkeley, on HIV, 1988*

Behind the Music of Our Time

- Think Creedence Clearwater Revival is a strange name? The band was performing as The Golliwogs before that.

- Led Zeppelin first performed as The New Yardbirds.

- Classic rockers Journey didn't always have such a catchy band name. The group was first called The Golden Gate Rhythm Section.

- John Lennon said the sound of a police siren gave him the idea for the Beatles' hit "I Am the Walrus."

- Ever wonder who the dude Steven Tyler is referring to in Aerosmith's "Dude Looks Like a Lady"? The song was written about Mötley Crüe frontman Vince Neil.

- The Guns N' Roses rock ballad "Don't Cry" features late Blind Melon vocalist Shannon Hoon doubling most of singer Axl Rose's vocals. Hoon—an old friend of Rose—also sang backup on the track "The Garden."

- Legend has long said the motorcycle sound at the beginning of The Shangri-Las' "Leader of the Pack" came from someone driving a real bike through a hotel lobby. The band didn't comment on it for four decades, but singer Mary Weiss now denies it ever happened.

- John Sebastian of The Lovin' Spoonful played harmonica on The Doors' "Roadhouse Blues." He's credited, though, as G. Puglese— supposedly to avoid a record contract conflict.

- 1960s pop star Lesley Gore missed her chance at a hit with the song "A Groovy Kind of Love." Gore was offered the track to record, but her producer thought it'd be a bad idea to do a song with the word "groovy." The Mindbenders released the single and watched it shoot to the top of the Billboard charts.

- The '60s recording of "Blue Moon" was actually an afterthought. The Marcels needed a fourth song to record during a session and decided to knock it out in the last 10 minutes of their studio time. It became a number-one hit song.

Word Histories

Encore: Although many people might expect an appreciative French crowd to yell this word at the end of a performance, the French actually call out *"bis bis!"* to show their desire for more. In fact, the word *encore* means "another" in French, which is why English speakers use it to request more of a performance.

Economist: This word first appears in the late 16th century and was used strictly in reference to housekeepers. It did not acquire its modern (and arguably loftier) meaning until centuries later.

Stripteaser: First recorded in 1938, this relatively recent addition to the world's lexicon describes a profession that goes back much further in human history. In 1940, the famous stripteaser Georgia Sothern asked linguist H. L. Mencken to coin a word to describe her profession; the result was *ecdysiast,* which refers to the process of molting undergone by insects. Many dancers, including the premiere stripper of her time, Gypsy Rose Lee, balked at being compared to an insect, and the word never gained popular footing. This explains why the seedier sections of town are not littered with Ecdysiast Clubs.

Googol: Around 1940, when mathematician Dr. Edward Kasner needed a word to describe the number one followed by a hundred zeroes, he turned to his nine-year-old nephew. The child responded with "google," which has since become familiar to Internet users who use the popular search engine Google.

Zipper: The inventor of this revolutionary fastening device, Whitcomb L. Judson, first introduced the zipper to the public in 1893 as the "Universal Fastener." It was an executive at the B. F. Goodrich Company who coined the term by which we know it today.

Payola: Referring to the practice of record companies paying radio deejays to play their artists's songs, the term "payola" is a combination of "pay" and "Victrola"—one of the largest manufacturers of turntables in America when the word was first used in the 1960s.

Abyss: One of the few words in the English language of Sumerian origin, it refers to the Abzu, the primordial sea of Sumerian tradition.

Busted!

Breasts. Hooters. Melons. Jugs. Whatever you want to call them, they are arguably the most prominent if not alluring part of the female anatomy. Men clamor after them and women flaunt them. Meet a couple who scammed women across America with promises of bigger busts.

A Man with a Plan

In the early 1960s, Jack and Eileen Feather (doing business as the "Mark Eden Company") began marketing a simple device that was "guaranteed to add three inches to your bustline." This "Mark Eden Bust Developer" was a plastic clamshell-shape device with a spring inside. By pressing the two plastic sides together using her hands, the tension of the spring reputedly increased the size of a woman's breasts. Sounded easy enough—the only problem was that it didn't work.

Prior to marketing the bust developer to the public, Jack tested it on his wife and the clients of his 14 figure salons. After noticing that the Bust Developer "subtly transformed his clients as women," Jack was ready to hit the big time.

The Burgeoning Business of Breasts

Each bust developer purchased was accompanied with an instructional pamphlet flaunting the cleavage of actress June Wilkinson. Inside the brochure, Jack promised that after using his device, "There is an incomparable difference in the entire feminine line, shape, and grace of her whole figure. Her very presence takes on a new and subtle glow of womanliness, of sex-appeal, and yes, of glamour that is undeniable and unmistakable." Not bad for only $9.95.

Complaints Pour In

After selling more than 18,000 Bust Developers, women began to complain that the contraption didn't live up to their expectations. At first, Jack happily refunded his customers' money. But by 1966, so many women had complained about being defrauded that the U.S. Postal Service shut down the Mark Eden operation and issued a fraud order with the federal government.

During subsequent hearings, both sides paraded a long line of experts, for and against the claims of the Mark Eden Company. The first claim to be attacked was Jack's statement that he was introducing a "scientific breakthrough" in breast enhancement. As it turned out, Jack had absolutely no scientific or medical training that would allow him to make such a statement.

Dr. Ralph Waldo Weilerstein, a noted specialist in obstetrics and gynecology, testified that there was virtually no connection between a woman's pectoral muscles and her breast tissue—a key factor in the suit. A physiologist and an orthopedic surgeon followed; they concurred that the only possible improvement that a woman might experience was their "breastline" and not the size of their breasts. Measuring a woman's breastline encompasses the muscles of the chest, back, *and* breasts. Few of the Mark Eden clients were interested in having more muscular backs.

Finally, June Wilkinson, the captivating model on the breast developer brochure testified that she had been well-endowed long before using the Mark Eden product. She told the court that she wore a special bra for the photographs to make her bust look better. Wilkinson also received $1,000 for the use of her likeness and 25 cents for every developer sold, earning about $4,500.

An End to Mark Eden

The hearings continued with a wide array of witnesses and experts until it was unanimously agreed that it was impossible to develop breast tissue through exercise; hence, no "scientific breakthrough" could occur using the Mark Eden Bust Developer. The court determined that Jack and Eileen Feather made false representations to their clients and that the bust developers failed to live up to the claims in the advertisements. Ultimately, the Feathers were indicted on 13 counts of mail fraud, ordered to remove their products from the marketplace, and pay a $1.1 million fine.

However, if you would like to buy a Mark Eden Bust Developer, it's not too late: They often show up for sale on eBay.

The Girls Are Writin' It for Themselves

Throughout history, the literary landscape has been dominated by male authors—but not because the female writers haven't been bringing their A-game. Read on for some fascinating "chick-lit" trivia.

Literary essentials such as *Uncle Tom's Cabin*, *Ethan Frome*, and *Frankenstein* are all classic novels with universal appeal that happen to be written by women. Still, the exposure female writers receive has often been paltry compared to the attention bestowed upon their male counterparts. Need an example? The Nobel Prize for Literature was first handed out in 1901, but so far, only 11 women have received the award.

- Barbara Cartland is the world's top-selling author, with more than 500 million copies of her books sold. Her career in writing romance novels began in 1923; when it ended with her death at age 98, it was estimated that she wrote 723 titles.

- *Gone With the Wind* by Margaret Mitchell (for which she won the 1937 Pulitzer Prize) still stands as one of the world's most popular books. Published in 1936 amid the Great Depression, *GWTW* sold more than a million copies in the first six months. More than 30 million copies of the novel have been sold worldwide, and it is estimated that 250,000 copies are still sold each year.

- *The Mouse Trap* by mystery novelist Agatha Christie is the longest-running play in history.

- Willa Cather, one of America's premier "frontier" authors, wrote such classics as *O Pioneers!* and *My Antonia*. Cather was openly attacked in the 1930s for her conservative politics and dodged rumors about her suspected homosexuality, as she often dressed in men's clothes and wore her hair short. Discouraged by negative criticism of her work, Cather became reclusive and burned most of her letters, destroying many of the details of her celebrated life.

- Harriet Beecher Stowe's *Uncle Tom's Cabin* was published March 20, 1852. It was the first American novel to sell one million copies.

- Louisa May Alcott wrote nonstop for two-and-a-half months. The result of her labor was *Little Women,* a novel based on her own experiences. Published September 30, 1868, *Little Women* immediately sold more than 2,000 copies.

- Lady Murasaki Shikibu, a Japanese noblewoman who was born in A.D. 970 and died in 1031, wrote the earliest novel on record, *The Tale of Genji.* Many critics consider the work a masterpiece.

- Famous for her prolific prose including the book *I Know Why the Caged Bird Sings,* Maya Angelou is also a poet, playwright, editor, actress, director, and teacher. President Bill Clinton commissioned her to write a poem for his 1993 inauguration. The poem, "On the Pulse of Morning," garnered as much attention for its content as for Angelou's reading at the inaugural ceremony.

- Jane Austen is one popular lady. In addition to being the author of classics such as *Emma* and *Sense and Sensibility* as well as her role as the patron saint of book clubs (or so it seems), Austen is the source for an amazing number of adaptations. In fact, it is estimated that more than 600 of her adaptations are being produced worldwide at any given time.

- Anna Katharine Green wrote the first American detective novel, *The Leavenworth Case,* in 1878.

- The three Brontë Sisters (Charlotte, Emily, and Anne) broke onto the literary scene with a book of poetry written under the pen names Currer, Ellis, and Acton Bell. The book sold only two copies. Still, Charlotte went on to write the mega-blockbuster *Jane Eyre,* Emily penned *Wuthering Heights,* and Anne churned out critically acclaimed but slightly less popular works such as *Agnes Grey* before her untimely death at age 29.

- Erma Bombeck, the comedy writer and newspaper columnist who wrote of the joyful (and not-so-joyful) work of the typical American housewife, earned between $500,000 to $1 million a year at the height of her success. Still, Ohio-born Bombeck didn't hire a maid to clean, grocery shop, or cook dinner. "If I didn't do my own housework, then I have no business writing about it," she said. "I spend 90 percent of my time living scripts and 10 percent writing them."

- Virginia Woolf wrote all her books while standing at her desk.

- In 1901, poet and avant-garde artist Gertrude Stein dropped out of medical school at Johns Hopkins. She said it was "boring" and decided to move to Europe. Known for her wit and inventive, often circuitous style of writing, Stein quickly became an integral figure in the hotbed of artistic activity that occurred in Paris in the early years of the 20th century. Some of her friends and colleagues included Spanish artist Pablo Picasso, French artist Henri Matisse, and American writers Ernest Hemingway and F. Scott Fitzgerald. Despite criticism regarding her (sometimes confusing) work, Stein refused to back down. "It is always a mistake to be plain-spoken," she said.

- Emily Dickinson never married, and after age 30, was a bona fide hermit. Her preference for seclusion surely contributed to her work output: She penned more than 1,700 poems. Only ten of these were published in her lifetime—and these without her permission.

- Anne Bradstreet has the distinction of being the first published American poet, appearing in 1650.

- Since her Edinburgh, Scotland, apartment was unheated J. K. Rowling wrote most of *Harry Potter and the Sorcerer's Stone* in a café. In fact, she was on the British equivalent of welfare (called "the dole") for most of the year she wrote the first book. However, in 2000, she became the highest-earning woman in all of Britain, bringing in around $30 million annually.

HOW IT ALL BEGAN

Down in Front
In the 1960s and '70s, physicist A. P. Pedrick sought patents for a number of interesting (and odd) inventions. For one, he designed a car that can only be driven from the backseat. Moreover, if things should go awry (as can often happen when backseat drivers are in control) the car has tracks to get it across fields and bogs. The car is also amphibious. Pedrick's patent description doesn't mention whether his car can also fly, though perhaps that's next on his drawing board.

Sleepovers
Before the fabulous inflatable bed-in-a-bag became popular, Dan Stephens came up with an inflatable rug to accommodate those unexpected over-night guests. His specifics, however, didn't mention what's to be done with any furniture that might be on the rug when it's suddenly blown up. Nor did they mention whether the rug is an Aubusson, Persian, shag, or quasi-astro turf. Maybe an old-fashioned cot is still the way to go.

Fancy Feet
Smelly, sweat-sopped runners are a curse upon those around them, which makes a shoe air conditioner a very useful invention. At least, so thought Israel Siegel, who came up with the idea in 1994. His patented air conditioner kicks in when a person walks, guaranteeing no more hot feet.

What's better, Siegel's design ensures no more cold feet either, as a heat exchanger and thermostat combine forces to heat your feet if they get cold. All one has to do is keep on walking.

The Last Bite
Obesity, the new bugaboo of public health professionals now that smoking has been more or less whacked out, is being combated in many ways: diet, exercise, saunas, and liposuction, to name a few. As if anticipating this "health problem of the month," in 1982, Lucy Barnly of Sacramento, California, patented the ultimate weight loss device: the anti-eating face mask.

Lucy's cup-shaped facemask is held over the mouth and chin by a complicated network of straps. It allows the wearer to speak and take liquids; however, most importantly, the device can be locked.

The Real "Spy vs. Spy"

❖ ❖ ❖ ❖

People love a good story involving intrigue and conflict.
One enduring tale has run for over 40 years in the form
of a much-beloved comic strip called "Spy vs. Spy."

Hidden Meanings

"Spy vs. Spy" was the brainchild of Cuban political cartoonist
Antonio Prohias. The artist came up with the idea for the word-
less strip during the late 1950s as a means of expressing his political
views and to call attention to the rapidly escalating Cold War.

In the strip, two spies—who look identical, except one is all
dressed all in black and the other all in white—portray two opposing
(though never stated) agendas and constantly attempt to sabotage
each other through a series of creative schemes and inventions.
Prohias never really informed his readers whom the characters
represented, leaving fans free to figure it out for themselves. Occasionally the strip will introduce a third, grey-clad female spy (thus
becoming "Spy vs. Spy vs. Spy"), who inevitably becomes the central
point of the conflict as the two suitors battle for her affection.

The Man Behind the *MAD* Comic

Prohias began drawing the "Spy vs. Spy" comic shortly after he fled
his native Cuba for the United States in 1960. After Cuban dictator
Fidel Castro took over the last "free press," Prohias feared that his
days were numbered. He spent his days working in a garment sweat-
shop and drew the strip in his kitchen at night. The wacked-out *MAD*
magazine picked up the continuing series; soon Prohias was able to
devote all of his time to drawing comics and honing his technique.
Still, he was always aware of the comic's origins. In a clever nod to his
underground days, he would sign "By Prohias" in Morse code underneath the title: -••• -•-- •--• •-• --- •••• •• •- •••.

After creating over 500 comics, Prohias relinquished the project to
the *MAD* magazine staffers in 1990. He died on February 24, 1998.
But his work lives on: Although the Cold War has ended, fans of the
strip still continue to enjoy the antics of Prohias's two hapless spies.

Sit, Honey!
How to Train Your Sweetheart

Men are often called dogs when it comes to their dating habits. So what if you could "train" your significant other the same way you train your canine? Turns out, it's not as far-fetched as it sounds.

Behavioral Basics

It's a fact: The science of psychology is the basis of most animal training. It's no secret that humans are animals, and, sure enough, the same kinds of techniques that work on pets can be used on people.

Behavioral psychology is the study of observable actions and responses. Most theories assume animals are born as "blank slates"; they are later shaped by their interactions with the environment. In its most basic form, this means we tend to repeat actions with positive consequences and avoid actions with negative consequences.

Seems simple enough, right? This sort of thinking is nothing new: For years, spouses have taken this approach to change their loved ones' behavior. Sandra Dee takes this approach with her husband, played by Bobby Darin, in the 1963 movie *If a Man Answers.* In it, her mother hands her a dog training manual and advises that what will work for the pooch will work for the hubby. Now, let's break down the core principles and see how they can work for you.

Understanding Reinforcement

The foundation of most animal training starts with the idea of reinforcement—something that increases a desired behavior. It could be positive: the addition of something to the environment, such as food or a belly rub. It could also be negative: the removal of something desirable from the environment, or a loud noise or disapproving look. Either can work, as long as the animal learns to associate the reinforcement with the behavior you're trying to teach. Now, let's put it into action.

Learning a Behavior: The Lazy Dog

In our first example, let's say we have a dog that won't go into its doghouse. Our initial thought might be to put a treat in the doghouse doorway to coax it inside. This, however, isn't likely to work; the dog will just grab the treat and dart away. Why? Because it's bribery, not reinforcement. Remember, reinforcement has to be linked with a specific behavior.

The trainer's answer is to ignore the dog while it's avoiding the house, and then reinforce it with the treat when it finally ventures inside on its own. The pup now knows a treat appeared because of what it did, and the behavior has been learned.

Learning a Behavior: The Lazy Boyfriend

Put this into a relationship setting: Let's say you want your boyfriend to dress up more often. Nagging him about it isn't likely to work in the long-term. The trick, then, is to avoid complimenting him or giving him extra attention on the nights he dresses like a slob. Then, on a night when he dresses nicely, you lay on the praise. Tell him with enthusiasm how great he looks, and—if you want to really reinforce it—give him some kind of special reward as soon as you get home. We'll leave it up to you to decide what the reward should be.

Maintaining a Behavior: The Dancing Dolphin

All right, the behavior's been learned—now it's time to maintain it. You may think the best thing would be to present a reward every time you see the behavior, but animal trainers have learned otherwise. They've found the more effective technique is what's called a variable schedule of reinforcement.

Think about it: A dolphin trainer won't usually give the animal a treat after every trick. Instead, the trainer will randomly reinforce the good behavior, giving the dolphin a treat on, say, the first, third, and sixth trick. That way the dolphin is more likely to keep working hard for the reward, since it doesn't know when it'll come, as opposed to thinking it can get lazy and do the absolute minimum to get the treat that comes every time.

Maintaining a Behavior: The Dancing Husband

It's no surprise that many men don't favor the dance floor. But once you've helped your husband learn the behavior (using the technique you learned above), you can keep him boogying by using the same kind of variable reinforcement used with the dolphin. In a similar scenario, after the second night of dancing, go easy on the compliments and rewards. Like the dolphin, if you lay it on thick every time, your hubby is going to realize he doesn't have to work hard to get his reinforcement. But if on, say, the third, fifth, and eighth nights, you deliver the full reward again, you'll enjoy continued success.

Stopping a Behavior: The Barking Dog

A barking dog is really annoying. But by using negative reinforcement, a trainer can teach it to keep quiet. Animals don't like having bright lights shone in their faces, so a trainer might use that as the unwanted addition to the environment. Every time the dog barks, he or she shines a bright light at it. As soon as the barking stops, the light goes off. Give it enough time, and the dog will learn what's happening and modify its behavior accordingly.

Stopping a Behavior: The Barking Boyfriend

Tired of dealing with your mate's horrible mood when he comes home from work every night? Try the same concept, but with more subtle tactics. When he starts getting cross with you, leave the room or stop responding to his mood. When he takes on a more pleasant tone, return to normal. He'll subconsciously make the connection.

That's just the start of how you can put animal training techniques to use in your personal life. Take the time to understand motivation and you can, within reason, have a lot more pull over people than you realize. Remember, it's all about reinforcement, no matter how small the gesture. Speaking of which, you looked really intelligent buying this book. Everyone noticed.

INSPIRATION STATION

Monet's Water Lilies

It might seem obvious that Claude Monet's famous paintings of water lilies were inspired by, well, water lilies; but the flowers he immortalized on canvas floated unnoticed by Monet for some time before he was inspired to paint them.

In the late 1800s, the painter designed and built a water garden full of water lilies near his house in Giverny, France. The pond's landscaping was inspired by Japanese gardens and design, with irregular contours and integrated features of the surrounding area. Monet said, "I planted my water lilies for pleasure; I cultivated them without thinking of painting them. And then suddenly, I had the revelation of the magic of my pond." Until his death in 1926, the lilies he had randomly planted in the water garden remained Monet's favorite theme. "I perhaps owe having become a painter to flowers," he remarked.

Shabby Chic: How Secondhand Became First Class

If you're a fan of the interior design style known as "shabby chic," then you know that one man's dusty old armoire is another man's pride and joy. Defined by heavily painted, chipped wood furniture, threadbare rugs and carpets, antique pictures, decorative accents such as quilts, and pretty much anything in a pastel color, shabby chic is a style inspired by hand-me-downs.

It all began when wealthy folks in Great Britain would move their old furniture into their summer cottages, in order to make room for newer, posher stuff. Their secondhand, well-loved, and mismatched furniture was often given a coat of white or pastel paint to spruce it up, creating a cozy, lived-in feel. The term "shabby chic" was coined in the 1980s by a style magazine and an interior design trend was born. These days, the shabby chic look is featured in home decorating magazines and Web sites, where readers can find tips to make brand-new furniture look tattered and old on purpose.

Space Is the Place: Astronaut Facts

❖ ❖ ❖ ❖

*Think being an astronaut is all glamour, weird tubes of
food, and putting flags into moonscapes? Read on to get a
further glimpse into what it's like to travel in outer space.*

It's the final frontier, so it may come as no surprise that life in space
is far from ordinary. Astronauts undergo all sorts of unusual procedures in their day-to-day life amid the stars; everything from their
dinners to their digs has fascinating facts behind them.

Cleanliness Concerns

Sloppy bachelors would feel right at home in orbit. Because of the
lack of laundry facilities, astronauts on missions change their socks,
shirts, and underwear just every two days and their pants once a
week. After that, the worn garments are sealed in airtight plastic
bags. (That might be a good policy for some guys on Earth, come to
think of it.)

As for showering, it's sponge-bath only for space crews. Water
droplets could escape and float out, posing a danger to expensive
electronics. To be safe, the astronauts step in a cylindrical stall,
where they have about a one-gallon ration of water to use. The dirty
water is sucked up by a vacuum and stored in special trash tanks.

Water isn't part of the tooth-brushing regime at all. NASA
developed a unique kind of toothpaste that astronauts swish around
without the need for liquid.

Waste Not

Contrary to common perception, most garbage is sealed in bags to
be brought back to Earth for disposal—it isn't just tossed into orbit.
As for the other, shall we say, "waste" produced onboard, astronauts
use toilets similar to those back home. Their facilities, though,
have no water; instead, the space toilet uses a constant vacuum-like
airflow in the bowl to keep things from floating back up in the zero
gravity. Crew members also have to strap in their feet and thighs to
keep themselves from floating away mid-act.

Slumber Situation

Sleeping takes a different turn in space. Astronauts zip themselves into specially designed sleeping bags that attach to their lockers. They can sleep either in the normal horizontal position or in a bat-like vertical stance—the two poses are indistinguishable when gravity isn't a factor. Some crew members may also rest in removable bunk beds.

Magnetic Attraction

Because of objects' tendency to float in space, magnets are a common commodity. Meal trays are magnetic and designed to keep forks, spoons, and knives stuck down, which can make eating a slight challenge. The food packages are also adhered to the trays with strips of Velcro.

Space in Space

At the International Space Station, it becomes a lot less crowded. Once finished, the station's set of solar panels will be big enough to cover the entire U.S. Senate Chamber three times. The whole facility will be about the size of a large five-bedroom house, with eight miles of electrical wire snaking through the walls. And get this: The completed station will weigh a whopping one million pounds—about the weight of 67 fully grown male elephants.

Did you know...

- The finished International Space Station will be a full 361 feet long. It'd take 57 Bob Saget clones stacked on top of each other to fill that much space.

- The station's robotic arm can lift 220,000 pounds—or nearly 900 American Gladiators—in a single swipe.

- By the time the space station is done, astronauts will have spent 800 hours on spacewalks working on the facility.

- Astronauts get out of doing the dishes: Crew members simply wipe off trays and utensils with disinfecting wipes and put individual containers into plastic bags.

Fast Facts

- *Frogs may say "ribbit" in the United States, but the word used to describe their sound isn't the same everywhere: In France, frogs say "coa-coa"; in Korea, they say "gae-gool-gae-gool"; and in Argentina, they say "berp!"*

- *The longest Shakespearean play is* Hamlet.

- *The name of the theme park Six Flags refers to Texas's history and the six flags it has flown: (in order) French, Spanish, Mexican, its own (as the Republic of Texas), United States, and Confederate.*

- *In fact, the first Six Flags that opened in Arlington, Texas, in 1961 was named "Texas Under Six Flags"—until proud members of the Daughters of the American Revolution argued that Texas had never been "under" anything. The name was quickly changed to "Six Flags Over Texas."*

- *Desert snails can sleep for three years. They hibernate during dry spells to retain moisture within their shells.*

- American Cookery, *published in 1796, is the first cookbook to call for ingredients found only in the American colonies—such as squash—and the first to feature recipes for pumpkin pie and turkey with cranberries.*

- *The term "First Lady" to address the president's wife was first used in President Zachary Taylor's 1849 eulogy of Dolley Madison: "She was truly our First Lady for a half century." It soon replaced earlier terms "Lady Presidentress" and "Mrs. President."*

- *The Turkish city of Istanbul is the only city in the world to straddle two continents: It is split between Europe and Asia by a narrow channel called the Bosphorus.*

- *India is the world's largest grower of bananas, producing 16 tons each year.*

Craziest Coke Claims:
Fact vs. Fiction

❖ ❖ ❖ ❖

Coca-Cola has quickly become a staple of the All-American diet. It's also a regular in the rumor mill.

For a common can of soda, you'd never guess all the strange things claimed about Coke. But fear not, faithful readers: Most of the matters are no more than myth. A few, however, are the real thing. It's time to separate fact from fiction.

Coke was originally green in color.

'Fraid not. The kind folks at Coca-Cola say their bubbly beverage has been brown since the first bottle was produced in 1886. However, the glass was green in the early days, which may have led to the rumor.

Coke once contained cocaine.

Believe it or not, this one's true: The original Coke formula used leaves from the coca plant. No one is entirely sure how much cocaine was used in a bottle of Coca-Cola, but some estimates place it at approximately two percent. Early ads even promoted the drink as a "brain tonic" that could cure headaches and chase away depression.

Once health experts began to realize the negative effects of cocaine, Coca-Cola modified its formula to use "decocainized" coca leaves that still have the same flavor—a process still in place today. A company called Stepan actually has a factory where workers remove the cocaine from the leaves and ship the drug-free product to the Coca-Cola warehouse. Surgeons then use the leftover cocaine, which is legal as a local anesthetic for minor surgeries. Stepan is the only legal U.S. supplier of cocaine for these purposes.

Coke can be used as a household cleaner.

True—and your kitchen counter will never taste better. The Coca-Cola Company says the drink's acidic nature could theoretically hold the power to clean. Coke points out, however, that many other acidic agents—vinegar, for example—are considered completely safe as food ingredients. As far as any health implications, Coke notes that "rubbing something in a cloth soaked in a soft drink is not at all like drinking a soft drink" because "people don't hold soft drinks in their mouths for long periods of time." Also, Coke says, your saliva neutralizes the acid before it moves any lower in your body.

Coke will dissolve corrosion.

This statement also has some truth to it. Because of the acidic level mentioned above, the drink could theoretically knock some rust off of corroded metals. The Coca-Cola Company, however, recommends instead using a product actually designed for that purpose.

Coke gives you kidney stones.

False, the soda sellers say. Coke claims its product has never been shown to cause stones and may, in contrast, help prevent them. Not having enough liquid in your diet can contribute to the problem, and Coke, its reps say, provides a "pleasant and refreshing way to consume part of [your] daily fluid requirements." These people are good.

Coke works as a spermicide.

We hate to be the ones to break the news, but no. The myth started after the debut of New Coke in 1985, when scientists began to notice an increase in birth rates in parts of Africa. As the story goes, two Harvard researchers looked into it and found women in the villages had, in fact, been using the drink as a contraceptive. The scientists decided to test both New Coke and the original Coke to see what was going on. They found New Coke was five times less effective than original Coke as a spermicide, which explained the increased rate. Both drinks, though, had too mild an effect to be considered even remotely practical.

There you have it: the fact and the fiction behind this little can with big legends. Who knew one drink could inspire so many strange stories?

FROM THE VAULTS OF HISTORY

Top That!

The first time that James Heatherington wore his newly invented top hat (also called the "silk hat" or "topper") in London, he caused quite a ruckus. He was immediately surrounded by crowds of onlookers trying to figure out what on earth was on his head. When the unruly crowds started pushing and shoving, dozens  of women fainted on the sidewalk and a young boy's arm was broken. Responding to the fray, the police arrested Heatherington, summoned him to court, and fined him £50 for "going about in a manner calculated to frighten timid people." Shortly after being released, Heatherington was overwhelmed with orders for the new top hat.

Another Bad Idea

Gaius Julius Caesar Augustus Germanicus (better known as "Caligula," meaning "little emperor's shoes") enjoyed a raucous and memorable reign from A.D. 37 to 41. Famous for his extravagance, cruelty, and sexual perversion, Caligula was at best a moderate ruler and a questionable general. After deciding to go to war with Poseidon, the Roman god of the sea, he ordered his men to randomly throw their spears into the water. We're guessing the outcome was a stalemate.

Morbid Moore

Anyone who has doubts about how public servants earn their money should have been present in 1971 when the Texas legislature unanimously (and astoundingly) passed a resolution to honor the Boston Strangler for his unconventional work in population control. Yes, this is a man who strangled 13 women to death between 1962 and 1964. Granted, the resolution was introduced by Representative Tom Moore Jr. as an "April Fools'" joke. He sought distinction for Albert de Salvo (also known as the "Boston Strangler") for his "dedication and devotion to his work that has enabled the weak and the lonely throughout our nation to achieve and maintain a new degree of concern for their future." Just to set the record straight, Moore later withdrew the resolution.

Going Green with the Zabbaleen

In Cairo, garbage is gold.

Hey, It's a Living

As the world's industrialized cities scramble to find solutions to over-flowing landfills, Cairo, an Egyptian city of 18 million people, is one of the few locations that may never have that problem. For genera-tions, the Zabbaleen (Cairo's garbage people) have been collecting and recycling the city's trash. They are so efficient that only 20 per-cent of the collected trash ends up in a landfill.

The Zabbaleen have to be thorough; their lives and those of their families depend on it. For them, going home after a hard day's work isn't a long commute. More often than not their homes are built from construction and demolition site refuse, literally in the dump. Still, it is here that the Zabbaleen have forged a community 50,000 strong.

Work starts at dawn. Fathers and sons in small jerry-built trucks and donkey carts make their way into the narrow city streets for the day's collections. Each unit has a separate route and pickup schedule. Laden, they return to their community, where women and children take up the task of sorting the findings, often in the family's front yard.

Waste Not, Want Not

Plastics, glass, metals, textiles, paper, batteries—all are separated and sold either to middle men who deal in volume or small manu-facturers, many of whom are also Zabbaleen. Animals' bones are collected and sold to fertilizer plants. Food waste is fed to the 40,000 pigs and the donkeys raised in the community's backyards. Their waste, in turn, along with inedible food, is composted. Then it too goes to the fertilizer plant.

The Zabbaleen have built paper compactors, cloth grinders, and aluminum smelters. Some of the profits from garbage collect-ing provide community services, such as literacy programs, schools, and medical facilities. An immunization program has dramatically cut infant mortality rates and eliminated tetanus. Financed by the community, some Zabbaleen have trained as doctors and lawyers and come back to serve the ones that helped them.

Political Waste Mismanagement

At the turn of the century, city politicians in Cairo, Alexandria, and Giza decided to modernize their waste management systems by contracting European companies to carry out garbage collection. In Cairo alone the contract was worth $50 million. Suddenly, the Zabbaleen way of life was threatened.

But citizens protested the substantial hike in garbage collection fees. The contractors weren't happy either. Their trucks were too big to negotiate the narrow crowded streets of the ancient cities.

Eco-Egypt

The Zabbaleen prevailed. They spent little time on celebration, however, as a new project has seized their enthusiasm. The Zabbaleen are going green. With assistance from an organization called Solar Cities, the Zabbaleen are installing solar-powered water heaters on their rooftops. Moreover, they are building the heaters from salvaged scrap materials. Previously, gas had been used for heating water, but in Egypt, as elsewhere, the price of gas has become prohibitive.

The water heaters could not be in a more prominent position. "Garbage City" is located in the Moqattam district, a barren limestone terrain that is also Cairo's highest point. On a clear day the ancient Giza pyramids are visible in the distance. Moqattam was quarried for the limestone used to build the pyramids, then abandoned as a wasteland until the arrival of the Zabbaleen, who were originally poor Coptic Christian farmers driven into the city from southern Egypt by drought.

Within Moqattam, the Coptic Christian faith remains strong. Their church is a limestone cavern known as the "Cave Cathedral." Not only is it equipped with a state-of-the-art sound system and closed-circuit television with seating for 20,000 people, it is the largest church in the Middle East. Father Sami'an, the church leader in Moqattam was once asked what the poor could teach. He replied, "Simplicity." Apparently, this is the case. The seemingly simple Zabbaleen model has been adopted with success in Lima, Manila, Bombay, and even parts of Los Angeles.

Art Work: When Guerilla Girls Attack

*The art world is a wild and crazy place, full of mammoth
sculptures, beautiful oil paintings, and thought-provoking
installations. In most of the world's museums, the majority
of the art on display is created by and about men—but
not if the Guerilla Girls have anything to say about it.*

New York City in the '80s

Manhattan has long been regarded as one of the most dynamic
areas on the planet. This was especially true in the 1980s—an era
of Reaganomics, cheap rent, AIDS, punk rock and hip-hop, and a
boundary-breaking art scene. Performance artists were blurring the
lines between art and life, and solo performers as well as ensembles
were causing quite a stir.

One such group, founded in 1985, called themselves the Guerilla
Girls. The development of their all-female, politically charged posse
was born out of the indignation they felt upon seeing an exhibit at
the Metropolitan Museum of Art called *An International Survey of
Painting and Sculpture.* Only 13 of the 169 artists represented at
this important show were women, and all of the artists were white
Europeans or white Americans. Many women were outraged at this
clear display of discrimination, but the Guerilla Girls decided to do
something about it. In the midst of the tumultuous '80s art scene,
this group of anonymous females swore they would "reinvent the 'F'
word: feminism."

Guerilla Warfare

The women who banded together to bring attention to the issue
at hand knew they'd have to be smart about it. Since the art world
is rather small—and many of the Guerilla Girls were artists themselves—they decided to act anonymously. After all, they figured, getting shunned for their activism wouldn't help get more female artists
into galleries. Also, the group wanted the public to focus on their
message, and not on whom they were as individuals.

The term "guerilla" was used in reference to guerrilla warfare: Who were these women, and where would they strike next? They solved the anonymity problem by wearing big, hairy gorilla masks whenever they were out in public. And they were out in public a lot. The group would sometimes be seen in public wearing fishnet stockings and high heels with their gorilla masks as a humorous counter to stereotypes of feminine sexuality.

The Guerilla Girls had arrived, and they had a lot to say. The group hung posters on city buses and in subway stations. The Guerilla Girl Web site recalls the story behind one of their most famous posters: "One Sunday morning we conducted a 'weenie count' at the Metropolitan Museum of Art in New York, comparing the number of nude males to nude females in the artworks on display. The results were very 'revealing.'" On the poster, a classic sculpture of a nude woman is pictured, though with a gorilla mask where her head should be. The slogan read: "Do women have to be naked to get into the Met Museum?" Below it, the gals show they've done their homework. "Less than 5% of the artists in the Modern Art sections are women, but 85% of the nudes are female." Another poster, plastered on walls around NYC's fashionable SoHo neighborhood, listed the names of 20 local art galleries: "These Galleries Show No More Than 10% Women Artists or None at All." Clearly, the Guerilla Girls were not afraid to call the art scene out.

Girl Power

If all this sounds pretty heavy-handed, it was; but it was also a lot of fun, both for the women involved and the public who received the message. One of the major weapons the Guerilla Girls always employed was humor. By poking fun at the system that ignored or repressed them, they were able to take some of the power out of it. They also found that humor was a good way to get people involved.

Whether you loved them or hated them, it was almost impossible to ignore the Guerilla Girls. Today their message continues to spread, extending beyond the Manhattan art scene. Guerilla Girl posters can be found worldwide, there are Guerilla Girl books, and the group continues to give lectures at museums and schools—even in some of the places they previously targeted.

The Times They Are A-Changin'

1983

- A U.S. Congressional committee formally condemns the internment of Japanese Americans during World War II.

- Michael Jackson's music video for the song "Thriller" premieres on December 2. It remains one of the most-aired music videos of all time.

- Astronaut Sally Ride is the first American woman in space.

- On January 3, Kilauea begins to erupt on Hawaii's Big Island. Named as one of the most active volcanoes on the planet, Kilauea was still flowing as of 2008.

- President Ronald Reagan calls the Soviet Union "an evil empire."

- More than 125 million TV viewers tune in to watch the final episode of *M*A*S*H*.

- The militant Islamic group Hezbollah ("Party of God") forms to offer resistance to the Israeli occupation of Lebanon.

- Sweden and the Vatican resume diplomatic relations broken off in 1534 when Lutheranism became the established church of Sweden.

- Crack cocaine appears in the United States. The "Just Say No" anti-drug campaign kicks off the same year.

- Harold Washington is elected the first black mayor of Chicago by a 3 percent margin. His first term in office is marked by a series of racially divisive battles in the City Council that earn Chicago the nickname "Beirut on the Lake" in the national media.

- The United States invades the small Caribbean island of Grenada, claiming that U.S. medical students living there are in danger and that Cuba intends to use the island to ship arms to Communist rebels in Central America.

- On November 2, the birthday of Dr. Martin Luther King Jr. becomes a national holiday.

ESCAPE!

SINKING CAR

*Thousands of drivers accidentally steer themselves into
lakes or rivers every year. Most cars take only a few minutes
to submerge—would you know how to get out alive? If you know how
to handle the situation, the disaster doesn't have to turn deadly.*

- **Stay calm and unbuckle**
  The first rule of thumb is never panic. Remain calm, unfasten your
  seatbelt, and get ready to exit the vehicle.

- **Roll down the window**
  Don't wait: Roll down your driver-side window as quickly as you can.
  Even electric windows will open if you try soon enough. If it doesn't
  work, you'll have to smash the glass. A heavy object is your best bet,
  but you can try to kick out the window with your feet, too. (Take an
  easy precaution and leave a screwdriver or hammer inside your glove
  box, just in case.) Aim for the bottom or corner edge of the window.
  Whatever you do, don't try to open the door—there's too much pressure from the water outside.

- **Work your way out**
  Take a deep breath and
  force yourself out through
  the open space. Then start
  swimming upward.

- **If the window won't open**
  If you can't get the window open or broken, your only option is to wait
  until your car has almost been overtaken with water. Climb into the
  back seat, as it'll be the last to fill up. Unlock the door right away so
  you don't forget. Then, once the water is as high as your neck, push the
  door open—once the water is inside the car, there should be enough
  pressure for the door to give without much trouble. As soon as it opens,
  swim as fast as you can out of the vehicle and toward the surface.

Fast Facts

- *On November 21, 1980, 83 million Americans tuned in to watch the finale to the* Dallas *cliffhanger "Who Shot J. R.?" A few weeks earlier, 85.1 million Americans voted in the Reagan-Carter presidential election.*

- *In 1981, when Nabisco purchased the Standard Brands Company—the original maker of Baby Ruth and Butterfinger— the recipes for these popular candy bars were misplaced. So Nabisco had to come up with new recipes that tasted the same as the old ones.*

- *The ancient Mayas believed the gods had created them for the sole purpose of cooking delicious foods for the deities—whom they presumed were made of corn. (Mayan actually means "men of corn.")*

- *The first fairy tale adapted into cartoon by Walt Disney was* Little Red Riding Hood, *released in 1922.*

- *Each of your nostrils registers smell differently. The right nostril detects the more pleasant smells, but the left one is more accurate.*

- *The original name of the game volleyball was "mintonette." It was created in 1895 when a YMCA gym teacher borrowed from basketball, tennis, and handball to create a new game.*

- *In Sri Lanka, nonverbal signals for agreement are reversed from those in Western countries: Nodding your head means "no" and shaking your head from side to side means "yes."*

- *The custom of men buttoning their clothes from the right and women from the left comes from the fact that men traditionally dressed themselves and were typically right-handed. Women were more often dressed by maids, who preferred to work from their right—the wearer's left.*

Marijuana: Fact vs. Fiction

❖ ❖ ❖ ❖

Marijuana is the most commonly used illegal drug in America, but when it comes to the straight dope about, well, dope, there's no shortage of misconception.

Despite its illegality, more than 70 million Americans admit to having used marijuana. Far fewer, though, understand just what it is and what it does. Countless myths and exaggerations have been spread about the substance, both in casual conversation and government-funded literature. It's time now to look at some scientific evidence to separate fact from fiction.

Marijuana and Addiction

Scientists say that marijuana has no physically addictive properties. But you *can* become addicted to marijuana, much in the same way you can become addicted to chocolate. People tend to repeat experiences that are pleasurable and rewarding. Multiple studies have indicated that even with the high number of people who have experimented  with pot, less than 1 percent of Americans smoke it on a daily or near-daily basis. Most users who do enter drug treatment for marijuana are also users of known addictive substances such as alcohol or cocaine. However, even with heavy, habitual marijuana use, withdrawal symptoms are typically mild to nonexistent.

Marijuana and Lung Damage

It's a fact: Smoking tobacco is bad for you. Tobacco use is linked to 15 different kinds of cancers, and it causes other lung diseases such as emphysema. But how does pot compare to tobacco? Well, it's a mixed bag. Marijuana does contain carcinogens and irritants and is largely similar to tobacco smoke outside of the active ingredients. Marijuana users also often inhale more deeply and hold the smoke in longer than tobacco smokers. On the other hand, marijuana smokers tend to inhale less dangerous material over time than tobacco users. Long story short: Pot isn't good for the lungs when smoked, but it's also not any worse than tobacco.

Marijuana and the Gateway Theory

Does pot lead users to other, more dangerous drugs? Some evidence might seem to suggest so; scientific studies have in fact found many hard drug users did use marijuana first. However, those studies only show a basic correlation, and not a cause-and-effect relationship. That is, the hard drug users may have smoked pot, but there's nothing suggesting it caused them to try the other drugs.

It's a matter of simple statistics: If marijuana is the most commonly used drug, it's logical that those who use harder substances would have tried pot first. Similarly, most cocaine users first tried alcohol and tobacco, but that doesn't mean those substances caused them to progress to coke. Most coffee drinkers probably had orange juice first, but that didn't cause their coffee habit. In reality, the majority of marijuana users never use other illegal substances.

Marijuana and the Law

Legalizing marijuana, many claim, would cause usage to skyrocket. Any speculation, of course, is guesswork. However, we can look at evidence from another country to get an educated idea. The Netherlands changed its stance in the mid-1970s to allow people over the age of 18 to legally buy pot. Interestingly, fewer young adults there use the drug than in the United States.

Marijuana and Brain Damage

Better find another explanation for your boyfriend's slow wit: Modern brain-imaging techniques have found no signs of brain damage or killed brain cells in marijuana users, even in those smoking multiple times per day. No widely accepted scientific studies have found proven long-term damage resulting from marijuana use, either.

Marijuana and Motivation

Yes, pot can make a person lazy. But its effects on motivation are no different than any other intoxicating substance: Someone stoned won't be productive, nor will someone drunk. Once the drug's effects wear off, though, scientists find no remaining effect on motivation or productivity. Studies suggesting students who have flunked out of school due to marijuana neglect to mention that the kids often were failing before they started using the drug.

Marijuana and Memory

It's a similar story with memory: Users currently experiencing the effects of marijuana are, as one might expect, less likely to remember current events, as short-term memory is affected. The impairment, however, ends once the short-lived intoxication is over. Also, studies find no evidence of previously learned knowledge being forgotten.

Marijuana and Reproduction

Many anti-drug campaigns claim the wacky weed can make a person infertile. It may make you too disoriented to figure out the process, sure, but as far as long-term effects, human studies have found no lasting impact on sex hormones for men or women. Granted, researchers have seen slight effects in people who had just smoked large quantities of marijuana. Even in those cases, though, the effects were found to be "insignificant and short-lasting"— coincidentally enough, a phrase also used by some of the subjects' girlfriends.

Marijuana and Drug Education

Anti-drug literature is everywhere these days. It turns out, however, that when it comes to marijuana the warnings may be having an unintended effect. Statistical data indicates the number of teens trying pot started increasing in 1992—right as anti-drug programs such as D.A.R.E. started becoming more common in classrooms—and the numbers have continued to climb in the years since. Studies also show no evidence that these kinds of campaigns, often focused on exaggerated claims rather than current scientific evidence, have any success in curbing drug use among teens.

Separating fact from fiction doesn't have to be difficult. Look carefully at the science behind any claim and you too can become a marijuana myth-buster. That is, if you can remember that much.

HOW IT ALL BEGAN

What's Black and White and Creamy in the Middle?

Oreo cookies have been a part of childhood in the West since 1912. In fact, by the time the Kraft company decided to bring their number-one product to the East, hundreds of billions of Oreos had already been consumed. Alas, since their introduction to China in 1996, the little black-and-white cookies failed to impress Chinese consumers, who thought the snacks were too sweet and expensive. For the first time in many decades, Oreos had to be taken off the assembly line and put back on the drawing board.

In 2006, Kraft reincarnated the Oreo in China as four sugar-reduced chocolate-coated wafer sticks with vanilla- and chocolate-cream filling. The traditional round chocolate cookies were still available for the few consumers who liked them. Also, by reducing the number of snacks in a box, Kraft was able to reduce the price. Between the two kinds of Oreo available, sales began to escalate.

Then, the Oreo aficionados in the Kraft research kitchens remembered a fundamental fact about the cookie: the delight in pulling apart the layers and licking off the filling. To solve this problem, the Krafty cooks came up with a cream-filled cylindrical wafer that, when the cream was sucked out of it, could be used as a milk straw until the wafer softened. The Oreo name stayed the same and so did the fun associated with eating the product. In 2007, Kraft saw their Oreo sales double in China and worldwide; according to Kraft and *The Wall Street Journal,* Oreo sales topped a billion dollars worldwide, making it the King of Cookies.

Of course, Oreo purists have groused about the new Chinese version—the cookies are supposed to be round, black, and white in the middle. But really, who cares as long as snackers young and old alike can enjoy them!

"Health food may be good for the conscience but Oreos taste a hell of a lot better."

—Robert Redford

Head Like a Hole:
The Weird History of Trepanation

❖ ❖ ❖ ❖

There aren't many medical procedures more than 7,000 years old that are still practiced today. Trepanation, or the practice of drilling a hole in the skull, is one of the few.

An Ancient Practice

Has anyone ever angrily accused you of having a hole in your head? Well, it's not necessarily an exaggeration. *Trepanation* (also known as "trephination") is the practice of boring into the skull and removing a piece of bone, thereby leaving a hole. It is derived from the Greek word *trypanon,* meaning "to bore." This practice was performed by the ancient Greeks, Romans, and Egyptians, among others.

Hippocrates, considered the father of medicine, indicated that the Greeks might have used trepanation to treat head injuries. However, evidence of trepanning without accompanying head trauma has been found in less advanced civilizations; speculation abounds as to its exact purpose. Since the head was considered a barometer for a person's behavior, one theory is that trepanation was used as a way to treat headaches, depression, and other conditions that had no outward trauma signs. Think of it like a pressure release valve: The hole gave evil spirits inside the skull a way out of the body. When the spirits were gone, it was hoped, the symptoms would disappear.

How to Trepan

In trepanning, the Greeks used an instrument called a *terebra,* an extremely sharp piece of wood with another piece of wood mounted crossways on it as a handle and attached by a thong. The handle was twisted until the thong was extremely tight. When released, the thong unwound, which spun the sharp piece of wood around and drove it into the skull like a drill. Although it's possible that the terebra was used for a single hole, it is more likely that it was used to make a circular pattern of multiple small holes, thereby making it easier to remove a large piece of bone. Since formal anesthesia had not yet been invented, it is unknown whether any kind of numbing agent was used before trepanation was performed.

The Incas were also adept at trepanation. The procedure was performed using a ceremonial tumi knife made of flint or copper. The surgeon held the patient's head between his knees and rubbed the tumi blade back and forth along the surface of the skull to create four incisions in a crisscross pattern. When the incisions were sufficiently deep, the square-shaped piece of bone in the center was pulled out. Come to think of it, perhaps the procedure hurt more than the symptom.

Trepanation Today

Just when you thought it was safe to assume that the medical field has come so far, hold on—doctors still use this procedure, only now it's called a craniotomy. The underlying methodology is similar: It still involves removing a piece of skull to get to the underlying tissue. The bone is replaced when the procedure is done. If it is not replaced, the operation is called a *craniectomy.* That procedure is used in many different circumstances, such as for treating a tumor or infection.

However, good ol'-fashion trepanation still has its supporters. One in particular is Bart Hughes, who believes that trepanning can elevate one to a higher state of consciousness. According to Hughes, once man started to walk upright, the brain lost blood because the heart had to frantically pump it throughout the body in a struggle against gravity. Thus, the brain had to shut down certain areas that were not critically needed to assure proper blood flow to vital regions.

Increased blood flow to the brain can elevate a person's consciousness, Hughes reasoned, and he advocated ventilating the skull as a means of making it easier for the heart to send blood to the brain. (Standing on one's head also accomplishes this, but that's just a temporary measure.) Some of his followers have actually performed trepanation on themselves. For better or gross, a few have even filmed the process. In 2001, two men from Utah pled guilty to practicing medicine without a license after they had bored holes into a woman's skull to treat her chronic fatigue and depression. There's no word as to whether the procedure actually worked, or if she's just wearing a lot of hats nowadays.

He Said, She Said

"What the country needs is dirtier fingernails and cleaner minds."
—*Will Rogers*

"Immigration is the sincerest form of flattery."
—*Jack Paar*

"For three days after death, hair and fingernails continue to grow but phone calls taper off."
—*Johnny Carson*

"A two-year-old is kind of like having a blender, but you don't have a top for it."
—*Jerry Seinfeld*

"You know your children are growing up when they stop asking you where they came from and refuse to tell you where they're going."
—*P. J. O'Rourke*

"Television: A medium. So called because it's neither rare nor well done."
—*Ernie Kovacs*

"A classic is something that everybody wants to have read and nobody wants to read."
—*Mark Twain*

"When I took office, only high energy physicists had ever heard of what is called the World Wide Web...now even my cat has its own page."
—*Bill Clinton*

"We didn't lose the game; we just ran out of time."
—*Vince Lombardi*

"Entertainment is a thing of the past, today we've got television."
—All in the Family *character Archie Bunker*

"You can't expect to hit the jackpot if you don't put a few nickels in the machine."
—*Flip Wilson*

"What I don't like about office Christmas parties is looking for a job the next day."
—*Phyllis Diller*

Heart of the Beat Generation: The Death of Joan Vollmer

The accidental death of Joan Vollmer, wife of writer William S. Burroughs, proved to be the catalyst of a literary movement.

The Beginnings of Beat

When writers Jack Kerouac, Allen Ginsberg, and William S. Burroughs first became friends in New York in the 1940s, they used to meet at an apartment on the upper west side of Manhattan, the home of Joan Vollmer and Edie Parker. Vollmer was a brilliant student at Barnard, an attractive woman in her early 20s, and well versed in philosophy and literature.

Vollmer also hosted amphetamine-fueled parties at the apartment and nurtured the literary revolution that became known as the Beat Generation. Her roommate, Edie Parker, was briefly married to Kerouac. Meanwhile, Vollmer became the common-law wife of the predominantly homosexual William Burroughs.

Benzedrine and Tequila Cocktails

By 1951, Vollmer and Burroughs were living in Mexico City with their young son and Vollmer's daughter from a previous marriage. Burroughs had left the United States to escape marijuana possession charges. It didn't help matters that both he and Vollmer had huge drug appetites. Vollmer was hooked on the amphetamine Benzedrine and consumed a copious amount of tequila every day. She was also suffering from a recurrence of childhood polio. The cumulative effect left her with swollen features, hair that was falling out, and a profound limp when she walked. At age 27, Vollmer's physical appearance was a long way from that of the bright young beauty who first acted as muse for some of the most gifted American writers of the 20th century.

On September 6, Vollmer's life tragically ended in what many believe was a drunken attempt to replicate the feat of William Tell, the legendary bowman who shot an apple from the top of his son's head. Vollmer and Burroughs were at a party where plenty of drugs and alcohol were being passed around. There, an allegedly drunk Vollmer agreed to allow an equally drunk Burroughs to place a glass on the top of her head and let him shoot it off with a .38 caliber handgun. Unlike Tell, Burroughs was not successful: He missed and the bullet pierced his young wife's forehead. Vollmer died at the Red Cross Hospital in Colonia Roma.

Burroughs was arrested and charged with homicide. He allegedly admitted to police that he was attempting to shoot the glass off Vollmer's head, but later, after conferring with his lawyer, claimed that the gun had accidentally gone off. In a 1965 interview with *The Paris Review,* Burroughs said, "I had a revolver that I was planning to sell to a friend. I was checking it over and it went off—killed her." He also called the William Tell rumor "absurd and false."

The Mexican judge agreed and ruled the shooting an accident. Having served just 13 days in jail, Burroughs was freed.

Joan Vollmer's Legacy

Whether it was merely an accident or a ridiculous drug-fueled stunt gone wrong, the death of Vollmer proved a pivotal moment in both the life of Burroughs and in the history of American literature. During his trial, Burroughs began to write his first novel, *Junkie.* By 1958, he had written the wildly imaginative *Naked Lunch,* a book that in 2005 *TIME* magazine listed as one of the best 100 English language novels written since 1923. Perhaps if Vollmer hadn't died, Burroughs might never have written it. "I am forced to the appalling conclusion," he wrote in the introduction to his book *Queer,* "that I would never have become a writer but for Joan's death."

Vollmer's death similarly influenced Allen Ginsberg, who wrote his most famous poem, *Howl,* after dreaming about his deceased friend. Jack Kerouac also drew upon Joan and her Benzedrine addiction to write passages of his 1957 classic novel, *On the Road.*

Welcome to the Jungle: Animal-Led Bands

They may be hairy, smelly, and totally wild—but that's not all these singers have in common with your average rock star. In fact, a handful of musicians have employed actual animals to front their bands.

Caninus

Claiming to be the world's first-ever animal-fronted band, Caninus features two pit bull terriers named Budgie and Basil performing with a bunch of death-metal dudes. The dogs, as one might expect, basically bark over loud, distorted guitars and lots of double bass drumming.

Hatebeak

Another metal act, Hatebeak, decided to go with a parrot vocalist named Waldo. The human members say they knew Waldo loved metal because he would stand on one leg any time they blasted their music. Fittingly enough, this band has worked together on a joint project with the dogs from Caninus. Squawk 'n' roll!

K9 Fusion

Looking to make your neighbors good and angry? Then K9 Fusion is another excellent option to blare from your stereo. A dog and his canine pals supposedly play all the instruments on this animalistic project, with the exception of programmed drums added by their owner.

Thai Elephant Orchestra

Perhaps the most inventive of the animal bands, the Thai Elephant Orchestra gives a group of 16 elephants from the Thai Elephant Conversation Center the chance to play on specially designed instruments. A worker at the center came up with the idea along with an American composer. We suggest they be forced to listen to eight straight hours of Hatebeak as punishment.

Talk to the Expert

THEME PARK COSTUME CHARACTER

Q: How long do you spend in the costume each day?
A: During the winter and fall seasons, we're in them for 30 minutes at a time. In summer, if it's 90 degrees or more, we're in them for 20 minutes. [The costumes] weigh about 25 pounds. But a lot of the taller characters are a little heavier.

Q: That must take a lot of physical stamina. How do you prepare?
A: At the beginning of our shift is a warm-up that we do. Half of it or so will be aerobics and cardio, and then we'll end with stretching. It's pretty much required, because they don't want anyone getting hurt in costume. There's also a "can and can't eat" [list]. They typically don't recommend eating something heavy before you get in costume. And they want us to stay away from sodas and caffeine.

Q: Have you ever fallen down because you don't have peripheral vision, or gotten overheated?
A: Not for overheating, though some people do. It's not very common, but it has happened. Peripheral vision depends. With each costume your vision is very different. I've tripped a couple of times on something that I didn't see. I can't say I've ever fallen, though.

Q: Theme park characters seem to bring out the best and worst in people. What are some of the strongest reactions you've gotten?
A: On the negative side, I'd definitely say people that like to be physical and think it's funny to mess with your costume pieces. There's a very short amount of time where you can see the characters, like I said, and some guests will get very angry, because they feel like we weren't out there long enough. On the other hand, you get to see a lot of great kids. Their eyes light up when they see the character, and they hug you and don't want to let go.

Do the Tighten Up:
A Brief History of the Corset

The medieval period was paradise for women's clothing: The flowing lines of women's gowns were comfortable and followed the natural figure. But it was too good to last. From the middle of the 15th century through the beginning of the 20th, with only brief respites, women forced their bodies into the shapes demanded by fashion.

Of Whalebones and Women

The first ancestress of the corset, worn from the mid-15th through the late 16th centuries, was a heavy under-bodice that laced up the sides or the front. A tapered "busk" of horn or whalebone was inserted in the front of the bodice to keep it rigid. At some point, whalebone was added to the sides and back. Interestingly, scholars report that the corset-wearers of the period were not necessarily uncomfortable—the infamously painful period of corsetry occurred later during the 19th century.

Boned bodices became fully boned stays in the late 17th century, when the preferred silhouette was long and narrow rather than broad and stiff. Stays that produced a slender line required more seams, tapering down to the waistline.

By the middle of the 18th century, extra shaping bones were sewn into stays to give the breasts some *oomph* and keep the back flat. Whalebone strips were laid diagonally on the sides to make the body long and narrow. Pregnant women were given a break—their stays laced at the sides, allowing more room.

Changing Styles

Women could breathe a little easier at the end of the 18th century. The popularity of fine cottons from India created a looser style using the natural drape of the fabric. Sashes narrowed and waistlines rose.

At first, women wore lighter stays under the new styles, made with more pliable materials and fewer bones. By the beginning of the 19th century, however, draped Greek statues were the ideal. Light muslin dresses clung to the body and underclothes that could spoil the silhouette were abandoned—at least in theory. In practice, even slender women often wore a cotton lining with two side pieces that fastened under the breasts, providing some support; heavier women experimented with stays that came down over the hips and tightly-fitted knitted silk body garments.

The respite was brief. A new silhouette emphasizing full skirts and narrow waists came into fashion with the end of the Napoleonic War, bringing the first true corset with it and ushering in the tight-lacing fad. Victorian women wanted tiny, wasplike waists, and the new corsets could give them that desirable figure. Usually laced up the back, the corset had a broad busk in the center front and narrow strips of whalebone at the back and sides. Gussets on the front at the top of the corset and on each side at the base produced roundness at the bust and the hips, emphasizing the smallness of the waist.

Over time, corsets became heavier and more restricting. Rubber-coated steel replaced the lighter, more pliable whalebone. Further changes in silhouette, including the bustle in the 1870s and the "S-curve" of the early 1900s, all exaggerated and distorted the female shape, requiring more heavily boned corsets.

Women's underwear underwent a change in the 20th century. Steel shortages during World War I and the introduction of rubber-ized elastic allowed women some freedom from tight stays. Finally, the free-for-all loose fashions of the '20s marked the end of the corset.

- *At the end of the 16th and beginning of the 17th centuries, some women with crooked spines were clamped into iron stays for orthopedic purposes.*

- *In the 18th century, both boys and girls were laced into stays as soon as they began to walk to encourage straight posture.*

- *During World War I, the U.S. War Industries Board claimed that by giving up their corsets, American women freed up enough steel to build two battleships.*

Fast Facts

- The word "salary" comes from the word "salt," which ancient Roman soldiers received as part of their pay.

- The bikini swimsuit, which debuted in July 1946, was named after the American detonation of an atomic bomb at Bikini Atoll in the South Pacific on July 1. Designer Louis Réard hoped his swimsuit would make a similar explosion in the fashion world.

- Celery was once considered a trendy, high-fashion food. It was served in its own vase, which was placed in the center of the table as a centerpiece.

- New York bookseller Harry Scherman started the first book-of-the-month club in 1926 to target people who lived in remote areas or were just too busy to keep up with new releases. The first selection was Lolly Willows, or The Loving Huntsman by Sylvia Townsend Warner, which was sent to 5,000 readers.

- The working title of the Beatles hit "With a Little Help from My Friends" was "Bad Finger Boogie."

- According to Hollywood lore, silent film actress Norma Talmadge started the tradition of stars putting their footprints in the cement at Grauman's Chinese Theatre when she accidentally stumbled onto the freshly laid sidewalk in front of it in 1927.

- The only active diamond mine in the United States is in Arkansas.

- Pepsi-Cola was the first foreign consumer product sold in the former Soviet Union.

- Ancient Romans believed the walnut was a physical model of the brain: The hard shell was the skull, the papery partition the membrane, and the two pieces of nut were the two hemispheres of the brain.

Everything Ventured, Nothing Gained (Yet)

Some people consider Oak Island, a small island off the coast of Nova Scotia, Canada, the repository of one of the world's most fantastic treasures. Others, however, think that it's a natural monument to the gullibility of man.

Stay Away

It's only a short boat ride across the channel (and an even shorter walk across the causeway) between the Nova Scotia mainland and Oak Island. Aside from the oak trees that give the island its name, there's little to distinguish the 140-acre island from the nearly 400 others that dot Mahone Bay. Nevertheless, boats are not permitted to land here, and the causeway is fenced off with a "No Trespassing" sign.

If the casual visitor could set foot on the island, however, they would find its surface permeated by hundreds of mine shafts. Thanks to plenty of folklore and gossip, for over two centuries Oak Island has been the focus of spectacular digging operations, with excavators using everything from pick and spade to modern industrial boring equipment. To date, these exertions have consumed millions of dollars.

Why All the Fuss?

Depending on the source (and there are many), Oak Island is the final resting place of any number of precious objects, including:

- Captain Kidd's pirate treasure
- Manuscripts proving that Sir Francis Bacon wrote Shakespeare's plays
- South American gold
- Marie Antoinette's jewels
- The Holy Grail
- The accumulated wealth of the Knights Templar and/or the Freemasons

The Legend Begins

As the story goes, in 1795 a boy named Daniel McGinnis ventured onto the island and gleaned from marks on a tree that rope and tackle had been used to lower something into the ground. The next day, he returned with two companions and initiated the first attempt to recover treasure from what has since become known as the Money Pit—a vertical shaft that by 1897 had already been excavated by a succession of individuals and companies. Depths ran to 111 feet with core samples drilled to over 170 feet deep.

The Problem

Flooding in the shafts, which many believe to be caused by special tunnels built as booby traps to foil treasure seekers, has always thwarted digging operations on Oak Island. Attempts to block these subterranean channels have been unsuccessful and have only revealed that the water from the shafts flows outward to the sea at various locations.

Despite the difficulties, treasure seekers continue to labor on Oak Island because the Money Pit, its auxiliary shafts, and the various features on the island's surface have yielded tantalizing indications that something of value lies beneath. Among the evidence: a stone inscribed with strange markings, a primitive pair of scissors, large amounts of coconut husk, and a piece of sheepskin parchment bearing what appeared to be an inscribed Roman numeral.

The Skeptics Have Their Say

Naysayers take plenty of issue with Oak Island's supposed treasure. They point out that while it may be likely that at one time pirates or even Freemasons landed on the island, that doesn't necessarily spell buried treasure. And there's nothing weird about sinkholes and subterranean chambers in limestone, they say. In fact, they're all over the region.

Moreover, skeptics note the lack of evidence of any digging on the island before the 1840s. They figure it's much more likely that a story about someone discovering a treasure cave got a few people excited. Legend built upon legend until, like the island itself, the story was muddied and mixed-up by the passage of time. Either way, perhaps Oak Island's greatest treasure is simply the human imagination.

Word Histories

Giraffe: This word is derived from the Arabic word for the animal. But as late as the 16th century, Europeans referred to the beast by the name coined by the ancient Greeks, *Kamelopardalis,* or Camelopard.

Bock Beer: From the German word for a male goat, because the beer's strength was said to make its drinkers behave just like the wild animal.

Lager Beer: Because it is aged in a storehouse before it is ready, this beer derives its name from the German word for "resting place."

G-String: Attributed to a variety of sources, including the thickest string on a fiddle; as a reference to "groin"; and the 19th-century strippers who referred to it as a "gadget." But the term "G-string" was first used to describe the loincloths worn by Native Americans. The modern version, of course, is much smaller.

Yule: The next time you feel some of the yuletide spirit, you may want to conjure images of pagan Viking celebrations—the word originally referred to the Old Norse Jol, a winter solstice festival.

Zap: This word comes to the English language courtesy of sci-fi writer Philip Francis Nowlan, who first used it in 1929 in connection with the "paralysis gun," wielded by his most famous creation, Buck Rogers.

Yacht: The word has its origin in the swift 16th-century German pirate ships called *jachts.*

Agent Orange: The experimental herbicide used to disastrous effect by the United States during the Vietnam War derived its name from the orange stripe on the side of its containers. The coloring distinguished it from the equally toxic but lesser known Agents White, Purple, and Blue.

World War I: One would think that they would wait for the second one to start before referring to the first as such, but some forward-thinking commentators were calling the European conflict of 1914–1918 the "First World War" before it was even over.

Knapsack: From the German word *knappen* meaning "to eat." German soldiers used the small sacks to carry their rations.

Iowa: The Final Frontier?

In the southeast corner of Iowa, lies a town where many a Star Trek *fan has gone before—we're talking about the town of Riverside, distinguished as the future birthplace of Captain James T. Kirk.*

To Boldly Go...

It was a seemingly inauspicious day in 1985 when Riverside resident, council member, and longtime *Star Trek* fan Steve Miller decided to put the town on the map. Miller was inspired by the show's creator, Gene Roddenberry, and his book, *The Making of Star Trek.* In it, Roddenberry indicates that Captain Kirk, commander of the USS *Enterprise,* was "born in a small town in the State of Iowa" in the year 2228. Miller presented his idea to the town council, and the group contacted Roddenberry and received his approval. They were also given a certificate, naming Riverside as the future birthplace of the dashing space captain. (Essentially, Riverside got the distinction because they asked for it first.)

As a result, Riverside, a town of less than 1,000 residents, plays host to Trek Fest each year on the last Saturday of June (a few months after the March 22 pre-anniversary of Captain Kirk's birth). During Trek Fest, visitors can find screenings of the television show, a *Trek*-themed swap meet, fan club meetings, a costume contest, and small-town carnival events including sports (demolition derbies, tractor pulls, and a rodeo have all appeared on the roster), a beer tent, and a parade down Main Street. Each year, Trek Fest draws 3,000 to 5,000 fans to Riverside's small corner of the universe.

Happy (Future) Birthday

If you can't make it to the festival, don't worry: There's a 20-foot-tall model of a ship resembling the *Enterprise* (dubbed the USS *Riverside* to avoid legal problems) on display year-round and not one but two plaques commemorating the town's status. The first sign can be found downtown behind a former beauty shop; the other is at Murphy's Bar, where on March 22, you can sing "Happy Birthday" to Captain Kirk with the locals.

FROM THE VAULTS OF HISTORY

Nonrequired Reading

Read any good books lately? If you've already read everything by Edgar Allan Poe, Agatha Christie, J. K. Rowling, and Dean Koontz, here's a list of some of the more offbeat titles you may have missed as well as the year they were published:

How To Cook Husbands, Elizabeth Strong Worthington, 1899

Do Snakes Have Legs?, Bert Cunningham, 1934

Teach Yourself Alcoholism, Meier Glatt, 1975

Sex Life of the Foot and Shoe, William Rossi, 1977

How to Make Love While Conscious, Guy Kettelhack, 1993

Lightweight Sandwich Construction, J. M. Davies, 2001

Bombproof Your Horse, Sgt. Rick Pelicano, 2004

Tooth Traditions

Can you remember the last time you lost a tooth and put it under your pillow so the tooth fairy could exchange it for a quarter? Or did you put your front tooth in a glass of water by your bedside so that she could leave you a silver dollar? Although it's a far-fetched concept, children have been leaving their teeth for the tooth fairy for hundreds of years.

The Vikings had a more direct method—parents would just pay their children for their recently lost teeth so they could add them to their necklaces or other jewelry. Adults believed that children's teeth gave them extraordinary power and would make them invincible in battle. Another commonly held belief is that recently lost teeth should be buried so that witches and evil spirits would not be able to use the power of the teeth to place curses on the child. Others thought that burying teeth in the garden would help children grow strong new adult teeth. But as people began to move from farms into cities, gardens became scarce; the tradition of "burying" teeth underneath pillows began as a result.

Marcus Garvey

❖ ❖ ❖ ❖

Jamaican-born activist Marcus Garvey came to the United States to pursue his campaign for black rights worldwide.

A Strong Start

When he arrived in New York in 1916, Marcus Garvey wasted little time in moving into action. He soon began recruiting members for the Universal Negro Improvement Association (UNIA), speaking first on street corners in Harlem, then in black churches. Garvey was a gifted orator, and blacks responded eagerly to his message of self-reliance and pride.

The UNIA provided more than a sense of community and a slogan. Decades before the Civil Rights movement, what the group accomplished was astonishing: Local branches helped launch small businesses, sold affordable insurance to their members, and acted as mutual aid societies. The Negro Factories Corporation, the financial arm of the UNIA, owned grocery stores, restaurants, a laundry, a fleet of moving vans, and a printing press. By 1920, the UNIA had nearly 1,000 branches around the world.

All Aboard the Black Star Line

In 1919, Garvey began his most daring project: a steamship company called the Black Star Line. Garvey envisioned Black Star ships transporting goods between black-owned businesses in North America, the Caribbean, and Africa. Shares were sold for five dollars at UNIA meetings. Garvey's followers eagerly bought more than $600,000 worth of shares.

On August 1, 1920, more than 25,000 of Garvey's followers gathered at Madison Square Garden to hear his opening address for the UNIA's First International Convention of the Negro Peoples of the World. Two-thousand delegates from 22 countries attended the monthlong convention. Garvey, wearing an elaborate uniform with a plumed hat, was elected the "Provisional President of Africa." But the convention was not all grandiose titles and ornate clothing—delegates presented complaints about the treatment of blacks worldwide and proposed specific remedies, summarized in the Declaration of Rights of the Negro Peoples of the World.

Trouble in Mind

Ultimately, the triumph of the convention masked the beginnings of trouble. The Black Star Line was a powerful symbol but a financial disaster, and the U.S. government was investigating Garvey. Meanwhile, Garvey's insistence on separatism rather than integration had alienated activists who were interested in equality and an integrated America. In June 1922, the black press blasted its own leader for meeting with the Ku Klux Klan. "I regard the Klan, the Anglo-Saxon clubs and White American societies, as far as the Negro is concerned, as better friends of the race than all other groups of hypocritical whites put together," said Garvey. The headlines on the black-owned newspaper *The Messenger* demanded, "Garvey must go."

In early 1923, Garvey was indicted on charges of mail fraud related to the sale of stock in the Black Star Line. The government's case was shaky: Company records showed serious mismanagement but no signs of fraud. During trial, the prosecutor ended his summation by asking the jury, "Gentlemen, will you let the Tiger loose?"

Aftermath and Legacy

Nevertheless, Garvey was convicted and after serving half of a five-year term, he was deported to Jamaica. Garvey continued working for the rights of blacks, first in Jamaica and then in London, but he never regained the influence he enjoyed before his conviction. Already ill, Garvey died of a stroke on June 10, 1940, after reading false notices of his death in newspapers.

In 1964, Garvey's body was returned to Jamaica, where he was declared the country's first national hero. Upon visiting Garvey's grave in Jamaica, Dr. Martin Luther King Jr. remarked that Garvey "gave millions of Negroes a sense of dignity and destiny and made the Negro feel that he was somebody."

The PEZ Candy Craze

*How much would you pay for a small plastic candy
dispenser? PEZ has inspired legions of obsessive fans who
are willing to shell out thousands for a rare find.*

The Beginning of Something Big

Eduard Haas couldn't have known what kind of monster hit he was
creating when he built the first PEZ prototype in Austria in 1927.
After all, it seems like a simple enough idea: a cute character with a
tilting head that spits out candy.

Haas first conceptualized PEZ as a smoking alternative, which
may be why the dispensers look conspicuously like lighters (the first
batch of PEZ actually came in metal tins). The candies were initially
made only in peppermint flavor. In fact, the name PEZ is derived
from *pfefferminz,* the German word for peppermint.

Legend has it that Haas's product was shot down when he first
tried to market it in America. He then got the idea to put a playful
face on the dispenser and sell it as a children's toy. Suddenly, PEZ
had found its place in the world.

These days, PEZ is made in Orange, Connecticut. The plant is
said to run 24/7, churning out crunchy little candies and colorful
dispensers around the clock. And boy howdy, are people ever eating
them up.

Most Expensive Dispensers

PEZ is a collector's dream. While there's no official list, PEZ dispensers can fetch a pretty penny. Some collectors report a transparent 1950s Space Gun model selling for more than $11,000. The
original Locking Cap model is said to have sold for $6,575, and the
Big Top Elephant dispenser is believed to have pulled anywhere
from $3,600 to $6,000 at auction.

Rarest Dispenser

Many collectors seem to agree the rarest dispenser is the elusive
Mr. Potato Head model. The design, like the Potato Head toys, has
a blank head with attaching face pieces. But this smiling spud didn't

last long; PEZ pulled it off the shelves after a few months over concern with kids choking on the detachable pieces.

The Original Head
The first head to appear on PEZ is a source of debate. Some say it was Mickey Mouse; others insist it was Popeye. In any case, there seems to be a clear consensus that it was a popular cartoon character who may or may not have had a constant hankering for spinach.

The Most Popular PEZ
The dispenser designs most commonly named as top sellers are Santa Claus and Mickey Mouse.

The Most Featured PEZ
The Tweety Bird PEZ makes regular primetime appearances, thanks to its immortalization in an episode of the TV show *Seinfeld.* In "The Pez Dispenser," the crowning moment occurs when Jerry places the dispenser on Elaine's lap during a piano recital, causing her to burst out in laughter.

The Tallest Dispenser
Marge Simpson's model takes the cake here with an impressive 5⅛-inch-tall stature. Other tall orders include Bugs Bunny, Asterix, Yosemite Sam, Uncle Sam, and Goofy.

PEZ-tastic Facts

- Americans alone eat more than three billion PEZ candies every year.

- There is a Bullwinkle dispenser, but no Rocky.

- The only real people to ever be featured on dispensers are Betsy Ross and Daniel Boone. Some say Paul Revere has a model as well, but its title was simply "Captain." The matter has become another PEZ controversy.

- An Elvis dispenser was shown in the 1994 movie *The Client,* but it was created as a prop by the filmmakers and was never an official PEZ issue.

- PEZ is available in Kosher flavors.

- There are two widely recognized PEZ museums: one in Burlingame, California, and one in Easton, Pennsylvania.

🎥 Behind the Films of Our Time

- One of the asteroids seen flying in *The Empire Strikes Back* is actually just a potato. Also, the infamous light saber sound from the *Star Wars* films was created by moving a microphone near a television and recording the interference noise.

- *Return of the Jedi* was originally titled *Revenge of the Jedi.* George Lucas says he changed it because the idea of revenge didn't fit in with the Jedi concept.

- *Star Wars'* Chewbacca is named after the Tunisian town of Chebika City. Some of the movies' scenes were shot close to there.

- The role of *Star Wars'* Princess Leia would have been offered to Jodie Foster if Carrie Fisher turned it down.

- Movie star Tom Hanks isn't only famous for his films—he's also related to Abraham Lincoln (his third cousin four times removed).

- The first film shown in the White House was 1915's *Birth of a Nation,* during the Woodrow Wilson presidency.

- *Back to the Future* may have made Michael J. Fox a household name, but the actor's screen name wasn't given by his parents: Fox's middle name is actually Andrew.

- The first motion picture to feature Sylvester Stallone, *The Lords of Flatbush,* paid its star 25 T-shirts for his work on the film.

- *Snow White's* seven dwarfs almost had different names. Filmmakers considered various names, including Snoopy, Dippy, Blabby, Woeful, and Flabby.

- The only Civil War flick without a single battle scene is *Gone with the Wind.*

- The stars of *Gone with the Wind* didn't make much money by modern Hollywood standards. Clark Gable is said to have worked 71 days for a total of $120,000, while Vivien Leigh was on the project for 125 days and received only $25,000.

Shemptastic!

❖ ❖ ❖ ❖

There are those who always seek the path less traveled—they like vanilla ice cream instead of chocolate, prefer Lou Gehrig to Babe Ruth, and think Star Trek *superior to* Star Wars. *Likewise, when it comes to the Three Stooges, they may be decidedly pro-Shemp.*

Declaring a Favorite Stooge

This is dangerous ground. You can argue politics or religion with someone for hours, but to mess with a person's favorite Stooge is to toss down the gauntlet. As one of the boys themselves might have said, "Them's fightin' woids!"

Sure, there's no denying that Curly is a great clown. Before the role of Moe's punching bag dissolved into a succession of Curly Joes, Curly was the first to suffer the lead Stooge's abuse. Fingers in the eyes, pliers to the nose, punches to the stomach, and ice down the pants were all absorbed without much protest by Curly, who could always be counted on to respond "Soitenly!" to any crisis and "Nyuk, nyuk, nyuk," when he was particularly pleased with himself. And who can forget that it was Curly who pioneered the unique art of running in circles while lying on the ground?

In Praise of Shemp

But Shemp didn't need any funny sounds or exaggerated movements. With a squashed potato for a nose, sad basset hound eyes, and a hangdog expression that rivaled professional clown Emmett Kelly, Shemp just naturally looked funny, as if somebody had worked him over and he had simply forgotten to get fixed up again.

Shemp, with his lank, jet-black hair, oddly resembled Moe. Indeed, when Moe was beating on Shemp he might well have been beating on himself, a fact that psychiatrists probably see as awfully telling—that is, until a lobster rises out of a soup bowl at some swanky dinner party and clamps a claw onto Shemp's nose. So much for social commentary.

A Bit of Backstory

All Stoogephiles know the story of Samuel "Shemp" Howard. As Moe's brother (as was Curly), Shemp had been part of the act early on, when the trio performed in vaudeville with Ted Healy, as "Ted Healy and His Stooges." In 1932, Shemp left for Hollywood to try his hand at a solo career. There he carved out a successful path for himself as a character actor. But when Curly was debilitated by a stroke in 1946, Shemp loyally returned to the group to save the Stooges from folding. Thereafter, Shemp became the main target of Moe's wrath. On November 22, 1955, Shemp died of a heart attack while lighting a cigar and telling a joke.

As a Stooge, Shemp hung in there and gave as good as he got. While it was accepted that Curly would never really get the best of Moe, Shemp could and did successfully fight back. That is, until Moe played his trump card—the fluttering hand going up and down in front of Shemp's face. Once he did that, poor Shemp was mesmerized, and never seemed able to remember that a slap was the inevitable conclusion.

Shemp managed to be a great clown without any of the typical clown tricks. He played it straight, and in doing so he extended the tradition forged in the time of Chaplin, Keaton, and so many others: the clown as everyman. Perhaps that's why, when Moe looks at Curly and utters his menacing, "Oh, a wise guy huh?" we watch to see what type of torment is about to be unleashed. But when Moe threatens to "moiderlize" Shemp, we turn away, fearful that the agony Shemp is about to feel will be felt by us all.

- *At 5'6", Shemp was taller than the rest of the Stooges.*

- *The birth of a nickname: His mother had a strong European accent. When she said his real name, Sam, it sounded like "Shemp."*

- *After high school, Shemp trained to be a plumber. He also delivered newspapers and set up pins at a bowling alley.*

INSPIRATION STATION

What a Woman

Considered one of the greatest rock songs of all time, composer Eric Clapton penned "Layla" in 1970, after combining two nuggets of inspiration: a poem and a woman.

Clapton's good friend, then-Beatles guitarist George Harrison, was married to Pattie Boyd, a model he had met while filming *A Hard Day's Night* a decade earlier. As time went on, Clapton realized that he was in love with Boyd. At around the same time, he read "Layla and Majnun," a Persian poem about unrequited love and madness. Those were two themes Clapton could relate to, and the song was written and recorded in just three short weeks.

All that wooing must have worked: Clapton and Boyd eventually married. Although they divorced ten years later, "Layla" would go down in history as one of the most beloved rock 'n' roll love songs ever written. The wrenching hit single "You Look Wonderful Tonight" by Clapton is also about Boyd. Interestingly, although the marriages to Boyd didn't last, the friendship between the two guitarists managed to stay strong.

The Thighbone's Connected to the Eiffel Tower

Gustav Eiffel's famous Parisian tower, built in 1889, owes much of its grace and beauty to an unlikely source: the thighbone. About 20 years prior, Swiss anatomist Hermann von Meyer had discovered that inside the human thighbone was an intricate latticework of tiny ridges creating perfectly formed lines of tension and stress. A Swiss engineer named Karl Cullman picked up on this knowledge and understood the implications the discovery had on architecture; the famous iron curves of the Eiffel Tower was thusly inspired by the curve in the head of the human femur. The curves are supported by an intricate latticework of metal studs and braces similar to the incredible engineering present in your skeletal system. Voila!

The Butcher and the Thief

❖ ❖ ❖ ❖

Meet the two charming fellows who inspired the children's rhyme:"Burke's the Butcher, Hare's the Thief, Knox the boy that buys the beef."

The Cadaver Crunch

In the 1820s, Edinburgh, Scotland, was suffering from a "cadaver crunch." Considering the city was regarded as a center of medical education, the lack of bodies for students to dissect in anatomy classes posed a problem. At the time, the only legal source of corpses for dissection in Britain was executed criminals. Interestingly, at the same time that enrollment in medical schools was rising (as well as the need for cadavers), the number of executions was decreasing. This was due to the repeal of the so-called "Bloody Code," which by 1815 listed more than 200 capital offenses.

The growing need for corpses created a grisly new occupation. "Resurrection Men" dug up the newly buried dead and sold the bodies to medical schools. William Burke and William Hare decided to cut out the middleman: Over the course of a year, they murdered at least 15 people in order to sell their bodies.

A Grisly Business

The pair fell into the cadaver supply business on November 29, 1827. At the time, Hare was running a cheap boarding house in an Edinburgh slum. Burke was his tenant and drinking buddy. When one of Hare's tenants died still owing four pounds, Hare and Burke stole the tenant's corpse from his coffin and sold it to recover the back rent. Dr. Robert Knox, who taught anatomy to 500 students at Edinburgh Medical College, paid more than seven pounds for the body.

Encouraged by the profit, Burke and Hare looked for other bodies to sell to Knox. Their first victim was another tenant at the boarding house, who fell ill a few days later. Burke and Hare "comforted" the sick man with whiskey until he passed out, and then smothered him. The result was a body that looked like it had died of drunkenness, with no marks of foul play.

Over the course of the next year, Burke and Hare lured more victims into the lodging house. They sold the bodies to Knox, who not only accepted them without question, but increased the pair's payment to ten pounds because of the "freshness" of the bodies they provided.

Their initial targets were strangers to Edinburgh, but Burke and Hare soon began to take more risks, murdering local prostitutes and "Daft Jamie," a well-known neighborhood character. People began to talk about the disappearances, and Knox's students began to recognize the bodies brought to them for dissection.

The End of Burke and Hare

Burke and Hare's mercenary killings ended on October 31, 1828, when Burke lured an old Irish woman named Mary Docherty to the house. James and Ann Gray, who were also boarders at the time, met Docherty there. Docherty was invited to spend the night, and arrangements were made for the Grays to board elsewhere. The next morning, the Grays returned and found the old woman's body under the bed. Although they were offered a bribe of ten pounds a week to keep quiet, the Grays ran for the police.

Hare testified against Burke in exchange for immunity. He was released in February 1829 and disappeared from the historical record, though popular legend claims he ended his life a blind beggar on the streets of London. Burke was tried for murder, found guilty, and hung. Although there was no evidence that Knox had any knowledge of the murders, angry crowds appeared at his lectures and tore his effigy to shreds. He eventually moved to London.

Fittingly, Burke's corpse was turned over to the Edinburgh Medical College for "useful dissection." A bit more oddly, skin from his body was used to bind a small book.

The murders led to the passage of the Anatomy Act of 1832, which provided new legal sources for medical cadavers and eliminated the profit motive that drove Burke and Hare to murder.

Fast Facts

- *The most frequently performed school plays are* Seussical *and* A Midsummer Night's Dream, *followed by* Grease *and* The Crucible.

- *The first speed limit in the United States was set in 1901 in Connecticut at 12 mph.*

- *Oregon is the only state with an official state nut: the hazelnut, a.k.a. the filbert.*

- *Three U.S. states have a state muffin: Minnesota (blueberry), Massachusetts (corn), and New York (apple).*

- *Maryland is the only state with an official sport—jousting.*

- *Milk is the official beverage of 19 states: Wisconsin, North Dakota, South Dakota, Maryland, Pennsylvania, Oregon, Oklahoma, Vermont, New York, North Carolina, South Carolina, Mississippi, Louisiana, Kentucky, Delaware, Minnesota, Arkansas, Virginia, and Nebraska. (Nebraska actually has two state beverages—the second one is Kool-Aid.)*

- *The most often portrayed characters in literature are Sherlock Holmes and Dracula.*

- *Silly Putty was the result of a failed attempt by General Electric to create a synthetic rubber for use in World War II. Seeing that it had no industrial uses, the sticky substance was marketed as a toy instead.*

- *Most American car horns honk in the key of F.*

- *The Library of Congress in Washington, D.C., is the largest library in the world, containing 28 million books and 532 miles of shelving.*

Zap! Boeing's Flying Laser Cannon

❖ ❖ ❖ ❖

Just when you thought the military has already come up with every conceivable way to wreak havoc on its adversaries, in 2008 the Pentagon announced that it had developed a new device that was so accurate, it could melt a hole through objects as small as a soda can from over five miles away.

Reach Out and Fry Somebody

Although the concept behind Boeing's Advanced Tactical Laser (ATL) began several years prior, the first ATL was tested in 2008. Weighing more than 40,000 pounds, the ATL was mounted in the belly of a C-130 Hercules turboprop cargo plane. The ATL is related to the Airborne Laser, a smaller weapon still under development that would use a modified 747 with a focus on ballistic missles. In addition to making Swiss cheese out of soda cans, the ATL is designed to fry trucks, tanks, ammunition dumps, and communication stations from a safe distance without the fallibilities of missiles and rockets that can be shot down and destroyed before they reach their targets.

The Three-Second Blast

Here's how it works: At the heart of the device are storage tanks that contain chlorine gas and hydrogen peroxide. When mixed together, a chemical reaction creates high-energy oxygen molecules that are sent through a mist of iodine. The resulting energy is converted into an intense form of light, or laser beam.

Stay with us here. After resonating through a series of mirrors, the laser beam travels through a long pipe and is adjusted for the external movements of the airplane and weather conditions. Just before the beam is delivered to its target through a revolving turret, it is "widened" to approximately 20 inches, condensed, and then focused on its target. A series of onboard computers help to make microscopic adjustments in its path before delivering a burst of a few seconds of energy to the target. Each laser-equipped aircraft is capable of delivering up to 100 laser blasts before it needs to return to its home base for refueling.

Hot Stuff
Similar to lasers used in the medical field, the ATL itself isn't hot, but it is capable of heating its target to more than several thousand degrees. If the target is a solid substance (such as an al-Qaeda jeep or a metal building), the laser is capable of melting it like ice cream on a hot summer sidewalk. While ATL technology is fascinating, its power is also disturbing: If the target is made from combustible material such as wood or paper, it will literally burst into flames.

A Safer Tool of Destruction
What makes the ATL such an effective weapon is that the laser beam can be delivered from a safe distance from the target, enabling the chance of an attack without having to actually be on location. The weapon can also send a number of lethal light beams to targets in different locations—all within a few seconds. Plus, unlike a gun or other arms, lasers are silent and invisible, enabling more covert operations.

But there are definitely some downsides to having such a complex weapon. For one, the ATL will toast anything in its path, such as people or a bird that has wandered into its trajectory. Another is that the laser's operation and accuracy depends largely on factors such as altitude, weather, and variables regarding geographic location—for instance, in the Middle East, visibility is limited due to blowing sand. But, all things considered, experts feel that the ATL is a much "safer" tool of destruction because it reduces the collateral damage that is typical even with smart bombs.

Although the ATL completed its critical design review in 2004, it is still considered under development. The weapon is currently being tested by the Department of Defense. There are also plans to develop smaller, more streamlined versions that can be mounted on surface vehicles such as tanks and trucks.

FLUBBED HEADLINES

"Antique Stripper to Demonstrate Wares at Store"

"Sadness Is No. 1 Reason Men and Women Cry"

"Mayor Says D.C. Is Safe Except for Murders"

"Check With Doctors Before Getting Sick"

"Neighbors Said Sniper Not Very Neighborly"

"Court Rules That Being a Jerk Is Not a Crime"

"Arson Suspect is Held in Massachusetts Fire"

"Enfields Couple Slain; Police Suspect Homicide"

"War Dims Hope for Peace"

"Killer Sentenced to Die for Second Time in 10 Years"

"Two Soviet Ships Collide, One Dies"

"Juvenile Court to Try Shooting Defendant"

"Plane Too Close to Ground, Crash Probe Told"

"Shot Off Woman's Leg Helps Nicklaus to 66"

"Reagan Wins on Budget, But More Lies Ahead"

"Soviet Virgin Lands Short of Goal Again"

"Stud Tires Out"

"Survivor of Siamese Twins Joins Parents"

"Safety Experts Say School Bus Passengers Should Be Belted"

"Is there a risk of flooding? Maybe, maybe not: Experts say it all depends on the weather"

"Meridian Woman Training for 20004 Games"

"No Gas Leak Found at Taco Bell Despite Bad Odor, Evacuation"

"Fisherman Arrested for Using Wife as Shark Bait"

"Sewage Spill Kills Fish, but Water Safe to Drink"

Pocket Egotism

It might be narcissistic and slightly voyeuristic, but so what? Where there's a photo booth, there's fun. Read on for the story behind those beloved self-portraits.

If You Build It, They Will Insert Coins

In 1926, a young Siberian immigrant and inventor named Anatol Josepho created his Photomaton machine, a large booth that could take a photographic image of a person and automatically develop it while the he or she waited. Josepho placed his creation in seedy-but-thrilling New York's Times Square. For a quarter, a person received eight photos of themselves within minutes. No one had seen anything like it and word got around. Immediately, the photo booth was a sensation.

People lined up around the block to get their photos taken. In 1932, a Photomaton station opened on Broadway and 47th. Despite the fact that Americans were within the depths of the Great Depression, people gladly forked over a quarter for pictures of family, friends, and even pets.

The photo booth craze continued to rage on; in the 1950s, visual artists such as Andre Breton, Salvador Dali, and Luis Bunuel all took artistic advantage of the photo booth's small and affordable images. Later, pop artist Andy Warhol would also frequent Times Square photo booths.

Keep On Clickin'

The chemical-dipped, eight-picture photo booths are no longer manufactured, but there are still many working, old-fashioned photo booths in bars, on fairgrounds, and in various unlikely places around the country. But the photo booth isn't fading away—it's just growing up. If you've been in almost any shopping mall in the past few years, you've probably seen digital photo booths set up in heavy traffic areas. Here, subjects can pick colorful backgrounds and add captions.

Like jazz, baseball, and the quilt, photo booths are a staple of American culture. Call us self-involved if you want, but don't we look great!

Rope: A Year Tied at the Waist

❖ ❖ ❖ ❖

Ever feel like you're tied down to your significant other?
In 1983, two performance artists decided to
take the idea to a literal extreme.

The Inspiration

It's easy to feel like you're attached at the hip to someone you see all the time. For Linda Montano and Tehching Hsieh, though, it was more than just a feeling. Montano (a female) and Hsieh (a male) actually had never met until she saw some examples of his work. A dialogue started, and they began to discuss a mutual project: a yearlong collaboration connecting art and life—literally.

In 1983, the performance artists decided to create an exhibit in which they would remain tied together by an eight-foot rope attached to their waists for exactly one year. The ground rules were simple: They would always be together, never remove the rope, and never touch. The artists say their inspiration came from the concept of communication and people's struggle to connect.

As you can imagine, things got interesting.

The Routine

An average day started with Montano waking first and meditating, exercising, or watching television until her attached associate awoke. Once they were both up, they'd run or walk Linda's dog, do some work, then go sit back-to-back at their respective desks and think for five hours.

As far as going to the bathroom, the two say it was usually a rushed affair. Part of the deal required them to always be in the same room if they were indoors, so privacy was out of the question.

The Sex

The other common subject of question, sex, was also crossed off the list. By virtue of the "no-touch" rule, the artists agreed to abstain from any sexual contact for the entire yearlong period. Even though they could have theoretically touched other people (that wasn't disallowed), they decided it would only be an escape, and so it was banned.

Montano explained it best in a 1984 magazine interview: "I believe that in the next 200 years, we will all be in outer space, so why not practice outer-space sex now by letting astral bodies merge."

Uh, yeah.

The Danger

Our dynamic duo had only two close calls they can remember: the elevator incident and the tripping trouble. In the first, Hsieh walked into an elevator and the doors closed before his companion followed. He was able to hit the "door open" button just in time, but Montano said she had nightmares of being sliced in half for days. In the second scare, a passerby ran between the two on a crowded street and was almost clotheslined. Once again though, disaster was averted. The only other physical danger the two reported revolved around their bike riding trips, when they rode in a single file fashion, artfully avoiding becoming tangled and/or mangled.

The Struggles

According to Montano and Hsieh, their relationship evolved over the months and brought about many less threatening challenges than one would think. In the early weeks, they spoke for hours every day. Eventually, they began getting annoyed with each other and pulled on the rope, leading to further anger. Next came the silent phase, when they would only gesture to indicate a need for food or bathroom. That led to an era of grunts and unintelligible noises—a time the artists referred to as a "beautiful regression."

It's worth noting that during the same period, Montano worked on a few other performance art pieces on her own: wearing only monochromatic clothes, listening to one note for seven hours every day, staying in a colored space for three hours a day, and starting to speak in a different accent every year.

We couldn't make this stuff up if we tried.

Misheard Lyrics

Pink Floyd, "Another Brick in the Wall, Part 2"
Correct: "No dark sarcasm in the classroom"
Wrong: "The ducks are hazards in the classroom"

Moody Blues, "Nights in White Satin"
Correct: "Nights in white satin"
Wrong: "Knights speaking Latin"

Ohio Players, "Love Rollercoaster"
Correct: "Rollercoaster of love "
Wrong: "Hold that bus sir, for love"

Bonnie Raitt, "Something to Talk About"
Correct: "Let's give them something to talk about"
Wrong: "Let's go get something at Taco Bell"

Bay City Rollers, "Saturday Night"
Correct: "S-A-T-U-R-D-A-Y night"
Wrong: "I say: 'Eat a rock! Eat a rock! Right!'"

The Go-Gos, "Our Lips Are Sealed"
Correct: "Our lips are sealed"
Wrong: "I licked a seal"

John Lennon, "Give Peace A Chance"
Correct: "All we are saying, is give peace a chance"
Wrong: "Yes we are sailing / Give Jesus Pants"

Red Hot Chili Peppers, "Can't Stop"
Correct: "Can't stop the spirits when they need you"
Wrong: "Can't stop the ferrets when they need food"

Skid Row, "18 And Life"
Correct: "18 and life you got it, 18 and life ya know"
Wrong: "18 and a licensed driver, 18 on the Maginot"

Bachman-Turner Overdrive, "Takin' Care Of Business"
Correct: "Takin' care of business"
Wrong: "Baking carrot biscuits"

Odd Ordinances

- The king of England is legally guaranteed the rights to the head of any dead whale found along the coastline. The queen is guaranteed the tail.

- Shooting a bank teller with a water gun during an actual robbery is considered a crime in Louisiana.

- Falling asleep in a South Dakota cheese factory could get you arrested.

- Becoming a professional fortune-teller is illegal in parts of Virginia.

- Virginia Beach has made it illegal to drive by the same place on a particular street—Atlantic Avenue—twice within 30 minutes.

- It's illegal to have any kind of peanut or popcorn stand on any city street or sidewalk in Greensboro, North Carolina.

- Riding a bike without both hands on the handlebars is a crime in Kill Devil Hills, North Carolina.

- You can't hold any official organizational meeting in North Carolina while members are in costumes.

- Bingo games are not allowed to last for more than five hours in North Carolina—unless they're being held at a fair, in which case it's okay.

- Pushing a moose out of a moving airplane is against the law in Alaska.

- Sorry, Californians: It's illegal to ride a bike in a swimming pool.

- Animals are not allowed to mate within 1,500 feet of any school, worship place, or tavern within the state of California.

- It's illegal to shoot at any animal while you are inside a moving vehicle in California; that is, unless that animal is a whale.

- Illinois actually made it illegal to speak English for about 45 years, from the 1920s to the 1960s. The law defined the official language as "American."

Too Much of a Good Thing

Ever felt overwhelmed while on vacation? Join the club. But if it's an extreme case, perhaps it's Stendhal Syndrome.

Vacation Interrupted

Suppose you've spent the day traipsing around the magnificent city of Florence. You sat at David's feet. You visited the Accademia Gallery. You took in the Uffizi. You end the day hiking up to the Piazzale Michelangelo to gaze over the city, but when you arrive at the summit, you don't have the picture-perfect moment you expected. Instead, you're struck by delirium. You're out of breath, panicked, and a bit dizzy.

In Italy, this affliction, suffered when one becomes overwhelmed by works of art or scenes in nature, is called Stendhal Syndrome.

Sketchy Syndrome?

The syndrome was brought to the medical community's attention in the 1970s by Italian psychiatrist Graziella Magherini. The doctor named it after Marie-Henri Beyle, a renowned 19th-century French writer who wrote (under the pseudonym Stendhal) about the disorientation visitors feel when viewing the artifacts of the Italian Renaissance, a feeling he'd also experienced when first visiting the historic city. Also known as the "tourist's disease," Stendhal Syndrome affects a few hundred people per year in Italy. Symptoms usually subside in a few days after the person leaves the area.

Although Italy is known for cities that are brimming with beauty and culture, it's not the only place you can fall ill with awe. In Jerusalem, a similar sickness is called Jerusalem Syndrome. There, the afflicted experience Stendhal symptoms, but they're caused by the weight of the city's religious importance. Doctors debate whether patients develop a psychosis as a result of their visit or if the visit is simply a trigger for a preexisting medical condition.

Whether it's real or imagined, the unique condition does make for a good story. So good, in fact, that it's been a plot point in many books, including Chuck Palahniuk's *Diary*, Robert Stone's *Damascus Gate,* and the horror movie, *The Stendhal Syndrome.*

Hitchcock's *Rope:* A Reel-to-Reel Murder

❖ ❖ ❖ ❖

When filmmaker Alfred Hitchcock set out to adapt Patrick Hamilton's play Rope, *he provided audiences with such a carefully crafted movie that some filmgoers might not be able to perceive its genius. Sure,* Rope *stands as one of Hitchcock's least-successful theatrical releases, but it remains a technical triumph.*

A Man with a Plan

Alfred Hitchcock set out to create a cinematic experience that would allow viewers to feel as if they were watching Patrick Hamilton's original play, *Rope,* up on the silver screen. Since the play takes place in real time, viewers, like the theater audiences, trav-eled with the performers while they unraveled a murder mystery at a dinner party.

The story begins in a darkened apartment, with the gruesome strangulation of a young man, David, by two other young men, Brandon and Philip. The killers then prepare for a planned dinner party—setting up the buffet on a chest, which secretly holds David's lifeless body. The party begins; the guests include David's fiancée, her ex-boyfriend, David's father and aunt, and the boys's prep school teacher and mentor, Rupert Cadell (played in the movie by James Stewart).

Viewers discover that Brandon and Philip planned this murder—of one of their prep school friends, no less—as nothing more than an experiment in murder. Though many cite the infamous 1924 Leopold and Loeb murder case as having influenced the plot, screenwriter Arthur Laurents remarked in an interview that Hitchcock and the film crew "never discussed that it was based [on the case]...of two rich boys in a Chicago school who decided to kill another boy" [in the spirit of adventure]. "They ignored it. I couldn't understand that."

A "Bewildering Technique"

Hitchcock wanted it to seem as if the camera were an invisible presence in the room. In doing so, he had to make several untraditional modifications to standard moviemaking. First, he wanted there to be no jarring edits or conspicuous camera jumps, but because reels of film at the time were only ten minutes long, each take had to be bookended by a zoom into a character's back.

Each take had to be absolutely perfect. The fluid camera movements were due to a specially built dolly—a remarkable feat, considering that the Technicolor movie cameras of the day were 1,000-pound machines that were not easily slipped through the set of a Manhattan penthouse (production stills show that even Stewart, who stood at 6'3", was dwarfed by one of these beasts). To this end, the set was equipped with movable walls, which had wheels and were hung from the ceiling (a great idea that led to another problem: The moving walls were noisy). In order to coordinate the delicate dance of actors, sets, and characters, 15 days of rehearsals were required before filming started. Hitchcock even reported that Stewart "couldn't sleep nights because of the picture. . . . It was the bewildering technique that made him worry."

A Trick of Light

Yet another technical problem lay in the fact that the story takes place at sunset. Since the back wall—which the audience sees in almost every shot—is a row of windows, the New York City skyline had to reflect the subtle changes in light as the night fell. This passage of time was accomplished, as the publicity material for the film put it, by a "magical . . . cyclorama—an exact miniature reproduction of nearly 35 miles of New York skyline lighted by 6,000 incandescent bulbs and 200 neon signs." Even Hitch's tradition of slipping himself into the film's action proved to be a challenge. According to Laurents, Hitchcock contemplated showing his profile, featured on the neon sign of a building seen over the shoulders of two actors. But he scrapped the idea as too gimmicky. Later, Hitchcock added himself as a sidewalk stroller outside the building during the movie's opening credits.

Fast Facts

- *Utah is the only state with a three-word capital: Salt Lake City.*

- *The first electronic handheld calculator, invented in 1967 by Texas Instruments, weighed nearly three pounds and could do only the four basic functions: addition, subtraction, multiplication, and division.*

- *The first radio station broadcast in the United States took place on November 2, 1920, on KDKA in East Pittsburgh, Pennsylvania. It announced that Warren Harding had been elected president.*

- *Gatorade is named for the University of Florida Gators, where the sports drink was created in 1965 by the UF kidney disease specialist Dr. Robert Cade.*

- *The Parker Brothers Company prints more play money each year than the U.S. mint prints real money.*

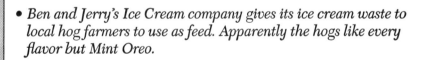

- *Oregon is the only state with a reversible flag: each side has a different design.*

- *Ben and Jerry's Ice Cream company gives its ice cream waste to local hog farmers to use as feed. Apparently the hogs like every flavor but Mint Oreo.*

- *More than 362 billion Oreos have been sold since their introduction in 1912, making the Oreo the best-selling cookie in the world.*

- *North Dakota has more golf courses per capita than any other state.*

- *Mosquitoes can mate in mid-air and often in as little as 15 seconds from start to finish.*

Positively Platypus

*What would you get if you could cross a duck with a
beaver, a venomous snake, a chicken, and an otter? Well,
it might look something like the duck-billed platypus.*

What on Earth...?

The oldest platypus fossil (of the platypus in its current form) dates
back more than 100,000 years. Indigenous to the southeastern coast
of Australia and Tasmania, the platypus is a *monotreme,* or egg-
laying mammal. In fact, it is one of only two mammals that reproduce
by laying eggs (the other is the echidna). In 1798, Captain John
Hunter sent sketches and the skin of a platypus back to England that
described a small, egg-laying animal with a pelt and a flat bill. They
thought he was joking. British scientist Dr. George Shaw, thinking it
was a hoax, tried to cut the
pelt with scissors, expecting
to find stitches attaching
the bill to the body.

It's no wonder: The platypus is
one strange-looking mammajamma.
With its fur and body shape, it resem-
bles an otter. The tail looks like that of a beaver,
but while beavers use their broad tails for propul-
sion, the platypus uses its tail for fat storage. It has four webbed
feet, but only the front two are used for swimming. The rear feet are
used for steering in water and aid in walking when on dry land.

And then there's the "duck bill." Actually, the platypus's rubbery
snout is decidedly different than a duck's, both in design and function. The bill of a duck is hinged and is used primarily for feeding.
The platypus's bill is actually a single piece of leathery skin with two
nostrils on the top and a small mouth on the bottom.

High Tech Meets Monotreme

Platypuses have a unique sense of perception called *electro-
reception.* Located inside the platypus's bill, electroreceptors can

---

detect electrical fields that are generated by muscular contractions of other animals in the vicinity. Since the platypus swims with its eyes closed, the electroreceptors enable it to detect even the smallest movement of its prey. If it senses an oncoming attack from a predator, the male platypus can sting with an ankle spur that is loaded with poisonous venom. While it is not lethal to humans, the venom is powerful enough to kill dogs and other animals.

Dining and Breeding

The platypus is a semiaquatic mammal and spends up to 12 hours a day searching for food under water. In order to survive, it must eat up to 25 percent of its body weight every day. And because it thrives on insects, worms, larvae, freshwater shrimp, and other small organisms, the platypus has to be an accomplished diver and stay submerged for up to 40 seconds at a time. A bottom feeder, the platypus normally forages shallow river bottoms, rooting around for things to eat. While underwater, the platypus fills its cheeks with prey until it reaches the surface, where it takes time to enjoy its meal. At the end of the day, the platypus retires to a nest dug out of a riverbank and furnished with leaves, grass, and twigs. While the platypus is admittedly more awkward out of water, it's still agile enough to run along the ground.

When it comes to the birds and the bees, the platypus is definitely one of the more interesting critters out there. Many are confounded by the fact that the platypus lays eggs, but yet is not a bird. The female usually lays two eggs two weeks after mating, and the eggs are incubated for 10 to 14 days, as the mother holds the eggs to her body. Even more baffling, instead of feeding from its mother's teats like other mammals, the baby platypus gets its milk by lapping it up from the hairs and grooves in the mother's skin.

You'd be hard pressed to think of an animal that has more unusual characteristics than the duck-billed platypus. But hey, after 100,000 years spent plodding around on the planet, it must be doing something right!

The Times They Are A-Changin'

1993

- On January 3, President George Bush and Russian President Boris Yeltsin sign the second Strategic Arms Reduction Treaty (START II), agreeing to reduce nuclear warheads by two-thirds.

- The song "I Will Always Love You," sung by Whitney Houston, tops the charts in January and February.

- In an agreement known as the "Velvet Divorce," Czechoslovakia is divided into the Czech Republic and Slovakia.

- President Bill Clinton agrees to compromise on the U.S. military's ban on homosexuals.

- Terrorists explode a car bomb in the garage beneath the World Trade Center in New York City. The bombers intended to topple the North Tower into the South Tower, causing it to collapse, but the concrete garage structure contains most of the blast.

- Toni Morrison wins the Nobel Prize for Literature.

- The FBI lays siege to the Branch Davidian compound in Waco, Texas. The 51-day standoff ends on April 19, after Attorney General Janet Reno approves removal of the Davidians from the compound by force. About 80 Branch Davidians, including 17 children, die in the attack.

- Israel and the Palestine Liberation Organization sign the Oslo Accords, formally recognizing each other and giving Palestinians limited autonomy in the West Bank and Gaza Strip.

- Basketball legend Michael Jordan breaks the hearts of fans by retiring from the Chicago Bulls. He returns to basketball 17 months later.

- The Maastricht Treaty on European Union goes into effect on November 1, replacing the European Common Market with the more comprehensive European Union.

You've Come a Long Way, Baby

During World War II, American employers faced a shortage of men. To make up for the lost workforce, thousands of women traded in their aprons for typewriters, rivet guns, and forklifts. Managing these women meant many supervisors had to change their mode of thinking.

The following article, "Eleven Tips on Getting More Efficiency Out of Women Employees," is taken from the July 1943 issue of *Transportation Magazine,* which instructed managers and supervisors how to hire women. Today, these tips would garner loads of lawsuits.

- Pick young married women. They usually have more of a sense of responsibility than their unmarried sisters, they're less likely to be flirtatious, they need the work or they wouldn't be doing it, and they still have the pep and interest to work hard and to deal with the public efficiently.

- When you have to use older women, try to get ones who have worked outside the home at some time in their lives. Older women who have never contacted the public have a hard time adapting themselves and are inclined to be cantankerous and fussy. It's always well to impress upon older women the importance of friendliness and courtesy.

- General experience indicates that "husky" girls—those who are just a little on the heavy side—are more even-tempered and efficient than their underweight sisters.

- Give every girl an adequate number of rest periods during the day. You have to make some allowances for feminine psychology. A girl has more confidence and is more efficient if she can keep her hair tidied, apply fresh lipstick and wash her hands several times a day.

- Be tactful when issuing instructions or in making criticisms. Women are often sensitive; they can't shrug off harsh words the way men do. Never ridicule a woman—it breaks her spirit and cuts off her efficiency.

Fast Facts

- *The first toothbrush was developed in China in 1498, featuring bristles made from hog hair. Later toothbrushes had horse and badger hair. DuPont introduced nylon bristles in 1938.*

- *The original London Bridge is in Lake Havasu City, Arizona. Millionaire Robert McCulloch purchased it—and shipped it over stone by stone—in the late 1960s, after London officials realized the 130-year-old bridge was sinking into the Thames River and needed to be replaced.*

- *The Tufts University mascot Jumbo the elephant is named for the elephant that circus magnate P. T. Barnum claimed was the largest that ever lived. After Jumbo's death in 1885, his preserved remains were put on display at the university.*

- *China is the world's largest apple producer, followed by the United States.*

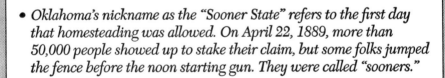

- *Guinea pigs are born fully developed, with fur, teeth, and their eyes open.*

- *Oklahoma's nickname as the "Sooner State" refers to the first day that homesteading was allowed. On April 22, 1889, more than 50,000 people showed up to stake their claim, but some folks jumped the fence before the noon starting gun. They were called "sooners."*

- *The colors of the Campbell's soup label—carnelian (dark red) and white—were chosen from the colors of the Cornell University football team.*

- *Nike shoes got their distinct waffle sole design in 1971, after track coach Bill Bowerman's wife served him breakfast. Inspired by the design, he put rubber in his wife's waffle maker and created what would become Nike's custom sole.*

The Strange World of Joe Meek

❖ ❖ ❖ ❖

The music business has produced more than its fair share of eccentric characters, but very few have been stranger than Joe Meek, the independent British pop-record producer of the 1950s and '60s.

A Complicated Man

Perhaps you have never heard of Joe Meek, but you've probably heard the musical recordings he produced and inspired: Meek was the first to develop the electronic effect reverb and sampling techniques. In 1962, he produced "Telstar," an electronics-soaked single by the Tornados that became a worldwide sensation. It was the first record by a British group to top the charts in the United States, more than a year before the arrival of The Beatles. "Telstar" sold more than five million copies around the world, making it one of the most successful instrumental records ever. Meek also recorded with then-unknown singer Tom Jones, although it was another two years (and with a different producer) before the singer made it big.

But that wasn't all there was to Meek. As well as being an innovative music producer, he was also an occultist, a paranoid eccentric, and, illegally at the time, a homosexual. Despite Meek's successes and influence on modern music, it's his strangeness that people remember.

304 Holloway Road

Joe Meek created his legendary home studio in a three-story apartment above a leather goods store in London. Meek's landlady operated the store below and frequently complained about the noise her tenant made. In the days before eight-track recording, records were recorded live with dubs added later. To obtain just the sound he was looking for, Meek would often have performers playing on the stairs or in the bathroom. When his long-suffering landlady complained by banging on the ceiling, Meek would simply turn up the volume to drown her out. It was a stressful situation that would come to a violent conclusion.

Meek's Downward Spiral

An obsessive Buddy Holly fan, Meek believed that the late rocker communicated with him from beyond the grave. He developed a similar obsession with the still-living bass player from the Tornados, Heinz Burt. When Meek confiscated a shotgun that Burt had brought to the studio one day, the components for violence were all in place.

In 1963, Meek was arrested in a men's public restroom after allegedly "smiling at an old man," which made the national press. Meek spiraled into depression, and his paranoia and outbursts worsened. On February 3, 1967, after yet another quarrel with his landlady, Meek blasted her with the shotgun that he had confiscated from Burt. He then turned the gun on himself. Coincidentally, it was also the eighth anniversary of Buddy Holly's death.

- *Like many musicians at the time, Meek was known to pop plenty of pills and experiment with LSD. The drugs may have accounted for much of his strange behavior.*

- *Meek was once seen running alone late at night along London's Holloway Road, dressed in pajamas and screaming that he was being chased by someone with a knife.*

- *When Phil Spector, a legendary (and legendarily whacked-out) producer in his own right called Meek to tell him how much he loved his music, Meek accused Spector of stealing his ideas and hung up on him.*

- *When drummer Mitch Mitchell (best known for his work with The Jimi Hendrix Experience) failed to do exactly as asked during a session, Meek stormed out of the control room with a shotgun and threatened to blow Mitchell's head off if he didn't do it properly.*

- *Buddy Holly wasn't the only dead guy talking to Meek—he also believed he was in spiritual contact with the ancient Egyptian Emperor Rameses the Great.*

HOW IT ALL BEGAN

Pin-ups

In 1900, Edwin Moore pinned his hopes on a single small invention. With $112.60 capital and an amazing amount of patience, Moore assembled by hand his creation: a "push pin with a handle."

Every afternoon and often into the night, Moore worked in a cramped room he had rented, hand-crafting his push pins. Every morning he would travel door-to-door to sell his pins at 17 cents a dozen. Turns out, he sold a lot of pins; his big break came when he sold an order of pins to the Eastman Kodak Company for $1,000. The Moore Push-Pin Company is still proudly pushing out pins from a large plant just outside of Philadelphia.

Glacial Golfing

No weekend duffer or follower of PGA-sanctioned golf tournaments would expect to find a golf course in remote Greenland, let alone an international golf tournament. After all, to most people Greenland is just a whole lot of ice and snow—surely, its sports would include dog sledding, ice fishing, perhaps skiing and snowboarding, and, for the hardier, arctic scuba diving, but certainly not golf.

Despite his surroundings, Greenlander Arne Neimann worked with what he had and in 1997 organized the first World Ice Golf Championship Tournament. He already knew a little something about the level of fanaticism rampant in the golfing world, and sure enough, the duffers came.

The tournament is still held each March in northwestern Greenland at the community of Uummannaq, a mere 370 miles north of the Arctic Circle. The annual tournament is played over a nine-hole, par-70 course, which changes every year because of glacier and iceberg movement. March is the ideal month for the tournament because the temperature often rises to a balmy 15 degrees below Celsius. Tournament officials recommend warm clothing, and graphite clubs are discouraged, since they tend to shatter in the cold.

Life on the Body Farm

When Mary Scarborough wrote the lyrics to "Old MacDonald Had a Farm," she probably didn't have a research facility in mind. In fact, one won't find cows, chickens, or pigs that go "oink" at the Body Farm—just scores of rotting human bodies.

E-I-E-I-Oh, Gross

The Body Farm (officially known as the University of Tennessee Forensic Anthropology Facility) was the brainchild of Dr. William Bass, a forensic anthropologist from Kansas. Its purpose, however nauseating, is to help law enforcement agencies learn to estimate how long a person has been dead. After all, determining the time of death is crucial in confirming alibis and establishing timelines for violent crimes.

After 11 years of watching and learning about human decomposition, Bass realized how little was actually known about what happens to the human body after death. With this in mind, he approached the University of Tennessee Medical Center and asked for a small plot of land where he could control what happens to a post-mortem body and study the results.

Bass's Body Farm drew the attention of readers when popular crime novelist Patricia Cornwell featured it in her 1994 book, *The Body Farm.* In it, Cornwell describes a research facility that stages human corpses in various states of decay and in a variety of locations—wooded areas, the trunk of a car, underwater, or beneath a pile of leaves—all to determine how bodies decay under different circumstances.

Reading the Body

According to Bass, two things occur when a person dies. At the time of death, digestive enzymes begin to feed on the body, "liquefying" the tissues. If flies have access to it, they lay eggs in the body. Eventually, the eggs hatch into larvae that feast on the remaining tissues. By monitoring and noting how much time it takes for maggots to consume the tissues, authorities can estimate how long a person has been dead. Scientists can also compare the types of flies that are indigenous to the area with the types that have invaded the body to determine whether the body has been moved. "People will have alibis for certain periods," says Bass. "If you can determine that the death happened at another time or location, it makes a big difference in the outcome of the court case."

But the farm isn't all tissue decomposition—scientists also learn about the normal wear-and-tear that a human body goes through. For instance, anthropologists look at the teeth of the victim to try to determine their age at the time of death. The skull and pelvic girdles are helpful in determining a person's sex, and scientists can also estimate how tall the person was by measuring the long bones of the legs or even a single finger. Other researchers watch what happens to the five types of fatty acids leaking from the body into the ground. By analyzing the profiles of the acids, scientists can determine the time of death and how long it has been at its current location.

Unfortunately, the perps are catching on. Some criminals try to confuse investigators by tampering with the bodies and burial sites, spraying the victim with insecticides that prevent insects (such as maggots) from doing their job.

Further Afield

At another facility at the University of New Mexico, scientists have collected over 500 human skeletons and store them as "skeletal archives" to create biological profiles based on what happens to bones over time. And in Germany, the Max Planck Institute for Computer Science has been working on a 3-D graphics program based on forensic data to produce more accurate likenesses of the victims.

Although many other proposed farms never got off the ground due to community protest, since the inception of Bass's original Body Farm, another farm has been established at Western Carolina University. Ideally, Bass would like to see body farms all over the nation. Since decaying bodies react differently depending on their climate and surroundings, says Bass, "It's important to gather information from other research facilities across the United States."

FROM THE VAULTS OF HISTORY

Corbett's Claim to Fame

As far as murderers go, few are more infamous than John Wilkes Booth, the man who assassinated President Abraham Lincoln. But second runner-up to Booth might be Thomas "Boston" Corbett, a.k.a. the man who shot and killed Booth.

Corbett was born in London, England, in 1832. He later came to New York where he worked as a hatter. After his wife died during childbirth, Corbett became an Evangelical Christian and took the new name "Boston," in honor of the city where he was reborn. In a move that historians are now speculating was affected by years of working with mercury in the hat business, Corbett castrated himself with a pair of scissors to escape the temptation of a group of prostitutes. Oddly, he then went to a prayer meeting, had dinner, and went for a walk before seeking medical care.

At the outbreak of the Civil War, Corbett enlisted in the Union Army. He apparently had found his calling, for he reenlisted three times. After Lincoln was assassinated in April 1865, Corbett was chosen as one of 26 cavalrymen to hunt down the slain president's killer. Eventually, the cavalrymen cornered Booth and a cohort in a tobacco barn in Virginia. After the barn was set on fire, Corbett shot Booth through a crack in the wall, later claiming, "God almighty directed me." Corbett was originally placed under technical arrest, but the charges were later dropped and he was given his share of the reward money: $1,653.85.

Worst. Shower. Ever.

If you're the type of person that hates to get caught in the rain, you definitely wouldn't want to be caught in a meat shower! In Kentucky in 1876, an elderly woman was tending the vegetables in her garden when she was suddenly showered with snowflake-size pieces of meat. Some nearby men grabbed a couple of the pieces and commented that it tasted like venison or mutton. After the samples were analyzed, it was determined that the meat was actually pieces of lung and muscle tissue that were regurgitated from a flock of flying buzzards on their way home. The incident is now known as "The Kentucky Meat Shower."

The Making of a Jelly Bean

*For a tiny candy, the making of a
jelly bean is one enormous process.*

You may not know it to look at them, but a handful of jelly beans
represent three whole weeks of work. Candymakers have the sugary
treats' creation down to a science, and one thing's for sure: It's not
simple.

Inside Out

Most jelly beans start with the inside. Confectioners stir up a boiling mix of flavors and
colors to form the inner goo. Some companies even go as far as putting in additions such
as real fruit puree. Afterward, it's time to cook up the middle and
work toward the outside.

    The still-liquid centers slosh to their next step, where machines
squirt them out one pop at a time into starch-filled molds. That's
where the candy gets their shape. After several hours of cooling,
the soon-to-be beans are taken out and brushed with sugar. At this
point, the candymakers set them aside for as long as 48 hours before
moving forward with making the outer shells.

Shake, Rattle, and Roll

Finally, the beans are ready to be finished. Workers bring the tasty
centers into a giant metal rotating pan. There, they shake the beans
around for two full hours, letting them gather several layers of external goodness. But the job isn't done yet—the crews still have to pour
glaze over the treats to give them their signature shine. A few more
days of seasoning, and these little treats are ready to be branded and
sent out. Many confectioners use a special kind of food coloring to
stamp the company name directly onto the bean. Then machines
move the jelly beans into boxes, seal them up for freshness, and
finally ship them away—the last step in a long journey from the factory and into your stomach.

Fast Facts

- *Babies are born with more than 300 bones. As they grow, some of the bones fuse together—adults have only 206 bones.*

- *Babies are born without kneecaps, which don't appear until children are between the ages of two and six years old.*

- *The first comic strip was* The Yellow Kid, *published in 1895. The most widely distributed comic strip is* Peanuts *(appearing in 2,400 papers worldwide), and the longest-running strip is* The Katzenjammer Kids, *which continues its run since 1897.*

- *In Gainesville, Georgia, the self-proclaimed "Chicken Capital of the World," it's illegal to eat fried chicken with a fork.*

- *The human stomach secretes two to three quarts of hydrochloric acid each day. To keep from digesting itself, the stomach has to produce a protective layer of mucus every two weeks.*

- *Delaware has only three counties—the fewest of any state. (Even Rhode Island, the smallest state, has five.)*

- *Louisiana is the only state without counties. It's subdivided into "parishes."*

- *The Leaning Tower of Pisa has eight stories.*

- *Duct tape was originally developed as "duck" tape. Early in World War II, the U.S. government commissioned Band-Aid maker Johnson & Johnson to make a strong adhesive that would keep ammo cases dry. Because the resulting tape was both green and waterproof, GIs called it "duck" tape.*

- *Most of the plants in Disneyland's Tomorrowland are edible fruits and vegetables. Guests are encouraged to help themselves to a bite.*

Pope Joan: Was She or Wasn't He?

❖ ❖ ❖ ❖

Posing as a man, a scholarly German woman of English descent entered the Catholic Church hierarchy, rising to become pope in A.D. 855. Her secret emerged, literally, when she gave birth to a son while riding in a papal procession through the streets of Rome. The populace, which just couldn't take a joke, tied her to a horse's tail and dragged her to death while stoning her.

So here's the question: Is this story fact or fiction?

What does the Holy See say?

Not a chance. They list Pope Benedict III, A.D. 855–858, with no suggestion that the Holy Father might have been a Holy Mother. The Church has long blamed anti-Catholic writers and saboteurs said to have doctored the evidence.

Surely that's plausible, given the avalanches of anti-Catholic hatred since the Reformation.

Up to a point, yes. Catholic-bashers pummelled the papacy with Pope Joan taunts. However, that cannot explain the pre-Reformation references, not all of which meant woe unto St. Peter's Basilica.

An example, please.

Take Jan Hus, the Czech heretic burned at the stake in 1415 (a century before Martin Luther picked up steam). In the trial record, Hus rebukes the papacy for letting a woman become pope. Why didn't they strappado him on the spot for rank blasphemy?

That indicates only that the Inquisitors believed the legend at the time, not that it's true.

Good point. But then there's Martin of Poland, a Dominican priest who wrote his history of the papacy in 1265. He's the primary source for Pope Joan and the hardest to dismiss. He didn't hate the church; he held high rank as papal chaplain. Did someone doctor our oldest copy of his account (circa 1300s)? Hard to say.

Could a woman have pulled off such a ruse?

Possibly. Medical checkups were even rarer than baths. The clergy shaved, solving the dilemma of facial hair. Papal garments were heavy and hanging. Every reference to Joan attests to her great intellect, a necessary aspect since no idiot could have been elected pope in drag. So, it wouldn't be easy to pull it off, but it's possible.

Okay: If Joan was so smart, then she knew she was pregnant. What did she plan to do with the child?

That's a big weakness in the pro-Joan theory. You can cover up your body and tonsure your head, but ask anyone who's ever flown commercially: You can't keep a baby quiet. How would she care for the infant if she managed to give birth in secret? If it's possible to insult a mythical figure's legacy, suggesting that she might abandon the infant would be that insult. She'd had to have known this pregnancy wouldn't end well.

So, what do we make of this? Legend or covered-up truth?

Stoning a pope to death in the streets would have been a big event, which should have spawned at least a few contemporary accounts. Where are they? There isn't enough strong evidence to say, "Pope Joan existed." There is just enough to make us wonder if the legend has some basis in reality.

How could that be?

Stories morph and change. About 700 years span the time between Joan and the Protestant Reformation—nearly the lifespan of the Roman Republic and Empire combined. The story could have wandered far enough into time's misty fog to place the papal mitre upon this mysterious woman's head.

But we do not know.

Without compelling new evidence, we never will.

He Said, She Said

"The secret of life is honesty and fair dealing. If you can fake that, you've got it made."
—*Groucho Marx*

"Name the greatest of all inventors—accident."
—*Mark Twain*

"Men don't care what's on TV. They only care what else is on TV."
—*Jerry Seinfeld*

"Men are only as loyal as their options."
—*Bill Maher*

"I love Thanksgiving. It's the only time in Los Angeles that you see natural breasts."
—*Arnold Schwarzenegger*

"When I played pro football, I never set out to hurt anyone deliberately—unless it was, you know, important, like a league game or something."
—*Dick Butkus*

"Cauliflower is nothing but cabbage with a college education."
—*Mark Twain*

"You've got to go out on a limb sometimes because that's where the fruit is."
—*Will Rogers*

"I once wanted to become an atheist, but I gave up—they have no holidays."
—*Henny Youngman*

"Christmas is a time when everybody wants his past forgotten and his present remembered."
—*Phyllis Diller*

"Men reach their sexual peak at 18. Women reach theirs at 35. Do you get the feeling that God is playing a practical joke?"
—*Rita Rudner*

"You've got bad eating habits if you use a grocery cart in 7-Eleven."
—*Dennis Miller*

Sound Secrets

❖ ❖ ❖ ❖

Take a Hollywood movie scene: A leather-jacketed hero scuffles with a bad guy and then walks through the snow before driving into the night. Sounds good, right? But what you really heard was a Foley artist punching a roasted chicken with a rubber kitchen glove and squeezing two balloons together while walking in a sandbox filled with cornstarch.

Things Are Not What They Seem

Whether you notice it or not, the sound of a movie can be as entertaining as the visual experience. But unbeknownst to many viewers, most sounds and special effects are not captured at the time of filming. Instead, they're either recorded in the studio by Foley artists or pulled from a library of prerecorded sound bites that are stored on computers until the sound is mixed for the movie.

The term "Foley artist" was used as early as 1927 when Al Jolson's movie *The Jazz Singer* became the first "talkie," or movie recorded with sound. In those days, recording the actors' dialogue superseded virtually all other sound or music recorded for the film. It wasn't until the early 1950s that producers discovered they could enhance the overall quality of the moviegoers' experience by adding specialized sounds that were purposely stripped away during filming in favor of an actor's spoken lines.

The profession's namesake, Jack Foley, was asked by his sound engineer to improve the quality of the audio tracks by introducing a series of "studio clips." Setting the industry standard, he discovered that in order to enhance the sound, three categories of sound were required, starting with "footsteps." Each actor executing a scene in a movie walks or runs with their own unique gait, on a variety of surfaces. By watching raw footage of the film, a Foley artist attempts to replicate and record the actor's pace and sound by walking on the most suitable surface, for instance, cement, gravel, or sand.

The second sound category that must be captured is the "moves." Moves accompany footsteps and include the sounds of skirts swishing, pants rustling, or leather jackets squeaking. Finally, all of the other special sounds required to make the experience more believable must be either pulled from thousands of computer-generated archives or shot especially for the film.

The Life of a Foley Artist

Foley artists are natural-born scavengers. When they're not actively involved in producing sound effects for films and television, you'll often find them scrounging around garage sales and piles of trash looking for anything that will generate a particular sound. A fertile imagination is key: What may sound like a couple passionately kissing in a movie may actually be a Foley artist sucking on his or her own forearm.

When Foley artist Marko Costanzo began freelancing for C5, Inc., he needed to come up with a variety of new sounds to use on his projects. Since most clips weren't available, he invented the following ingenious additions to his audio library:

- For a two-minute sequence of a dragonfly in *Men in Black,* Costanzo clipped off the ends of the blades of a simple plastic fan and replaced them with duct tape. When the fan was turned on, he could control the quality of the resulting flapping sound by brushing his fingers against the duct-taped blades.

- For a knifing scene in the crime drama *Goodfellas,* Costanzo tried stabbing raw chickens, beef, and pork roasts with the bones intact.

- To achieve the sound of walking on freshly fallen snow, he walked on kosher sea salt covered with a thick layer of cornstarch.

- To emulate the sound of a dog walking across a hardwood surface, Costanzo glued press-on nails onto work gloves and clickity-clacked the nails on wood. The size of the dog could be controlled by the thickness of the nails used.

The motion picture industry thrives on creating fantasies. From the moment that the actor steps onto the soundstage, nothing is what it seems. Without Foley artists, our movie-going experience would be a lackluster one.

Odd Ordinances

- Texas has a law preventing people from carrying concealed ice cream cones.

- Calling a girl a "slut" could land you a $1,000 fine and six months in jail in Utah.

- The city of Globe, Arizona, has made it illegal to play cards with a Native American.

- Women are not legally allowed to wear pants in Tucson, Arizona.

- It's illegal to mail a complaint about a hotel having cockroaches in Los Angeles.

- Horses are under no circumstances allowed to wear cowbells in Tahoe City, California.

- It was once illegal to sneeze on a train in the state of West Virginia.

- It is illegal for an ambulance to go faster than 20 mph in Port Huron, Michigan.

- All public vehicles are required to have spittoons—those old-fashioned receptacles for spitting out your chewing tobacco refuse—in the city of San Francisco.

- Stepping out of a plane while flying over Maine is strictly against the law.

- You're a criminal if you use hair curlers without a license in Oklahoma.

- Similarly, wearing make-up requires a permit in the small city of Morrisville, Pennsylvania.

- Ontario, California, will not tolerate any roosters crowing.

- Giving a lit cigar to a pet is against the law in Zion, Illinois.

- Clawson, Michigan, found it necessary to pass a law that farmers can't sleep with their pigs, cows, horses, goats, or chickens.

There's More to Know About Tycho

A golden nose, a dwarf, a pet elk, drunken revelry, and... astronomy? Read about the wild life of this groundbreaking astronomer.

Look to the Stars

Tycho Brahe was a Dutch noble-man who is best remembered for blazing a trail in astronomy in an era before the inven-tion of the telescope. Through tireless observation and study, Brahe became one of the first astronomers to fully understand the exact motions of the planets, thereby laying the groundwork for future generations of star gazers.

In 1560, Brahe, then a 13-year-old law student, witnessed a partial eclipse of the sun. He reportedly was so moved by the event that he bought a set of astronomical tools and a copy of Ptolemy's legendary astronomical treatise, *Almagest,* and began a life-long career studying the stars. Where Brahe would differ from his forbearers in this field of study was that he believed that new discoveries in the field of astronomy could be made, not by guesswork and conjecture, but rather by rig-orous and repetitious studies. His work would include many publica-tions and even the discovery of a supernova now known as SN 1572.

Hven, Sweet Hven

As his career as an astronomer blossomed, Brahe became one of the most widely renowned astronomers in all of Europe. In fact, he was so acclaimed that when King Frederick II of Denmark heard of Brahe's plans to move to the Swiss city of Basle, the King offered him his own island, Hven, located in the Danish Sound.

Once there, Brahe built his own observatory known as Uraniborg and ruled the island as if it were his own personal kingdom. This meant that his tenants were often forced to supply their ruler (in this case Brahe) with goods and services or be locked up in the island's prison. At one point Brahe imprisoned an entire family—contrary to Danish law.

Did We Mention That He Was Completely Nutty?

While he is famous for his work in astronomy, Brahe is more infamous for his colorful lifestyle. At age 20, he lost part of his nose in an alcohol-fueled duel (reportedly using rapiers while in the dark) that ensued after a Christmas party. Portraits of Brahe show him wearing a replacement nose possibly made of gold and silver and held in place by an adhesive. Upon the exhumation of his body in 1901, green rings discovered around the nasal cavity of Brahe's skull have also led some scholars to speculate that the nose may actually have been made of copper.

While there was a considerable amount of groundbreaking astronomical research done on Hven, Brahe also spent his time hosting legendarily drunken parties. Such parties often featured a colorful cast of characters including a Little Person named Jepp who dwelled under Brahe's dining table and functioned as something of a court jester; it is speculated that Brahe believed that Jepp was clairvoyant. Brahe also kept a tame pet elk, which stumbled to its death after falling down a flight of stairs—the animal had gotten drunk on beer at the home of a nobleman.

Brahe also garnered additional notoriety for marrying a woman from the lower classes. Such a union was considered shameful for a nobleman such as Brahe, and he was ostracized because of the marriage. Thusly all of his eight children were considered illegitimate.

However, the most lurid story of all is the legend that Brahe died from a complication to his bladder caused by not urinating, out of politeness, at a friend's dinner party where prodigious amounts of wine were consumed. The tale lives on, but it should be pointed out that recent research suggests this version of Brahe's demise could be apocryphal: He may have died of mercury poisoning from his own fake nose.

The Lady is a Vamp

Meet Theda Bara—Hollywood's first "bad girl."

Publicity Makeover

Theodosia Burr Goodman was born in Cincinnati in 1885, the eldest daughter of a prosperous Polish tailor and a Swiss-born wigmaker. Dullsville, right? However, when Goodman became known as film star Theda Bara, a more flamboyant bio was concocted to match Bara's exotic on-screen persona: the Egyptian-born daughter of a French actress and an Italian sculptor. Bara held press conferences in a steamy hotel room fashioned to resemble a Sultana's chambers. Never breaking character, she gave interviews in a sultry French accent. Bara's willingness to participate in such outlandish stunts helped propel her into stardom—she now ranks among the top silent film stars, trailing only Mary Pickford and Charlie Chaplin in popularity.

A Brief but Memorable Career

Bara landed her first screen role in 1914 as an extra when she was nearly 30 years old. Soon, a Fox film director lobbied for her to star in the 1915 vampire flick, *A Fool There Was*. The immortal catchphrase "Kiss me, my fool" helped propel her to stardom; suddenly, the good Jewish girl found her silver-screen niche as a blood-sucking femme fatale. When Bara took on the title role in her most famous film, *Cleopatra* (1917), her publicists hyped her alias, "Theda Bara," as an anagram for "Arab Death."

Her career flourished, but it ultimately went bust in 1919 after Fox began promoting flat-chested flappers over the buxom Bara. Unfortunately, Bara was unable to shake her vampy typecasting, which made it difficult to find work as censorship in Hollywood became stricter. She continued to make movies until 1926. Bara made more than 40 films, but sadly, all but three have been lost, giving her the highest percentage of lost work for someone with a star on the Hollywood Walk of Fame. Despite the film industry moving on without her, Bara remains one of the most memorable figures of early filmmaking.

Behind the TV Shows of Our Time

- Nancy Cartwright, internationally known as the voice of Bart Simpson on *The Simpsons,* first tried out for the part of Lisa.

- Milhouse, Bart's best friend, has the middle name Mussolini.

- Homer Simpson's e-mail address is ChunkyLover53@aol.com.

- *The Simpsons*'s Krusty the Clown has been given two real names in different episodes: Herschel Schmoikel Krustofski and Herschel Pinkus Yerucham Krustofski.

- *Grey's Anatomy* hunk Patrick Dempsey tried out for the part of Dr. Chase on *House* before accepting his spot on *Grey's.*

- *South Park*'s Mr. Garrison's first name is Herbert.

- *South Park* creator Trey Parker named Cartman's mom, Liane, after his former fiancée. He has said that she cheated on him, so he wanted to immortalize her with the cartoon's most promiscuous character.

- An average episode of *South Park* takes only five days to create.

- A sticker on Dwight Schrute's desk in the American version of *The Office* says "Froggy 101"—the name of an actual country music station in Scranton, Pennsylvania.

- Some shots shown in the opening sequence of the American version of *The Office*—such as the water cooler and copy machine—are taken directly from its British counterpart.

- The outside building shown as Dunder-Mifflin in *The Office* is actually located in the real town of Scranton, Pennsylvania; coincidentally enough, across from an old bar that was named "The Office."

- The computers used in the Dunder-Mifflin offices on *The Office* are actual functioning, Internet-enabled computers. Actors say they sometimes surf the Web while in the background of shots to pass the time.

- *The Office*'s John Krasinski and B. J. Novak went to high school together and were in the same grade in Newton, Massachusetts.

The Rise of the Rubber Duckie

❖ ❖ ❖ ❖

America's favorite bath toy dates back centuries.
He makes bath time lots of fun, but your tub buddy
has a lot of history under his belt, er, beak.

The Early Birds

This yellow bath bird is believed to have made his first appearance sometime in the 1800s, when rubber became common in toy production. Historians say the first ducks were actually made of a hard rubber and were far less squeaky than the modern variety.

Duckie's Debut

You can credit *Sesame Street*'s Ernie with bringing rubber duckies into the spotlight. The Muppet's ode to his bathtime buddy catapulted the duck into mainstream culture. The song, first performed on *Sesame Street* in 1970, idolizes the "cute and yellow and chubby" friend who's always waiting in the "tubby." Doo-doo-be-doo, indeed!

The Modern Duck

These days, most rubber ducks are not rubber at all. Instead, they're created from a vinyl plastic made to mimic the original product's appearance.

A Worldly Traveler

Once in a while, a rubber duckie likes to take a dip outside the tub. In 1992, storms sent cargo from a ship into the ocean. One of the boxes happened to hold 29,000 rubber toys, including thousands of duckies, all of which broke free and swam the open sea. The ducks drifted all the way from the International Date Line to Alaska, where they washed up 10 months later.

Duck Love

To some, the ducks are more than just toys. Hundreds of devoted collectors spend their days scouring for every possible model. The Guinness World Record holder currently owns more than 2,600 different ducks—and, we assume, not too many dates.

Candy That Time Forgot

❖ ❖ ❖ ❖

Between the First and Second World Wars, there were almost 6,000 candy companies in the United States. Then, in the 1970s and '80s, the big companies—Mars, Hershey's, and Nestlé—started snapping up the competition. Suddenly, candy became less varied and more streamlined. Here are some of the candies of yesteryear.

Choco-Lite
Don't be fooled by the name of this candy bar—Choco-Lite wasn't guilt-free chocolate, though it *was* slightly smaller than most bars. The "lite" likely referred to the dozens of small holes that were punched through the bar, making it seem airier.

Marathon
Mars made this funny-looking, awesome-tasting candy bar in 1973. It featured eight inches of braided caramel covered in milk chocolate. At that length, it was much longer than most of the other candy bars on the shelves. Sadly, it wasn't popular enough to go the distance. Mars discontinued it in 1981.

Chicken Dinner
The Sperry Candy Company created the Chicken Dinner Bar in the early '20s and no, it didn't taste like chicken. The bizarre name was meant to convey the feeling of wellbeing and prosperity associated with "a chicken in every pot." Instead, the bar was chocolate-flavor caramel rolled in nuts, similar to today's Nut Roll. The candy was phased out in the '60s.

Forever Yours
This confection, created in 1923, was distributed as two bars in one pack—one chocolate, one vanilla. In 1936, the vanilla bar (which was covered in dark chocolate) left the pack and struck out on its own as the Forever Yours bar. It was discontinued in 1979, but it came back ten years later as the Milky Way Dark Bar. In 2000, it was renamed Milky Way Midnight.

Nestlé's Triple-Decker

This bar was discontinued in the early '70s, probably because it was too expensive to produce. The bar had three layers of chocolate: white, dark, and milk. Fans say that the bitter/creamy/sweet combo was unparalleled; there are more than a few online message boards where chocoholics swap recipes for homemade versions.

Bit-O-Choc

Many candy fans out there will recognize the Bit-O-Choc's successful brother, Bit-O-Honey. The latter candy, a sweet, almond-flavored nougat bar, is still being produced 80 years after the Schutter-Johnson candy company created it. Bit-O-Choc, on the other hand, didn't last long. By all accounts, the "molar-ripping" bar was only slightly better than another incarnation, Bit-O-Coconut. The candy was phased out after a few years on the market.

Fat Emma

In Minneapolis in the 1920s, nougat was big business. Pendergast Candy Company had developed a way to use egg whites to create lighter, fluffier nougat that folks loved. Though Frank Mars would eventually use the nougat recipe in his most popular bars (Milky Way and 3 Musketeers), Pendergast made a puffy candy called the Fat Emma, which, though discontinued, is still used in the industry when referring to a candy bar with fluffy nougat filling.

Caravelle

Fans of the Caravelle bar say that eating one was almost a religious experience. The creamy chocolate was wrapped around dark, moist caramel and malted-flavored crisp rice. When Cadbury acquired its producer, Peter Paul, in 1988, the Caravelle was discontinued.

Seven Up

If you were a kid in St. Paul, Minnesota, in the 1950s, you might have enjoyed one of Trudeau Candies' Seven Up bars. This bar was composed of seven small, candy box–style chocolates welded together with chocolate. Boasting four types of caramel, Brazil nuts, coconut, jelly, chocolate-slathered mint, fudge, nougat, butterscotch, and butter cream, this Frankenstein of a confection was phased out in 1979.

Word Histories

Woman: Although there are some feminists who spell the word "womyn," to remove the implied derivation from "man," the origin of this word is actually much more neutral—it comes from the Old English *wif-man,* or "female human being."

Admiral: A title of rank adopted by Western seamen in the 13th century who came into contact with Arabic ship captains who called themselves *Amir-al-bahl* ("commander of the sea"). Still, the word originated in the desert, as the title of Abu Bakr who was called *Amir-al-munin* or "commander of the faithful."

Workaholic: An American counselor named Wayne Oates coined this term in 1971. He recognized his own condition after his young son asked for an appointment to see him.

Wildcat: This word, used to refer to risky business ventures, originated with a failed Michigan bank. Before the bank collapsed in 1830, it printed its own currency depicting a wild panther.

Venezuela: When Spanish explorers encountered the canal-building South Americans, they were reminded of Venice, Italy. *Venezuela* literally means "little Venice" in Spanish.

Snacks: The tasty treats have been consumed since the 1600s, when the word was first used to describe small portions of food hastily snatched between meals.

Quarantine: This word comes from the French *quarante,* which means "forty," and *-aine,* which adds a degree of approximation (equivalent to "-ish" in English). This is because sailors whose ships were suspected of carrying disease were restricted from shore contact for about 40 days upon arriving in a port.

Ain't: A widely used contraction of "am not," the term was first used in early 18th-century England, where it was considered proper English by all classes.

Hazard: One of the many things that Crusaders brought back to Europe from the Middle East were games using dice, or *al zahr* in Arabic, which led to the use of "hazard" to describe similarly risky pursuits.

World War II Baseball and the One-Armed Outfielder

In January 1942, President Franklin D. Roosevelt responded to a letter from Baseball Commissioner Kenesaw Mountain Landis, advising that baseball should continue during World War II because it was good for American morale. He should have specified, "Good baseball, that is."

Service-able Baseball

World War II-era baseball is known for many things: a one-legged pitcher, a 15-year-old pitcher, and a perennial doormat team, the St. Louis Browns, finally winning a pennant. However, there was nothing more memorable than a one-armed outfielder named Pete Gray.

Although baseball was allowed to continue during the war, many of its players went into the armed forces. Dozens of players entered the military, including stars such as Bob Feller, Joe DiMaggio, and Ted Williams. Teams scrambled to find replacements. The Boston Red Sox held open tryouts, while the Cleveland Indians found a fellow with feet so large—he wore size 17 shoes—that he was rejected for the army.

The Cincinnati Reds tried 15-year-old Joe Nuxhall as a pitcher. He gave up five runs in less than an inning for an Earned Run Average of 67.50. Bert Shepard, who had lost a leg in the war, fared better during his short stint with the Washington Senators: He held the opposition to one run in five innings. However, 41-year-old Paul Waner summed up the best reason for recruiting wartime players. A former star with the Pittsburgh Pirates, Waner found himself in the outfield for the New York Yankees. When asked by a fan why he was back on the field, Waner replied matter-of-factly, "Because DiMaggio's in the army."

By 1944, the quality of play found in a Major League Baseball game had hit an all-time low. Fittingly, that year the St. Louis Browns, who usually finished last or awfully close to it, won the American League pennant for the first and only time in their history.

Not Quite Far Enough

In 1945, the Browns decided to give a one-armed outfielder named Pete Gray a shot. He was born in 1915 as Pete Wyshner in Nanticoke, Pennsylvania. Right-handed, Gray lost his right arm as a young boy when it was amputated just above the elbow after an accident. At age 17, he hitchhiked to Chicago to see the 1932 World Series between the Cubs and Yankees. Thereafter, Gray was determined to play Major League Baseball.

Gray had previously played in several successful minor-league seasons, including with the Brooklyn Bushwicks and the Trois Rivieres Renards of the Canadian-American League. On the field with the Browns, critics derailed him by saying he was a curiosity playing because of the dwindling talent pool. Gray had plenty of talent, but despite devising a method of fielding that was so quick he had to demonstrate it in slow motion, Gray found that he could not hit major-league pitching because he had no second hand to temper his swing when pitchers threw him off-speed balls. Even his quickness on the field could not stop runners from taking an extra base on him. Gray hit .218 in 1945, which was his only major-league season. Many of the balls he hit just didn't have enough force and died on the warning track just a few feet from the fence.

"Just not quite far enough," Gray said ruefully.

Back to Normal

In 1946, players returning from the service helped boost the quality of play—and just in time. The 1945 World Series had been so miserable it was dubbed "the fat men against the tall men at the office picnic." This made a prophet out of Chicago sportswriter Warren Brown, who when asked to pick which team would win before the start of the series said: "I don't think either of them can win it." As for Gray, he was dropped from the Browns in 1946 and went on to play in the minors until 1949. Still, he continues to serve as a source of inspiration for many disabled people and amputees.

Fast Facts

- Like plants, children grow faster during spring than any other season.

- In India, sunburns are typically treated with honey and boiled potato skins.

- The world's oldest still-existing amusement park is Bakken in Denmark, which opened in 1583.

- The best-selling fiction writer of all time is Agatha Christie, whose murder mysteries have sold more than two billion copies worldwide since 1920. Only the Bible and some guy named William Shakespeare outsell her.

- Herbert Hoover, born in 1874, was the first U.S. president born west of the Mississippi River.

- Virginia is the birthplace of more U.S. presidents than any other state (eight), followed by Ohio (seven).

- Nine-banded armadillos have identical quadruplets every time they give birth.

- Filipino warriors developed a version of the yo-yo in the 16th century as a weapon. Their version, however, was a four-pound ball attached to a 20-foot cord.

- Walt Disney has won the most Academy Awards ever (22). Katharine Hepburn has won the most of any woman (4).

- In the United States, all swine under 180 pounds are "pigs"; those over are "hogs." In the UK, there is no distinction—all swine are called "pigs."

- After the Revolutionary War, the site known as Big Salt Lick became Nashville, Tennessee.

What a Way to Go!

❖ ❖ ❖ ❖

*Some people are choosing to buck the bummer burial
tradition by creating customized coffins that are to die for.*

African Beauties

The Ga people of Ghana fashion coffins into shapes that reflect the
lifestyles or livelihoods of the deceased. For instance, a leopard-shape
coffin signifies the deceased was a powerful person; a chicken represents a maternal figure. Carpenters have respectfully carved caskets
into various symbolic animals, including cows, elephants, crocodiles,
lobsters, sharks, and objects such as shoes, hammers, pineapples, cell
phones, Coca-Cola bottles, cigarettes, and cars.

However, as unusual as some of these coffins are, the one designed
for a gynecologist out-weirds the rest: a giant uterus complete with
ovaries. Apparently, what was good enough to carry him into this
world was good enough to carry him out.

Anglo Innovation

In England, one can find picture-box coffins that use the entire outer
surface of the casket as a colorful canvas. Giving new meaning to
the term "still" art, these coffins are painted with landscapes, floral
arrangements, sports motifs, etc. Buyers even have the option of pre-
designing their own coffins.

However, even the stiff-upper-lip set can get loose with their burial
boxes, commissioning specialty shaped coffins such as a giant satin
ballet shoe, a replica of a beloved guitar, and a large garbage Dumpster. One Brit even ordered a sleek wooden egg and requested to be
buried upright in the fetal position. (No yolk!)

Americans take a much more pragmatic approach to their coffin
creations. These dualistic coffins also serve as entertainment centers,
coffee tables, or beer-can-shaped coolers. With just a little know-how,
an oak coffin becomes a wooden shelving unit. Top a casket with glass,
and it serves as a unique conversation starter. Fill the cooler coffin
with beer and it becomes a fitting centerpiece for a living wake—
albeit a potentially sobering experience for the guest of honor.

INSPIRATION STATION

The Tsars of the Midway

The next time you're dangling upside down in a roller coaster 10,000 feet in the air, take a second to give props to the Russians. During the 17th century, Russian winter sled rides were a hugely popular pastime; the more daring the rides, the more people came to participate or just watch from the sidelines. Slides were built between 70 and 80 feet high and employed breathtaking 50-degree vertical drops. Entrepreneurs looking to take the trend worldwide soon replicated these "ice mountains." When the rides were built for warmer climates, engineers used wheeled cars on wooden tracks instead. In many countries, roller coasters are still referred to by their inspiration: "Russian Mountains."

Planting the Sydney Opera House

It's hard to say what is the most impres-
sive feature of Australia's Sydney Opera
House—its enormous size at over
4.5 acres, or its power supply,
which is enough for a town of
25,000 people. But for many,
the coolest thing about the
opera house is the roof itself.
Designed by Danish architect Jørn Utzon in 1957, the roof of the venue is a collection of enormous concrete "shells." Some say the shells look more like boat sails, but neither the shapes of shells nor sails were in Utzon's mind when he was designing the structure. His inspiration? Palm fronds.

One for the Kids

"Hey Jude," the Beatles' most successful song in the United States, had sad beginnings. At the time, Paul McCartney was witness to the divorce proceedings between John Lennon and his wife Cynthia. Inspired, McCartney began to write "Hey Jude," initially as a sympathetic note to the couple's five-year-old son Julian. But "Hey Jude" wasn't an entirely selfless gesture—McCartney wrote the rest of the song as a sympa- thetic note to himself.The rest of the song deals with his break-up with fiancée Jane Asher and his qualms with dating Linda Eastman. The track, released in 1968, stayed on the charts for 19 weeks with 9 weeks at number one.

Meet the Bug Men

*About one in three movies features at least one scene containing
an insect, whether it's a single fly landing on a windowsill
or a swarm of 3,000 locusts terrorizing an entire town. Stay
seated for the end credits and you'll likely spot a credit for an
"insect wrangler." Alternately known as a "bug wrangler" or
simply "bug man," an insect wrangler is a trained entomologist
responsible for not only providing various creepy-crawlies
used in a movie or TV show but also for manipulating
them onscreen so they swarm, run, or fly on cue.*

So, how do you train an insect?

You don't. Insects can't be trained—they
can only be manipulated. Wranglers have
to understand why insects do things and
then work out how you can manipulate
that behavior to fit the needs of the
script. Spiders, for example, refuse to
walk on Lemon Pledge furniture wax. If
you spray the area you don't want them to go, they will unfailingly
avoid it. Similarly, cockroaches will always run from a light source.

To make an insect fly toward a window, wranglers will place a
bright light out of shot behind the window. To make an insect fly
away and then return to the window, they attach a tiny harness made
of very fine silk and control the bug like a puppet.

Is there a casting process for bugs?

It may sound strange, but casting is very important. You need to
choose the right insect according to the demands of the shot. In the
1990 movie *Arachnophobia,* in which deadly tropical spiders terror-
ize a small California town, the insect wranglers deliberately chose
to use the New Zealand Avendale spider for the swarm scenes. After
testing a variety of other species, they found it was the only spider
that would run when it was crowded rather than just attack the other
spiders.

What about makeup for insects?

Absolutely! When the insect wrangler on *The Silence of the Lambs* set couldn't obtain specimens of the rare moth needed for the movie, he had to use common moths instead. He anesthetized each moth and painted on the distinctive markings (resembling a human skull) of the death's-head hawk moth onto its body. In *Spider-Man,* the insect wrangler had to paint the tiny blue-and-white Steatoda spider that bites the Peter Parker character. The wrangler used water-based, nontoxic paint, of course, so that it would easily wash off without harming the spider.

Are insects ever harmed during filming?

No. The U.S. Humane Society monitors most movie and television sets. If moviemakers want the "No Animals Were Harmed" end-credit disclaimer, they have to meet the Humane Society's strict guidelines. Wranglers work closely with the actors on how to handle bugs so as not to mistreat them. In the 2005 movie *The Three Burials of Melquiades Estrada,* for example, Tommy Lee Jones's character comes across a dead body covered in ants. In the first shot, the insect wrangler used real ants on a dummy body. But for the shot when Jones sets fire to the corpse, the real ants were replaced with rubber ones so that no ants would be harmed.

Tricks of the Trade

- To create a cockroach death scene, a bug wrangler will administer just the right dose of carbon dioxide. This will make the cockroach run a few feet before flipping onto its back and lying unconscious for several minutes. It will regain consciousness just in time for a second take.

- To get spiders to run up a wall, an insect wrangler will hide out of shot and blow a hair dryer up the wall toward the spider.

- Parts of a floor can be heated or cooled to control the direction of swarming spiders. Electric fields or shivering wires will stop the spiders from swarming too far.

🎥 Behind the Films of Our Time

- The American musical classic *Grease* is known as *Vaselina* in the country of Venezuela.

- It's not just the glasses: While the character of Superman is scripted as being 6'2", the character of Clark Kent—played, of course, by the same actor—is written to be only 5'11".

- Actress Charlize Theron first got noticed while she was throwing a fit at a Los Angeles bank. Legend has it the A-list actress freaked out when a teller wouldn't accept her check. A talent manager handed her his card as she was being thrown out.

- *Rocky IV* is considered the highest-grossing sports movie. *Jerry Maguire* is second.

- One of the longest movies ever released ran 25 hours long: Andy Warhol's ****. At the very top of the list is the experimental film *The Cure for Insomnia*, which clocks in at 87 hours long.

- The Aston Martin car driven by James Bond in *Goldfinger* later auctioned at a cool $275,000, making it one of the most expensive props ever to appear in a film.

- Harrison Ford was producers' first choice to play the lead role in both *Dragonfly* and *JFK*. Both parts, however, went to Kevin Costner.

- Fruit is a strong symbol in all three *Godfather* movies: Every time an orange appears, someone is facing death.

- The movie *Buffy the Vampire Slayer* featured a then-unknown Ben Affleck. The actor spoke just one line.

- The cult classic *Monty Python's Life of Brian* was never shown in some countries. Ireland and Norway were among several nations that banned the movie upon its release.

- The HAL computer in *2001: A Space Odyssey* is short for "Heuristically program ALgorithmic computer."

- Every single still photo featured in the film *Forrest Gump* shows the character with his eyes closed.

Down the Drain

❖ ❖ ❖ ❖

Dismayed at the high prices of traditional funerals?
Why not wash the remains down the drain?

The Pressure Cooker

Funerals are big business. A traditional funeral can cost upward of $15,000, while an "inexpensive" funeral runs around $2,000. This can cause big problems—perhaps the bereaved is unable to foot the bill. Or maybe it was the deceased's wishes to have a less expensive, more eco-friendly method of disposing of his or her remains.

Enter an interesting approach. In 1992, scientists came up with a unique way to dispose of animal carcasses used in medical research: alkaline hydrolysis. Today the method is used on human remains as well. The process uses a combination of a high-alkaline product (usually lye) and a temperature of about 300 degrees Fahrenheit. It also takes a specially designed stainless-steel container that acts much like a large pressure cooker.

After a moderate amount of "cooking," the carcass is reduced to a coffee-color syrup, with the approximate consistency of motor oil. The liquid is sterile and is generally safe enough to be poured down the drain. For those who would like to have something more tangible to remember their loved ones by, bone residue can be captured, dried, and placed in an urn, similar to cremation. The cost would also be akin to that of cremation.

The New Alternative to Burial

The process is actually nothing new. For years, Hollywood movie plots have incorporated similar methods—think of gangster flicks in which some wise guy's body is dissolved in a bathtub full of lye. But there are real-life benefits: Alkaline hydrolysis is gaining favor because of its environmental benefits. Unlike cremation, there are no dangerous emissions like carbon dioxide or the ill effects of the disposal of mercury and silver dental fillings.

Even so, alkaline hydrolysis has been a tough sell. While human burial and cremation have become mainstream methods for disposing human bodies, there's something unsettling about watching grandma circle down the drain. Minnesota and New Hampshire have legalized the process, but only one funeral director has stepped up to offer the service.

Many detractors of the service are uncomfortable with the idea. "We believe this process, which enables a portion of human remains to be flushed down a drain, to be undignified," says Patrick McGee, a spokesperson for the Roman Catholic Diocese of Manchester. A number of detractors are more concerned with the process of disposing human waste. On the other hand, George Carlson, an Industrial Waste Manager with the New Hampshire Department of Environmental Services, says that things the public might find more troubling routinely flow into U.S. sewage treatment plants all the time—including blood and embalming fluid from funeral homes.

But others, such as New Hampshire State Representative Barbara French, agree that it might be time for a change toward hydrolysis. "I'm getting near that age and thought about cremation but this is equally as good and less of an environmental problem," she said. "It doesn't bother me any more than being burned up."

The Big Kahuna of Hydrolysis

The chief proponent of the process is Brad Cain, president of BioSafe Engineering. The company manufactures the required steel containers and estimates that as many as 50 facilities (including veterinary schools, universities, pharmaceutical companies, and the U.S. government) use his equipment to dispose of animal carcasses and other types of medical wastes. Cain would like to offer the service to the public as an alternative to cremation.

Currently, there are only two facilities in the country that use the process—the University of Florida in Gainesville and the Mayo Clinic in Rochester, Minnesota. Both are research facilities and neither of them offer the service to the public. Chad Corbin, a Manchester funeral director, was issued a permit to operate a hydrolysis tank in 2007, but the process became mired in delays and red tape. Now he has to begin the approval process all over again. "I don't know how long it will take," he said, "but eventually it will happen."

ESCAPE!

CHARGING BULL

Think you've got what it takes to beat a charging bull? An average bull weighs in the ballpark of 2,000 pounds—more than ten times the weight of a typical man. Unless you're a trained rodeo performer used to sidestepping an angry bull, you probably want to follow these steps if you find one staring you down:

- First of all, stay still. Bulls tend to attack when they're angry, so the last thing you want to do is provoke that massive hunk of meat.

- You may have run track in high school, but the bull can outrun you. Use your wits to find a nearby place where it won't be able to follow you, such as a building with an open door or a high fence you can quickly climb. If you spot such a place, make a mad dash for it. Otherwise, stick with staying still.

- Assuming escape's not an option, take a deep breath and get ready to play the rodeo clown. Those clowns throw around red cloths for a reason: They work. Pull off your shirt and wave it around to distract the bull. But it doesn't have to be red; bulls respond more to the movement than to the color itself.

- Once the bull starts heading toward the shirt, toss it as far away as you can. The bull should charge toward it, leaving you a window to run like the wind while it's distracted.

- In the case of a full-on stampede, don't mess with the distraction part—it's too tough to divert an entire group's attention. Your only options are to get out of their path or to run with them to keep from getting run over. Once those fellas are charging, though, don't stay still, or they will trample right over you—and that's no load of bull.

Fast Facts

- Francis Scott Key wrote the lyrics of "The Star-Spangled Banner" to the tune of the 18th-century British drinking song "To Anacreon in Heaven." The pub tune was the theme song of London's Anacreontic Club, which took its name from the ancient Greek poet known for his devotion to the god of wine.

- The maiden name of Blondie Bumstead in the comic strip Blondie is "Boopadoop."

- Newly hatched queen bees fight to the death to kill all other newly hatched—and unhatched—queens, until only one is left standing. There can only be one queen in a hive.

- Human beings are the only animals that cry emotional tears.

- The phrase "last laugh" is derived from the laughlike sound a bullet shot through the heart sometimes causes in its victim before death.

- Contrary to popular belief, the gladiators of ancient Rome did not kill each other. Because the government invested so much money in their training and preparation, they fought only to the "first blood," at which point the injured gladiator would raise his finger in surrender.

- More than 50 percent of people admit to checking their e-mail in the bathroom.

- The tradition of the white wedding dress dates back to Queen Victoria, who in 1840 chose white not as a display of purity but of wealth, since white fabric was an expensive luxury. (Not to mention impractical, because of its difficulty to keep clean.)

- A laugh expels air out of the body at speeds up to 70 miles per hour, a sneeze at more than 100 miles per hour.

The Wilhelm Scream

In the early days of the film industry, it was hard to find a good scream. Before the invention of sound bites, directors who required a blood-curdling shriek from actors often got rather paltry-sounding yelps. That is, at least until Private Wilhelm entered the scene.

That Hurts!

In the 1951 war classic *Distant Drums,* a soldier is dragged underwater by an alligator as he wades through a treacherous Florida swamp. After the filming was completed, sound engineers recorded a series of screams that were added during post-production. Two years later, in *The Charge at Feather River,* a soldier named Private Wilhelm (played by Ralph Brooke) takes an arrow in the leg. Similar to modern sound engineering processes, the *Distant Drums* scream was resurrected from a vault and added to Wilhelm's impalement scene.

The Real "Wilhelm"

What became known as the Wilhelm Scream is actually thought to be the handiwork of a popular television and screen actor named Sheb Wooley. He and other actors from *Distant Drums* were asked to contribute various sound bites to the film. Wooley later went on to play in classics such as *High Noon* with Gary Cooper, Clint Eastwood's *The Outlaw Josey Wales,* and the hit television series *Rawhide.* But it was Wooley's contribution to radio, the hit song "Purple People Eater," that overshadowed his success as the originator of the Wilhelm Scream.

Over the years, the Wilhelm Scream has enjoyed something of a cult following. One of the scream's biggest fans was Ben Burtt, the sound-effects creator for the original *Star Wars* in 1977. While perusing the sound archives of Warner Bros. Studios (who owned the rights to the Wilhelm Scream), he came across the scream and decided to use it in his film. He became so fond of it that it became his signature sound bite in other productions including the *Indiana Jones* series. More than 50 years later, moviegoers can still hear Private Wilhelm.

Jersey Jumper

With enough ingenuity, a person can get famous
in all sorts of ways. Just ask Sam Patch, who made
a name for himself by going over the falls.

Factory Boy

Sam Patch was born circa 1807 in Rhode Island. As a young boy, Sam worked in the Pawtucket mills, often for 12 hours a day. It was dull, hard work, but he found something to keep him occupied and his friends entertained: waterfall jumping.

Waterfall jumping was an art. Jumpers dove in feet first, and they sucked in a deep breath just before they hit the water. Once underwater, they stayed under long enough to start frightened spectators buzzing. Finally, when all appeared lost, they burst out of the water like a fish on a line, much to the delight of a relieved audience.

In his mid-20s, Patch left Pawtucket for Paterson, New Jersey. Beside being a factory town, Paterson was also home of Passaic Falls, an idyllic waterfall with a 70-foot drop that was second only to Niagara on the East Coast.

Taking the Plunge

On September 30, 1827, Patch dove off a cliff and into the swirling waters of the falls. He emerged from the waters with a gasp; the "Yankee Leaper" had been born. Patch realized that he could either work for pennies in a hot, sweaty factory or parlay his jumping skills into fame and possibly fortune.

Patch developed a routine. He would lay out his coat, vest, and shoes on the ground, as if he may not need them again. He gave a speech containing one, or both, of his favorite sayings: "There's no mistake in Sam Patch," and "Some things can be done as well as others."

Soon, word of Patch's jumps got around. He attained celebrity status, and with fame's siren song ringing in his ears, Patch set out to jump whenever and wherever. On August 11, 1828, he jumped

100 feet from a ship's mast into the Hudson River at Hoboken, New Jersey. Patch's antics earned him much publicity, as hundreds of onlookers would gather to watch him jump from increasingly tall heights. In addition to being the "Yankee Leaper," he also became known as "Patch the Jersey Jumper."

On October 7, 1829, Patch leaped into immortality by jumping 85 feet into Niagara Falls from a platform off of Goat Island. This time, he was billed as the main entertainment. As an onlooker recorded: "Sam walked out clad in white, and with great deliberation put his hands close to his sides and jumped." Ten days later, he jumped Niagara again from 120 feet, netting a cool $75 for his work.

In November, Patch, now accompanied by a pet black bear, showed up in Rochester, New York, to jump the thundering Genesee Falls. He performed the jump on November 6, 1829; some reports say he threw the bear over the side as well. Showing that there was "no mistake in Sam Patch," he decided to repeat the plunge on Friday, November 13.

He may have chosen an ominous date to jump the Genesee, and he may or may not have been drunk, but he was certainly tempting fate. Sure enough, a third of the way down, he lost his form and hit the water like a sack of potatoes. One report later said that he had ruptured a blood vessel on the way down. Either way, thousands of spectators anxiously watched the water, but Patch never resurfaced.

Post-Patch

Still, even in death Patch was controversial. Some say his body wasn't found for months, while others say that it was found just two days later. After his body was found, he was buried in a grave with a marker reading: "Here Lies Sam Patch. Such Is Fame."

But death did not stop Patch. He lived on for years in novels, comics, and popular plays such as *Sam Patch* and *Sam Patch in France*. There was a Sam Patch-brand cigar, and President Andrew Jackson even named his favorite riding horse Sam Patch.

Clearly, Sam Patch was not all wet.

WHO KNEW?

Light-Fingered Finn
The next time you go out with friends for a drink, be careful what you order. According to some historians, Mickey Finn was a notorious Chicago bartender who plied his wares in the late 1890s. When his customers weren't looking, he would spike their drinks with chloral hydrate. After a few minutes, they would pass out and Finn would rob them blind.

F-Word Firsts
Have you ever wondered who first uttered the F-word onscreen? That dubious honor goes to Marianne Faithfull, who said it in the 1968 film *I'll Never Forget What's 'Isname*. But director Brian De Palma broke all the records in his 1983 film, *Scarface,* starring Al Pacino. The F-word was spoken exactly 226 times, or on average, four times every three minutes.

Where's the Tag Tournament?
Those of you who wrangled your way out of doing the dishes as a kid by playing Rock, Paper, Scissors with your brothers and sisters will be happy to learn that the childhood game lives on. Every year, the World RPS (that's Rock, Paper, Scissors) Society hosts their world championship, designed to pit the best players against each other. Players can also go at it with other aficionados at the Sami Tournament in Norway; the New Zealand Rock, Paper, Scissors Championships in Auckland; the Australian RPS Championships on the Gold Coast; or challenge your fists against the best at the Camden Riversharks Tournament in Camden, New Jersey. And, for the slightly more cultured, try the Sixth Annual Roshambo Winery Rock, Paper, Scissors Tournament in Sonoma, California.

Of Monks and Chefs
White chef hats date back to the 15th century, when several Greek nobles hid from the invading Turks in monasteries. The nobles dressed as monks—in tall black hats and robes—and were given cooking responsibilities. The monks grew frustrated that they couldn't tell the nobles apart from other monks, so they changed the nobles' uniforms from black to white.

Heterochromia: The Eyes Have It

*If the eyes are the windows to the soul, the color
of a person's irides, (the plural of iris) is the window
dressing. The vast majority of human beings have two
eyes that are the same color, usually brown, blue, grey,
green, or hazel. But some people just can't commit.*

What's Up, Doc?

Put plainly, *heterochromia* is the presence of different-colored eyes
in the same person. The condition is a result of the relative excess or
lack of pigment within an iris or part of an iris. The causes for having
mismatched eyes vary, and some are more worrisome than others.

Heterochromia is largely hereditary; many people are born with
eyes that don't quite match and nothing seems to be wrong with
them. Females experience it far more than males, and most cases of
genetic heterochromia have been found to occur between ages two
and nineteen. Some folks who had different-colored eyes as a child
report their eyes eventually matching when they reached adulthood.

Diseases such as glaucoma, neurofibromatosis, and Waardenberg
syndrome can also cause the condition. Waardenberg syndrome is
a rare disorder that affects skin pigmentation and is responsible for
varying degrees of hearing loss. Most people with Waardenberg syndrome have two different-colored eyes, making the presence of, say,
one green eye and one blue eye, cause for a trip to the doctor.

Another way two eyes might be different colors is due to eye
injury. A foreign object in the eye (we're talking about more than an
eyelash), ocular inflammation, or other eye injuries can cause trauma
to the eye and alter its color.

Now, heterochromia doesn't just mean a person has one brown
eye and one green eye; many people with this trait will have one eye
that is two colors—part green and part blue, for example. And whatever the color of the iris happens to be, it doesn't have any bearing
on the ability of the eye to see. Having heterochromia doesn't mean
that a person has poor eyesight.

What (Color) Is It, Lassie?

Animals can also show signs of heterochromia, including cats and horses. However, much more common than heterochromia in humans is heterochromia in dogs. Many breeds, including Siberian huskies, Australian sheep dogs, Great Danes, dalmatians, and Alaskan malamutes exhibit striking cases of the condition—perhaps you've seen a Siberian husky with one ice-blue eye and one dark brown eye. Just as is the case with humans, the dog's vision is completely normal; unlike humans, however, heterochromia in canines is rarely considered a cause for medical concern.

Got Heterochromia? Cool!

If you see multicolored eyes when you look in the mirror, and you have a clean bill of health, then celebrate! Chances are good that you'll never have to think up something interesting to talk about at a cocktail party.

Many people find folks with different-colored eyes fascinating. Some say they find it mysterious (and more than a little sexy) because it's such a rare characteristic. Largely, heterochromia is often seen as really cool, the prevailing notion being that people with mismatched eyes are smarter, more intriguing, possess greater depth, and are generally cooler than everyone else. Lucky you!

If you have heterochromia, you're in good company. Check out this list of celebrities and historical figures that have boasted dual-tone eye-color:

- actress Kate Bosworth
- actor Christopher Walken
- king and conqueror Alexander the Great
- actress Mila Kunis
- comedian and actor Dan Aykroyd
- singer Carly Simon
- actress Jane Seymour
- actress Sally Rogers

Bad Ad Grab Bag

"Lost Cat—Last Seen: On Sunday April 27 at the Park County Rod & Gun Club Shooting Range."

"Artificial Christmas Tree For Sale. Like New. Needs stand, ornaments, lights and branches. $99.00 firm."

"Misc For Sale: $600."

"Due to the lack of interest by friends & relatives, the birthday party for Becky Pritchard has been cancelled."

"Perfection in Mountain Park Ranch—Pride of Ownership—3 BR, 2 Ba—Open and Spacious. Ceiling in Every Room."

"Found: Wedding dress. Kwik Car Wash, 2016 South Otsego."

"1989 Thunderbird, V6, AT, brn, great cond, speaks spanish, $4,550."

"Wanted: Somebody to go back in time with me. This is not a joke. You'll get paid after we get back. Must bring your own weapons. Safety not guaranteed. I have only done this once before."

"Youth Programs: Skydiving for Tots (ages 10 mos.-2 years). Introduce your toddler to the fun and thrill of skydiving before he or she develops unwarranted fears of freefalling."

"Turkey—FOR SALE. Partially eaten. Only eight days old. Both drumsticks still intact. $23.00 obo."

"Hariobért—If we can't make you look good…you ugly!"

"Baby Items: HUGGIES used diapers for sale, $4."

"Imitation Crap Meat lb. $2.99"

"Bar-S Franks, 16 Oz., Tasty Dog Chicken or All Meat, 2 for 88¢"

"Four poster bed, 101 years old. Perfect for antique lover."

"Buy: "I love you only" Valentine cards: Now available in multi-packs."

"Wanted. Man to take care of cow that does not smoke or drink."

If These Bones Could Talk

❖ ❖ ❖ ❖

Early in the 20th century, archaeologists searched
frantically for the "missing link"—a fossil that would
bridge the gap between apes and man. What was found,
however, made monkeys out of everyone involved.

Fossil Facts or Fiction?

In November 1912, a story appeared in the English newspaper
Manchester Guardian: Skull fragments had been found that could
be of the utmost significance. "There seems to be no doubt whatever
of its genuineness," wrote the reporter, characterizing the bones as
perhaps "the oldest remnant of a human frame yet discovered on
this planet." The story generated feverish speculation. On the night
of December 18, 1912, a crowd jammed into the meeting of the
Geological Society of London to learn about this amazing discovery.

What they heard was that solicitor and an amateur archeologist
Charles Dawson had discovered two skull fragments and a jawbone
from a gravel bed near Piltdown Common in East Sussex. He had
been interested in this area ever since workmen, knowing of his
archeological interest, had given him some interesting bone fragments
from the pit several years before. Dawson had since been making his
own excavations of the pit, aided by Arthur Smith Woodward, keeper
of the Department of Geology at the British Museum.

The skull fragments were definitely human, but the jawbone was
similar to an ape. If they came from the same creature, as Woodward and Dawson both hypothesized, then they had discovered
the missing evolutionary link between ape and man. Woodward
announced, "I therefore propose that the Piltdown specimen be
regarded as a new type of genus of the family *Hominidae.*"

A Deep Divide

Almost immediately, two distinct camps were formed: doubters and supporters. In Woodward's favor were the facts that
the remains were found close together, that they were similar in color and mineralization, and that the teeth were worn

down in a flat, human way—unlike those of an ape. Doubters contended the jawbone and skull fragments were too dissimilar to be from the same creature. American and French scientists tended to be skeptical, while the British generally accepted the validity of the discovery.

Woodward's side scored valuable points when a canine tooth missing from the Piltdown jaw was discovered in 1913 close to where the jaw-bone originally had been found. Hard on the heels of that find came another—an elephant bone that had been rendered into some type of tool and supposed to have been used by Piltdown Man.

In 1915, there came perhaps the most conclusive evidence of all: Dawson found the remains of a similar creature a scant two miles away from the site of the first discovery.

Bone Betrayal

So Piltdown Man entered the archaeological record. After Dawson died on August 10, 1916, no significant new Piltdown discoveries were made, but no matter. Even when a few scientists identified the jaw as that from an ape, they were ignored.

However, as other fossil discoveries were made in subsequent years, it became evident that something wasn't quite right about Piltdown Man. Things really began unraveling in 1949, when a new dating technique called the fluorine absorption test was used on Piltdown Man. It revealed that the skull fragments were relatively modern and the jawbone was just a few decades old. Finally, in 1953 a group of scientists proved conclusively that Piltdown Man was a hoax. The jawbone had been stained to look old, the teeth filed down, and the bones placed at the site.

Although the identity of the Piltdown Man hoaxer has never been revealed—even Sir Arthur Conan Doyle, author of the Sherlock Holmes series of mysteries, is considered a suspect by some—most suspicion falls on Dawson, who was later found to have been involved in other archeological frauds. Ultimately, it seems that if seeing is believing, then Piltdown Man is proof that people will only see what they want to believe.

Fumbling Felons

When Honesty Is the Worst Policy

A clerk at a New Zealand food store was describing to police the man who had just robbed the store at gunpoint. Since the clerk had said that the man wasn't wearing a mask, the cop asked him to describe whatever he remembered to a police sketch artist.

As the clerk worked with the artist, it was clear that he had an amazing eye for detail. He noted specific features of the robber's face—a remarkable feat, especially for someone who had been held at gunpoint.

At last the artist finished and handed the picture to the investigating officer. The officer did an immediate double take. The clerk had described himself! When confronted with the fact, the clerk confessed that it was indeed he who had robbed the store. When the cop asked him why he had so accurately described himself to the sketch artist, the clerk responded: "I was just being honest!"

Wedding Bell Blues

An Alabama female police officer had previously worked prostitution stings, and she had seen a lot of odd things in her time. So she didn't think much of it when, while she was working undercover, a man dressed in a tuxedo pulled up in a car alongside her and propositioned her. The officer played along, and soon the man found himself under arrest. Then the cop discovered why her "john" was dressed so nice: It was his wedding day. He had gotten married just a few hours before and had dashed out from the reception to buy more beer. But once out he apparently decided that booze wasn't enough to quench his thirst.

It's a good bet that her husband's arrest warrant was the one "gift" the bride didn't expect to receive on her wedding day!

No Sale

Sometimes you have to know when to walk away. A man from South Carolina bought substandard cocaine from his dealer. But instead of just feeling burned, he indignantly stormed into a police station. Throwing the bag of drugs disdainfully onto an officer's desk, the man demanded that the police arrest the dealer who had sold him the mediocre coke.

Becoming Fluent in Body Language

❖ ❖ ❖ ❖

What does your body language convey about your thoughts? Learning to read the effects of nonverbal communication can help you better convey your own motivation—and understand that of others.

You can say a lot without ever opening your mouth. The science of body language theorizes that everything from hand placement to eye activity speaks volumes about our true intentions. Learn the dialect and you can gain a whole new kind of communication power.

Power of the Palms

Psychologists say the palms are among the most telling signs of body language—and not in the fortune-telling sense, either. Subconsciously, people tend to hold their palms out and open, facing another person, when they are being particularly honest. In contrast, hiding one's palms is usually associated with lying or trying to conceal something.

Some other palm moves to pick up include:

- Rubbing the palms together: shows excitement or expectation
- Hands clenched together: indicates an unspoken feeling of anxiety or negativity
- Palms up and flat against each other in a steeplelike position: shows a feeling of superiority and confidence
- Hands held together behind the back: shows a position of authority
- Stacking the hands on top of each other and resting the face on it: a sign of courtship, most often used by women to unwittingly indicate interest in a potential partner

All About the Arms

You may have heard that arms crossed in front of the chest indicate a sense of discomfort. Scientists agree: Studies have found that taking on the standard crossed-armed position actually leads others to develop a more negative impression of you. The stance is consistently interpreted as being disagreeable or even hostile, particularly if the fists are also clenched.

It makes sense, then, that not crossing one's arms indicates a sense of confidence and superiority. It's theorized to be a function of evolution, as the stance would have shown an open and vulnerable body to potential predators centuries ago.

Another common variation (limited to men) involves leaving their arms hanging down in front with their hands clasped together in the middle, directly over their, uh, nether region. Observers see this most frequently when a man is standing in front of a large group or when he is otherwise intimidated or dejected. It's considered a protective position (think about it) and is also thought to have an evolutionary function.

I Spy Your Eyes

A person's eyes can tell you a lot about their intentions. Lowering the eyebrows indicates dominance, while raising them shows submission. Widening the eyes, particularly in women, creates a baby-like appearance that encourages men's protective instincts. Also, a woman tilting her head down and looking upward shows submission for the same reason—a move usually thought to increase a man's attraction. Researchers say the ultimate ammo a woman can use is tilting her head down, lowering her eyelids, looking up, raising her eyebrows, and slightly parting her lips—all at the same time. Better start practicing.

Liar, Liar

While not foolproof, psychologists have found a string of common body language signs that often indicates a lie. Touching your nose, rubbing your eye, placing your hand over your mouth, scratching your neck, or pulling at your collar can all be signs of dishonesty.

That's just the tip of the iceberg when it comes to the hidden code of body language. The signs are right in front of you, just waiting to be read. Skeptical? We can tell.

Fast Facts

- Americans choke to death on toothpicks more than any other object.

- A woodpecker can peck 20 times a second.

- The phrase "to go scot free" comes from an Old English tradition, when "scot" referred to a payment or fee. "To go scot free" meant to escape the charge.

- Rome's historic Ponte Milvio, built in 206 B.C., is known as the Lovers' Bridge. According to urban legend, young couples will find eternal happiness if they write their names on a padlock, attach it to a lamppost on the bridge, and fling the key in the Tiber River below. Tired of removing some 820 pounds of padlocks each year from lampposts, in 2007, the mayor of Rome installed a chain for lovers to use instead.

- Mockingbirds can mimic the songs of 39 other bird species, as well as other high-pitched sounds, including a piano and a squeaky door hinge.

- Cattle branding began in the United States in Connecticut, where farmers were required to brand all of their pigs.

- Of all the fingers, the nail on the pinkie finger grows the fastest.

- Four U.S. states do not allow billboard advertising: Alaska, Hawaii, Maine, and Vermont.

- The Barbie doll first appeared in an astronaut uniform in 1965. Nearly 20 years later, Sally Ride became the first American woman in space.

- From 1975 to 1977, Mattel sold a doll called "Growing Up Skipper" whose breasts grew as her left arm was turned.

519

Talk to the Expert

FOOD SCULPTOR

Q: When did you decide sculpting with food was a good idea?
A: At first I wasn't really sure if it was a good idea, because how serious is food? It's not serious—and I'm a serious sculptor. But I had the opportunity to do Mickey Rooney and Ann Miller in chocolate for the 100th performance of *Sugar Babies* [in 1980]. Then in 1995, my brother saw an ad for a butter sculptor and called me. From butter, I went to cheese. And now I'm even doing things in fruits and vegetables.

Q: What are the easiest and hardest foods to work with?
A: Cheese can be very easy to work with, because you just get a block of cheese and carve away—you don't add, you just subtract. But the fact that you can't add sometimes does present problems. Butter can be easy, because you can both add to it and subtract from it, but it doesn't have much in the way of support.

Q: What are some of the wildest sculptures you've done?
A: We did a 3,000-pound cheese car. It really was just a skin of cheese on a car—there were maybe three to four inches of cheese on it. The rest was an armature; and all of the cheese had to be screwed onto the car and then caulked.

Q: So, traditional sculpting tools don't always work on food.
A: I use all kinds of different tools. I use woodcarving tools on chocolate. For cheese, I use plaster tools. I use food tools, like a cheese grater. I'm always looking for stuff that I think will work.

Q: Most of your sculptures are done for one-time events. What happens to the food afterward?
A: Right now, a lot of the butter is being turned into biofuel. You can also use it as animal feed. Cheese very often goes to a food bank. And I've had people eat the chocolate sculptures.

More Than a Minor Contribution

How a Civil War surgeon-turned-madman helped
shape our understanding of the English language.

An Unlikely Contributor

The *Oxford English Dictionary* (*OED*) is widely considered the definitive record of the English language. For more than a century, readers have turned to it to understand and pronounce millions of words.

Less well known, however, is the fact that one of its earliest and most important contributors was William Chester Minor, a Civil War surgeon who murdered a man in England, sliced off his own penis, and wrote all his contributions for the world-renowned dictionary while locked inside the padded walls of an insane asylum.

The son of Congregational Church missionaries, Minor was born in Ceylon (now Sri Lanka) in June 1834. At age 14, he was sent to the United States to attend medical school at Yale. After graduation, he enlisted in the U.S. Army, where he served as a physician during some of the Civil War's fiercest skirmishes, including the bloody Battle of the Wilderness in 1864.

The Definition of Madness

Though he had admitted to previously having had "lascivious thoughts" in Ceylon, there is some speculation that exposure to the brutality of war hastened Minor's descent into madness. Whatever the case, he wound up in New York City shortly after the war. While there he developed an unhealthy taste for prostitutes and other assorted "pleasures" found in the city's less savory areas.

By 1868, his erratic behavior landed him in St. Elizabeth's asylum in Washington, D.C. Soon after his release, Minor was relieved of his military commission. He eventually settled overseas in London.

If the move to England was intended to halt his increasing insanity, it failed—a year after his relocation, Minor shot and killed George Merrett, whom he suspected of breaking into his home. After a subsequent jury found Minor not guilty by reason of insanity, he was marched off to England's Broadmoor asylum in Berkshire.

A New Hobby

Because of his military pension he was afforded comfortable quarters at Broadmoor, including two rooms, one of which he constructed into a library to house his growing collection of books. Shortly after his "incarceration," a public request was released, asking for volunteers to contribute to the *OED*. With plenty of free time on his hands and a large collection of books at his disposal, Minor began enthusiastically contributing entries to the fledgling dictionary—a pastime that would take up most of the remainder of his life.

For the next two decades Minor pored through his library, finding quotations for thousands of words in the dictionary by keeping lists of recurring words that matched the current needs of the *OED*. Minor's lists became so prolific that the editors of the *OED* eventually sent Minor their lists of words they needed filled.

Minor's contributions, said to have numbered more than 10,000 entries, were so frequent and numerous that he eventually developed a friendship with the *OED*'s editor, Dr. James Murray, who made the trip to Broadmoor to visit the institutionalized contributor. Murray would later say that Minor's contribution to the *OED* was so enormous that it "could easily have illustrated the last four centuries [of words] from his quotations alone."

Further Descent

Whatever satisfaction Minor took from his meaningful work on the *OED*, it did nothing to stop his lunacy, which had grown to such a state that he amputated his own penis in 1902. Still, Murray helped guarantee Minor's release from Broadmoor, which was approved by Home Secretary Winston Churchill in 1910. Upon his liberation from the asylum, Minor returned to America, where he would remain until his death in 1920.

Behind the Music of Our Time

- The KISS mid-'70s hit "Beth" was originally named "Beck." It's believed to have been written for the songwriter's girlfriend, Becky. Legend has it KISS bassist and vocalist Gene Simmons changed the name so fans wouldn't think it was about guitarist Jeff Beck.

- The first album to reach number one on the charts in the United States without ever being released on vinyl was Vanilla Ice's *To the Extreme* in 1990. The album was available only on cassette and CD.

- The main guitar riff from Guns N' Roses' only number-one hit, "Sweet Child O' Mine," actually was a result of guitarist Slash doing a musical exercise. Singer Axl Rose happened to hear him playing it and decided to turn it into a song. Slash always hated the idea.

- The seemingly out-of-place distorted guitars in the last verse of the Radiohead song "Fake Plastic Trees" were, in fact, a mistake: The man in charge of mixing the album inserted them at the wrong point (they were supposed to be at the beginning of the verse), but the band decided to keep the accidental arrangement.

- Three different drummers played on recordings of the Beatles song "Love Me Do." Original drummer Pete Best played on the first recording. Ringo Starr soon replaced him and rerecorded it. The story goes, though, that the producer didn't like Ringo's version, which led to session drummer Andy White stepping in. All three versions have been released on various albums over the years.

- The catchy six-note riff that serves as the melody of Missy "Misdemeanor" Elliott's hit "Get Ur Freak On" was played on a tumbi, an unusual single-stringed guitar. Producer Timbaland wrote the part.

- The title for Funkadelic's "One Nation Under a Groove" came from a comment bandleader George Clinton's girlfriend made to him one morning while they watched the flags go up in the United Nations Plaza.

- The rock 'n' roll classic "Johnny B. Goode," written by Chuck Berry, originally contained the controversial lyric "that little colored boy can play." It was later changed to "that little country boy can play."

Chill Out: The Popsicle Story

As luck would have it, some of the best inventions actually happened by accident. The world would be a sadder place without penicillin, microwave ovens, ice cream cones, Post-it Notes, potato chips, Super Glue, Slinkies, or heaven forbid—Popsicles.

A Chilly Start

The Popsicle was "invented" by an industrious 11-year-old boy named Frank Epperson on an unseasonably cold San Francisco evening in 1905. After accidentally leaving his drink in a cup on the front porch overnight, Epperson discovered that the drink had frozen around the wooden stir stick. The next morning, he pulled the frozen drink out of the cup by the stick and voilà...the Popsicle was born.

Actually, Epperson's frozen invention originally took the neighborhood by storm as the "Epsicle." It wasn't until 1923 while running a lemonade stand at the Neptune Beach amusement park in Oakland, California, that he realized the money-making potential of his discovery. His own children loved the cool treat, begging him for one of "Pop's 'sicles." In 1924, Epperson applied for the first patent of the "Popsicle," the first "drink on a stick."

The Popsicle Goes Big Time

A year later, Epperson sold the patent and rights to the brand name "Popsicle" to the Joe Lowe Company in New York. As it turned out, he made a wise business decision—during the first three years, he earned royalties on the sale of more than 60 million Popsicle ice pops. Popsicles soon began to appear all over the world—they were affectionately known as "Ice-lollies" in Great Britain and "Icy Poles" in Australia.

Popsicles grew in popularity with kids and adults alike. As soldiers returned home from World War II and began building families, the average breadwinner could afford the convenience of having their own refrigerators and freezers. That meant that busy homemakers could buy large quantities of Popsicles in "multipacks" and store them indefinitely in the freezer, dispensing them to the kids whenever they deserved a treat (or needed a bribe). In the mid-'40s, cartoonist and adman Woody Gelman created the "Popsicle Pete" mascot to help market the product in magazines, comic books, and television commercials. Eventually, cardboard advertisements were distributed to vendors touting the new marketing slogan, "If it's Popsicle, it's possible."

Popsicle Spin-Offs

The treats continued to sell well and, in 1965, they became part of the Consolidated Foods Corporation lineup. At that time, 34 different flavors were offered by the company. Several years later, "Creamsicles" (a sherbet pop on a stick with a vanilla ice cream center) were sold in orange and raspberry flavors. The new item became so popular that "National Creamsicle Day" is now celebrated every August 14.

The Popsicle continued to make the corporate rounds when the Gold Bond Ice Cream Company purchased the U.S. operations of Popsicle Industries; it was purchased three years later by Unilever. In 1993, the Popsicle underwent another change when the Unilever company name was changed to the Good Humor–Breyers Ice Cream Company, where the brand remains today.

- *Popsicles also are used in craft projects, as children, adults, and just about anyone who went to camp create bridges and houses made from Popsicle sticks. But the "stick bomb" is one of the more notorious creations made from used Popsicle sticks. After weaving five sticks together in a specific pattern, the stick bomb is thrown to the floor, where it "explodes" with a loud pop.*

- *Woody Gelman was also the writer and co-creator of the Bazooka Joe comics found in Bazooka gum, as well as the sci-fi trading card series Mars Attacks.*

Fast Facts

- *The name "Ouija," as in the popular toy "Ouija board," comes from the French and German words for "yes"—oui and ja, respectively.*

- *The bee that stings you probably isn't a honey producer. Of 20,000 bee species in the world, fewer than 500 are considered to be honeybees. Of these, only four have been domesticated.*

- *The U.S. Congress created the Patent System in 1790. Before a patent could be approved, the system originally required the patent examiner (then Thomas Jefferson), the secretary of war, attorney general, and the president to sign off on it. Since then, the Patent Office has approved more than 5 million patents.*

- *Not surprisingly, the first TV remote control, designed in 1950, was called "Lazy Bones." However, it wasn't until 1956 that Dr. Robert Adler, a research engineer with Zenith Corporation, developed a commercial remote control, thereby becoming the patron saint of couch potatoes.*

- *In 1873, an Illinois farmer named Joseph Glidden was credited with designing the most popular barbed wire, winning in court battles and in the marketplace over 570 other patented designs.*

- *In 1843, the first commercial Christmas card was printed in England, using illustrations by John Calcott Horsley, a noted London artist at the time. The press run was 1,000 cards. Today, 2 billion cards are sent every Christmas in the United States alone—something of a hallmark.*

- *By legal definition, every living creature in Tennessee is a "dumb animal."*

- *Most fish never sleep—they are in perpetual motion marked only by periods of inactivity.*

The Sheep Wars

*Read on for a little-known tale of rivalry, property
damage, and death in the Old West.*

The reputation of the American cowboy dominates and defines the
West: As anyone who's ever enjoyed a steak can attest, even the cattle
that cowboys protected and steered across the plains have become a
part of America's identity. But before the cowboy, and the cattle he
tended, ruled the landscape, they first had to do battle with an equally
romanticized group that encroached upon their stomping grounds—
shepherds and their flocks of sheep.

Part of the problem was that the shepherds seemed to have their
own way of doing things. Whether riding a donkey or traveling on
foot, shepherds moved slowly with their grazing flocks. When they
met with a fence, instead of turning aside, they would often simply
cut it to cross ranch lands. It didn't help that the sheep competed with
the cattle for food. In addition, many of the shepherds were Mexican;
their cultural differences seemed an affront to the cowboys' "American" way of life.

The two groups continuously butted heads in what was to be
known as the "Sheep Wars." The cowboys were often swift to move
when a flock was discovered crossing their land. In 1875, cowhands
in west Texas drove 400 sheep into the Canadian River. Many other
territories and states witnessed even greater calamities. In separate
incidents in Wyoming, cattlemen drove 10,000 sheep into the
mountains to die and more than 12,000 sheep off a cliff. In northern
Arizona, things between cattlemen and shepherds got hot enough to
escalate into what is known as "The Graham-Tewksbury Feud"—
a decade-long series of reprisals between two families. Before it was
over, 26 cattlemen and 6 shepherds were dead, along with scores of
beasts.

The Sheep Wars ended circa 1900 with the closing of the free
prairie and the introduction of laws that made fence cutting a felony.
Though sheep and cattle exist peacefully side-by-side, today it is the
cowboy, and not the shepherd, who defines the American West.

ANAGRAMS

An anagram is a word or phrase that exactly reproduces the letters in another word or phrase. The most interesting of them reflect or comment on the subject of the first.

A gentleman—Elegant man

Microwave—Warm voice

T. S. Eliot—Toilets

Eleven plus two—Twelve plus one

The meaning of life—The fine game of nil

A shoplifter—Has to pilfer

A domesticated animal—Docile, as a man tamed it

Garbage man—Bag manager

Bob Marley—Marble boy

Belgium—Big mule

Breasts—Bra sets

Achievements—Nice, save them

Year two thousand—A year to shut down

Weapon—One paw

The answer—Wasn't here

Nice seat—I can't see

Stripes—Persist

Poetry—Try Poe

Guinness draught—Naughtiness drug

Apple, Inc.—Epic plan

Dancing with the Stars—Winners had tight acts

Conversation—Voices rant on

The Fate of the Freedom Ship

❖ ❖ ❖ ❖

The Freedom Ship was conceived as a new kind of boundary-free community—a luxurious neighborhood that would constantly circumnavigate the globe. But a decade after its inception, construction has yet to begin. Here's what the Freedom Ship would be like—that is, if it ever got afloat.

A Grand Idea

Imagine a luxury-filled community that offers the best in business, entertainment, and education. Now imagine it slowly floating around the world in an ongoing two-year cycle. According to its Web site, the Freedom Ship is pitched as a 4,500-foot-long barge that would consist of individual neighborhoods. Each 'hood would house a number of different living units ranging from $9,136,600 (plus a $14,716 monthly maintenance fee) to an economy unit at $153,000 (plus a $492 monthly maintenance fee—and no kitchen). There would also be space for shops, restaurants, and businesses. For visitors, an onboard hotel would provide high-end guest lodging.

The Freedom Ship's plans also call for plenty of entertainment. The ship would feature a "world-class" casino, along with a convention center large enough to accommodate concerts and sporting events. Museums, aquariums, and nature preserves round out the entertainment options. But if boredom's an issue, getting on or off the ship would be no problem. Designs include plans for a flight deck for turbo-prop aircraft and a marina to let residents come and go at their leisure. And don't worry—there would even be storage for private planes.

But this isn't just a cruise ship. Not leaving anything out, the Freedom Ship's planners made sure that education and healthcare are key parts of the plans—a school system and state-of-the-art medical facility are also included in the budget.

A Docked Dream

It's all impressive, but in reality, the estimated $11 billion project hasn't amounted to anything more than an idea; and so far, this idea is showing no signs of sailing off any time soon.

Odd Ordinances

- Drinking beer from a bucket while sitting on a street curb is illegal in St. Louis, Missouri.

- Selling doughnut holes is absolutely against the law in Lehigh, Nebraska.

- New York City has outlawed any entertainment-based acts of throwing a ball at someone's head.

- You can't take a lion into a movie theater in Baltimore, Maryland.

- In Carlsbad, New Mexico, if you artificially color a baby chick, duckling, gosling, or rabbit, you are no longer legally allowed to sell it, raffle it off, display it in a shop, or give it away as a prize.

- Carrying a set of wooden teeth across state lines is illegal in the United States—unless you are a dentist.

- Imitating the mascots Smokey the Bear or Woodsy the Owl is not legally allowed anywhere in the United States.

- Bothering a butterfly will result in a $500 fine in California.

- Goatees are illegal in Massachusetts.

- Oral sex is illegal in 18 states: Alabama, Arizona, Florida, Idaho, Kansas, Louisiana, Massachusetts, Minnesota, Mississippi, Georgia, North and South Carolina, Oklahoma, Oregon, Rhode Island, Utah, Virginia, and Washington, D.C.

- Having sex with the lights on is illegal in Virginia.

- Having sex in any position other than missionary is illegal in Florida, Massachusetts, Montana, and Virginia.

- Trains are not allowed to move faster than an average person can walk in the city of Andalusia, Alabama.

- Drivers in Pennsylvania who encounter multiple horses coming toward them are required to pull off the road and cover their cars with blankets until the animals pass.

Primed to Be a Private Eye

❖ ❖ ❖ ❖

*Think being a PI is all high-speed chases and sultry
suspects? Actually, for the most part, working as a private
investigator can be a lot like any job—you stare blankly
at a computer screen in a dimly lit cubicle for eight hours
a day—only for less money. But the good news is that
working in the private investigation field can be just about
anything you make of it—just look at Thomas Magnum!*

Questionable Origins

The first private eye on record was a French
criminal and privateer named Eugene
Francois Vidocq, who founded a private
investigation firm in 1833. But Vidocq was
hardly a man with a spotless record, and
neither were his employees: Most of his
investigators were his friends who were
ex-convicts and other citizens of questionable character. Vidocq was periodically arrested by the police on a series of
trumped-up charges, but he was always
released after they failed to produce
enough evidence to support their claims.
Despite his questionable background, Vidocq made a number of significant contributions to the field of investigation, including record
keeping, ballistics, indelible ink, and unalterable bond paper.

The Modern PI

Fast forward to recent statistics from the U.S. Department of Labor,
which state that in 2006, there were approximately 52,000 working
gumshoes. While more than a third of working private investigators
have college degrees, many have only high school diplomas or Associate degrees, and some have neither. Those with college degrees
come from varied backgrounds, such as accounting, computer science, business administration, or the dozens of other majors whose

curriculum lends itself to specific types of investigative work. Interestingly, most private investigators do not have a degree in criminal justice.

The Nature of the Work

Talk to anyone who's knowledgeable about the private investigation business and they'll tell you that the prerequisites for success are an unquenchable thirst for answers and the ability to root out details after everyone else has come up empty handed. Superior communication skills and a special area of expertise, say, in computers, also come in handy. The most successful private eyes are people who can think logically, apply their unique knowledge to a problem, and consistently come up with creative means to their ends.

A Day in the Life

Depending on their background, private investigators can end up working for a variety of employers: individuals, professional investigative firms, law firms, department stores, or bail bondsmen. Many set up their own private practice. One place they can count on *never* working is for the local police department or the FBI. Government agencies rarely interface with private investigation firms. Unfortunately, that nixes the dramatic movie image of a lone-wolf PI getting a call in the middle of the night because the police are stumped and desperately need help.

The type of work private investigators do is largely dependent on the type of company they work for, the types of cases they take, and what their clients ask of them. The majority of cases have to do with locating lost or stolen property, proving that a spouse has been unfaithful, finding missing friends or relatives, conducting background investigations, or proving that a business associate absconded with the company cash.

Much of the work that private investigators do involves long hours sitting behind the wheel of their car doing surveillance with binoculars and cameras with telephoto lenses. Only the highest-profile cases involving investigative firms with large operating budgets can afford sophisticated surveillance vans loaded with high-tech equipment. Other cases require collecting facts the old-fashioned way: by interviewing suspects, witnesses, and neighbors in person. Facts that can't be collected that way are often obtained by perusing public records by computer, or researching tax records, business licenses, DMV records, real estate transactions, court records, and voter registrations.

The PI Paycheck

But how much can a private eye expect to make? Fortunately (or unfortunately, whatever the case may be), the entertainment industry has painted a rather broad picture of the private investigation business. For every television show about a PI living on a Hawaiian estate, there's another show about a PI living in a dilapidated trailer house on the beach. The truth is, the median salary for private investigators in May 2006 was $33,750. The middle 50 percent earned between $24,180 and $47,740; the lowest and highest 10 percent earned $19,720 and $64,380, respectively. Not too shabby, but probably not the lap of luxury, either.

Still Want to Be a Private Eye?

For those who remain undaunted by the proposition of drinking their dinner out of a thermos and spending ten hours a day in a car or cubicle for $25,000 a year, here's some insight on how to pursue a career in private investigation:

Many private investigators have retired early from military, police, or fire department careers. Having pensions or retirement funds can help with "getting over the hump" until the earnings as a PI increase.

Some states require specific schooling while others require new investigators to spend time completing on-the-job training before applying for their license. Most states have licensing requirements for becoming a PI, so it's important to look into what's required and how long it takes before one can expect to begin to make a decent living. If the type of work requires that private investigators carry a firearm, a private eye will need to look into the local ordinances for carrying a concealed weapon.

If nothing else, private investigation can certainly be a fascinating and challenging career choice that promises a break from the ordinary job doldrums. So grab that Beretta, rev up that Ferrari, and get ready for your new life as a gumshoe!

He Said, She Said

"Be thankful we're not getting all the government we're paying for."
—*Will Rogers*

"If the NBA were on channel 5 and a bunch of frogs making love were on channel 4, I'd watch the frogs, even if they were coming in fuzzy."
—*Bobby Knight*

"We don't need refs, but I guess white guys need something to do."
—*Charles Barkley*

"Washington, D.C., is to lying what Wisconsin is to cheese."
—*Dennis Miller*

"The reason the golf pro tells you to keep your head down is so you can't see him laughing."
—*Phyllis Diller*

"What is the difference between a taxidermist and a tax collector? The taxidermist takes only your skin."
—*Mark Twain*

"I'm completely in favor of the separation of Church and State. My idea is that these two institutions screw us up enough on their own, so both of them together is certain death."
—*George Carlin*

"If winning isn't everything, why do they keep score?"
—*Vince Lombardi*

"It is fast approaching the point where I don't want to elect anyone stupid enough to want the job."
—*Erma Bombeck*

"Politics is the art of looking for trouble, finding it everywhere, diagnosing it incorrectly, and applying the wrong remedies."
—*Groucho Marx*

"Golf is a good walk spoiled."
—*Mark Twain*

"This is really a lovely horse and I speak from personal experience since I once mounted her mother."
—*Ted Walsh (racing horse commentator)*

The Most Dangerous Legal Drugs

❖ ❖ ❖ ❖

*Just because a doctor prescribes it doesn't necessarily mean
a drug is safe. A research study published in 2007 indicates
that some medicines may warrant a closer look.*

10. Etanercept

A little more than 1,000 deaths were attributed to this immune-
system controller between 1998 and 2005. The drug, sold under the
brand name Enbrel, is typically prescribed for rheumatoid arthritis,
psoriatic arthritis, and ankylosing spondylitis (inflammation of the
spine).

9. Risperidone

This antipsychotic, marketed as Risperdal, is
blamed for 1,093 deaths in the same seven-year
period. It is used in cases of schizophrenia and
bipolar disorder and also to treat autistic children
who show signs of irritability.

8. Interferon beta

With 1,178 deaths between 1998 and 2005, you
may want to approach interferon beta with caution. The drug (most
frequently sold as Avonex, Betaseron, or Rebif) is prescribed to help
people with multiple sclerosis.

7. Infliximab

Also an immune-system modulator, infliximab (more commonly
known as Remicade) is used for treating arthritis, Crohn's disease,
and plaque psoriasis. It is known, however, to increase risks of cancer and autoimmune disorders. Just over 1,200 deaths were linked
to it between 1998 and 2005.

6. Methadone

This drug is used for helping people kick narcotics habits, but it may
help them kick the bucket, too. It has 1,258 deaths next to its name
in the seven-year analysis.

5. Acetaminophen
Trusty ol' Tylenol and others like it are connected to 1,393 deaths in the study. The reason? It can cause liver damage that's irreversible and often deadly—and at doses not much higher than the recommended amount. The take-home message: Never take a single pill more than is recommended.

4. Morphine
This closely controlled painkiller is given only for severe pain. Known to be addictive, it is linked to 1,616 deaths over the seven-year study period.

3. Clozapine
Another antipsychotic, clozapine (sold as Clorazil and FazaClo) actually alters how the chemicals in the brain work. Most commonly prescribed for schizophrenia, its death count from 1998 to 2005 was a whopping 3,277.

2. Fentanyl
Fentanyl (brand name Fentora) is attributed to 3,545 deaths in the same time frame. The painkiller is usually used only for the most extreme cancer-related pain.

1. Oxycodone
The top contender, with 5,548 deaths under its belt, may not come as a surprise. Most notoriously known by the name OxyContin, this narcotic pain reliever is among the most addictive medications out there; as such, it has become highly abused by drug users.

Other drugs that get the red flag include the asthma medication Advair, diabetes drug Avandia, pain reliever Celebrex, antibiotic Ketek, acid reflux treaters Prilosec and Nexium, and any decongestant with pseudoephedrine. Each has been found to cause potential serious problems with directed use.

Take the time now to talk to your doctor and make sure you understand everything you're taking to prevent becoming another statistic in a seven-year study.

HOW IT ALL BEGAN

By the Glass or Gallon

In modern times, when people think gin, they picture complicated, elegant, and expensive cocktails: martinis, Singapore Slings, and gin and tonics. But for about a century after a Dutch doctor invented gin in 1650, it was actually cheaper in Britain than beer. By 1690, Londoners were drinking half a million gallons of gin a year; by 1750, consumption of the drink had risen to 11 million gallons in London alone. The term "Dutch courage" was born because much of the stuff was imported from Holland.

In 1751, however, the British government passed the Tippling Act to reduce gin consumption by reducing its availability. Prohibition in the United States further sullied gin's reputation. "Bathtub gin" was no misnomer—gin is so easy to make that it can be done at home, even in the bathtub, if a person so chooses (and many have).

So much for gin's original application: as a liquor formulated to cure kidney and stomach disorders!

Stick-ups

In 1980, Art Fry and Spencer Silver came up with the Post-it Note. Their invention suddenly made "I'm sorry, I forgot to write it down," the lamest excuse in the Western world.

Back in the early '70s, Fry and Silver were employed by office equipment producer 3M. The duo pitched their idea, but the company didn't dig it. Then Fry and Silver began handing out samples to their coworkers. Their colleagues clamored for more; eventually the head honchos at 3M came around. Post-it Notes were launched nationally in 1980 to great success.

Notable Notes:

- Post-its have always been recyclable.

- It would take approximately 506,880,000 Post-it Notes to circle the world (using 2⅞-inch square notes).

- The most expensive Post-it Note sold in an auction went for £640—it featured a charcoal drawing by artist R. B. Kitaj.

A Weapon for Peace

*How an eccentric genius caused a stir over
ray guns—30 years after his death.*

Tech Dissention

The U.S. government has never been one to throw away a good idea—
after all, it might come in handy someday. In a May 1977 issue of
Aviation Week & Space Technology, Major General George J. Keegan,
retired head of Air Force intelligence, asserted in an article that the
Soviet Union was in the final stages of developing a particle beam
weapon capable of neutralizing intercontinental ballistic missiles. Yet
soon afterward another article appeared in the *Baltimore Sun* entitled,
"Moscow Yet to Develop Laser Weapon, [President] Carter Says." It
seemed U.S. intelligence needed to get their story straight.

The United States had experimented with developing a particle
beam weapon as early as 1958, but they eventually abandoned the
device, deeming it unfeasible. Why then, nearly 20 years later, was
there a need to deny the existence of such a weapon in the enemy's
hands? What possible edge could the Soviets have over the United
States that might lend a semblance of credibility to Keegan's claims?

The edge lay in the work of Nikola Tesla, the brilliant scientist and
inventor who claimed to have developed the plans for a "teleforce"
weapon against which there could be no defense.

Enter Nikola Tesla

Tesla's particular area of specialty was electricity, but unlike Thomas Edison—his
contemporary, rival, and onetime employer—
Tesla's knowledge of the medium seemed
more akin to sorcery than science. He claimed
that his discoveries and inventions came in hallucinatory flashes. In his laboratory, he entertained
luminaries such as Mark Twain and president
Theodore Roosevelt with displays of electrical wonder.

As Tesla grew older his genius led to increasingly bizarre claims and concepts for inventions. Many of these were born from the inventor's hatred of warfare. He was convinced that the future peace and prosperity of mankind lay in the development of weapons so terrible, yet so universally available, that all nations would cease to consider warfare a practical means of settling disputes.

Death Rays for Peace

In 1931, Tesla conceived of an invention he later termed a "New Art of Projecting Concentrated Non-Dispersive Energy through Natural Media"—what we now call a particle accelerator. The press, always a big fan of Tesla's dramatics, chose to call the invention a "Death Beam." In a 1934 article in the *New York Times,* Tesla characterized the invention as one that would make war impossible because every nation would possess the ability to send highly concentrated bursts of energy through the air with enough power to "bring down a fleet of 10,000 enemy airplanes at a distance of 250 miles."

Tesla sought funding for the device. With World War II imminent, Tesla sent his proposal to all the Allied nations in the hope that they would cooperate to manufacture the weapon in time. Only the Soviets took an interest and provided Tesla with $25,000 for plans to develop the "teleforce" weapon.

Tesla's increasingly bold assertions led many of his contemporaries to consider him a crackpot. After his death in 1943, it was discovered that certain items, including a notebook, had been removed from his belongings by an unknown agent (suspected of being Russian). The U.S. government quickly moved to confiscate his remaining papers.

From Stalingrad to Star Wars

When reports of Soviet experiments in high-velocity particle beam weapons began to proliferate in the 1970s, the U.S. government definitely paid attention. Many experts already believed that the Soviets, capitalizing on the knowledge gleaned from their dealings with Tesla in the '30s, had successfully tested such a weapon as early as 1968. The furor was sufficient to reinvigorate U.S. interest in particle beam weapon applications, which soon gave rise to the heavily publicized (but ultimately fruitless) Strategic Defense Initiative, or "Star Wars," program of the Reagan administration.

Freaky Frog Facts

❖ ❖ ❖ ❖

Kermit, Jeremiah the Bullfrog, Prince Charming—frogs are clearly special creatures with many talents. They're also sort of gross. Check out these freaky frog facts that are sure to delight and disgust.

- At about four weeks old, tadpoles get a bunch of very tiny teeth, which help them turn their food into mushy, oxygenated particles.

- Horned lizards are often called horny toads, though they're not actually amphibians. Horny toads can squirt blood from their eyeballs to attack predators. This only happens in extreme cases, but they can shoot it up to three feet, so watch out.

- The Goliath frog of West Africa is the largest frog in the world. When fully stretched out, this sucker is often more than 2½ feet long!

- When frogs aren't near water, they will often secrete mucus to keep their skin moist.

- Frogs typically eat their old skin once it's been shed.

- One European common toad lived to be 40 years old, making it the oldest known toad on record.

- While swallowing, a frog's eyeballs retreat into its head, applying pressure that helps push food down its throat.

- A frog's ear is connected to its lungs. When a frog's eardrum vibrates, its lungs do, too. This special pressure system keeps frogs from hurting themselves when they blast their seriously loud mating calls.

- The earliest known frog fossils were found in Arizona and are thought to be about 190 million years old.

Fumbling Felons

A Developing Crime

Two boys from Louisville, Kentucky, stole a woman's Polaroid camera as she strolled through the park. Alerted by the woman's screams, a police officer gave chase, but the two thieves already had a head start.

Fortunately for the cop, the two boys had stopped and were taking pictures of one another. But much to their chagrin, the pictures that emerged from the Polaroid were all black, which, as many people know, is simply how Polaroid pictures look before they develop. Muttering about broken cameras, the boys continued on their way, occasionally stopping to take a photo. Each time a picture emerged from the camera all black, the thieves discarded it. All the pursuing cop had to do was follow the trail of rapidly developing photographs to find the technology-challenged crooks.

Who Ya Gonna Call?

With all of the informational resources available today, such as the Yellow Pages and the Internet, it's surprising that some people still have trouble finding the right person to contact for a particular task.

This was certainly the case for an Arizona woman who decided that she just couldn't stand her husband anymore. But instead of taking the obvious road and asking for a divorce, she contacted a company called "Guns for Hire" that staged mock gunfights for Wild West theme parks and the like. The woman asked them if they could kill her husband for her.

Now, while advertising is supposedly a key to a success-ful business, it's unlikely that a hired killer would go about broadcasting his or her services. After all, it tends to make the whole anonymity thing a bit difficult. On the plus side, however, at least the woman's prison sentence gave her a years-long vacation from her husband.

Crime Quickie: A mugger robbed a couple visiting a zoo in Blomfield, South Africa. Fleeing the scene, the mugger ran inside a tiger enclosure. The couple's belongings were recovered. The mugger was not.

All Shook Up

*Achy back? Sleepless nights? Simply bored in your
motel room? Put Magic Fingers to work!*

In the 1960s, although motel rooms were cheap at $25 a night, inde-
pendent motel owners still had to be mindful of the competition. After
the Motel 6 chain started adding free color televisions, telephones,
and coffee makers to its rooms, competitors were left scrambling for
amenities to add value to their rooms. Enter the "Magic Fingers"
machine.

Gently Shake You to Sleep

John Houghtaling invented Magic Fingers in 1958; initially it was sold
as a device guaranteed to solve many of the medical problems that
occur when traveling: back pain, stress, and sleeplessness. In reality,
it was nothing more than an electric motor that, when fastened to the
underside of a mattress, shook the guest until they fell asleep or were
pitched off the bed. Originally selling for more than $200, the Magic
Fingers included not only the vibrator but the mattress as well.

After months of dismal sales, Houghtaling realized that replacing
the mattresses in each motel room was cost prohibitive for owners,
so he retired to his basement "research facility" to develop a portable
model. The earliest units were far too big and shook violently. He
finally came up with a much smaller version that could be used with
existing mattresses and were coin-operated at 15 minutes for a quarter.

New and Improved

Franchisers sold the new models to motels for $45. After installation,
the franchisers collected 80 percent of the revenue, and motel owners
got the remaining 20 percent. The average haul for a week was $2 per
room. Houghtaling sold a lot of franchises, and the monthly sales
exceeded $2 million.

Eventually, the novelty of the units wore off, and motel owners
found that guests were prying open the coin boxes and stealing the
proceeds. Magic Fingers machines were discontinued, but you can
still buy a home version of the gadget online.

The Times They Are A-Changin'

2003

- Former Pennsylvania governor Tom Ridge is named the first Secretary of Homeland Security.

- Tennis champ Serena Williams defeats her sister Venus at Wimbledon.

- The space shuttle *Columbia* explodes over Texas as it re-enters Earth's atmosphere, returning from its 28th mission. The space shuttle program is suspended soon after.

- Singer Norah Jones cleans up at the Grammy's, winning Record of the Year and Album of the Year.

- The United States and Britain declare war on Iraq on March 19.

- On March 20, U.S. troops, backed by British forces and smaller contingents from Australia, Denmark, and Poland, invade Iraq from Kuwait. Coalition forces occupy Baghdad on April 9, toppling the Hussein regime. Hussein is captured on December 13.

- The South African government agrees to pay reparations totaling $85 million to the families of more than 19,000 victims of apartheid.

- The U.S. Human Genome Project completes the identification and genetic mapping of the three billion DNA letters in the human genome.

- Volkswagen ceases production of the classic Beetle, 65 years after the car's original launch. The 21,529,464th and final car is made in Puebla, Mexico, and shipped to Germany for display in Volkswagen's museum.

- On August 14, more than 50 million people in 8 states and parts of Canada lose electricity in the largest blackout in North American history.

- Pope John Paul II beatifies Mother Teresa on October 19, giving her the title Blessed Teresa of Calcutta.

- On October 24, the Concorde makes its final flight, after 27 years of commercial supersonic air service.

Buried Under Memories

❖ ❖ ❖ ❖

*At one time or another, most of us have forgotten where
we left our car keys or paused because we lost our train of
thought. Call them lapses in memory or "senior moments,"
but wouldn't it be nice if you could remember everything you
wanted throughout your entire life? Well, for one California
woman that capability is both a gift and a curse.*

Life on Automatic Rewind

Jill Price, a woman in her 40s living in
Los Angeles, California, can remember
every detail of her life from when she
was 14 years old to the present. And not
just hazy, familiar memories but detailed
minutia from much larger events, such
as the date, time, and day of the Mount
St. Helens eruption or the time of day
that the Rodney King beating took

place. "My life is like a split-screen," says Price. "Though I'll be living in the present, a dozen times or more a day I'll be pulled back
into reliving specific memories of the past." All it takes is a song,
a familiar smell, or seeing something on television to send Price
back decades in time. She can tell you what she was doing, what
her friends said, and even what her mother ordered for lunch at a
restaurant.

Price traces the beginning of her unique "gift" to a traumatic
time as an eight-year-old when her family moved from their East
Coast home to California. The move triggered a series of traumatic
recurrences of anxiety and depression—bouts she has learned to
control over time. After marrying at age 37, she suffered a miscar-
riage, and her husband died after suffering a stroke. The onslaught
of memories, both good and bad, was relentless. For years, Price
tried to suppress her unpleasant memories, but they always returned
with a vengeance.

A New Diagnosis

After enduring these flashbacks for more than 20 years, in 2000, Price finally wrote to Dr. James McGaugh, a neuroscientist and a leading memory researcher affiliated with the University of California, Irvine. She was looking for answers as to why she held onto such vivid memories. McGaugh was astounded by Price's dilemma. Relying on historical almanacs and a diary that Price had kept since she was ten, McGaugh and his research team tested her recollection of events going back to her childhood.

McGaugh performed a series of evaluations on Price, including CAT scans and MRIs, which determined that a part of her brain was three times the size of other women her age. The medical team published a research paper about Price and proposed a new name for her condition called "hyperthymestic syndrome," or quite simply, having a superior memory. According to McGaugh, the enlarged parts of Price's brain are consistent with people diagnosed with obsessive-compulsive disorder. For instance, just as many OCD patients have a tendency toward compulsive collecting, Price has a doll collection totaling in the hundreds.

Company in Numbers

After Price was diagnosed with hyperthymestic syndrome, two other people with similar symptoms surfaced. However, unlike Price, who has struggled with reliving vivid and traumatic childhood memories, the other people seem to have more control over their memories and the impact they play on their current lives. Perhaps this is because the others didn't have the trauma that plagued Price as a child. In 2008, Price published a memoir about her condition entitled, *The Woman Who Can't Forget.*

"The constant onslaught of memories is both a blessing and a curse," says Price, noting that sometimes the pleasant memories serve as a form of comfort. "I have this warm, safe feeling that helps me to get through anything." Unfortunately, she also has to deal with reliving unpleasant memories that replay in full detail. "Over the years, it has paralyzed my life. It has eaten me up."

Fast Facts

- In one day, a single cow discharges enough methane to fill 400 one-liter bottles.

- A flink is a group of 12 or more cows—perhaps cattle ranchers and dairy farmers should be called flinkers.

- Entomologists have learned that mosquitoes have 47 teeth—quite a mouthful for a bug on a liquid diet.

- The Haskell Free Library and Opera House is an official heritage site in both the state of Vermont and province of Quebec—the international border runs right through the building. The books and the opera house stage are in Canada, but seating for the opera audience is in the United States.

- We know of boneheads, but as for muscleheads, caterpillars have the edge: The average caterpillar has 248 muscles in its head.

- A sloth is sometimes so slow that moss grows on its back. But slow is one thing, stationary is another—snails can sleep for three years straight.

- In Paraguay, only registered blood donors may legally duel.

- An average shower uses 30 gallons of water.

- The shotguns used by American forces during World War I proved to be so effective that the Germans cried, "Foul!" and tried to have them banned.

- In some countries, guinea pigs aren't cute, cuddly, children's pets—they're a diet staple. Peruvians, for example, annually eat 63 million guinea pigs. In a church in the town of Cusco, a guinea pig is on the table in a painting of the Last Supper.

Women You Wouldn't Want to Mess With

As the stories of these legendary "ladies" attest, class and distinction doesn't necessarily mean an elevation over evil. Read on for horrifying tales beyond imagination.

Wu Who?

Empress Wu, China's sole female leader, displayed a talent for ruthlessness and cruelty that belied her station as a member of the so-called "weaker sex." Born in A.D. 624, she became a fifth-level concubine to Emperor Taizong at age 14. Educated, beautiful, and gifted, she quickly caught the emperor's eye and earned the pet name "Charming Lady."

"Cunning lady" would have been more appropriate. Wu soon learned attention equaled power. Elevated to "second grade" concubine under Emperor Kao Tsung, Wu still wanted more. After securing the new emperor's favor by bearing him two sons, she devised a plan to eliminate her competition by strangling her own infant daughter and blaming the baby's death on the jealous actions of the empress and head concubine.

The emperor sided with Wu and elevated her to the throne. Empress Wu then ordered the "murderers's" deaths, allegedly first having their hands and feet amputated and then drowning them. That level of cruelty set the tone for the rest of her reign. When a stroke incapacitated the emperor, she took over his duties and dispatched any opposition by means of exile, murder, or forced suicide.

After her husband died, Wu installed her weakest son as emperor so that she could continue to rule through him. When he eventually proved difficult to manage, she facilitated his abdication and formally assumed the crown. But while Wu was inarguably brutal, she was also brilliant. The empress is credited with elevating the stature of women in Chinese society and with advancing agriculture and lowering taxes.

Bloody Bathory

Though born into nobility in A.D. 1560, Erzsebet (a.k.a. Elizabeth) Bathory was anything but noble. Known as "Hungary's National Monster," she was a sadistic serial murderess who is rumored to have tortured and killed up to 650 women, aided by a motley crew consisting of her children's wet nurse, a dwarflike manservant, and a brawny servant woman rumored to be a witch.

Frankly, Bathory's cruelty sounds like the stuff of legend. She reportedly began torturing peasant girls for entertainment by lashing and bludgeoning them. She moved on to dragging the women naked through the snow, and then drenching them with water until they froze to death. After Bathory's husband died, she moved to their castle at Cachtice. There she befriended Anna Darvulia, a sadist like herself (and rumored to be her lover).

The relationship with Darvulia emboldened Bathory to engage in even more atrocious behavior. Legend has it that one time when Bathory was too weak to partake in more vigorous torture activities, she had a servant girl delivered to her bedside so she could bite the flesh from her. Other rumors persist that Bathory bathed in the blood of virgins to maintain her skin's youthful appearance.

It's hard to point to an exact cause for her outlandish actions. Bathory's parents were cousins, part of Hungary's elite aristocracy. Some believe this inbreeding caused her madness; others attribute Bathory's heinous crimes to her volatile temperament and unrestrained sense of upper-class privilege.

Since Bathory's victims were peasants, the ruling class (mainly consisting of Bathory's relatives) tended to turn a blind eye to her vicious pastimes. But things changed after Darvulia died in 1609. Bathory then met Erszi Mjorova, the widow of one of Bathory's tenant farmers. It was Mjorova who may have encouraged Bathory to refine her tastes toward more genteel victims.

When it was discovered Bathory's appetite had changed to girls of noble birth, her cousin the King of Hungary ordered her arrest. Convicted of 80 counts of murder, Bathory's noble heritage protected her from the death penalty. Instead, she was sentenced to be walled up alive in her castle. Unrepentant to the end, she lived in such a state for four years, until she was discovered dead by a guard in 1614.

LaLaurie the Gory

Delphine LaLaurie is another woman who has inspired countless tales and ghost stories. The wife of a prominent New Orleans dentist (her third husband, whom she married in 1825), she led a dual life. Publicly she was a gracious hostess, well known for her lavish parties and charmingly flirtatious disposition. But to the servants at the family's mansion in the city's French Quarter, Madame LaLaurie was a brutal mistress capable of unspeakable evil.

LaLaurie's life was by all accounts privileged and perfect. Eventually, however, the malevolent side of her behavior surfaced publicly. One night, a neighbor reported seeing a young servant girl fall (some say jump) to her death from the top of LaLaurie's three-story home while being chased by her hostile mistress. As a reprimand, the authorities removed the house slaves and fined the couple $300. The servants were then auctioned off to the highest bidders—who, coincidently, were LaLaurie's relatives. She repurchased the slaves and returned them to her service.

Things appeared to settle down at the LaLaurie home until a fire broke out in 1834. When firefighters arrived to put out the blaze, they discovered two slaves chained to the stove. Apparently, the servants had set fire to the kitchen on purpose to attract attention to the atrocities taking place inside the mansion.

This is where it gets ugly. Implored by the servants to look in the attic, the rescuers uncovered horrifying evidence of LaLaurie's evil. Although no one's entirely sure what was found, there are stories of horrifying experiments being done on the slaves. Some describe more than a dozen naked bodies, both dead and alive, chained to the walls or strapped to operating tables. One man had a hole cut in his head with a stick inserted to stir his brains. A caged woman had her arms and legs broken and reset at angles to resemble a crab. Body parts were scattered everywhere.

Although Dr. LaLaurie is rumored to have known about his wife's grisly hobby, he was not thought to be a participant in her gruesome experiments. His wife, meanwhile, escaped the city before she could be brought to justice. However, a marker in Alley 4 of St. Louis Cemetery No. 1 indicates her body was returned to New Orleans from Paris for burial following her death in 1842.

FROM THE VAULTS OF HISTORY

Scarlet Woman

Contrary to popular belief, not all so-called "witches" were burned at the stake. Just look at Bridget Bishop, the first person hanged during the Salem witchcraft trials of 1692. Bishop held the dubious honor of being accused by more individuals of witchcraft than any other defendant. Bishop was a widow who remarried to Thomas Oliver in 1666. From the start, the match was abusive—Bishop's face would often be bruised, and many times the couple were publicly chastised for fighting. Her husband claimed that Bishop "sat up  all night conversing with the Devil." Ultimately, after Oliver died, hysteria against Bishop (and the belief that she was a witch) grew, and a warrant was issued for Bishop's arrest on the charge of witchcraft. A long list of detractors took the stand against her, including her brother-in-law. Within eight days, Bishop was charged, tried, and hung. As it was recorded, "Now the honest men of Salem could sleep in peace, sure that the Shape of Bridget would trouble them no more."

Surprising Sommelier

Given that you have to be 21 to legally drink in all U.S. states, it might surprise you to learn that a teenager invented Dom Perignon champagne. In 1653, the blind 15-year-old Perignon entered a Benedictine monastery. Blessed with an acute sense of taste and smell, Perignon perfected his ability to ferment champagne in the bottle. Moet et Chandon vineyards were so impressed by the young man's accomplishments that they named its best vintage after him.

Muff 'n' Stuff

Kids invent the darndest things: take, for example, earmuffs, the brainchild of Chester Greenwood, a 15-year-old Maine farm boy who hated getting cold ears in winter. He kept at his dream, opening an earmuff factory in 1877. By 1936 he was selling 400,000 sets a year.

From Addiction to Art

*With a little creativity, a North Carolina-based artist
turned a machine designed for feeding nicotine addictions
into a high-tech dispenser of art: The Art-o-mat.*

Crinkling Inspiration

It was the sound of cellophane that first struck artist Clark Whittington with inspiration. Watching a friend's reaction and interest upon hearing the crinkling material, Whittington realized that a simple wrapper could grab attention. With that in mind, Whittington prepared for a 1997 art show at a local café by wrapping his black-and-white photographs in cellophane. As an added kick, he sold them at a dollar each out of a recently banned cigarette vending machine. The gimmick was such a hit that the café owner decided to keep the machine permanently. Whittington recruited other artists to help stock its slots, and from there, a cultural phenomenon was born.

Widespread Sensation

There are currently more than 80 Art-o-mat machines scattered across 25 U.S. states, and others in Quebec, Canada, and Vienna, Austria. Whittington oversees each one, making sure every Art-o-mat vending machine is functional and well stocked. And what stock! Hundreds of artists from around the world contribute their small creations to be sold in the Art-o-mat. Pieces range from photos and earrings to screen prints and miniature watercolor paintings.

Micro Economics

Some of the machines sell thousands of items each year, which is no surprise when the price is kept low: With the pull of a knob, most of the works are available for as little as $5 to $7. The proceeds are split between Art-o-mat, the artist, and sometimes the venue.

It's not every day you see a deadly habit turn into a culture-maven creation, but the Art-o-mat has accomplished the unlikely transformation—no small task, indeed.

Hellish Headlines

"Map Can Help Determine Direction"

"Psychics Predict World Didn't End Yesterday"

"'Save the Whales' Trip Cut Short After Boat Rams Whale"

"Soap and Water Still Cleans Well"

"Critics Say Sunken Ship Not Seaworthy"

"Circumcisions Cause Crybabies"

"State Says Cost of Saving Money Too High"

"Absentee Votes Can Be Made in Person"

"Sun or Rain Expected Today, Dark Tonight"

"Milk Drinkers Are Turning to Powder"

"NJ Judge to Rule on Nude Beach"

"Child's Stool Great for Use in Garden"

"Dealers Will Hear Car Talk at Noon"

"Lawmen From Mexico Barbecue Guests"

"Two Sisters Reunite After Eighteen Years at Checkout Counter"

"Nicaragua Sets Goal to Wipe Out Literacy"

"Autos Killing 110 a Day, Let's Resolve to Do Better"

"Death Causes Loneliness, Feeling of Isolation"

"Smokers Are Productive, but Death Cuts Efficiency"

"Child's Death Ruins Couple's Holiday"

"Blind Woman Gets New Kidney from Dad She Hasn't Seen in Years"

"Man is Fatally Slain"

"Man Loses Legs, Vows to Continue Arms Protest"

"Federal Agents Raid Gun Shop, Find Weapons"

When Bicycles Ruled the (Sporting) World

❖ ❖ ❖ ❖

What sport lasted a day longer than the ancient Olympics, broke the race barrier before baseball, and caused more injuries than modern football? Turn-of-the-century bicycle racing, of course.

Blood, Guts, and Determination

In 1900, the most popular sport in North America was the grueling phenomenon known as the six-day bicycle race. Usually held on indoor velodromes with wooden tracks, teams of two riders would compete for 144 hours, taking turns accruing laps and competing in sprinting events.

These six-day events were not a sport for the faint of heart. At a race, as many as 70,000 fans would thrill to the sight of these powerful riders sustaining serious, often fatal, injuries and pushing themselves to the limits of endurance. Here are some of the sport's major players.

Reggie McNamara (1887–1970)

Dubbed the "Iron Man" of cycling, Australian Reggie McNamara had a seemingly inhuman capacity for the punishment and exertion that defined the six-day events. On the fourth day of a competition in Melbourne, McNamara underwent an emergency trackside operation without anesthesia to remove a large abscess "from his side." Though he lost a considerable amount of blood, he rose from the dust and, ignoring the entreaties of his trainer and doctor, resumed the race. In fact, his injuries on the track put him in the hospital so often that he wound up marrying an American nurse after a 1913 competition in New York. He achieved several world records and defeated the French champions so soundly that they refused to ride against him.

Bobby Walthour (1878–1949)

During his career, bicycling champion Bobby Walthour of Atlanta, Georgia, suffered nearly 50 collarbone fractures and was twice assumed to be dead on the track—only to rise and continue riding. By the time he was age 18, he was the undisputed champion of the South; soon he held the title of international champion and kept it for several years. In addition to making himself and cycling familiar to people all over the world, Walthour brought a great deal of prominence to his native Atlanta. Invigorated by his accomplishments, Atlanta built the Coliseum, one of the world's preeminent velodromes at the time.

Marshall "Major" Taylor (1879–1932)

African American cyclist Major Taylor, the son of an Indianapolis coach driver, proved that endurance bicycling was a sport in which individual talent could not be denied. In an era of overt racism and discrimination, he rose through the ranks to become one of the highest paid athletes of his time. After relocating to the somewhat more race-tolerant Worcester, Massachusetts, Taylor began to rack up a string of victories in the six-day and sprinting competitions. Dubbed the "Worcester Whirlwind," Taylor toured the world, defeated Europe's best riders, and set several world records during his professional career.

Enter the Machines

Like modern stock car racing, six-day cycling events used pacing vehicles. Originally, these were bicycles powered by two to five riders. But in 1895, English races began using primitive motorcycles. These new pace vehicles allowed the cyclists to travel faster, owing to the aerodynamic draft produced by the machines. Crowds thrilled to the speed and noise of these mechanical monsters, which weighed about 300 pounds each. It took two men to operate the motorcycles, one to steer and one to control the engine. They were also quite dangerous: A tandem pacer forced off the track in Waltham, Massachusetts on May 30, 1900, killed both riders and injured several fans. The advent of motorcycles increased the popularity of the six-day races for a time, but it waned with the arrival of a new vehicle spectators preferred over bicycles: the automobile.

Bad Ad Grab Bag

"Cuisine of India—Nashville's BEST Italian Restaurant."

"Toaster: A gift that every member of the family appreciates. Automatically burns toast."

"Now is your chance to have your ears pierced. Get an extra pair to take home."

"Lost: small apricot poodle. Reward. Neutered. Like one of the family."

"We do not tear your clothing with machinery. We do it carefully by hand."

"Tired of cleaning yourself? Let me do it."

"For sale: an antique desk suitable for lady with thick legs and large drawers."

"Dog for sale: eats anything and is fond of children."

"Get rid of aunts: Zap does the job in 24 hours."

"Dinner Special—Turkey $2.35; Chicken or Beef $2.25; Children $2.00."

"Human Skull, Used once only. Not plastic. $200 OBO Dr. Scott Tyler."

"Thanks to my DENTIST...I'm wearing my favorite jeans again!"

"1995 Nissan Maxima, green, leather, loaded, CD, auto start, sunroof, 4-door, good condition, $4500. Not for sale."

"China Cabinet, buffet, hutch solid pine, 6.5-foot tall by 4.5-foot wide, lighted windows, few cat scratches but cat has been killed. $700."

"For Sale—collection of old people."

"AS ADVERTISED—Shurfresh Whole Peeled Baby—2LB $1.69."

"Oscar Mayer Bilingual Turkey Franks 3 for $4."

"Amazing Smashing Wig Sale. A Beautiful Blend of Human & European Hair."

"Family Pride Cleaner—Tailoring—Mammograms—Shoe Repair"

"One of the greatest gifts you'll ever give your family may be your funeral."

Oofty Goofty

Thanks to a tumble, a young man capitalized on an unlikely talent.

First, the Freak Show

Shortly after the California Gold Rush of 1849, a German army deserter named Joshua Marx fled his motherland and arrived in San Francisco to launch a career as a dramatic actor. After failing miserably, Marx came up with the idea of passing himself off as a "wild man from Borneo" in a Barbary Coast freak show.

Marx covered himself from head to toe with sticky road tar and horsehair. He climbed into a cage where he would slobber and growl at people who paid ten cents to gawk at him. His "trainer" heightened the experience by poking him with a heavy stick and tossing large chunks of raw meat through the bars of his cage. Marx acquired his stage name after ravenously tearing into the meat, growling, shaking the bars, and yelling "Oofty Goofty!" at the top of his lungs.

As the Wild Man of Borneo, Oofty enjoyed critical success for all of a week until he became ill and was rushed to the hospital. There, doctors determined that the root of his problems was his inability to sweat through the tar. After weeks of futile efforts, they finally discovered that the tar would come off with a common solvent if they laid Oofty out in the sun.

A New Career

Oofty later passed on a number of other character acts to pursue a career singing and dancing at a beer hall, but he was so bad that he was tossed out after only one number. Interestingly, it was after landing on a stone sidewalk that he discovered that he was relatively impervious to pain. Capitalizing on his unique gift, Oofty eked out a living by taunting bystanders to physically accost him—10 cents for a kick, 25 cents for a thump with a walking stick, or 50 cents for a wack with a baseball bat.

Oofty's career came to an untimely demise when John L. Sullivan, the famous boxer, whacked him across the back, breaking two of his vertebrae. His claim to fame now a distant memory, Oofty shriveled away into obscurity.

Index

❖ ❖ ❖ ❖

G

Gadsby (Wright), 231
Gaedel, Eddie, 130
Gall, Franz Joseph, 124
Gandhi, Mohandas, 65
Garbage, 109–10, 417–18
Garfield, James, 211
Garvey, Marcus, 443–44
Gatorade, 467
Gearren, Leslie Hamilton, 163
Geller, Sarah Michelle, 126
Gelman, Woody, 525
Geophagia, 209
"Get Ur Freak On," 523
Ghost forests, 146–47
Gin, 537
Ginsberg, Allen, 431, 432
Ginsburg, Douglas, 277–78
Giraffe, 440
Gladiators, 506
Glassey, Donald and John "Africa," 317–18
Godfather, 502
Goldfinger, 502
Golf
    balls, 83
    courses in North Dakota, 467
    Jeanne Carmen, 314–15,
    World Ice Golf Championship
        Tournament, 475
Gone with the Wind, 15, 80, 402, 447
GoodFellas, 485
Googol, 399
Gore, Al, 313
Gore, Lesley, 398
Gourmet, 167
Graceland, 177
Graduate, The, 80
Graffiti, 266–67
Graham, Jack, 47–48
Grauman's Chinese Theatre, 437
Gravity dips, 294
Gray, Pete, 495–96
Grease, 502
Great Gatsby, The (Fitzgerald), 15
Great Wall of China, 87
Green, Anna Katharine, 403
Grenada, 421
Grese, Irma, 328–29
Greyhounds, 244
Grey's Anatomy, 490
Griffiths, Frances, 45
Grootveld, Robert Jasper, 100
G-string, 440
Guerilla Girls, 419–20
Guillotine, 167

Guinea pigs, 472, 546
Guinness Book of World Records, 196, 265
Gull, 167
Gum, 31
Gunpowder Plot, 379
Guns N' Roses, 398, 523
Gurning, 119

H

Haas, Eduard, 445–46
Hair, 209, 283. *See also* Beards.
Halcrow, Marjorie, 81
Hamilton, Alexander, 358
Handcuffs, 201
Handshake customs, 332
Hanks, Tom, 338, 447
Harding, Warren G., 113, 357
Hare, William, 451–52
Harley-Davidson, 244
Harrison, George, 450
Hart, Gary, 358
Hartmann, Sadakichi, 157–59
Harvard University, 83
Hashshashin, 212–13
Hatebeak, 433
Hats, 416, 510
Hawaii, 169, 341, 374, 421
Hazard, 494
Hazelnuts, 453
Head binding, 151
Headlines, 131, 356, 456, 552
Heartbeats, 231
Heatherington, James, 416
Hecht, Ben, 157–59
Heinz products, 87
Helium, 392
Hell, Michigan, 217
Hello, 167
Helmsley, Leona, 223
Henbane, 196
Henson, Jim, 139
Heroin, 58
He Said, She Said, 55, 68, 137, 183, 206,
    222, 300, 353, 430, 483, 534
Heterochromia, 511–12
Hewitt, Foster, 168
"Hey Jude," 499
Hezbollah, 421
Hiccups, 231
Hilley, Marie and Frank, 136
Hippos, 168
Hitchcock, Alfred, 126, 465–66
Hitler, Adolf, 59, 113, 116, 164, 178–79,
    328–30
HIV, 88, 306

Hoblophobia, 126
Hobo slang, 33
Hockey, 168
Holly, Buddy, 49, 307, 392
Hollywood. *See Movies and Hollywood.*
Holmes, Sherlock, 453
Homosexuality, 181–82
Honey, 283
Honey Mushroom, 161
Hoover, Herbert, 497
Hope Diamond, 204–5
Horses, 32, 196
    as service animals, 19
    racehorses, 24
Hot dogs, 240
Houghtaling, John, 542
Houston, Whitney, 470
Howard, Samuel "Shemp," 448–49
How It All Began, 24, 74, 122, 240, 405
Hsieh, Tehching, 458–59
Hubbard, L. Ron, 200
Hudson, Rock, 306
Hughes, Bart, 429
Hulme, Juliet (Anne Perry), 296–97
Human Genome Project, 543
Human Growth Hormone (HGH), 28
Hummers, 313
Hummingbirds, 244
"Hungry Like a Wolf," 170
Hunt, Helen, 255
Hutchence, Michael, 367
Hyde, Edward, 67
Hydrophobia, 126

I

I Am Legend, 171
Ice cream, 31, 244, 467
Icke, David, 71
Iditarod Trail, 191
Ignoramus, 84
Illuminati, 71
I Love Lucy, 260
Impotence, 87
Incredible Hulk, 139
India
    bananas, 413
    man-dog marriage, 61
    plastic bags and cows, 63–64
    sunburn treatment, 497
    toxic places, 173–74
Infliximab, 535
In Search of Lost Time (Proust), 95
Insects, 500–501
Insults, 335
Interferon beta, 535

International Space Station, 412
Inventions, 405
Iraq war, 543
Ironing, 38
Iroquois Theater fire, 143–44
Islam, 212–13, 421
Israel
    Oslo Accords, 470
    postage stamps, 111
Istanbul, Turkey, 413
"I Will Always Love You," 470
Iwo Jima flag raising, 281

J

Jackpot, 251
Jackson, Horatio Nelson, 18
Jackson, Janet, 307
Jackson, Michael, 421
Jacobson, Max, 51–52
James, Jesse, 270
Japan, 246, 372–73, 381
Japanese Americans, 421
Jaws, 15
Jaws 3-D, 338
Jazz, 167
Jefferson, Thomas, 39, 221, 358
Jell-O, 58
Jelly beans, 479
Jeopardy!, 62
Jerry Maguire, 502
Jesus Christ, 270, 304
Jet Propulsion Laboratory (JPL), 199
Joan of Arc, 67
Jockstraps, 390–91
"Johnny B. Goode," 149, 523
Johnson, Lyndon B., 21
Jones, James Earl, 338
Jones, Norah, 543
Jones, Tommy Lee, 313
Jong-il, Kim, 253–54
Jordan, Michael, 470
Josepho, Anatol, 457
Journey, 398
Jousting, 453
Judas Iscariot, 270, 304
Juliana (queen of the Netherlands), 219
Jung, George, 245–46
Junk mail, 108

K

K9 Fusion, 433
Kalakuta Republic, 238–39
Karate, 150
Karloff, Boris, 16–17
Kemmler, William, 271–72

Rite of Spring, The (Stravinsky), 309–11
Riverside, Iowa, 441
Roads, 87, 235
Robot, 84
Rock, Paper, Scissors game, **510**
Rocketry, 199–200
Rocky IV, 502
Roddenberry, Gene, **53**
Rodin, Auguste, 305
Roller coasters, 499
Roller derby names, **237**
Rome, 519
Roosevelt, Franklin Delano, 164, 215
Root beer, 313
Rope, 465–66
Rosenberg, Julius and Ethel, 260
Rosenthal, Joe, 281
Roses, 374
Rowling, J. K., 404
Rubber duckies, 491
Run (from Run-DMC), 54
Russia, 174, 273, 372. *See also* Soviet
    Union (USSR).
Ruth, Babe, 83

S
St. Anthony's Fire, 249–50
St. John's Dance, 249–50
St. Louis Browns, 130
St. Vitus's Dance, 249–**50**
Salamanders, **264**
Salary, 437
Sandwich, 323
Santa Claus, 363
Sauncy Diamond, 205
Savoy, Douglas Eugene "Gene," 96
Sawbuck, 84
Schenectady, New York, **244**
School plays, 453
Schwarzenegger, Arnold, 28, 313, 338
Science predictions, 298–99, 396–97
Scientific American, 292
Scofflaw, 251
Scot free, 519
Scrabble, 262
Screwdrivers, **331**
Scrubs, 377
Seabiscuit, 80
Sea-Monkeys, 232
Séances, 291–92
Search and Rescue crews, **325**
Sears Tower, 366
Sebastian, John, 398
Seinfeld, 62, 160, 393
Sergio III (pope), 190

Service animals, 19–20
Sesame Street, 62, 88–89, **491**
7-Up, 262
Seven Up candy bar, 493
Shabby chic, 410
Shakespeare, William, 243, 269, 335, **413**
Shaking hands, 332
Shangri-Las, 398
Sharif, Nawaz, 235
Sharks, 127, 263, 319
Shaving, 262
Shaw, Phil, 38
Sheep wars, 527
Sheldon, William, **117**
Shoebills, 263–64
Shoes
    facts about, 361–62
    Nike, 472
    sneakers with lights, 201
    X-ray Shoe Fitting Machines, 132–**33**
Showers, 127, 546
Shows, Bobby, 141–**42**
Shrikes, 264
Shrimp, 168, 263–**64**
Siegel, Israel, 405
Silence of the Lambs, The, 80, 501
Silly Putty, 196, 453
Simon and Garfunkel, **307**
Simon Says, 70
Simpsons, The, **490**
Sin eating, 72–**73**
Singing sands, 333
Six Flags theme park, **413**
Sixx, Nikki, 369
Skin, 231
Skin of Our Teeth, The (Wilder), 286
Skylab, 366
Slang
    con talk, 112
    diner-English glossary, 140, **187**
    hobo slang, 33
    word history, **273**
Slapstick, 251
Sleeping Beauty, **305**
Slinky toys, **123**
Slogan, 84
Sloths, 546
Slot machines, 32
Smoking, 85–86, 127, **231**
Snacks, 494
Snails, 39, 413
Snap! Crackle! Pop!, **355**
Snow White, 447
Soap operas, **331**
Soccer, 83

Contributing Writers

Michael Allen is a Los Angeles-based writer with credits in television, print, and the Web. Learn more about this fascinating (kinda) fellow at http://sanvicentemedia.com/.

Jeff Bahr is an author and motorcycle-journalist who fancies life in the fast lane. With eight Armchair Reader™ books currently under his belt, this "hired pen" appears to be on the fast track to Armchair Reader largesse.

Robert Bullington earned his master's degree in English from the University of Virginia. He currently makes his home in Richmond, where he spends his time writing, raising a family, and performing with Nettwerk recording artists The Hackensaw Boys.

Ryan L. Cole has worked as a speechwriter and aide in the U.S. Department of Health and Human Services, U.S. Department of Education, and White House during the presidency of George W. Bush. His freelance work has been published in *The Wall Street Journal, The Washington Times,* and *The Weekly Standard.* Ryan holds degrees in history and journalism from Indiana University.

Katherine Don is a freelance writer who hails from a Chicago suburb and currently lives in New York City. When not typing away on her trusty Macbook, she volunteers for nonprofit organizations that deal with health-care and penal-system reform and researches for her book-in-progress. She is currently a student at New York University's Graduate School of Arts and Sciences.

Mary Fons-Misetic is a Chicago-based professional freelance writer and performer. Her popular blog, PaperGirl, can be read at www.maryfons.com.

Anne Holub is a Chicago-based writer and all-around Web Girl Friday. She's always on the lookout for subway tokens, sea glass, and old wool coats that smell like wood smoke.

Erika Cornstuble Koff is a freelance writer who has worn many hats, from stand-up comic to public relations executive to copy editor. In spite of her work on *The Gigantic Reader,* Erika remains a lousy Trivial Pursuit player. She currently resides in Naperville, Illinois, with her husband Ben.

Shanon Lyon is a Seattle-based writer specializing in game content and trivia. She's the author of *Gifts with Meaning,* and her work has appeared in a number of national publications, including *Kiwi, ID, Natural Health,* and *American Girl.*

Susan McGowan is a poet who, despite her best efforts, has found employment as a freelance writer and functionality expert. She lives in Columbus, Ohio, with her husband, impish daughter, and too many pets named Murph.

Art Montague is a Canadian freelance writer whose publication credits include *The Ottawa Book of Everything,* a bestseller now in its third printing. Since 2002, he has also contributed to 13 Uncle John's Bathroom Reader collections as a member of the Bathroom Readers Institute and Hysterical Society.

JR Raphael is a seasoned journalist, who, incidentally, enjoys seasoned fries. His work has appeared in dozens of publications, including *PC World, The Washington Post,* and www.msnbc.com. This book, however, marks the first time he's written about animal-fronted death metal bands. Visit JR online at www.jrstart.com.

Russell Roberts has written more than three dozen books for both adults and children. He currently resides in New Jersey with his wife, daughter, and their scheming calico cat.

Lawrence Robinson is a Los Angeles-based novelist and screenwriter who has contributed to several Armchair Reader™ series titles. He can be found at http://britwriter.com/.

Allen Smith is a freelance writer living in Vail, Colorado, specializing in human interest, humor, and health and fitness stories. He has written for magazines, newspapers, and the Web, including www.livestrong.com and www.trails.com. You can contact him at www.snowwriter.com.

Pamela D. Toler is a freelance writer with a lot of curiosity and a PhD in history from the University of Chicago. She is particularly interested in the times and places where cultures meet and change each other.

Ken White lives in Missoula, Montana.

Jennifer Plattner Wilkinson is a writer and teacher enjoying life in her current home in Wisconsin.

Kelly Wingard has a hyperactive mind, a short attention span, and an insatiable curiosity; in other words, writing for *The Gigantic Reader* seemed to be a natural fit. (Although, after wandering off-topic for hours, not a very profitable one.) Wingard lives in Decatur, Illinois, with her husband, Ken; a hand-me-down dog; and their part-time-resident-granddaughter, Ella.